Adèle Hugo
La Misérable

Adèle Hugo

-La Misérable-

LESLIE SMITH DOW

GOOSE LANE

Published by Goose Lane Editions with the assistance of the Canada Council, 1993.

Book design by Brenda Steeves.
Edited by Laurel Boone.
Interior photographs courtesy of Musées de la Ville de Paris © by SPADEM 1993; photograph collection, Public Archives of Nova Scotia; Heritage Trust of Nova Scotia.
Printed in Canada by The Tribune Press Ltd., Sackville, N.B.

10   9   8   7   6   5   4   3   2

Canadian Cataloguing in Publication Data

Dow, Leslie Smith
Adèle Hugo

Includes index
ISBN 0-86492-168-3

1. Hugo, Adèle, 1830-1915.   2. Hugo, Victor, 1802-1885 —
Biography — Family.   3. Hugo Family   I. Title

PQ2295.7.S65 1993   848'.709   C93-098647-4

Goose Lane Editions
469 King Street
Fredericton, New Brunswick
Canada E3B 1E5

*F*or Kyleakin Stuart Donal, my labour of love;
and for Donald, who gave him to me.

Adèle Hugo, Guernsey, 1855-1863 *(Musées de la Ville de Paris)*

Contents

Acknowledgements *ix*

Chronology *xi*

Introduction *xiii*

Family Ties *23*
Paris, 1830-1852

A Princess in a Tower *51*
Jersey, 1852-1854

The Quick and the Dead *66*
Jersey, 1854

A Passage to Freedom *81*
Jersey, 1855, and Guernsey, 1855-1863

A Dangerous Liaison *103*
Halifax, 1863-1864

"She of Crazy Love and Folly" *123*
Halifax, 1864-1865

The Sympathy of Strangers *134*
Halifax, 1865-1866

Los Barbados *146*
Barbados, 1866-1871

". . . More Dead than the Dead" *158*
Paris, 1872-1885

An Uneasy Death *177*
Paris, 1915

Hugo Family Tree *181*

The Pinsons *182*

Bibliography *185*

Index *191*

Acknowledgements

My greatest gratitude goes to my husband, Donald Dow, for supporting me and encouraging me to complete this project.

Thanks are also due to Dr. Barry Jones of the Royal Ottawa Hospital, an expert on schizophrenia, for confirming my suspicions that Adèle more than likely suffered from schizophrenia; to Laura Currie, for her invaluable research into mental illness and other topics; to the Regional Municipality of Ottawa-Carleton for a travel and sustaining grant; to the Canadian Authors' Association for bestowing the Air Canada Award for the most promising Canadian writer under age thirty upon me (and so enabling me to conduct research in Paris); to the staff of the Canadian War Museum, particularly Cameron Pulsifer and Jean Langdon-Ford; to Lois Kernaghan Yorke and the staff of the Public Archives of Nova Scotia; to the staffs of the Ottawa Public Library, the Canadian Currency Museum, the National Gallery, the National Library and the National Archives for their continued assistance; to Master Corporal Derek Egan of the Cambridge Military Library, Halifax; to Warren Alleyne, researcher and writer, Barbados; to Elizabeth Collard, historian, Ottawa; to Bruce Ellis, curator, Citadel Hill Army Museum, Halifax; to Ron MacDonald, Garrison Library, Halifax; to John Dagger, researcher, London, England; to Doug Hendry, researcher, Ottawa and London, England; and to Claire McIlveen, Ed Head and Dave Morefield, for providing the necessities of life while I undertook research in Halifax.

Grateful acknowledgement is made for permission to quote from: Cameron Pulsifer, *The 78th Highlanders in Halifax*, Vol. 2, *The Officers* (unpublished report: Parks Canada, 1985) and *British Regiments in Halifax* (unpublished report: Parks Canada, 1980); Raymond Escholier, *Hugo, roi de son siècle* (Paris: Arthaud/Librairie Flammarion, 1970) and *Victor Hugo, cet inconnu* (Paris: Librairie Plon, 1951); Henri Guillemin, *L'Engloutie: Adèle, fille de Victor Hugo, 1830-1915* (Paris: Éditions du Seuil, 1985); André Gide, *Anthologie de la poésie française* (Paris: Éditions de la Pléiade/Éditions Gallimard, 1949); Arnaud Laster, *Victor Hugo* (Paris: Éditions Pierre Belfond, 1984); Ruth Jordan, *George Sand* (London: Constable, 1976); Jean de Mutigny, *Victor Hugo et le spiritisme* (Paris: Fernand Nathan, 1981); Herbert Juin, *Victor Hugo*, Vol. 2 (1844-1870) and Vol. 3 (1870-1885) (Paris: Flammarion, 1984); Irving Gottesman, *Schizophrenia Genesis: The Origins of Madness* (New York: Freeman, 1989); and unpublished materials held by the Public Archives of Nova Scotia.

Chronology

1802 Birth of Victor Hugo

1803 Birth of Adèle Foucher

1822 Marriage of Adèle Foucher and Victor Hugo
      Eugène Hugo goes mad

1823 Birth and death of Léopold Hugo

1824 Birth of Léopoldine Hugo

1826 Birth of Charles Hugo

1828 Birth of François-Victor Hugo

1829 Hugo family lives at 11, rue Notre-Dame des Champs

1830 Hugo family moves to 9, rue Jean-Goujon in the
      Champs-Élysées
      Birth of Adèle Hugo

1837 Death of Eugène Hugo

1843 Death of Léopoldine Hugo Vacquerie

1848 Hugos live in an apartment at 6, Place-Royale, then move to 4,
      rue d'Isly briefly, finally lodge at 37, rue de la Tour-d'Auvergne

1852 Victor Hugo and family go into exile on Jersey, Channel Islands
      Adèle first hears about Albert Pinson

1854 Adèle meets Pinson

1856 Hugo family deported from Jersey; move to Guernsey

1863 Adèle Hugo runs away to Halifax

1866 Adèle follows Pinson to Barbados

1868 Death of Adèle Foucher Hugo

1871 Death of Charles Hugo

1872 Adèle brought back from Barbados and incarcerated at Maison Rivet, Paris

1873 Death of François-Victor Hugo

1885 Death of Victor Hugo

      Adèle moved to Château de Suresnes, Paris

1915 Death of Adèle Hugo

Introduction

I'm creative, sensitive. I believe in mysteries, magic, rainbows, and full moons. I wonder why it's expected that I be quieted, medicated, whenever it seems I'm stepping out of the boundaries of "reality". . . . Music . . . envelopes me and becomes alive, breathing high and low notes, and I'm floating on the movement.
— *a schizophrenia sufferer*[1]

Adèle Hugo was the youngest child of French literary hero Victor Hugo, then the world's most famous writer. She began her life in the most brilliant company; Europe's most celebrated artists, musicians and writers regularly visited the Hugo home. Adèle knew Paganini, Rossini, Clésinger, Lamartine, Dumas, Balzac and many others. She herself was an accomplished pianist, composer and writer, and her beauty astounded many — Balzac wrote that he had never seen any woman as attractive as the thirteen-year-old Adèle. The young woman who was already at ease sharing her ideas with Europe's best seemed destined to make a magnificent marriage and lead an equally interesting life.

But somewhere along the line, everything went terribly wrong. The spectre of mental illness, which had ruined the life of her uncle Eugène while enhancing her father's creativity, reared its ugly head. The quiet, pious Adèle became unhappy and defiant and remained resolutely unmarried despite many proposals from some of Europe's most eligible bachelors. Tormented by her growing mental instability, Adèle yearned to escape what had become a stifling life. She chafed under the strictures applied to unmarried women and lamented that she could not even go out to buy a newspaper unchaperoned.

In 1863, at the age of thirty-three, Adèle took matters into her own hands. She ran away from home. Her goal was Halifax, where her former lover, an English officer named Albert Andrew Pinson, was garrisoned. When Pinson had proposed marriage to Adèle, she had refused, but later, when she changed her mind, Pinson would have none of it. Pinson's brutal rejection plunged Adèle into despair. Eventually, she succumbed to what was then termed madness.

In 1866, Pinson's regiment was transferred to Barbados; Adèle followed. When he and his regiment left in 1869, Adèle, by then hopelessly demented, stayed on, unaware of his departure. She wandered the streets in rags and was finally taken in by a local woman. It was not until 1872 that the mentally and physically broken Adèle was finally brought back to Paris. Her independence had come at the price of her sanity, and, on the advice of doctors, Victor Hugo had his daughter committed to an insane asylum.

The order denying Adèle her liberty was never rescinded, even upon Hugo's death in 1885. She lived for thirty more years behind asylum walls, albeit in considerable style, until she died in 1915. It was a sad end for the high-spirited, sensitive and intelligent woman.

While Adèle sat cocooned inside her pavilion, wild tales began to spring up about her and her earlier adventures. Even her own experiences could not match the unsubstantiated stories of her past recounted in her father's obituary in the *New York Times*. In the article, no fewer than three versions of Adèle's life were advanced: Adèle was either kidnapped by an English officer or married him against her parents' wishes; she then travelled to Nova Scotia with her new husband, where he died. Or, Adèle and her husband were posted to India; he beat her, their two children died in infancy, and her husband committed suicide; Adèle made her way to Singapore where she became a vagrant; some sympathetic strangers found her, dirty and in rags, and when she announced she was Victor Hugo's daughter they saw to it that she was sent home. Or, stated the *Times*, "As a girl she was kidnapped at Guernsey by an English officer. All Europe was searched for her by her parents, but they obtained no trace of her whereabouts. Several months later a girl found wandering alone in the streets of New York, apparently demented, declared, 'I am the daughter of Victor Hugo.' This was the only statement she ever made." This event allegedly took place years after Adèle's experiences in India and Singapore.[2]

Perhaps the only grain of truth the *Times* journalist managed to un-cover was that eccentricity was not unknown in the Hugo family. The newspaper blamed Hugo himself for fostering this trait. He was, the *Times* claimed, the "enemy of discipline and subordination" and prob-ably spent little time on his children's moral instruction. "It is unlikely that he did more than urge upon them the importance of liberty and the brotherhood of man, and to trust his wife to keep them away from his literary labours."[3] While it is true that Hugo was a great defender of freedom of speech and collective liberty, his refusal to grant his own daughter even the smallest personal freedoms, and the rigours of his moral instruction to his children while he himself behaved in quite the opposite manner, infuriated Adèle. His inability to recognize in his daughter anything more than a marriageable female — rather than seeing her as a talented musician, composer and writer — contributed to the tragedy her life became.

An article occasioned by Victor Hugo's death in the *Halifax Morn-ing Herald* tells a fuller story, one that is somewhat less fanciful because it originated with a Halifax lawyer, Robert Motton, Jr., Q.C. Adèle had retained Motton, who was about her own age, in her never-ending battle to try to force Albert Pinson to marry her. Theirs had been a purely professional relationship; nonetheless, Motton felt it was his duty to protect Adèle's memory from the inquisitive *Halifax Morning Herald* reporter who came to his office hoping for an anecdote about the Hugo family, and particularly about the mysterious Hugo daughter.

Motton knew there were several sides to Adèle's unusual story, and he picked one which he felt would do the least damage to his former client. "I knew Adèle Hugo well," he said, leaning back in his leather-padded chair. "She told me her story several times. But of course, professional honour requires that I shall not divulge her story." The reporter saw the tale of Adèle Hugo's secret life slipping away; he half-rose to leave.

Motton motioned him to sit down again. "I shall be happy to give you an outline of it as she often told it to others — to the lady with whom she boarded in Halifax, and to other friends; a story the accuracy of which I have no reason to doubt." Sticking his thumbs firmly in his waistcoat, and leaning a little farther back in his comfortable chair, Motton began his tale:

When Victor Hugo was exiled from France, he lived for a while in Brussels. A wealthy English family named Pinsen[4] lived there at the same time. The two families became intimate, and the poet's youngest daughter, Adèle, fell in love with a son of the Pinsens. It became an infatuation. They became engaged. But Hugo was in exile and in poverty and the Pinsens did not favour an alliance of their family wealth with the brains of a Hugo. It seems, however, that the young couple went through a sort of secret marriage, and Pinsen promised in due time to publicly marry Adèle in an English church. In due course he purchased a commission in the army and was gazetted a lieutenant in the sixteenth regiment. The regiment was ordered to Halifax, and he wrote to Adèle telling her of the fact, saying that he would take her to Halifax as his wife and requesting her to meet him in London where they would be publicly married. Victor Hugo and his wife would not listen to any such proposition, and insisted that if Pinsen wanted to marry, he must come to their home and marry as any other man would. But Adèle was madly infatuated with him, and insisted on going to London as he desired. Finally she got her way and her mother accompanied her to the British metropolis. When they arrived they found that Pinsen had left for Halifax with his regiment. It looked very much as if he had deserted Adèle.

Motton was a popular after-dinner speaker and well known for his dexterity in telling tall tales. He continued as the fascinated reporter sat with his mouth agape, pencil scratching feverishly on his notepad:

> She was a remarkably handsome woman, tall and well built, with a Roman nose, wavy jet black hair, piercing black eyes, and dark complexion. She wrote a beautiful hand, almost like copperplate, and spent a good deal of time writing — accumulating a large pile of manuscript while here. On one occasion she offered it to me, saying, "Publish it some day; you will startle the world and make a fortune." I have been sorry many times that I did not accept the manuscript.[5]

Unbeknownst to the reporter, most of Motton's tale was untrue.

Adèle and her story were largely forgotten until 1892, when an article in the *Athenaeum*, a London review, cited the discovery of two thousand pages of *Diary of Exile*, ascribed to Victor Hugo. That same year, other articles appeared in *Scribner's* and *Le Figaro* discussing the marvellous *Diary*, which so cleverly traced events and personages of Hugo's years in exile. Upon closer examination, cracks began to appear in the theory that the journal had been kept by Hugo himself; one theory, advanced in an 1896 article, was that the diary was the rough draft of Mme Hugo's biography of her husband. It was not until 1952, when Réné de Messières, cultural counsellor with the French Embassy in New York, gave a talk at Harvard University titled "The Journal of Exile of Adèle Hugo," that Adèle's authorship was recognized.

In 1950, a box of papers was deposited by the Hugo family at the Victor Hugo Museum in Paris; the documents had been found in a drawer of a bureau sold by Julie Foucher Chenay, Madame Hugo's sister, who was responsible for putting Hauteville-House (the Hugo home in Guernsey) in order following Victor Hugo's death. These were what remained of Adèle's papers, including parts of her secret journal. Julie Foucher had evidently thrown away the rest of Adèle's papers; she had made a draft and a final copy of most of her writing.

Some of Adèle's journal was acquired by American millionaire J.P. Morgan for the Pierpont Morgan Library in New York City sometime between 1896 and 1905. Her manuscripts, acquired from a London dealer, were said to be among Morgan's first purchases for the library, acquired from a London dealer. Closer examination revealed that the Pierpont Morgan Library would often be in possession of her final copy while the Victor Hugo Museum would have the draft, and vice versa. From 1926 until his death in 1956, Professor Frederick Hoffherr of Columbia University worked to decipher these journals, which Adèle had written in an idiosyncratic code; he was not allowed to publish his work.

In 1962, the Pierpont Morgan Library acquired from the personal library of Marc Loliée of Paris three sheaves of paper totalling one hundred pages, which had also formed part of Adèle's journal. These documents had been found between the pages of a sixteenth-century Geneva Bible owned by a chair repairman; he had sold them to the French diplomat Jean Delalande, and M. Delalande in turn eventually sold the papers to M. Loliée.

Lastly, a typewritten transcription of hitherto unknown pages of Adèle's diary, translated into English, was discovered at the Victor Hugo Museum; the original pages were never found.

In the early 1950s, Professor Frances Vernor Guille began working on the manuscript, rendering its many encoded words and passages into a readable text. Her faithful reconstruction of Adèle's *Journal of Exile* was first published in 1968 as *Le Journal d'Adèle Hugo, Volume 1.*[6] Guille began to divulge the hitherto murky details of Adèle's tragic life. That first volume of Adèle's diaries covered only 1852; the second, published in 1971, covered 1853; the third, published in 1984, covered 1854. Sadly, Guille's plans for a fourth volume were cut short by her death, leaving more diaries and other of Adèle's papers still undeciphered.

Adèle's journal actually appears to be two works. In the first, she compulsively recorded almost verbatim the daily events and conversations in the Hugo household. Guille's three books, consisting of these records, have been an invaluable aid to biographers of Victor Hugo, thanks to Adèle's precise recording of conversations between her father and other socially, politically and artistically prominent people of the time, as well as his views on widely diverse topics. In the second, secret, diary, Adèle confided her innermost thoughts in a kind of code. To further complicate matters, it would appear that Adèle scribbled her thoughts on whatever paper was at hand rather than in a bound journal. Sample pages from these diaries show how, in her precise handwriting, she inverted words to form anagrams and substituted abbreviations and initials for names. In some cases, someone else has corrected her manuscript, rendering it almost illegible, with words scratched out and comments written in the margins. Often, Adèle wrote quite dissimilar entries in her two diaries on the same day — one public, and one private; or she did not date her entries at all, making reconciliation of events and chronology difficult for her posthumous readers.

In 1969, French film director François Truffaut chanced to read Guille's strange-but-true tale of Adèle, and he instantly saw her story's potential as a film. Yet it was not until 1975 that he was able to realize his vision. That year, *L'Histoire d'Adèle H.* (or *The Story of Adèle H.*, as the English version was titled) was released, with Isabelle Adjani in the title role. Although the film focuses mostly on Adèle's three-year stay in Halifax, it departs from Guille's painstaking research on numerous points, often sacrificing historical fact in favour of romantic fiction. The departures are unnecessary, for in the life of Adèle Hugo, truth is far stranger than fiction. Henri Guillemin's *L'Engloutie* deals with the tragedy of Adèle, and she figures peripherally in numerous biographies and critical treatments of Victor Hugo and his work. Some Canadian and American magazine and newspaper articles, ranging from prosaic to wildly speculative, also attempt to unravel the mystery and madness of Adèle.

The life of Adèle's lover, Albert Andrew Pinson, remains largely unknown, save for the emotion-charged ramblings of Adèle's diary and the unflattering opinions of colleagues and journalists. His officer's service records, which would have provided additional and, perhaps, less biased insight into the man, have not survived. Nor have any of his letters. His motives, like his personality, remain as hidden as his origins. Much of what is contained in these pages regarding Pinson has had to be reconstructed through guesswork and second-hand accounts, placing Pinson in the unhappy position of being unable to defend himself.

Adèle Hugo, in effect, rejected a nineteenth-century French value system which excluded women at best and, at worst, rendered them nothing more than the chattel of their fathers and husbands. Despite her great ability to contribute to society, there were few places within that society for her. Although other women of her time did manage to succeed and even triumph over the odds against them, Adèle was in many ways less fortunate than her bold sisters. Although possessed of a superior intellect, she lacked their emotional single-mindedness. Like most people who have been long dominated and suppressed, she ultimately failed to surmount the many obstacles in her path to freedom. And her mental illness and finally her incarceration made effective action impossible. In some ways the story of Adèle Hugo is the story of all women past and present, whom a patriarchal culture has reduced to their base value as brides, wives and mothers. Like all frustrated and oppressed women, Adèle wanted most of all to be free.

⚜

1. From: *Schizophrenia Genesis: The Origins of Madness* by Irving Gottesman. Copyright © 1989 by W.H. Freeman and Company. Reprinted with permission, p.48.
2. Anon., "The Tragedy of Hugo's Daughter," *New York Times* (May 2, 1915), Sec. V, p.20.
3. "The Tragedy of Hugo's Daughter," p.20.
4. The surname of Adèle's lover is spelled Pinson, Pinsen, and Penson by different writers. Pinson is the preferred spelling, since it is the one used in his own and his relatives' army records. However, in quotations, the alternate spellings will appear without comment.

5. "A Romantic Story of the visit to Halifax of Adèle, the favorite daughter of Victor Hugo," *Halifax Morning Herald* (May 27, 1885), p.3.

6. Frances Vernor Guille, *Le Journal d'Adèle Hngo*, Vol. 1 (1852) (Paris: Minard, 1968); Vol. 2 (1853) (Paris: Minard, 1971); Vol. 3 (1854) (Paris: Minard, 1984). All translations from these volumes are my own.

"Dédé," sketched by Adèle Foucher Hugo, 1833 *(Musées de la Ville de Paris)*

Chapter 1

Family Ties
Paris, 1830-1852

Like alms, child, offer then your prayer
To your father, to your mother, to the fathers of your father.
— *Victor Hugo*, "La Prière pour tous" [1]

*M*adame Adèle Hugo lay gasping on her bed. The curtains had been drawn and, despite the heat, the windows were tightly closed. Periodically, the reverential quiet of the room was punctuated by her groans and by the sounds of shot scraping across the roof tiles overhead.

It was July 28, 1830. Outside, the three-day revolution later known as *Les Trois Glorieuses* was only half over. Shops were closed, streets barricaded and printing plants taken over by gendarmes. From the rooftops, young insurgents pelted police street patrols with garbage; the police and their military reinforcements fired back. Despite the relative isolation of the Hugos' rented home at 9, rue Jean-Goujon in the Champs-Élysées, the family found itself in the thick of the action. Only two days before, the setting had been bucolic. The Champs-Élysées, full of woods and parkland, was a popular picnic and recreation spot for Parisians. But then the former cow pasture erupted into violence.

Inside the house, a drama of equal concern to the Hugo family was unfolding. For the moment, the family consisted of Madame Hugo; its patriarch, the poet, novelist and playwright Victor Hugo; their six-year-old daughter Léopoldine (called Didine); and their sons, Charles, four (known as Charlot), and François-Victor, two (nicknamed Toto). As a cloud of gunsmoke floated by the windows of Madame Hugo's room, another member of the Hugo family entered the world with a lusty cry. Named after her twenty-nine-year-old mother, Adèle (Dédé) was the Hugos' fifth and last child. Their first, Léopold, had lived just three months.

Hugo could not have asked for a more dramatic moment; it was the stuff of his own melodramatic plays. "My wife was in labour while the shot was breaking the slates on our roof," Hugo wrote excitedly to his friend and fellow poet Alphonse de Lamartine shortly after the event.[2] Hugo seemed unable to decide whether his proximity to the conflict or the birth of his daughter was the more noteworthy.

Les Trois Glorieuses broke out in the wake of elections held on June 23 and July 3, which had given a large majority to the opposition party. On July 7, King Charles X suspended freedom of the press, dissolved the Chamber of Deputies and changed the electoral laws. On July 26, the day after the changes became law, Liberal journalists signed a petition of protest. On the night of July 27-28, Republican students and workers declared that insurrection was the only solution. Most Parisians agreed; they hated Charles X.

On Adèle's birthday, the students and workers and their supporters quickly erected barricades throughout central and eastern Paris. The rebels, with borrowed rifles, attacked the Swiss Guard station, the Palais-Bourbon and City Hall. By the final day of *Les Trois Glorieuses,* July 29, some two hundred soldiers and eight hundred rebels had been killed. The king, who had not left his palace at Sainte-Cloude, finally agreed to revoke his ordonnances, but it was too late. By the time the uprising ended, Charles X had been deposed and the popular Louis-Philippe installed as the new king of France.[3]

Madame Hugo had never expected to give birth in the middle of a revolution. The family had only recently moved to the not-yet-fashionable Champs-Élysées district. The change in households, when Madame Hugo was seven months pregnant, was made not by choice but by necessity. The Hugos had been evicted from their apartment at 11, rue Notre-Dame-des-Champs because their beleaguered landlord would no longer put up with the constant comings and goings of friends, foes and family. The Hugos could not disturb the neighbours at their new address; theirs was the only house on the street.

Much of the commotion which their landlord had found so disruptive had come in the wake of the premiere of Hugo's latest and most scandalous play, *Hernani*. It was not the content of the play that was so objectionable, but its form. *Hernani* seemed to embody the upstart Romantic movement's unconventional and naturalistic philosophy of literature. The play pitted Victor Hugo and his not inconsiderable band of supporters against the staid and inflexible Classicists — better known as the *chauve-têtes* to their irreverent young detractors. Every time the curtain rose on *Hernani* there was literally a battle for seats between the two groups — one intending to cheer what it felt was a masterful production, the other to jeer at this travesty.

Soon after the tumult of Adèle's birth, the Hugos found themselves in the middle of another crisis, this time a personal one. Their marriage was rapidly deteriorating, and the catalyst was Charles Augustin Sainte-Beuve (1804-1869). A devotee of the Romantic movement and member of the Académie française, Sainte-Beuve's output included literary histories such as *Port-Royal*, *Portraits littéraires*, and *Causeries du lundi*.

When Hugo was apprised of the love affair between his wife and this close family friend, whom he had perceived until now as a rather stodgy old bachelor (Sainte-Beuve was, in fact, only two years his senior), he had no cause to doubt the news: it had come from Sainte-Beuve himself. The affair had begun innocently enough. Madame Hugo had long enjoyed the company and conversation of the popular Sainte-Beuve, but his gentle attentions soon turned more ardent. Madame Hugo found his concern for her well-being moving and very unlike the mostly sexual attentions of her spouse. What Sainte-Beuve lacked in charisma he more than made up for in genuine tenderness and sincere emotion. Unlike her self-centred husband, Sainte-Beuve was also interested in Madame Hugo's opinions and intellectual musings; his ability to listen and absorb information was one of his strengths. If the truth be known, the cerebral and highly-educated Sainte-Beuve could write rings around Hugo, who was better at passionate verbosity than at well-reasoned argument. Drama critics later accused Hugo of being too calculating in using the drama of life as mere fodder for his plays.

The affair between Madame Hugo and Sainte-Beuve was at its most intense in 1830 and 1831, and so the whispers began that the critic, not the poet, was the father of the newest addition to the Hugo brood. Indeed, Sainte-Beuve had so successfully insinuated himself into the family that Hugo immediately and innocently chose him as Adèle's godfather. He later regretted his impetuosity, but Sainte-Beuve couldn't have been more grateful. When she was baptised on September 19, 1830, in the church of Sainte-Philippe-du-Roule, it was Sainte-Beuve, the man who considered himself Adèle's spiritual father (if not her biological one) who held her tiny head over the font. Sainte-Beuve would later write that baby Adèle was "pure, and containing nevertheless something of me."[4]

Sainte-Beuve would not keep his feelings secret. Tormented by his futile love for Adèle senior, and often astonished at the shabby treatment Hugo meted out to her, Sainte-Beuve finally told his friend of his feelings for his wife. Although their friendship did not break off immediately, it naturally dwindled. Hugo was especially wounded when he received from the critic some of his wife's ardent letters. "You are the person I have most loved," she had written to Sainte-Beuve, "and I do not except my children." She did not mention her husband.

Enraged and hurt, Hugo forced his wife to choose between himself and Sainte-Beuve. She was a pragmatic woman, so she chose Hugo. She undoubtedly was thinking of her children, but perhaps she also reflected on her early, forbidden love for Victor; perhaps she hoped that the episode might somehow precipitate a return to those halcyon days. Sainte-Beuve, for his part, wrote that little Adèle was the bond between him and Madame Hugo, whom Victor no longer permitted him to see. "Through her, I love you still, and all shadow of hate is erased in the memory her presence brings," he wrote.[5] For Hugo, the child symbolized his worst suspicions about his wife.

Hugo had been a tender and ardent courtier of his childhood

sweetheart, the beautiful Adèle Foucher, and the fate that had had a hand in bringing them together in the first place may have helped keep them together through thick and thin. Their marriage had been joking-ly foretold even before their births by Hugo's father, Léopold. Léopold Hugo, then an army officer, and Sophie Trébuchet were married, fol-lowed into matrimony three weeks later by their good friends Pierre Foucher and Anne-Victoire Asseline (who would later become the par-ents of Adèle Foucher). At the Foucher's wedding breakfast, Léopold raised his glass high in a toast to his friend and exclaimed, "It is my wish that you should quickly have a girl. I will have a boy and we will marry them." Twenty-five years later, the promise came true, but not without a great deal of patience and perseverance on the part of the young lovers.

Victor and Adèle had first met in 1809, at Les Feuillantines, the Paris home of Victor's mother, Sophie Trébuchet Hugo. Victor was seven years old; his bride-to-be was six. They spent many of the en-suing days, and much time over the ensuing years, together. On April 26, 1819, Victor, aged seventeen, and Adèle, aged sixteen, dared each other to reveal their greatest secret. "Je t'aime," he whispered to the raven-haired beauty. "Moi aussi, je t'aime," she replied. They immedi-ately became engaged, although their love remained secret. Surprisingly, when they finally revealed it, both sets of parents objected to their union and the pair had to wait three more years before they could take their marriage vows.

For her part, Sophie Hugo refused to be swayed by any of her son's arguments in favour of his marrying Adèle Foucher, whose family she no longer regarded as having the same social standing as hers. At the same time, the Fouchers worried that Victor could not possibly support a family. Once again, fate intervened. In 1820, Hugo's poem "Ode sur la mort du duc de Berry" reached the eyes and touched the heart of King Louis XVIII, who awarded him a small pension. The following year, Sophie Hugo died, and with her the major obstacle to her son's union with Adèle Foucher. In 1822, his first book, *Les Odes et poésies diverses*, appeared, and at last it was evident that Victor Hugo had begun to establish himself as a writer. The matrimonial path was now clear. On October 12, 1822, Adèle Foucher and Victor Hugo were married.

But even that day was marked by tragedy. Victor's brother, Eugène, had been secretly in love with Adèle, and Eugène, too, was a poet — when he was eighteen, his "Ode sur la mort du duc d'Enghien" had won him the admiration of the Académie des Jeux Floraux de Toulouse in 1818. He was volatile, like his younger brother, but it soon became apparent that he lacked Victor's self-possession. Two months after the literary prize was awarded, Monsieur Biscarrat, an instructor at Pension Cordier, noted in a letter to Victor that he felt Eugène was suffering from what he described as "dementia."[6]

It did not help matters that Victor had already begun to eclipse his elder brother in poetry, which was Eugène's chosen field. In the end, the sight of Adèle, for whom he cherished a burning passion, marrying his brother and rival was too much for Eugène to bear. On that day, Eugène Hugo had a mental breakdown.

Although Victor's wedding day had been marred by the incident, he did not abandon his brother. Eugène stayed with the newlyweds for three months. Being so close to the happy couple must have added to the afflicted brother's trials, and soon it became painfully obvious that the patient needed more care than Victor and Adèle could give him. Victor, who until then had been dutifully supporting his brother financially and emotionally, was forced to write to their father on December 20 that Eugène was "ill, and dangerously ill. I have often told you about the deplorable state of his mind. It had been growing worse for more than a month, in a way which greatly alarmed us all, and we could not find any proper cure, since he had kept the free exercise of his will, and he stubbornly refused all help and care."[7]

In January of 1823, Léopold Hugo, himself a writer and now a general, came from Blois to assess Eugène's condition for himself. He evidently agreed with his youngest son, for he took Eugène home with him. Shortly afterwards, General Hugo had Eugène confined to an insane asylum at Charenton, where, curiously, he was not allowed to receive visitors. He died in 1837, apparently without ever recovering his sanity. Perhaps due to the family's reticence to divulge details, or due to the lack of medical knowledge at the time, the exact nature of his ailment remains unknown.

Certainly, the three Hugo brothers — Abel, Eugène and Victor — had an unconventional upbringing; neither their mother nor their father had been exemplary parents. Both had a predilection for extra-marital affairs that overrode their parental duties. In the year of Victor's birth, 1802, his mother had conducted an intense affair with his father's compatriot, General Victor Lahorie, who was later executed for trying to carry out Sophie's plan to incite a revolution. It was an open secret that she had named the young Victor for the General. That same year, Léopold and Sophie separated. They briefly reunited in Naples in 1806, and Sophie and her three sons remained there while Léopold pursued glory — and younger women — across Europe. In 1809, Léopold received his promotion to the rank of general, and he was appointed governor of the Spanish province of Avila. A year later, he was given the title of Count of Siguenza; by then, he was openly co-habitating with Catherine Thomas. At the same time, Joseph Bonaparte was appointed King of Spain by his more powerful brother, Napoléon. King Joseph soon discovered that Léopold was living "in concubinage" with Catherine Thomas and had long been estranged from his wife. The shocked monarch ordered Sophie and her three young sons to rejoin their patriarch.

In 1810, Sophie, Abel, Eugène and Victor arrived in Spain. But Léopold had finally gotten wind of his wife's affair with Lahorie and demanded a divorce. He vowed to keep his sons with him, and he enrolled them in a local school. Once again, King Joseph intervened and insisted that Léopold leave his mistress, release his children and let the entire family depart for France. Despite Léopold's subsequent return to France, the couple did not reconcile. In 1815, the Hugos obtained a judicial separation and Léopold married his longtime mistress.

Such dollops of real-life drama awakened the writing talent of the Hugo brothers. Not only did Victor's stormy upbringing provide him with grist for his writing mill, it also shaped his character and undeniably influenced his own domestic behaviour. By his early teenage years, Victor's literary genius and his penchant for pomposity had begun to show. At the age of fourteen, he grandly declared he would be "Chateaubriand or nothing." By the time he was twenty, Hugo's successes were quickly heaping up and he was becoming ever more self-centred and domineering. The attendant obligations of genius soon made him a difficult man to live with.

Although Hugo had remained passionately in love with his wife up until the contretemps with Sainte-Beuve, she had grown tired of catering to his whims. She did not share his insatiable sex drive, for one thing, although she was obliged to bear the fruits of his conjugal labours. All of her pregnancies had been difficult and the five births extremely painful; she vowed to have no more children. In the absence of reliable birth control, Madame Hugo had little choice but to remain cold to her husband's continual advances. Whether the relationship between Madame Hugo and Sainte-Beuve became a physical one either before or after the birth of little Adèle remains unclear. Given Madame Hugo's resolute decision to have no more children, it is possible that their relationship remained unconsummated, although perhaps not wholly platonic.

The upheaval following Sainte-Beuve's revelation lasted upwards of six months. By January of 1832, relations between Hugo and the critic had settled back into a cordial, albeit reserved, mode. In January of 1833, the young novelist George Sand wrote to Sainte-Beuve (whom she had never met) asking for two complimentary tickets to the opening of Hugo's latest play, *Lucrèce Borgia*. Sand received the tickets soon after, proof that Sainte-Beuve and Hugo were once again on good terms.

But loving memories evidently lingered between Madame Hugo and Sainte-Beuve: when little Adèle was ten, Madame Hugo sent Sainte-Beuve a portrait she had drawn of her daughter, and she also sent him "as a precious souvenir" her marriage veil. Sainte-Beuve replied by publishing *Livre d'Amour*, a book of love poems about and to Madame Hugo, much to the embarrassment of everyone involved.

Although Hugo exchanged affectionate notes with young Adèle when he was away from Paris, his suspicions about her paternity subtly lessened his affection for her, or at least cooled his responses to her childhood needs. The rest of the family seemed to form a community from which Adèle was excluded; later, Madame Hugo castigated them for acting as if Adèle "did not exist." Nevertheless, Hugo was a devoted father with advanced ideas about child rearing. From the beginning, it was clear to everyone that Léopoldine was not only her father's favourite but her mother's as well. Charles, François-Victor and Adèle proved no competition for the lively Léopoldine. Hugo doted on his eldest little girl in an era when male children were much more eagerly desired, not only to carry on the family name but to satisfy France's desperate need for soldiers. (Even so, by this time, female children could inherit money and property equitably with males.)

The sensitive Adèle, who bore an astonishing resemblance to her older sister, was quick to perceive that her three siblings took precedence in the family pecking order. Adèle received no less outward care than her brothers and sister, for Madame Hugo, too, had enlightened ideas about child-rearing. Madame Hugo blamed herself for the death of her first child, Léopold, because she had entrusted him to nurses. She insisted on feeding and caring for the rest of her children herself, although wet nurses were in vogue and breast feeding was considered distasteful for a woman of her position.

Nor was young Adèle deprived of material things. As an infant, she was taken in her pram by her mother, or, more likely, a maid, to the Tuileries, the Luxembourg Gardens or the woods of the Champs-Élysées. Like all French children of the time, she enjoyed far more parental attention, affection and indulgence than her German and English counterparts, whose mothers and fathers believed firmly, not only that corporal punishment led to virtue, but that children were by nature savage beasts whose evil ways had to be beaten out of them. French parents, fortunately, had enjoyed the enlightened wisdom of Jean-Jacques Rousseau on the subject of child-rearing for more than half a century. Rousseau was one of the first to profess faith in the essential goodness and innocence of children and in the benefits of love and attention, even if he did not always adhere to his own teachings.

Victor Hugo certainly loved his children, but the single-mindedness that undoubtedly contributed to his literary genius, as well to his famous concentration and his prodigious output, did not make for a serene and equitable domestic life. Young Adèle learned the often-painful lessons of love, desire, jealousy, betrayal and even revenge early on. Later, as a young woman, she did not avoid their pitfalls but embraced the operatic dimensions of life as it was enacted in the Hugo household.

Following his wife's liaison with Sainte-Beuve and her refusal to resume sexual relations, Hugo began a series of affairs, often with more than one woman at a time, and many of them long-standing. This habit lasted until his dying days. The first and most durable of his extra-marital relationships was with Juliette Drouet, a young actress whose lack of talent did not prevent her from acting in several of Hugo's dramas. Her first role for Hugo was that of Princesse Négroni in *Lucrèce Borgia*, which premiered in February, 1833. By the middle of that month, Hugo and the pretty, delicate Juliette — who had once been a sculptor's model — had become lovers. At the time, George Sand (who by then was a correspondent of Hugo's, although they never actually met) was infatuated with a more famous and accomplished young actress, Marie Dorval. In a letter dated January 27, 1833, Gustave Planche tried to prevent Sand from getting too closely involved with Dorval. He wrote that he had been told by "an intimate acquaintance" of Juliette Drouet's — possibly Hugo — that Dorval "had once had for J____ the same sort of passion that Sappho had for the ladies of Lesbos."[8] It is not known whether Sand took Planche's information as a warning or a recommendation.

In the summer of 1845, one of Hugo's dalliances very nearly proved his undoing. In the previous century and during the Napoleonic years, adultery had been not only tolerated but encouraged. But by 1845, although extramarital affairs continued to be commonplace, the strict laws governing adultery that had long been on the books were once again being enforced. Hugo found out just how seriously the current regime took such transgressions when he imprudently became enmeshed with Léonie Biard, the wife of a prominent painter. "You are an angel," he wrote to her in one letter. "I kiss your feet. I kiss your tears."[9]

Under the name Lafon, Hugo rented the apartment in the rue Saint-Roch where their trysts took place, perhaps unaware that renting an apartment under an assumed name for such purposes was also illegal. At dawn on July 5, a gendarme interrupted Léonie and Hugo *in flagrante delicto*. (Eugène Ionesco gives a hilarious, if somewhat fanciful, account of this incident in his satirical work, *Hugoliad*.) Léonie, it seems, had aroused her husband's suspicions shortly before the scandalous event by asking for a divorce. The request convinced Biard, always suspicious of his wife's actions, that something was going on. Finally, he ascertained just what it was. Tracking the pair to the rue Saint-Roch, the vengeful husband had his wife arrested. The unfortunate Léonie was sent to the loathsome St. Lazare prison for women.

Hugo, however, was not touched. Much to his discredit, the poet immediately invoked his rights as a Peer of the Realm, which entitled him to be judged by a gathering of peers and no one else. He did not have to submit himself to the *code civil*, and he refused to co-operate with the officers. The brouhaha died down only after King Louis-Philippe I intervened personally, soothing Biard's manly pride by commissioning several works for one of his palaces. Hugo managed to escape without prosecution or even censure.

Hugo made no effort to get his mistress out of jail, nor did he visit her. Astonishingly, it was Madame Hugo who called on the forgotten Léonie in prison and arranged for her release. The two women had apparently joined forces some time before in a bid to oust Juliette Drouet from Hugo's heart — and his bed. Léonie, despite having already served time in prison, was then forced to spend six months in a nunnery before being granted her freedom. In the end, though, she got her wish: her husband filed for divorce. In 1851, Léonie sent Hugo's love letters to Juliette; later that year, she took up her pen and pursued a writing career which lasted for six years.

Adèle Hugo *(Musées de la Ville de Paris)*

Hugo's family suffered as a result of his extramarital affairs as much as it did from his growing capriciousness and his megalomania, but, on September 4, 1848, a worse catastrophe rocked it to its very foundations. On that day, Léopoldine and her husband of seven months, Charles Vacquerie, went boating on the Seine at Villequier, the village where the Vacquerie family lived. The pair were accompanied in a small racing skiff by Charles's uncle, Pierre Vacquerie, and Pierre's ten-year-old son. Somehow, the boat capsized in the tricky currents. Attempts to save Léopoldine then three months pregnant, from the cold water were fruitless. Her young husband, an excellent swimmer, refused to abandon his wife to her fate and died with her. His uncle and cousin also drowned. On September 6, a quadruple funeral was held at Villequier. Madame Hugo, who was beside herself with grief, did not attend. For several weeks afterwards she lay in bed wishing to die herself. For days she refused to speak and cradled her drowned daughter's long, dark hair, which had been cut off after her death, in her arms.

Victor Hugo, who had been on holiday in Spain with Juliette Drouet, knew nothing of the tragedy. Then, "on September 9, returning to France, the two travellers stopped in a café in Rochefort for refreshments and to read the newspapers which they hadn't read for several days. Opening one of them by chance, Hugo exclaimed 'It's horrible!' and looked as though he had been struck by lightening."[10]

None of the Hugos was ever the same again. Victor Hugo found himself unable to write novels or plays and turned his attention to poetry. The thirteen-year-old Adèle, eager to play the dutiful daughter, busied herself comforting her family during this period, to the detriment of her own well-being. Despite her best efforts to distract both herself and her family from the tragedy, life never quite got back to normal, and for many years the family mourned Léopoldine's death with considerable melodrama. A decade later, they displayed the dress in which the favourite daughter had drowned in their home in Jersey, and they came to believe that Léopoldine came back from the grave to speak to them at nightly séances. But of all the family members, Adèle was the most affected by her sister's death, finally becoming fixated on Léopoldine.

Adèle kept the depth of her distress mostly to herself, but photographs taken by her brother Charles (who had recently taken up the new fad) show a wistful, even melancholy young woman of haunting beauty. Although it was the fashion of the time to strike a serious pose for the photographer, painter or sculptor, Adèle could not disguise her emotional vulnerability. She had serious eyes, a delicate face and an aquiline nose like her mother's. Under her corsets, layers of petticoats, and heavy, dark-coloured dresses (the height of French chic), Adèle hid a slight figure. Her crowning glory was her thick, dark hair, which, when loosened from the two huge braids coiled on each side of her face, tumbled to the floor. Even Juliette Drouet proclaimed without reservation that Adèle was a "sweet and ravishing girl."[11] She was not the only one to feel that way. The pious, elegant and reserved Adèle was considered the perfect "*jeune fille accomplie.*" While still a teenager, she was hailed by many who knew her as a good and interesting writer, as well as an accomplished pianist and composer.

It must have been difficult for the beautiful and talented young woman to behave as virtuous French girls were expected to do and to obey her father without question. Despite the lack of formal education for girls (schooling was not thought to prepare them to be wives and mothers, to run a household or to grace a salon), Adèle had a lively, enquiring mind which often turned to matters considered far too serious and impenetrable for the fair sex. Moreover, Adèle had inherited her father's passion, and this, combined with her beauty, made her a sought-after companion for the opposite sex. No wonder Hugo felt compelled to follow the lead of other upstanding French fathers and lock up his daughter until she married.

Despite her father's caution and the watchful eyes of family and servants, Adèle managed to requite her passion at least twice as a teenager. The first time was at age sixteen with her future fiancé, Auguste Vacquerie, the brother of Charles Vacquerie, who had died so tragically with Léopoldine. Under the shady arcade which ringed the Place-

Royale, and out of sight of the family's third-floor apartments, Adèle shared her first kiss with the twenty-six-year-old Vacquerie. In due course, she and Vacquerie shared much more. At one assignation, he confessed, "I read Molière; Molière was more unhappy than I. I do not want your body without your heart; I will not treat you like a prostitute — I have more respect for you."

"Yes, you suffered," Adèle replied. "I gave myself to you because you suffered. Prostitution can be a sublime devotion and we don't know that the public girl is not a sister of charity."[12]

Their conversation indicates that Adèle had a rather relaxed attitude towards sexual intimacy, and that this may have made Auguste uncomfortable. Although it was not unusual for men at the time to have mistresses, similar behaviour in a woman, especially an unmarried girl, would have been scandalous. Yet Adèle obviously shared her father's passion, for her liaison with Vacquerie was only the first of her youthful encounters. Her infatuation with Vacquerie, a severe-looking man with a razor-sharp profile, was likely partly inspired by her curiosity about physical intimacy. She had hoped that in becoming engaged to him she might discover the same rapturous love her sister Léopoldine had found with his brother, Charles. But the first blush of love soon paled. Later that year, Adèle fell in love anew. This time, she chose Jean-Baptiste Auguste Clésinger, an unsavoury but talented sculptor with a reputation as a drunkard and a seducer of young women. In 1854, upon hearing that he was dying, Adèle confided to her diary that Clésinger, who was a good deal older than she,

was one of the men who had lit the fire of love in my heart, who could light it again. Will I never see again his glances — so hot and so cold — which I felt for three years? Clésinger! I remember the last time I saw you. It was in Paris. You were close to me the whole night. You courted me, you were absorbed in my love. Oh! you were a genius: the genius is in your hands, the genius is in your eyes. I loved you. When you were with me, I was happy.[13]

Clésinger's wild genius, so different from Vacquerie's melancholy, had dazzled her. Her turgid diary descriptions suggest that she may have been sexually intimate with him as well, ignorant, perhaps, of his crude and violent side, which manifested itself in a predilection for beating his pregnant mistress. He soon lost interest in her, but the bewildered Adèle could not understand that she had been used and cast aside by the rapacious artist. She remained fixated on Clésinger, even after he met, seduced, and married Solange Sand, the teenage daughter of George Sand.

Adèle and Solange didn't know each other, but they were close in age, of similar background and social accomplishments, and exceedingly passionate. At the time, Solange was engaged to marry a M. de Préaulx, and had come to Paris with her mother to shop for her trousseau. While there, they also decided to have Clésinger sculpt their busts in marble. After three or four sittings with Clésinger, who was at his charming best, Solange announced to her mother that she would marry, not her fiancé, but the penniless sculptor. "Jean-Baptiste Auguste Clésinger was far from being a mother's dream of a son-in-law. He was uncouth like the cuirassier he had once been, fond of the bottle and above all, an inveterate spendthrift."[14]

He and Solange were married in the spring of 1847, only a few weeks after Solange jilted M. de Préaulx. Two months later, Solange was pregnant. The relationship proved tumultuous, and Clésinger soon drank his way through his wife's considerable dowry. On a drunken visit to Sand's estate, Nohant, he nearly killed his brother-in-law, and he even struck his mother-in-law. Sand, who was no shrinking violet when it came to standing up for herself, was terrified. "That fiendish couple left last night," she wrote, "head over heels in debt, jubilant in their insolence, leaving behind a scandal they will never be able to live down. For three days I had been living in my own house in fear of murder. I never want to see them again, they will never soil this place again with their feet."[15]

Despite her lamentations about her lost love, Adèle was better off free of Clésinger. But she didn't see it that way. Years later, she still mourned his loss. "I had the sky in my soul," she wrote. "I loved, I felt that you found me beautiful. I was eighteen. Love, happy love, there is nothing but that in the world."[16]

Not long after Clésinger dismissed her, Adèle had a strange dream. "One night while I slept," she wrote, "in the dreams which precede one's deepest sleep, the face of an Englishman appeared before me and told me that he would play the role of lover in my life."[17] She never forgot the dream — or the handsome stranger in it.

By the age of twenty, Adèle had grown bored with the vapid routine of Parisian social life, with its empty gallantries and stiff formalities. Her loneliness was obvious, even to strangers. Over lunch at Chez Robelin, Eugène Vivier, a musician and composer, said to her, "You are an extraordinary woman. I am certain, without having seen you before, that you are very unusual. You have no friends among the young ladies of your own age."

"No," she responded, "I have none."

Adèle's solace lay in listening to her father and the illustrious guests who so often filled the family salon with lively discussions of politics, literature and social justice. The same room was just as likely to be occupied by Europe's most famous musicians, who came to dine, discuss and — to Adèle's delight — to perform. She had never quite recovered from the shock of Léopoldine's death, nor had she managed to become a replacement in her father's eyes for his favourite daughter. Her lengthy fixation on Clésinger, when there were so many other eligible men around — including Auguste Vacquerie — was the first indication that something might be wrong with the otherwise brilliant Adèle.

Emotional upheaval seemed to be stalking her, and the whole Hugo family. In 1851, Charles and François-Victor were imprisoned, and by December of that year, Victor Hugo himself was a fugitive from his homeland. Hugo had brought the exile upon himself, the result of an attempted political double-cross which backfired. During the 1851 election campaign, Victor Hugo loudly trumpeted his support of La-\martine for president of the republic in speeches and in *L'Événement*, a daily newspaper that he had helped to found in the summer of 1848.

By 1851, *L'Événement* was run by Charles and François-Victor Hugo, Auguste Vacquerie and Paul Meurice, who were also its chief writers. Following a visit from Charles Louis Napoléon, Hugo changed his mind and threw his support — and the newspaper — behind Napoléon Bonaparte's nephew.

It was a disastrous bit of bad judgement. Despite Louis Napoléon's sops to democracy, his real aim was dictatorship. Hugo was completely taken in, despite the fact that he, of all people, should have been able to read the warning signs. In 1836 and again in 1840, Louis Napoléon had attempted to overthrow Louis-Philippe. He was finally imprisoned for life, whereupon he set to work on a treatise favouring the eradication of poverty. This did not occupy all of his attention, however, and in 1846, posing as a bricklayer, he escaped and went to London. Two years later, Louis Napoléon was back in France. That year, popular discontent over the unfairness of the voting system, combined with rapid industrialization, explosive growth in French cities and a financial crisis, had forced the abdication of King Louis-Philippe in favour of the Comte de Paris. But public faith in the monarchy had been undermined, and Lamartine seized the moment to declare a provisional government, of which he became the leader.

The Second Republic, proclaimed on February 24, 1848, started out badly. In her diary, Adèle recorded her father's opinion of the events of the four months which followed:

> It was a strange and terrible time. All of France was stupefied and disconcerted, seemingly joyous yet secretly terrified. Everyone was blinkered by doubt and floundered in the vacuum created in the wake of the abdication. In the search for creditable leadership, it was impossible to distinguish the false from the true, the good from the bad, the just from the unjust, sex from sex, day from night, this woman who called herself Lamartine from this man who called himself George Sand.[18]

In other words, the world as the French had known it was turned on its ear. The president of the new Republic had a feminine-sounding name; one of the most famous writers of the day was a woman who had taken a man's name. Nothing seemed certain or predictable any longer.

Sand, whose real name was Baroness Aurore Dupin Dudevant, had helped fire the nascent women's movement to action, and almost single-handedly broke down many social, moral and sexual prejudices of the time. Having left a loveless marriage to pursue life as a writer, Sand astounded polite society by dressing up as a man, smoking cigars and taking numerous lovers, including Frédéric Chopin and Alfred de Musset. Hugo did not trouble to read any of Sand's books (he rarely devoted much time to other writers' works), but they did exchange views and share the same circle of friends, although not the same drawing rooms. Sand's opinion of Hugo was low. She described his 1839 play *Ruy Blas* as "stupidity," "absurdity" and "idiocy." "It is because his heart lacks fire that his muse lacks taste," she observed. To her, Hugo was "a man of genius who has been lost by praise, and is going straight to the lunatic asylum."[19]

Hugo must have regarded the strong-minded and outrageously independent Sand as a dangerous model for young French women, particularly his own daughter, who was already beginning to get ideas about how a modern young woman should behave. Adèle could hardly have escaped reading Sand's radical first novel, *Indiana*, and it may have shaped her later views on marriage. This book's "basic message was revolutionary. Women were made to realise with clarity that their marital problems were not individual cases of incompatibility, but the results of a social structure invented and perpetrated by men. They began to question an order of things that made wives the chattel of their husbands and denied them freedom of choice. Men of letters were impressed. Sainte-Beuve called it 'a darling work'; Balzac, 'the reaction of truth against fantasy.'"[20] From Hugo's point of view as a father, *Indiana* would certainly have represented an alarming attitude.

Yet Hugo must have secretly agreed with Sand's most important and vigorously held view, that passion should take absolute precedence over society and its prejudices. Like Hugo, she was concerned with the rights — or lack of them — of the common people, and with improving the miserable conditions of the majority of French working people. She took up the workers' cause, and, even more fervently, that of equal rights for women during the tumultuous years before and after the 1848 revolution.[21]

On June 4, 1848, Hugo had been elected to the Constituent Assembly; on June 23, four days of street fighting began over high unemployment and the Assembly's rash decision to assign work to unemployed men regardless of their trades and training. Hugo went to the barricades in an attempt to restore calm; instead, the insurgents occupied the Hugos' third-floor apartment at 6, Place Royale[22] and forced his family to flee. The Hugos stayed temporarily at 4, rue d'Isly before moving to 37, rue de la Tour-d'Auvergne a few months later.

But the Republicans had made inroads. By December 10, 1848, the confusion lifted long enough for elections to be held — the first in which universal *male* suffrage was allowed — and Louis Napoléon to be elected president of the Republic. The feminist campaign for female suffrage and the right to vote in the May, 1849, elections gathered steam. But Sand herself declined an invitation by early feminists to run for the National Assembly in no uncertain terms.

The new women's movement and Sand's adamant views changed forever the way Adèle saw life and her role in it. As her later diary entries show, Adèle became a staunch believer in the rights of women and, in particular, the tyranny of marriage. Up until her mid-teenage years, Adèle had been a quiet, obedient girl, earning praise for her femininity, her empathy and her beauty. Now she found herself drawn to the new rebellion. Adèle had begun to resent the attitudes of men like her father, who did not feel that women could occupy any meaningful place in society beyond the drawing room. His liberal views did not extend as far as granting women the right to a say in the government, and he even opposed Queen Victoria's right to rule, saying that women were unfit to govern despite ample evidence to the contrary. When the

Victor Hugo and his two sons *(Musées de la Ville de Paris)*

feminists also failed to win the right to vote in the 1849 elections, Adèle's disappointment was acute.

Louis Napoléon quietly worked to thwart the hard-won democratic gains the French populace had made. On December 2, 1851, he dissolved the National Assembly and, supported by a plebiscite, he installed an authoritarian regime. This regime, too, proved provisional, and he was soon transformed into a hereditary monarch. Astoundingly, this move would also be ratified by plebiscite, and Louis Napoléon would become Emperor Napoléon III.

In 1851, new restrictions had been imposed on journalists. Charles Hugo paid no attention, and on May 16, he attacked the death penalty in the pages of *L'Événement*. He was accused of showing contempt for the law and put on trial on June 11. Victor Hugo defended his son. Charles's trial proved to be Hugo's finest hour, at least oratorically. He performed his task admirably, scoring powerfully on point after point. Even his detractors could only admire the poet's ardent and eloquent defence, so unlike his usual speeches, riddled as they were with unwieldy rhetoric and meandering pronouncements which rendered them at best boring, at worst unintelligible. But Hugo's impassioned plea for his son lacked originality, a charge which was to be levelled at him again and again in later years, and in the end, his outstanding performance was not enough to save Charles. He was sentenced to six months in the notorious Concièrgerie and fined five hundred francs. Then François-Victor, arrested for tirades in *L'Événement* for the right of asylum for foreign exiles, was tried on September 15 of the same year. He was sentenced to nine months in jail and fined 2,000 francs. But it was widely held that the regime's real target was the poet himself.

Hugo was disgusted not only by Napoléon III's betrayal of his support, but by the heavy-handedness of the new regime, and he railed publicly against the ruler's duplicity. In retaliation, Napoléon closed down *L'Événement* and clapped Vacquerie, too, into prison. Madame Hugo had also written two articles for the newspaper, but they were not politically inflammatory enough to send her to prison along with her sons, or perhaps the opinions of a woman were not taken seriously. Soon after François-Victor's trial, Hugo went into voluntary exile in Brussels, where he kept up his agitation for the overthrow of Napoléon III.

One night Adèle had a peculiar dream:

I was in the bedroom that I occupied at the Place-Royale, and all of a sudden my mother entered and told me, "Your father wants to talk to you. He has gone crazy. He is exasperated. He is smashing the windows. . . ."

I ran to the salon, where my father bid me enter. "I am furious with Eugène Delacroix, who has the temerity to ask for your hand. I have sent him back the letter in which he makes this request, and I am now writing him a letter full of insults which will offend him, so that he will renounce all of his pretensions toward you."

In the dream, Adèle decided, against her father's wishes, to marry the painter (who was older than Victor Hugo), although she had never met him:

All of a sudden I perceived the torches which lit the altar and the darkness which enveloped the rest of the chapel. "Bah!" I said, "I am not married. It is a dream, because it is night and the torches are lit. It is a dream, it is a dream."

Painfully, I made this judicious reflection as I opened my eyes and saw before me in my bed at 37, rue de la Tour d'Auvergne, an enormous bowl of chocolate which my chambermaid, Elise, had brought.

"Mademoiselle would not wake up, so I had to make a lot of noise."

"My goodness, Elise," I responded, "you have done well. At the end of sleep and dreams lives reality and chocolate!" And I ate with a hearty appetite![23]

For the next six months, the two Adèles lived quietly in Paris, visiting François-Victor and Charles in prison daily. In November, they visited the patriarch in Brussels. Upon their return home, Madame Hugo wrote to her husband that Adèle had tired quickly on the journey. "The poor child doesn't carry her poverty as willingly as I do. We lead, we two, as retiring a life as possible, as befits our situation."[24] On December 6, Adèle fell ill, apparently suffering from some sort of psychological disorder, but she soon recovered.

At the expiry of his sentence in December, 1851, Charles left Paris to join his father in exile. It was not until April 22, 1852, that Adèle was able to announce to her father, "Toto is free." Thanks to a pardon by Napoléon III, François-Victor did not have to serve the remaining two months of his sentence — much to his disgust. "The poor boy refused with all his might the pretentious favour that he was forced to accept," Adèle wrote. "[Napoléon III's] pardon of Toto is unfortunate good luck; his sentence was already more than half served and he would have preferred to stay in prison."[25] Nevertheless, François-Victor's release freed all three of the remaining members of the Hugo family from their unhappy captivity in Paris.

Meanwhile, Hugo's political activities had resulted in expulsion by the edgy Belgians, who were eager to please the new French regime. The poet chose Jersey, one of the English-owned Channel Islands, for the next phase of his exile. Despite his violent dislike of England and the English, Hugo knew the island harboured a substantial French expatriate population. It was, moreover, relatively close to France, and its gloomy climate and coastline suited his morbid imagination perfectly. Besides, his idol, Chateaubriand, had once spent time there. His choice did not delight the rest of the family, particularly Madame Hugo. Jersey was small, unsophisticated and isolated. It was hardly convenient for trips to Paris or Brussels. Getting to Jersey from either capital was difficult at the best of times; often, the circuitous land route combined with the uncertain seas to make any voyage to the island a protracted adventure. Moreover, no one save François-Victor spoke or understood

English with any fluency. Despite this, Hugo's decision stood, and he summoned the clan to make its preparations to join him.

On May 28, 1852, Monsieur Ridel, the auctioneer, came to the family's huge apartment to inspect the goods they were putting up for sale. Adèle could feel the excitement building inside her as she and her mother picked through their belongings, trying to decide what would best serve them in exile. Among the few things which Madame Hugo kept were Hugo's bed and the Sèvres china given to them by King Charles X.

On June 4, Adèle began her *Journal of Exile*.

The following day, she recorded:

The apartment is sorted out. My father's room is arranged. I prepared his office myself. His desk is in front. To the left and right are his two seals. A bronze paperweight and a globe in the middle of the table. Then his copying paper decorated with his designs, four little boxes of cards, a water jug of metallic silver occupied the back of the desk.[26]

Crowds gathered outside on June 9, the day the goods were open to public inspection. The apartment had a panoramic view of Paris, of which Hugo was justly proud, and, down below, Adèle could see that the street was jammed with carriages. She was thrilled. Finally, she felt fully involved in a family adventure; the future, from her perspective, was delightfully uncertain:

A queue of carriages occupies the whole of the rue de la Tour d'Auvergne. The crowd is so dense that in opening the windows one can feel their breathing, and on closing them one fears asphyxiating the visitor. Their cries — "God but this is beautiful"; "Look at the bust of Madame Hugo!" "What a beautiful bed!" "I want to sit in Victor Hugo's armchair!" — reached up to me.[27]

The next day, June 10, M. Ridel auctioned most of the Hugo possessions. They sold quickly. For nearly a month afterwards, Adèle and her mother lived in the huge and virtually empty apartment. François-Victor, immersed in the charms of a Parisian actress after his long prison stay, refused to take any part in the preparations; he had no intention of leaving the capital, no matter how much his father blustered. Charles, for his part, was happy in Brussels, and saw no reason to subject himself to the rigours of Jersey, either.

Adèle had no such power to refuse her father, nor did she want to. She welcomed the stormy winds of exile as if they were a Mediterranean breeze. She had grown sad amidst the gaiety of Paris; to her, exile was not a trial but a romantic adventure. Jules Janin, a friend of the Hugos, described the melancholy Adèle during her last few days in Paris:

> At the open window, a young girl in a white dress, her arms crossed over her chest, her black hair done in the fashion of Camille de Corneille, watches in silence, the enormous city at her feet! Chaste and naive apparition of an honest and sincere regret! What does this child think of, what abandoned dreams are in this young heart, what says this spirit, full of sadness for her exiled father? . . .
>
> I see you there, alone in this empty, abandoned house, waiting for the hour that will bring you, dignified sister of Léopoldine, beauty that the poems and the writers of this time have saluted with such pride! One and all they seem to say, in seeing this charming, resigned beauty . . . "There is the most beautiful poem of the century." Serious child, in the middle of such glory, searching the silence stronger than all this noise, a great courage, a great heart. . . . She has seen, stoic and without letting fall a tear, the disaster of this day. . . . She waits, silent and immobile and calm at the open window.[28]

On July 15 Adèle said her final *adieux* to Paris and, with her mother and Auguste Vacquerie (who had been released from prison May 8), she went to spend ten days in Villequier, Vacquerie's hometown. From there, they travelled to Southampton, England, and finally they sailed for Jersey and exile on the last day of June. Adèle wrote, "At 10:30 in the evening we left Southampton. We left by the Royal Mail on a superbly calm night, little resembling the previous night. I went to sleep in my cabin."

The following morning, Adèle rose early. "I woke and went up to the bridge. The sea was calm as a mirror. Many rocks, and then more rocks, such is the view. We passed Guernsey. The port of St-Pierre is built in an amphitheatre of houses situated close to the sea. Rocks, and more rocks, and then, in the distance, the shores of what is called Jersey."[29]

1. Victor Hugo, "La Prière pour tous," lines 214-215, dated June 15, 1830. Translations of this and other works by Victor Hugo are my own unless otherwise indicated.

2. Joanna Richardson, *Victor Hugo* (London: Weidenfeld and Nicolson, 1976), p.45.

3. Jacques Boudet, *L'Histoire de France par image: de Louis XIV à la Révolution de 1848* (Paris: Bordas, 1982), Vol. 2, p.133.

4. Raymond Escholier, *Hugo, roi de son siècle* (Paris: Arthaud, 1970), p.118. All translations from this work are my own.

5. Escholier, pp.135-36.

6. Arnaud Laster, *Victor Hugo* (Paris: Belfond, 1984), p.18. My translation.

7. Richardson, p.22.

8. Ruth Jordan, *George Sand* (London: Constable, 1976), pp.70-71.

9. Victor Hugo to Léonie Biard, letter #4, from the collection of the Maison de Victor Hugo (on public display). My translation.

10. Anon., *Collection les géants* (Paris: Paris-Match, 1970), p.30. Translations from this work are my own.

11. Henri Guillemin, *L'Engloutie* (Paris: Éditions du Seuil, 1985), p.20. Translations from this work are my own.

12. Guille, Vol. 3, pp.414-15.

13. Guille, Vol. 3, p.60.

14. Jordan, p.240.

15. Jordan, p.244.

16. Guille, Vol. 3, p.61.

17. Guille, Vol. 3, p.37.

18. Guille, Vol. 3, p.141

19. George Sand, *Correspondance* (Paris: Calmann Lévy, 1892), Vol. 3, p.223.

20. Jordan, pp.62-63.

21. Boudet, Vol. 2, p.139.

22. Now known as the Place des Vosges, it is the oldest square in Paris, having been laid out by Henri IV early in the seventeenth century. The apartment houses, made of pink stone, are still handsome, and the square itself, filled with trees and lined with quiet cafés, echoes with the shouts of children. It is now the site of the Maison de Victor Hugo, the museum dedicated to the poet.

23. Guille, Vol. 1, pp.178-80. Raymond Escholier, *Victor Hugo, cet inconnu* (Paris: Plon, 1951), pp.249-50. Translations from this work are my own.

24. Guille, Vol. 1, p.54.

25. Guille, Vol. 1, p.55.

26. Guille, Vol. 1, p.196.

27. Guille, Vol. 1, p.198.

28. Jules Janin, *Histoire de la littérature dramatique* (Paris: Levy, 1854), Vol. 4, p.422.

29. Guille, Vol. 1, pp.224-25.

Chapter 2

A Princess in a Tower
Jersey, 1852-1854

The island of Jersey . . . is a bunch of flowers dipped in the ocean, a bunch which has the fragrance of the rose, and the bitterness of the waves.

— *Adèle Hugo*[1]

*W*ith the hood of her black travelling cloak pulled low over her brow, and clutching her mother's arm, a slightly seasick Adèle Hugo stepped off the Royal Mail packet boat and onto the small island in the English Channel which would be her home for the next three years. They landed at St Helier, Jersey's tiny capital, on July 31, 1852, three days after Adèle's twenty-second birthday. "We arrived on Jersey," she wrote. "Maman was nearly recognized, but what does it matter! We are among the English. We are beginning exile, just as a year ago we began imprisonment in the persons of my two brothers."[2]

The two women checked into the the Hôtel de la Pomme d'Or while they awaited the arrival of their patriarch. On August 2, evidently bored with their routine after only two days, Adèle recorded curtly:

We await my father. We drove to St-Aubin to look for lodgings. Few lodgings. Everything is taken. An English woman, more or less impertinent, closed her door in our faces. We await my father. M. Auguste and Maman have gone down to the pier.[3]

On August 3, the *Jersey Times* announced the arrival of "Madame and Mademoiselle Hugo, mother and daughter of the illustrious poet of this name who himself is expected daily." On August 4, the great man himself appeared. Adèle wrote:

> My father finally arrived at 12:30 this morning. I haven't seen him since December 3, 1851. I would never have believed anyone who would have told me "you will leave your father on December 3, 1851, in the rue de la Tour d'Auvergne in Paris; you will not see him again until August 5, 1852, on the island of Jersey, on board a ship." Nevertheless, that is how it happened.
>
> There was a large crowd of Jerseymen, English, and French exiles waiting at the pier. My father embraced me and then saluted and talked to the French exiles all around him. After that, we went to the hotel.[4]

Her father, Adèle recorded, took this outpouring of good will in stride and immediately assumed the role of leader of the *proscrits*. "Another ovation from the exiles. My father delivered a touching speech to them on equality, and on the good hope that they would one day triumph. . . . They shouted twice, with my father: 'Vive la République!'"[5] Royalty could hardly have received a better reception.

The family stayed at the Hôtel de la Pomme d'Or until August 16, when it was finally decided that they would live at Marine Terrace, situated a quarter of a mile from St Helier. The house had not been Hugo's choice, and, Adèle says, a "great battle" had taken place over where they would live. Their new home was spacious but austere, consisting of

> two semi-detached houses, leading into two separate gardens. The Hugos' part was furnished in a very simple English style. The ground floor consisted of a conservatory opening onto the garden, and a room which became a studio for amateur photography. There was also a kitchen, domestic quarters and a

drawing room. On the first floor were the bedrooms of Madame Hugo and Adèle, a visitor's room and a dining-room. On the second floor were the bedrooms of Charles and François-Victor, and Hugo's room, which looked over the sea, towards the French coast.[6]

Soon, the Hugos assembled their peculiar extended family. Juliette Drouet, Hugo's mistress, rented a house a discreet distance away, a move which soon had the conservative Jerseymen frowning at Hugo's moral turpitude. But for Juliette, there really had been no choice. She, like Hugo's family, had come at his insistence, to be with him during his exile. Charles Hugo, like his father, had been followed into exile by his mistress, Augustine Allix, whose brother Jules would arrive in 1853 when he himself was condemned to exile. And Auguste Vacquerie, Adèle's first lover, had arrived in July with Adèle and her mother. Described in the *Jersey Times* as a well-known writer and former editor of *L'Événement*, Auguste lived in the Hugo household at Marine Terrace.

In the first few months of entries in her *Journal of Exile*, Adèle dwells on the family's contentment at being reunited. She recounts, in minute and often wry detail, the goings-on in the Hugo home, her father's political opinions, and her reflections on some of the most important men and women of letters of the time. Her approach is fresh and insightful, and the diary is littered with comic drawings of some of the family's many guests. This journal, written for others to read, contrasts starkly with the cryptic, encoded entries in her secret, personal diary, which reveals a confused, lonely girl who was often at the mercy of her personal demons.

But the hearty Victor Hugo was as oblivious to the unhappiness of his daughter as he was to the mighty sea winds which blew up from the beach. He immersed himself in his new life, taking vigorous walks and swimming daily in the sea. Hugo was particularly flattered by the crowds of French exiles who called at Marine Terrace to hear him hold forth on economics, politics, and life in general. On their first public excursion as a family, an evening at the local theatre, the Hugos were

Adèle Hugo *(Musées de la ville de Paris)*

given places of honour in the Governor's box. Adèle was unimpressed with the "small, badly lit" theatre, and the English-language play turned out to be mediocre, but the family — especially Hugo — enjoyed the attention they received from the audience.

All too aware of the dangers of idleness, Hugo insisted that everyone in the house engage in some constructive work for the better part of the day, just as he did. Accordingly, the family threw itself into the business of exile, with daily bouts of reading, writing and fulminating. François-Victor finally tore himself away from the delights of his young actress and arrived on September 22; he undertook the staggering task of translating all of Shakespeare's works into French. Charles was writing a book and dabbling in photography. Madame Hugo, too, took up her pen. She was something of an expert on her topic, her famous husband, but her book, *Victor Hugo raconté par un témoin de sa vie*, was not published until 1911, long after her death.

Adèle made every effort to imitate her busy kin. She commenced writing a book about female emancipation, perhaps as a kind of homage to George Sand, perhaps as a compensation for her own lack of liberty. She vowed that the work was a serious one which "no one would laugh at in a hundred years." The idea was a daring one, and perhaps as near as Adèle could come to rebuking her father for the constraints he placed upon her freedom. Writing came naturally to every member of the Hugo clan, and Adèle was anything but discouraged from pursuing the gift they shared. But Adèle appeared to wish to earn her living by writing, which was unthinkable for a woman; her only vocation was to marry and have children.

The business of writing was at best a perilous existence, and for women it was a difficult path indeed. In the United States, where there was no longer any stigma attached to female writers, they frequently earned less than men and were also expected to perform arduous household and mothering duties. Becoming a governess was really the only occupation to which a well-brought-up young woman such as Adèle might aspire, but then only if she found herself single and in straitened circumstances. In 1852, Alice B. Neal remarked in her article

"American Female Authorship," published in the popular *Godey's Ladies Book*, "The salary of many a governess equals, if not exceeds, the largest income we have ever known an American authoress to receive." Even in America, the desire of a woman such as Adèle to pursue a literary career purely for love of writing was considered distasteful and unfeminine. "We have said nothing of simple literary ambition," Neal continues, "because we do not recognize it as a worthy motive. It savors too much of vanity, and its returns are too often only vexation of spirit."[7]

Adèle had other frustrations to vex her spirit. She alone of the Hugo clan was endowed with a gift for music. At twenty-two, having dedicated long hours each day to her writing and her music, Adèle had begun to come into her own as a composer. Auguste Vacquerie wrote about Adèle's evening recitals for the family:

> We have the sweetest nights. When we have worked hard, Mademoiselle Hugo recompenses us by playing the piano, and we hear what melodies she has composed. Charming, original music, which she has created all by herself, far from the Opera, far from the Conservatory, exits spontaneously from nature and from the heart. . . . A great musician, whom no one has ever seen, distributes Himself through the flowers, the waves, the oaks. . . . She listens to these concerts, this daughter of the poet. She hears the instruments and the voices. She cultivates the murmurs and the noises and she mixes them with her soul, her destiny, her lost country . . . and she creates from this nature and this life profound music, free, real, sad and happy.[8]

By 1856, the Guernsey *Comet* could report that, on May 8, Adèle's setting of her father's poem, "Nuits de juin," was on the program of a public concert. Adèle also initiated plans to publish her compositions with a Belgian firm.

Perhaps Adèle's talent had been enhanced by the parade of musicians with whom Hugo had long associated; many of these, along with new musical acquaintances, visited him in exile. But she certainly derived none of her musical talent from him. Although he admired his friend Franz Liszt's talent, Hugo described his instrument as "infamous"; in a letter to Théophile Gautier written on April 17, 1852, Hugo complained, "You know I hate the piano," that "wooden beast."[9] Perhaps Adèle's constant practice, added to his continuing personal dislike of her, contributed to his distaste for the instrument and his inability to appreciate the depth of his daughter's talent.

Adèle had no financial reason to earn her own living, and artistic ambition for its own sake was considered unworthy; her family tolerated and encouraged her desire to write and compose only so long as she remained single. They constantly reminded her that her first and only duty was to marry and have children, and, to fulfil it properly, she would have to abandon her other interests. The choice was repugnant, for she had no interest in or mastery of any of the other "womanly arts." She preferred playing the piano and composing settings for her father's poems to working a piece of embroidery. The family had always had a retinue of servants to see to their daily needs, and although Adèle might be expected one day to oversee her own household, that day seemed remote. The actual cooking of a meal was a complete mystery to her.

Despite her preoccupation with writing and composing, Adèle's initial expectations of her life as an exile proved not only naive but dismally unfounded. As the endlessly repetitive weeks wore on, Adèle's enthusiasm for the exile's life waned. "The ambience on Jersey," she wrote, "was, all things considered, unbearable. On the island were three hundred exiles, extremists, dying of inaction and of nostalgia, bursting with unemployable ardour."[10]

Yet Adèle retained some measure of faith in the future. Her father tried to persuade her to accept life as it was. "The possible is possible, and the impossible is impossible," he told her. "Everything that has been discovered up until now springs from human attributes and does not go against nature, but what you believe goes against and reverses all the laws of nature."

She replied, "Is it not also said that the printing press astonished, that electricity, that steam, that chloroform, that the daguerreotype, that even séances go against nature? . . . You believe in progress within the limits of the possible, but I believe even in the limits of the impossible. I believe that it will be possible for man to become an angel, and that it will be human to be superhuman."[11]

Adèle felt especially confined and stifled because she realized that her femininity, not her talent, posed the biggest obstacle to her artistic success. It was an obstacle which her brothers and other men around her, like Vacquerie, had never had to confront, and she began nursing a resentment toward their easy freedom. Adèle had always had an artistic, even melancholic, temperament, but as month succeeded tedious month on Jersey, she became more and more withdrawn, dreaming alone in her room for hours on end, confiding only in her secret diary, written in her special code. "It is difficult," François-Victor complained, "to live with Lord Spleen [his father] and Lady Nostalgia [Adèle]."[12]

Adèle's emotional difficulties were compounded by the fact that her family insisted on treating her like a giddy girl. The limits of her freedom were sharply defined, not only by family decree but by social convention. Her chief manacle was her father. Hugo, unable to forget the incident between his wife and Sainte-Beuve, seemed determined that his only remaining daughter would not betray him in the same way. Either he was unaware that Adèle had already had at least two love affairs, or else he had decided to make sure she would never transgress again. As an unequivocal ally, he had centuries of French custom, which forbade unmarried women or those who had not reached twenty-five, the age of majority, from appearing in public unescorted. Nor did she get much sympathy from other family members. Instead of intervening on his sister's behalf, her brother Charles told her bluntly that marriage was the only path to her independence from their father's dominance. That the family no longer lived on French soil did not weaken their enforcement of French behavioural codes.

Their prohibitions did not entirely thwart Adèle. Although she had once been obedient to the point of submission, a new Adèle was emerging. She began to defy her parents by going out alone and petulantly refusing to marry. Under French law, Hugo would have been well within his rights to confine his daughter to her room for a month, faced with such rebellion, but he did not. Still, his forbearance did not stop Adèle from noting bitterly that she felt like a piece of her father's property, and her repeated violations earned her severe chastisement. Hugo went so far as to censor what Adèle read; even works by his colleagues were not safe, particularly the novels of Alexandre Dumas, a good friend of the family and well known to Adèle. S.P. Oliver, an English resident on Guernsey who was the poet's neighbour for some time, observed, "One day, the subject discussed at table was the education of ladies, apropos of a series of lectures then being given by a young professor (present at table) to the young ladies of Guernsey. On some of those present objecting to the excessive love of novel-reading by young girls, Victor Hugo launched out a masterly defence of novelists, from Homer down to Dante and Cervantes; at the same time, he allowed the evil of young girls being allowed to read certain works by Dumas and Paul de Kock."[13]

It was made clear to Adèle that her situation would be quite different if only she would marry. Auguste Vacquerie was the family's first choice, no doubt at least partly because they still mourned Léopoldine and her beloved husband Charles, Auguste's brother. A few years earlier, he had been Adèle's choice, too. Vacquerie was still devoted to Adèle, and he held advanced ideas about women's equality. He knew of, and supported, Adèle's insistence on personal freedom. For years he had been her *de facto* fiancé, yet she had so far refused to take the fateful step into matrimony.

Adèle's passion for Vacquerie had long since passed, but that in itself should not have been a matter of great significance; love and matrimony rarely went together in upper-class French marriages. Adèle recognized, too, that her brother Charles was right: marriage would bring her a measure of independence from her domineering father. But she also knew that, unless she chose a sympathetic man, the matter of her independence and her career would likely remain in the same state of arrest as it had under her father.

The Hugos, like most French families of their class, believed that for women all liberty outside of marriage and the family home was dangerous. So were single women. The medieval view that girls must marry, and marry early, was still adhered to. Marriageable age for French girls was anywhere between fifteen and twenty. Sometime during their mid-teens, they began attending their first balls and were expected to become engaged within a year, or two at most. A girl who lingered too long at home lost some of her market value, since it was suspected that something must be wrong with her. The longer she remained unmarried, the greater the risk that she would also lose her greatest attribute — her virtue.

So the Hugo family advised Adèle with some urgency. She was already in danger of becoming an old maid and an embarrassment to the family, and Victor Hugo could not tolerate embarrassment. He promised Adèle a generous dowry, which, he told her, he hoped would render her "marriageable." Adèle found his remarks tasteless, and she responded by proclaiming marriage "a humiliating thing for a woman," a mere transfer of property from patriarch to husband. She added, as if to appease her father's famous pride, that she would not miss for the world being called Miss Hugo.[14]

As their daughter aged into her mid-twenties without showing any serious inclination toward marrying, the Hugos became more and more worried, not only that she would not make a good marriage, but that she was increasingly unhappy. For her unhappiness they could offer no solution. Suitors, discreetly encouraged by Hugo, came to call; between 1852 and 1863, Adele received five marriage proposals from some of the continent's most eligible bachelors. She refused them all. Meanwhile, the spurned Vacquerie nonetheless remained in the household and very much in love with Adèle.

While Adèle was a prisoner of the monotony of life on Jersey and the strict rules imposed on her, her neurotic behaviour increased. In her secret diary she began to praise her own beauty and accomplishments extravagantly, and now, too, the disquieting dream she had had in 1846 in Paris about the strange man preordained to change her life returned to haunt her. Adele first referred to an elusive Englishman in her secret diary on December 27, 1852, although she did not yet recognized him as the mysterious man of her prophetic dream. In fact, she professed little interest in Albert Andrew Pinson, mentioning him only in the context of another assignation. Two days after Christmas, Adèle had gone next door on the pretext of borrowing a boat from the Hugos' landlord, Monsieur Rose. The landlord was not home, as she well knew, but his son, whom she identifies only as J___ Rose, was. Adèle knew the young man was strongly attracted to her; the feeling seems to have been mutual. "I went back; I talked of insignificant things. I was ravishing, dazzling; I had a veil of tulle which rendered me incomparable. I was on fire."[15]

Adèle had time and again been called a beautiful young woman, yet the high praise was a curious way for the normally modest Adèle to describe herself. The harbouring of grandiose delusions (later she would claim to have composed all of the European operas popular at the time) is a symptom of severe manic depression or schizophrenia, and these diary entries may be evidence of Adèle's own mental illness. Her father indulged in the same boastfulness, but his strengths were well-established. Unlike him, Adèle never took any concrete, sustained steps to prove what she believed to be her superiority.

That December day, on the pretext that he would teach her English while she taught him French, J___ Rose and Adèle agreed to read to each other. Rose's choice was an English version of the memoirs of Jean-Jacques Casanova de Seingalt, better known simply as Casanova, and he selected for Adèle's instruction the bawdy descriptions of a young couple's nuptial romps. Adèle pretended to find the passages shocking, but she did not end their mutual tutorial nor make any attempt to leave. When they finally did stop reading to each other, Adèle records, Rose grew even bolder. "The lesson over, he said to me, Mademoiselle, kiss me, I will not, I assure you, make the slightest resistance. Start with me, finish with P___."[16]

Rose and his brothers had often mentioned Monsieur P___. "They say that he is in love with me," Adèle noted, unimpressed. When she returned to the Rose household the following day, December 28, Rose implored her to wait a moment, and she would surely meet P___. "No, I can't, I must return for dinner," Adèle answered coldly,[17] professing little interest in the dashing young man with a reputation for adventure. But, despite Adèle's insistence on beating a hasty retreat this time, Rose managed to walk her to the door and kiss her. Far from being repelled by his forwardness, Adèle later confessed to her diary that she enjoyed it.

Rose promised to bring Pinson to visit Adèle the following Wednesday. But the meeting never took place. Adèle quickly realized she had gone too far in her amours with the infatuated Rose, who might now want her to be his mistress or even his wife. She was not sufficiently interested in him to want either, and she resolved not to see him again. Rose soon took to his bed, partly due to Adèle's rebuff. On January 17, 1853, Adèle noted in her diary that the young man was gravely ill (likely with tuberculosis, which was rampant) and was pining for a visit from her. Suspecting that he wanted to play on her sympathies, Adèle refused to call on him, and she never saw him again — he died on July 6, 1853.

It would be two more years before Adèle and Albert Andrew Pinson finally met, and by then, Pinson's circumstances would be greatly changed.

On April 2, 1853, a curious thing happened, the first in a series of unusual occurrences. "It was nine o'clock in the evening," Adèle wrote:

> We were going to dine. Night had completely fallen. All of a sudden the door to the salon opened and Victor Hugo saw enter a tall woman, pale and blonde, visible only by the weak light of the fire. This tall woman advanced, singing, and said to him, "Monsieur Hugo! Monsieur Hugo!" then sat down at the piano and sang again, "France! Poor France!"[18]

The woman, who was English, then asked to have dinner with the family. Hugo, who had experience dealing with the mentally unbalanced, calmly agreed and escorted her into the dining room. A short time later, a doctor arrived and took her away. The Englishwoman was a guest of their neighbour and landlord, Mr. Rose. Suddenly, in the middle of a quiet conversation, the woman had risen and announced she was going to visit Victor Hugo. "And before anyone could stop her, she took two leaps. In a minute, she was at our door."[19]

The strange goings-on didn't stop with the madwoman. Adèle couldn't help but hear the tall tales spread about by the islanders. Some said the devil had appeared to them and armed themselves with crosses to protect themselves. Others claimed to have seen the Virgin Mary and had erected a chapel. Marine Terrace had its own demon or guardian angel, known as the White Lady. To evoke her, Adèle wrote, one had to go to the end of the terrace, where there was a large black cross on the wall separating the terrace from the sea:

> One night, three months ago, a young workman was coming home from work. He went by Saint-Luc's church which is near Marine Terrace. Suddenly, he saw at the end of the road a shape, white and immobile. . . . Startled, the workman did not dare advance or retreat. To advance would be to offend the apparition; to retreat would be to invite it to follow him. But to stay where he was would have been impossible. . . . The worker decided finally to continue on his way, and running, flying and lost, closed his eyes, with his hair standing on end, passed full of terror in front of the spectre.[20]

Adèle relished the ghostly island tales; they fit with her own macabre leanings, particularly her fixation on Léopoldine. She could hardly have ignored her dead sister's presence. Portraits of the dead girl abounded throughout the house. Scraps of her clothing and locks of her hair had been preserved in Madame Hugo's room. To Adèle, it seemed that only her own death could put her on the same pedestal as Léopoldine. She even dreamed of dying with Auguste, in a similar tragedy. "Why not die, exceptional woman, young, beautiful, well-brought up, important, loving, dignified daughter of Victor Hugo?" she lamented,

"Die as a dignified woman with an exceptional man, important and unique in spirit and in heart?"[21]

At Marine Terrace, Adèle constantly felt the brooding presence of Auguste Vacquerie weighing upon her. He burst out in uncontrollable fits of jealousy almost daily and watched her every move. The only thing which now bound them together was the tragic deaths of his brother and her sister, and a cloud of melancholy descended over her whenever she was near him. Even when they were not together, she had periods of black despair. She yearned to begin a life of her own and to share her love with someone who inspired her passion, just as her sister had done. Indeed, Adèle could no longer hide the strain of life on Jersey. She had become childishly unreasonable and stubborn; her bouts of defiance and withdrawal continued.

One evening, Charles voiced Adèle's sentiments exactly. "I will not regret Jersey," he blurted out. "I will have no grief in leaving it. I will have no more grief in leaving Jersey than I had in leaving the Concièrgerie. It is a mistake to think that one longs for the moments of sadness in life and the places where one has suffered."

But Victor Hugo could not abide the point of view of his eldest son and most outspoken child, who was simply putting into words the well-guarded opinion of the rest of the family. Hugo, who had found the island the perfect place to write uninterrupted, extolled its virtues. "You are wrong," he told Charles. "I find that it is necessary to long and to know longing. I will look back fondly on this house, the Terrace. I will not forget the sweet life, the profound liberty that one has here. Here one feels free. And to crown it all, we have the sea and the sky."

Charles would have none of it. "Jersey might be liberty," he retorted, "but it is also inactivity. Me, I need to construct barricades, to fire rifles, to go to Spain, to make noise, to make an uproar. I don't like this life in Jersey; it is too calm. Life is useless if one does not use it."[22]

The chasm of uselessness and despair yawned widely before Adèle.

1. Richardson, p.122.

2. Richardson, p.120.

3. Guille, Vol. 1, p.230.

4. Guille, Vol. 1, p.236.

5. Richardson, p.122.

6. Richardson, p.123.

7. Alice B. Neal, "American Female Authorship," *Godey's Lady's Book* 41 (June, 1852), p.147.

8. Guille, Vol. 1, pp.61-62.

9. Guille, Vol. 3, p.425.

10. Jean de Mutigny, *Victor Hugo et le spiritisme* (Paris: Fernand Nathan, 1981), p.13.

11. Guille, Vol. 2, p.117.

12. Bernard Boringe, "Adèle, l'autre fille de Victor Hugo," *Historia* 347 (October, 1975), p.76.

13. S.P. Oliver, "Victor Hugo at Home," *The Gentleman's Magazine* (London, 1870), p.721.

14. Guille, Vol. 1, p.69.

15. Guille, Vol. 2, p.457.

16. Guille, Vol. 2, p.458. Throughout her diaries Adèle signifies Albert Pinson with the initial P.

17. Guille, Vol. 2, p.462.

18. Guille, Vol. 2, p.52.

19. Guille, Vol. 2, p.53.

20. Guille, Vol. 3, p.153.

21. Boringe, p.77.

22. Guille, Vol. 3, pp.324-30.

Chapter 3

The Quick and the Dead
Jersey, 1854

Jersey is an island full of legends. There is not a rock, not an old ruin which is not haunted by apparitions.

— *Adèle Hugo*[1]

*E*arly in June of 1854, Adèle was more than a little surprised to find a handsome young stranger sitting at the dinner table, a blond-haired, fine-featured and smartly dressed Englishman. His blue eyes and wry smile enchanted her, and she discovered, to her delight, that he spoke fluent French. It was only when Albert Andrew Pinson was introduced that she realized he was the same young man her late neighbour and would-be suitor J___ Rose had so often spoken about — and the man who had appeared to her in her prophetic dream. He was every bit as dazzling as the dream (and J___ Rose) had promised he would be. Fittingly, their first encounter had actually taken place, unknown to Adèle, not far from Jersey's windswept beach, near the place where Adèle had so recently despaired of ever finding love and happiness. "He saw me for the first time on a bench on the terrace in Jersey," she confided to her private diary. "I was sitting down, reading; I was absorbed in my book and I didn't see him. But he saw me, and from that day . . . he loved me."[2]

That evening transformed Adèle's life forever. "Reményi [a violinist often called the "Hungarian Paganini"] played," she wrote. "At the back of the room was Pinson. His fine and gracious face appeared to me sweetly through the space choked with cigar smoke. At that moment, I recalled how eight years before, at the Place Royale in 1846, perhaps in October of the same year, I loved Auguste. I thought of nothing else." But then she had had the portentous dream about the Englishman — Pinson — who would become her lover. "It has taken Albert eight years to realize this dream."[3]

The pair met often after that; Pinson came regularly to dinner, sometimes several times a week. On June 7, Adèle boldly invited him to join the Hugo household in a séance. These séances had begun the year before. Delphine Gay de Girardin, who had perfected the new fad of table-rapping, had arrived on September 6, 1853, for an eight-day visit. A favourite in Parisian circles at the time, Madame de Girardin was a friend of Lamartine as well as Hugo, and her ardent fans considered her a sort of romantic deity. In fact, Chateaubriand greeted the announcement of her marriage to a prominent publisher with groans, for he felt he had lost his greatest inspiration. Naturally, Madame de Girardin's conversation with the Hugos turned to the subject of greatest importance to her. "Do you do the tables?" she asked.

Victor Hugo was skeptical despite himself; his wife, with her characteristic good sense, simply smiled. Of course, like everyone on Jersey, the senior Hugos had tried "the tables," but so far without success. In the corner of the parlour sat the little table with which they had tried to summon the spirits, but Madame de Girardin had quickly pointed out that, for a proper séance, the table had to be round, with a single supporting pedestal ending in three legs. Furthermore, every member of the family had to take part or the spirits would not appear. Madame de Girardin soon unearthed a table with the appropriate dimensions at a local antique dealer's shop, and attempts to contact the spirit world began in earnest.[4]

Even with the requisite elements in place, the first séances at the Hugo household were dismal failures, and it was not until September 11 that the seekers managed to contact the spirits. To everyone's shock, the otherworldly visitor at that first successful séance said her name was Léopoldine. "From that moment on, Delphine de Girardin had no further need to stimulate her hosts. And during two and a half years, from 1853 to 1855, séances were held practically every day and sometimes several times daily."[5]

Madame de Girardin soon sensed that Adèle's brother Charles was an excellent medium. Although he was dubious about spiritism at first, it soon became apparent that he did indeed have some sort of direct conduit to the netherworld. With Charles at the table's helm, the spirits began visiting the Hugo household in droves. Most of the time, Charles and his mother directed the séances, assisted by Auguste Vacquerie, Adèle, and an assortment of guests. The illustrious assembly often included General Charles Le Flô, a diplomat expelled from France during the revolution, and the Hungarian revolutionary Colonel Alexandre Teleki. The sessions could last for hours, with Victor Hugo propped in a corner scribbling down the spirits' delphic utterances. The recording and transcription of the messages was painstaking, since the spirits tapped out their long and complex messages by tapping once for *a*, twice for *b*, and so on. The Hugos roused a pantheon of personalities from the dead, including Napoléon, Hannibal, Jesus Christ, the lion of Androcles, the Shadow of the Tomb, and even Shakespeare, who dictated a romantic drama to Victor Hugo — in French. One critic later theorized that Hugo was suffering from parapsychologic delusions (*la paraphrénie fantastique*). Symptoms of this malady include extravagant ideas and hallucinations succeeded by megalomania. Sufferers often reveal themselves to be Jesus Christ or a similarly powerful figure, and feel themselves to be possessed by evil spirits. When asked about the subjects of their dementia, victims often respond with obscure word plays, invented words and unusual sentence constructions that seem similar to those of the ancient Greek oracles. In other respects, the afflicted appear completely normal.[6]

On June 7, 1854, Albert Andrew Pinson, motivated perhaps by curiosity, perhaps by the opportunity to hold hands with Adèle in the dark, agreed to help the Hugos contact the spirits. In an attempt to convince the table-rappers of the inanity of their belief, Pinson insisted that he would ask the spirits questions in English, which no one else present understood well, save François-Victor. He and Charles Hugo led the encounter that night, helped by Madame Hugo, Adèle, Teleki, Vacquerie and other guests.

Soon after everyone had assembled, the table began to move and shake, the usual sign that a spirit wished to make contact. Charles asked, "Who is there?"

"*Frater tuus* [your brother]," came the reply.

"You aren't my brother," said Charles coolly. "Are you the brother of Monsieur Pinson?"

"Yes. André," the spirit replied.

A look of astonishment crossed Pinson's face. No one at the table could have known that he did indeed have a brother named André, or that he had disappeared twelve years ago without a trace.

Pinson then asked a question in English; the table responded. He asked a second question, and again he received a reply. The Hugos and the other guests apparently did not understand the nature of the messages Pinson was receiving, but he was visibly shaken by what he had heard. Rising to his feet, his voice filled with emotion, he asked that, since what had just transpired was of a deeply personal nature and related to his family, nothing should be recorded. His wishes were observed. But there is no record of the mysterious André (or Andrew) Pinson. Later, rumours that Albert Andrew Pinson was not using his real name were rampant; perhaps, worried lest someone in the Hugo family had found out that he was trying to hide his identity, he concocted this tale of a lost brother as a cover story.

Although he continued to profess skepticism about the phantasmagoric ravings of the spirits, Pinson was nonetheless entranced by the goings-on in the Hugo household, and he returned to take part in the séances several more times, on June 10, June 12, July 2, August 6, August 17 and September 8. The spirits weren't Pinson's only fascination: he had been thoroughly intrigued by Adèle's smouldering intensity — and her money. Within a few months, they had apparently fallen in love. Adèle knew she was walking on dangerous ground with Pinson, and it thrilled her. Quickly, their attraction developed into a love affair that pointed toward marriage.

In truth, Pinson had not come to Jersey seeking a wife, nor was rest and relaxation his object. His situation might have been delicately described as a sort of temporary fiscal exile. After he had returned to England from Jersey two years earlier, he had encountered only bad luck. His particular weakness was horse racing. He was an avid participant and an equally avid, if less accomplished, bettor. In the summer of 1854, he had been forced to flee his homeland, leaving behind a stack of unpaid gambling debts and an equal number of disgruntled creditors. Meeting the gullible, rich and beautiful Adèle was the answer to his prayers.

It was not Pinson's style to shower Adèle, or any woman, with affection and attention. Often, he didn't visit for days at a time, and when he did show up, he was blunt about what he wanted. Even this sporadic attention was good enough for Adèle, who had finally found a man to rouse her deepest passions. She knew, too, that Pinson, unlike Vacquerie, was not one to stand by and wait for any woman; more often, they came to him. His rakish, aloof behaviour was so different from that of the fawning courtiers who attempted to win her attentions that Adèle was entranced. Soon, the confidence man had the attention-starved young woman under his spell. Pinson, with his gambler's instincts, was sure of his mark. He proposed.

Pinson had already told Adèle that marrying a woman for her money was repugnant to him; yet marriage to Adèle would bring him a splendid dowry — enough to pay off his gambling debts and then some. For obvious reasons he decided it was better for Adèle, no matter how head-over-heels in love she was with him, to remain ignorant of his free-wheeling past, at least for the moment. He said his father, whom he claimed was an Anglican minister, was quite wealthy and that, despite rumours to the contrary, he had no need for money. In fact, there is no record of Pinson's father's having been a clergyman, only "a gentleman"; even if his father was indeed a man of the cloth, he would have been poor if he depended on his stipend for his livelihood. While membership in the clergy would be enough for the Pinson family to qualify as gentry — barely — it would scarcely put them among the ranks of the wealthy unless the family had some private source of income. In Pinson's case, it is almost certain that his infatuation with Adèle was based on his desperate need for money.

In order to become engaged to Adèle, Pinson would first have had to pass muster with her parents; Adèle, in turn, would have had to submit herself to his mother and father. Once both sets of parents had approved the match, the young couple could be considered affianced. Courtship, which would continue for several weeks or months, required the fiancé to pay an afternoon or evening call on his beloved every day from then on, bearing flowers. But none of this happened, for all did not go according to Pinson's plan. Adèle had principles as well as beauty, and, still embracing George Sand's brand of feminism, she fervently opposed marriage. She refused his proposal.

Rejected as a husband, Pinson no longer made even a passing attempt to play the suitor. Only marriage could bring him Adèle's dowry. Alarmed at Pinson's sudden change of feeling for her, Adèle soon regretted her impetuous refusal of marriage to the man of her dreams. By the end of the summer, she could not wait to become Madame Pinson and leave Jersey forever. One September evening, Adèle recorded in her diary her feelings for Pinson and the obstacles she knew they would have to surmount:

> Englishman, you love a French woman; Monarchist, you love a republican; blond, you love a brunette; man of tradition, you love a woman of the future; materialist, you love a woman of ideas.
>
> So why do I love you, can you tell me?[7]

Meanwhile, Auguste Vacquerie, still lingering at Marine Terrace in the vague hope that Adèle might change her mind and marry him after all, was bitterly disappointed by the change in Adèle. She told him bluntly that she would never marry him, and that she was in love with someone else. Vacquerie was understandably in anguish. Adèle flaunted her new lover before him, and he took offence at every slight. On August 28, Pinson came for dinner and gave Adèle his arm as they went into the dining room. The gesture enraged Vacquerie, and, perhaps out of malice, he told Adèle shortly afterwards that he wanted to become the lover of Margaret Allen, a trusted English friend of Adèle's who was then visiting. A few months later, he even dedicated one of his poems to Margaret. Yet a bond of friendship still existed between Adèle and Vacquerie, which only increased his pain. Adèle had no one else to talk to, and she desperately needed someone to understand her. On the night of September 12, she went to his room. "He was alone," Adèle wrote. "He had a piece of verse which he had written for me and which he had burned. . . . While the paper burned I smoothed the mattress, trying to forget how I once loved him. I sat and cried my tears all over the drapes [of his four-poster bed], weeping over the miserable situation."[8]

Vacquerie, too, was miserable. "It will be difficult to reconcile a woman's charm with her emancipation," he lamented. "But what does it matter? Certainly under this gracious exterior there is a heart which bleeds. Man, you will be a slave when woman is free!"[9]

At the end of September, Pinson left Jersey. Much later, rumour had it that the real reason for his departure was that he had been unable to ignore a British magistrate's ultimatum any longer: be sent to debtor's prison or join the army. This was a common way of decreasing the prison population and satisfying the British army's constant need for soldiers. In fact, it was not Pinson's fate. While he quite likely joined the army to escape his debts, he was not forced to do so. Still, what he told Adèle was not quite the truth, either. Ignorant of his past, she was led to believe that his father had purchased a commission for him in the British army. In fact, Pinson joined the West Yorkshire Militia, an outfit which did not require purchase of commissions. The pay was a pittance, but his chance of facing action in the newly declared Crimean War or on any other front was slim. While a line regiment would have offered him more money (ensigns received £95 per annum), it would also have put him in harm's way.

Despite what he told the lovesick Adèle, Pinson did not join the West Yorkshire Militia's third battalion until November 6, 1854. Just what he got up to between the end of September and the date of his enlistment is lost to posterity, although he apparently did return to England. Certainly, he did not take the opportunity to return to the Channel Islands. Lord Palmerston, confirming Pinson's appointment, described him to the Earl of Harewood as a "gentleman," implying that he had some private means of support without indicating what this might have been. Nevertheless, the story persisted that Pinson was chronically short of cash and something close to being a professional gambler. He also enjoyed another advantage of being in the militia: a good deal of liberty. What Pinson did during his considerable time off-duty is unknown, but gambling was likely at the forefront of his activities. In any case, having more or less rectified his financial problems by joining the militia, all ideas of matrimony seem to have fled Pinson's mind. He had begun to sense that Adèle's mental and physical intensity was more than a little out of the ordinary; she and her family had begun to seem bizarre. His new status was undoubtedly something of a relief. Had he joined the regular army corps, he would have required the permission of his commanding officer to marry Adèle, a privilege granted to an average of six out of a hundred officers, all ranking higher than himself. In the militia, which assembled only rarely, such a rule would have been impractical, but the canny Pinson appears to have kept this information to himself.

Adèle, distraught, had not yet dared tell her parents all that had transpired between herself and Pinson, but her strange behaviour had not gone unnoticed. Madame Hugo attributed Adèle's emotional disequilibrium to her unhealthy isolation. In her opinion, exile had clouded her daughter's judgement, allowing her daydreams and fantasies to be magnified in a way they would not have been in a more sophisticated and vibrant milieu. Adèle, she argued to her husband, needed female friends her own age and the variety and spontaneity of life on the Continent. She did not add that the girl's mother needed the same diversions.

Madame Hugo adored Paris and could not abide life on the rocky outcropping of which her husband had become so fond. Hugo was loath to let any of his family return to the Continent, particularly to

France; they were supposed to be in exile, he said, although, in reality, only he himself had been expelled. But Madame Hugo finally wore down his intransigence and persuaded him to allow her and Adèle to leave the island on a trip to Paris. Adèle enjoyed her time in the city of her birth, and her physical and mental well-being visibly improved. But within a few days of their return to Jersey, Adèle reverted to her old, moody self; the change of scenery did more for Madame Hugo's constitution than for her daughter's.

In matters of the heart, Adèle took her cue from her father, or at least from his books. The passion with which she conducted her three love affairs was equal to or greater than the passion of Victor Hugo's greatest heroes and heroines. Her mental instability, combined with the heady world of her father's fiction and the subdued and lonely life she led on Jersey had, as her mother feared, a detrimental effect on Adèle, leaving her unable to distinguish between true, lasting love and devotion and the exciting flush of infatuation. This lack of judgement contributed to the strange situation in which she found herself with Albert Pinson. He was unlike any man she had ever met. He was unimpressed by her father, for one thing. His quietly mocking attitude, his abundant self-confidence, and his penetrating insight into people's personalities fascinated her as much as his personal magnetism and delicate, almost feminine good looks. She felt that he could see straight into her own heart. Compared to Vacquerie's elaborate politeness and reserve, Pinson's straightforward desire was exhilarating.

Adèle did not doubt that Pinson was the man in her dream of eight years ago, and that his destiny was to be, quite simply, the love of her life. In her secret diary, she wrote:

> [He] refused everything in order to stay in Jersey. His family offered him a commission in the army, the chosen career of the English gentry. He refused. What did he care about the army, a career, ambition? His career was to love me, his ambition was to see me. But life has its hard and practical side. When love is near, you have to think of marriage, and he had to have a position. In

order to be able to marry me, he finally accepted a commission in the army. He left distraught, in tears, alone, and he took courage only from the idea that he could be my husband.[10]

Adèle launched a frantic campaign to get Pinson to give up his commission and come back to her; she had transformed him into her only means of escaping the life she detested. On October 12, she concluded ominously that she had been Clésinger's Béatrice, the woman immortalized by Dante in his *Divine Comedy*; now, Pinson would play the same role for her. In desperation, she consulted the spirits in private séances, but nothing worked. In one night-time session, at the beginning of October, 1854, the table instructed her to tell Pinson she was going to have a baby.

"Will this produce the intended effect?" Adèle asked the spirits.

"Yes," the table replied. "Say, 'I will die if, abandoned, I have a child.'"

"Is this the way to keep him?" Adèle asked.

"Yes," the table unequivocally replied.[11] Adèle decided to keep this dramatic gesture in reserve.

When she consulted the table again that same night, Jesus Christ himself visited her. She was not in the least surprised to receive such an exalted guest.

"In eternity, you will be divine," Jesus told her. "In eternity you will be beautiful. In eternity you will be The Woman. In eternity you will be mother, mistress, sister, daughter, wife."

"What will happen to my spirit?" asked Adèle.

"In eternity you will be made of beauty. In eternity you will be made of fire. In eternity you will be made of light. In eternity you will be made of flames."[12]

The episode convinced Adèle that she was doing the right thing in pursuing Pinson. But while she agonized over the absent Pinson, Vacquerie's brooding presence was taking its toll on her. Adèle felt guilty and, at times, harassed by her jealous ex-lover. She knew that she had to break with him, but she hesitated, since Pinson's affection was doubtful and he showed no signs of returning to her. Once again the spirits advised Adèle: get rid of Vacquerie. On December 18, 1854, she asked them, "Why do you tell me to throw Auguste out right away when Albert loves me so little and might not return? Will you respond to that question?"[13]

The spirits would not. They promised, though, that Pinson would visit in a few weeks, and that there would be trouble, very likely ending in catastrophe, if Vacquerie were still present. Believing she was acting to avoid the possibility of one or the other of the men being killed in a duel or similar tragedy, Adèle pleaded with her mother to send Vacquerie away. Madame Hugo was shocked and saddened by her daughter's request, but she nevertheless agreed to it, suggesting that perhaps Vacquerie could return in the spring. The compromise suited Adèle, but when she turned again to her table, the spirits were not happy. They insisted Vacquerie had to go — forever. The distressed Adèle did not listen to her own better judgement and, in the end, the spirits got their wish. Adèle's isolation was nearly complete.

Now she could devote all her time to what had become shameless efforts to manipulate Pinson into marriage. She tried ever more desperate tactics. She told him that she was engaged to someone else and used the ploy suggested by the spirits, that she was pregnant. Later, she threatened to commit suicide if Pinson did not return and marry her. In December, 1854, Adèle learned that Pinson had told her brother that he wanted to marry a fourteen-year-old girl he had met. Adèle was livid. "The thing made me sick, without regard to who she was," she wrote. "I wanted to write a letter breaking with him. . . . If the thing is true, it is our absolute rupture, the irreparable death of my love."[14] The news, likely a ploy on Pinson's part to get rid of Adèle, did not have the desired effect. In an urgent letter dated December 28, hand-delivered to Pinson by Margaret Allen (who had returned to England), Adèle wrote:

In your second letter, you begged me to marry you, without renouncing your commission, which you might lose. But, at that moment, it was impossible for me to marry, since I was attempting to hold myself up as an example in the fight against prejudice. . . .

Auguste Vacquerie, by Charles Hugo *(Musées de la Ville de Paris)*

It is clear that, after having used all the reasoning possible, and having used it futilely, it was necessary to use less subtle methods. I used two: my death, and jealousy. I tried the first: it didn't work . . . I tried immediately the second method, it being the most sure and the only one feasible. . . .

Obviously, if you prefer to see me with another than to renounce your commission, you don't love me.[15]

To Pinson, fed up with Adèle's antics, the appeal was simply another pathetic attempt by a woman whose sanity he already thought questionable to hijack him into marriage. Accordingly, he took nearly five days before penning his negative reply. Adèle, undaunted, tried once more:

Having borne your child, but not daring to say so because of your lax conduct toward me, I will marry a very handsome and very spiritual man, and the only method of stopping this marriage would be for you to renounce your commission.

Still Pinson would not relent; but Adèle was not so easily cast aside. Their summer romance had pitched them both into a maelstrom of passion and bitterness.

1. Guille, Vol. 3, p.153.
2. Richardson, pp.150-51.
3. Guille, Vol. 3, p.37.
4. de Mutigny, p.24.
5. de Mutigny, p.26.
6. See de Mutigny, pp.82-84.
7. Guille, Vol. 3, p.36.

8. Guille, Vol. 3, p.26.

9. Guille, Vol. 3, p.453.

10. Guille, Vol. 3, p.151.

11. Guille, Vol. 3, p.32.

12. Guille, Vol. 3, p.33.

13. Guille, Vol. 3, p.45.

14. Guille, Vol. 3, pp.58-59.

15. Guille, Vol. 3, pp.522-23.

Adèle Hugo in exile *(Musées de la Ville de Paris)*

Chapter 4

A Passage to Freedom
Jersey, 1855, and Guernsey, 1855-1863

Everyone preached marriage at the poor girl. "It is the role of a
woman," said her father. "It is your only way to liberate yourself," said Charles.

— *Frances Vernor Guille*[1]

*I*t was a calm summer evening. The incessant pounding of the surf had
slowed, and a light breeze blew up from the beach. The bougainvillea,
roses and shrubs so lovingly cultivated by Madame Hugo and Adèle
were at the height of their glory, and their fragrance drifted in through
the open French doors to where the Hugo family were dining. Inside
the house, the air was stiflingly hot, despite the building's high ceilings
and plastered walls. Adèle's cheeks were flushed, and she fidgeted as
she waited for the meal to end. Finally, after what seemed like hours,
dinner was finished and Adèle escaped to the seaside terrace. She was
promptly joined by Charles, carrying the family cat, Agneau, whose
name belied her outbursts of viciousness. Agneau's temperament may
have been influenced by her origins; her mother had been born in the
Concièrgerie prison in Paris; Auguste Vacquerie found her during his
incarceration there and brought her to Jersey with him.

Charles and Adèle strolled toward a stone bench on the far side of
the formal gardens, the same one on which Adèle had been sitting
when Pinson first saw her. Within a few minutes, the sea air had revived
them both. As Charles sat absently stroking the protesting Agneau,

Adèle gazed out over the surging water, which was illuminated by the silvery light of a new moon. Charles had been as glad to escape from dinner as his sister. The most outspoken of the three Hugo children, he was often at loggerheads with their father. Because he was a son, and the eldest, Charles was often allowed more latitude than the compliant François-Victor, and certainly more than Adèle. Yet, he, too, often protested Hugo's heavy-handed demand for absolute obedience and agreement with his opinions.

Adèle suffered the most, as Charles well knew, and she had finally made up her mind to ask for his help in breaking free of her father, of Marine Terrace, of Jersey, and of the restrictive life she found increasingly intolerable. She gazed out over the ocean for a few more minutes, shuffling her shoes on the flagstones as she searched for the right words to frame her question. Was there any way, she finally blurted out, of emancipating herself from her father? Smiling cynically, Charles answered that legally there was nothing she could do, but that if she wished to pursue illegal means she could always become a thief or a prostitute. Adèle was not shocked by his answer. In a low tone, she responded that thievery and prostitution were contrary to her conscience; she would not do such things to support herself.[2]

"One should be only partly responsible for one's passions," Adèle murmured, still gazing at the water. Just then, Victor Hugo ambled down the path. He stopped near the sea wall, his hands in his pockets. "Do you find Othello and Claude Frollo [the villain of Hugo's play, *Notre-Dame de Paris*] guilty?" Adèle asked her father, raising her voice slightly so as to be heard over the waves and wind.

"No," he replied, taking a few steps closer to the pair, "despite the fact that both of them killed the women they loved. They did so in the heat of passion, which is an extenuating circumstance. I would not condemn them to death, but to life in prison." His remarks were prescient; at the moment of Adèle's rebellion, still far in the future, Victor Hugo would condemn his daughter's betrayal of him, and, when the time came for revenge, the punishment he exacted on her would be strikingly similar.

But Charles was right about marriage. For an upper-class, unmarried young woman, there were virtually no other opportunities. Unlike her lower-class sisters, Adèle could not hire herself out for pitifully low wages in a factory sweatshop, go to work in the fields, nor work as a dance-hall girl. She must marry.

There were notable exceptions, among them writers like Eugénie Nyobet, George Sand, and, in the previous century, painter Elisabeth Vigée-Lebrun. All three were married and yet were perfectly free to do as they wished, regardless of whether they neglected their domestic duties. Certainly, in the nineteenth century, more women than ever before were taking up their pens and entering the field of journalism (Sand had worked on *Le Figaro* and *La République*; Eugénie Nyobet founded the feminist newspaper, *La Voix des femmes,* in 1848) as well as publishing books. But there was a difference. All of these women had the support and permission of their husbands or fathers to pursue their profession; Adèle, despite her gifts, had neither permission, nor, as it turned out, the requisite determination to become a career woman. Instead, her attention was increasingly diverted by strange obsessions.

At the age of thirteen, Adèle had been described by Honoré de Balzac as the most beautiful young woman he had ever seen. As the years of exile wore on, she had begun to wither in body and spirit. She had metamorphosed from a dazzling young Parisian woman, enthusiastic about life and her place in it, to a reflective, bitter exile. Her continued fixation on Pinson robbed her of happiness, and she had ceased to try to free herself from this foolish, futile love. No longer did Adèle share the qualities which had made Léopoldine so delightful. Her kind-heartedness, generosity and piety had given way to restlessness, withdrawal and neurosis. Nor could Charles coax a smile from his sister in any of the many photo sessions to which he subjected the family. Charles had developed a mania for photography and liked nothing better than clicking his camera at anything that did, or, preferably, did not move. But each plate showed the same sad Adèle. At first, her wistfulness had been engaging, making her look like a damsel in distress. Now, her slight frown and vacant eyes made her look old and taciturn. Moreover, Adèle was beginning to lose her shapely figure, and the face which had once inspired so many writers was beginning to look heavy; her far-away look had hardened into aloofness.

Victor Hugo had become increasingly critical of his daughter, whom he had come to perceive as self-centred and disobedient, and was piqued by her continual refusal of marriage proposals. One night, as she sang for the family and their guests, her father ordered her to stop, grumbling that her diction was terrible. Hugo had no hesitation in applying the same standards of criticism to Adèle's informal serenade as he would to a competitor's play. Pompously and publicly, he counselled his daughter, "Study hard and enunciate distinctly. . . . I gave the same advice to Madame Marie Dorval, who, despite her admirable talent, had very bad diction."[3] If Adèle was wounded by her father's remarks, she didn't show it; she had other things on her mind.

Adèle's continuing obsession with the low-ranking English army officer puzzled not just her family and friends but her retinue of admirers. One of them was Jules Allix, who had followed his sister, Augustine, Charles Hugo's mistress, into exile. Allix, naturally, was a frequent visitor to Marine Terrace because of his sister's connection to the family. But the real reason for his presence in the Hugo household was Adèle, with whom he had been secretly in love for years. Jules Allix often took part in the Hugo family séances, but one night at the beginning of October, 1855, something went terribly wrong. As the evening progressed, Allix's personality changed. By the time the séance had finished, the young man had become transfixed. For the next several hours he simply stared, glassy-eyed, into space. Madame Hugo, alarmed by his strange behaviour, asked him what was wrong. "I have seen things this night," was his cryptic response. It was the first sign that Jules Allix was suffering what was described at the time as a "mental crisis."

In the days that followed, there was little change in Allix's behaviour. One day, he broke out of his lethargy to lunge furiously at Auguste Vacquerie; he then struck Charles Hugo. It was decided that he should be sent home to his family in France, but on the way he tried to break out of his carriage. His relatives were forced to put him in a mental hospital, in a private cell for his own protection.[4] The episode was short, however; by 1856 Allix had recovered his faculties enough to be able to teach French in Brussels.[5] Even so, the incident frightened everyone. It was the second time someone either close to, or part of, the Hugo family had gone mad. At Madame Hugo's insistence, the family séances came to a halt.

Shortly afterwards, Victor Hugo became embroiled in another controversy which would result in the family's once again having to change its address. The circumstances leading to the Hugos second exile began, curiously, with a public meeting held September 22, 1855, in London, England. At the meeting, a Frenchman, Félix Pyat, had read a letter in French which attacked Queen Victoria for paying an official visit to Napoléon III. It was published in several English newspapers but created no stir, despite its crude and violent anti-monarchist sentiments. The letter was also published in *L'Homme*, the French-language newspaper of the Jersey exiles, but here Pyat's inflammatory statement did not go unnoticed. In fact, the English-speaking residents of Jersey were so appalled they asked the French expatriates responsible for its publication to leave the island. "The group of exiles asked Victor Hugo to draw up their protest. He did so, with vehemence, and François-Victor and Charles added their signatures. 'And now,' ended Hugo, 'expel us, too!'" The Jerseymen lost no time in granting Hugo his wish. "On 27 October he was ordered to leave the island. On 31 October, with the tin trunk in which he kept his papers, Victor Hugo left for Guernsey."[6] On November 9, Adèle and her mother also left Jersey for Guernsey, and before long the rest of the Hugo entourage followed its leader.

In the beginning, at least, the change seemed to suit Adèle. Guernsey, although much smaller than Jersey, was a paradise in comparison. Flowers grew everywhere in abundance, up to eight feet in height, producing radiant blooms even in November. Shortly after the family's arrival in Guernsey's capital, Saint-Pierre-Port, Hugo purchased Hauteville-House, a Georgian-style mansion, for 25,000 francs. It was the first home the Hugos had ever owned. Built around 1800, the house underwent a massive transformation under the hands of Hugo, whose Romantic imagination knew no bounds, at least as far as architecture was concerned:

> What is striking about it is the grandiose scale, the mixture of the classical, the medieval and the exotic. One mantelpiece is made of components which date from the Middle Ages, the Renaissance and the reign of Louis XII. Chinese silks and Norwegian panels are found in a single drawing-room.[7]

The bustle of renovation brought Adèle out of the gloom and lethargy which had plagued her on Jersey. Madame Hugo remarked that her daughter seemed content playing her new role of *châtelaine* of the household and was happy with her lovely new room. In the summer of 1856, Adèle even consented to follow her father's example of bathing in the ocean, a practice which her doctor had long recommended and which her mother had urged. That year, one of her compositions was played at a Saint-Pierre-Port concert. Her family was relieved, for it seemed Adèle's disquieting melancholy had evaporated. But it hadn't; Adèle had simply decided to keep her unhappiness to herself. Madame Hugo failed to note that, in so eagerly adopting the role of housekeeper, Adèle was setting herself up for a life as an old maid — the doting spinster who took care of nieces and nephews with no real life of her own.

Internalizing her unhappiness and fears had an extremely negative effect on the imaginative young woman. On December 6, 1856, Adèle was suddenly taken ill with an intense fever, delirium, and a bout of gastroenteritis. The mysterious affliction was initially put down to an attack of nerves. She suffered for four days. On the fifth day, her fever was so high that the family physician, Dr. Émile Allix, also an exile and a personal friend of Hugo's, and a local physician, Dr. Terrier, predicted that she would not last until morning. But Adèle rallied, and the illness departed as quickly as it had come. By Christmas Day, a relieved Victor Hugo was able to announce in a letter to a friend, "My daughter is out of danger."[8] The strange malady had lingering effects; Adèle never resumed the spirited and sympathetic personality that was hers before exile.

The sadness which enveloped Adèle soon began to hover like a fog over the whole family, with the sole exception of Victor Hugo, who remained as robust and inspired as ever. But there was something even more unsettling about Adèle, which no one could quite put a finger on. To Madame Hugo, it was evident that her daughter had begun to show signs of deranged behaviour, much like Eugène's. In part, Adèle's difficulties stemmed from her father, who had never ceased trying to mould her into the image of the dead Léopoldine. It seemed she could never please him, no matter how hard she worked, serving long hours as her father's secretary and also expending considerable energy, at her father's behest, on both writing and composing.

Adèle had no compunction about refusing several offers of marriage on the grounds that she felt marriage to be degrading to women, an argument which Hugo dismissed as nonsense. Nonetheless, his effort to entice Adèle to marry by parading a string of eligible bachelors before her was not successful. Yet Hugo did not go so far as to arrange a marriage himself; he simply made life difficult for his recalcitrant daughter. Living under the increasingly watchful eyes of her parents became more and more trying for Adèle. She felt they treated her like an infant.

Eventually, though, even Madame Hugo had had enough of her husband's heavy-handed behaviour towards Adèle, whom she was trying so hard to encourage. She took Hugo to task for his shabby treatment of their youngest daughter in a letter dating from 1858:

> You said this morning, while lunching, that your daughter loves no one but herself. I did not want to argue in front of the children, because it is not good. Adèle has given you her youth, without complaint, without demanding any recognition, and you find her conceited.[9]

What Hugo mistook for conceit was, in reality, his daughter's ever-increasing tendency to withdraw into herself, her feeling of restlessness and claustrophobia at not being able to leave the tiny island, and the subjugation of her independent mind. She had become obsessive in cataloguing her belongings, making endless lists with headings like "artificial flowers," "jewellery," "hats" and "summer dresses." Clearly, she needed another outlet for her intellect.

Following her illness in 1856, Adèle had been forbidden by Dr. Allix to practise the piano or experience the slightest stress; he had also recommended a change of scenery to put her on the road to recovery. Hugo refused to let her travel, and it was some time before Madame Hugo succeeded in gaining her husband's permission to take Adèle to Paris again — and then only after the intervention of François-Victor. They departed on January 18, 1858, and remained in the French capital until May. The chief object of their visit (at least, as Hugo understood it) was to find a husband for Adèle.

During this time, Madame Hugo renewed her acquaintance with Sainte-Beuve (whom Adèle called "Uncle"), and they saw each other often. They wrote often, too, and the subject of their correspondence was frequently young Adèle. Sainte-Beuve agreed with Madame Hugo that a change was needed, and he encouraged her to bring Adèle to Paris the following winter for three months. However, mother and daughter could not obtain the required permission, and stayed put in Guernsey. Not until May 11, 1859, did Hugo allow the pair — and Charles — to leave the Channel Islands. This time, their destination was London. The visit was to have been brief, only a few weeks, but Madame Hugo managed to prolong their stay for the entire summer. In August, François-Victor joined them. Not until September 6 did the quartet depart for Guernsey. But even this lengthy stay abroad was not enough, as Sainte-Beuve had hoped, to cure Adèle of the melancholy which enveloped her, nor to get her sufficiently interested in other men that she forgot about Pinson.

Despite her firmly held views against marriage, it became clear to Adèle as the years advanced that, no matter how much she despised the idea, surrendering her status as "Mademoiselle Hugo" was likely the only way out of her Guernsey captivity. Steadfastly, though, she refused to marry just anyone; Adèle, like her parents before her, had resolved to marry for love. The family had no objection to this, only to her choice of mate. The greatest objections to Albert Pinson were, first, that despite his assertions to the contrary, he had little or no means of support. Second, he was English. Hugo despised England and had little love for the English people; that his daughter should marry one was unthinkable. But Adèle was determined to marry the man of her choice, whatever his ambitions and assets — or lack thereof.

By 1856, Pinson had begun his climb up the army's promotional ladder. The Crimean War over, he felt safe in transferring from the militia to a line regiment, the Sixteenth Regiment of Foot, known variously as the Old Birks and the Featherbeds. The regiment, through a quirk of fate, had managed to miss all the major battles of the nineteenth century, including the Napoleonic Wars, the Crimean War and the Indian Mutiny, having been posted instead to the far-flung reaches of the British Empire — including Ceylon, Jamaica and Canada — while other regiments fought the wars. The regiment saw some action in the battle for Dutch Guiana, but were then, unfortunately, chosen to garrison the new colony's dank and malaria-infested fortress. The soldiers of the Sixteenth were called up several more times for active duty, but by the time they arrived the conflicts had invariably ended, earning them another nickname, "the Peacemakers." (After 1881, the Sixteenth Regiment of Foot became known as the Sixteenth Bedfordshire Regiment. It has since merged with the Forty-Fourth Foot Guards, and is now known as the Third East Anglian Regiment.)

Pinson's choice was a popular one at the time. There were tantalizing incentives for new recruits to join up, largely the result of the Crimean War, in which thousands of officers and soldiers had been killed. Officers who had purchased a commission and been killed in the line of duty were replaced by men who were not required to pay the purchase price. As well, commanders were allowed to award a certain number of commissions each year to deserving recipients, or to those with connections. Moreover, as Lieutenant-Colonel Garnet Wolseley (later Field Marshal Viscount Wolseley) noted in his memoirs, *The Story of a Soldier's Life*, "any Militia officer who could then induce a certain number of his men to volunteer for the Line was given a commission."[10]

In a letter dated February 17, 1856, the militia's Colonel Commanding, Ferrars Loftus of the Third Battalion, recommended Pinson and three other officers for a line regiment.[11] The recommendation was enough to absolve Pinson from having to purchase his commission. At the time Pinson joined, the Sixteenth Regiment was stationed in Jamaica, and it was later sent to Quebec. The prospect of his being so far away for an indefinite period of time no doubt added to Adèle's depression. Fortunately, she did not have long to wait for Pinson's return. The following year, the Sixteenth was recalled to Britain. In 1858, Pinson went to Ireland to enlist in the Sixteenth's newly formed second battalion. Still, he managed to benefit from the change: on March 23, 1858, he was promoted to lieutenant, a promotion which, despite the the practice of the time, he did not purchase.

Only a few non-purchasable commissions existed, and Pinson had to wait for one to become available. The promotion to lieutenant boosted his pay to £118 per annum. It was hardly a fortune and did little to solve his financial problems. Officers' pay amounted to about half that paid to civil servants of similar rank in the British War Office. Even skilled tradesmen made about £100 a year. A well-off physician would earn £300, and members of the upper class could live comfortably on £500. Most officers, also being gentlemen, had private incomes which supplemented their meagre army earnings. Officers who did not purchase commissions rarely had private incomes, nor did they fit the stereotypical portrait of a British army officer.

Pinson became an instructor of musketry and likely attended the school of musketry at Hythe, Kent, which had been established in 1854; soldiers from every British regiment were sent there to qualify themselves as marksmen. But Pinson craved a different sort of action. Being in the Sixteenth Regiment's second battalion on a colonial posting was hardly a coveted position, but it suited his tastes perfectly.

Pinson, with his devil-may-care attitude and penchant for gambling, women and horse-racing, was just the sort of subaltern Wolseley despised. His aptitude for soldiering was questionable, a not-uncommon shortcoming of British officers at the time. Aldershot, a military base formed by Queen Victoria's consort, Prince Albert, in 1856 as a training ground for officers, was a haven not for learning, according to Wolseley, but for dissipation: "I can conscientiously assert that I never learnt anything there, nor heard of any regimental officer who did." The camp, he added,

> was then a somewhat rowdy place. A considerable number of officers went to town every afternoon to amuse themselves there, getting back by an early train next morning that enabled them to be in time for parade. . . .
>
> Late hours were kept, and the evenings at our mess often ended in an attack upon the quarters of one or other of four lately joined subalterns who had practically no pretensions to the rank of gentleman.

"These four Ensigns," Wolseley continued, "were absolutely useless as officers, and we soon got rid of them."[12] He might have been talking about Pinson, who soon earned the dislike of his comrades-in-arms for his prissiness.

Wearing the rose-coloured glasses of love, Adèle had easily been able to overlook her reluctant lover's faults. Her blindness to his darker side is surprising, given not only her staunchly defended independence but her considerable experience in matters of the heart. Even her short time with Clésinger seemed rapturous compared to the agonies of the heart Pinson was causing her; she was forced to admit that the current situation was far from ideal: "If Albert doesn't give me happy love, I will not love him any more."[13] But it was not so easy to evict Pinson from her heart, and her resolve to end the affair soon melted. They wrote often and met in Brighton when he was on leave in 1859 and again the following year.

After several years in Ireland, Pinson's regiment moved to the infamous Aldershot in April of 1861. This was good news for Adèle. Not only was camp discipline decidedly lax, but Pinson was more accessible to her in southeast England. In May of 1861, Adèle managed to slip out from under her father's hawkish protection to continue the liaison, which she had continuously shored up.

It was not easy for her to break away. The previous February, Madame Hugo had left for a long trip to Paris, and Adèle was to join her mother either in Paris or Brussels at an unspecified later date. But, without warning, Adèle departed for the Isle of Wight instead, accompanied by her trusted maid, Rosalie. She told no one of her whereabouts until some time later, causing great consternation within the family. Her real objective was to see Pinson, who was stationed less than a hundred kilometres away. Although the couple managed to meet, once again Adèle failed to extract from Pinson a promise to marry her.[14] Adèle's ruse was short-lived; her deception was discovered, and she was forced to return home, where it was made clear that she had dishonoured her family by her absence. From then on, her every move was watched by her parents, who were determined that their daughter would not slip away from them again. Adèle was not permitted to leave the house alone for any reason; she felt, with good cause, that she was being kept a prisoner. Far from acting suitably remorseful for her behaviour, Adèle only grew more determined to escape what she viewed as enslavement. It was now that she made her fateful decision to be with Pinson at all costs.

Pinson remained in Aldershot with the Sixteenth until late December. At Christmas, he visited the Hugos at Guernsey. Adèle had, by then, succeeded in overcoming her father's anglophobia and had won his consent to her marriage with Pinson. Her chief weapon had been one her father could not resist: the written word. On December 20, 1861, Adèle wrote her father the following letter, reminding him of how he had also objected to Léopoldine's marriage, which, however brief, had turned out to be wildly happy:

Another time, you resisted another marriage, and your son-in-law brought to your first-born daughter the splendid dowry of a great love. You had said, moreover, "sad marriage, poor marriage," you disdained this noble young man, and then one day you avowed to the world that you were proud, because this obscure young man was Devotion himself. The obscure young man whom you disdain today could be Courage.

Adele's heartfelt plea worked. Hugo wrote in his notebook, "I received from my daughter an admirable letter. I am giving to my daughter 50,000 francs for her dowry."[15]

But Pinson's lack of commitment to Adèle had not changed; he did not ask Victor Hugo for permission to marry his daughter, despite her urging. Hugo apparently thought he was consenting to his daughter's formal engagement to Pinson — he officially received Pinson at Hauteville-House on Christmas Day — yet on December 26 Pinson departed for England. It should have been obvious to everyone that Pinson had long since ceased to be serious about courting Adèle. Her erratic behaviour and crude attempts to dominate him and trick him into marriage had done a good deal to scare him off permanently. But there was another reason for his reluctance: he had just learned that his newly created battalion was about to be sent on its first colonial posting, to the British garrison at Halifax, Nova Scotia.

The regiment's mission was to intervene in the Trent Affair. The incident was sparked by an American frigate, the *San Jacinto*, which had stopped a British packet boat, the *Trent*, and removed two Confederate agents. A diplomatic crisis ensued. Relations between the United States and Great Britain became hostile, and British forces were put on the alert, with reinforcements sent to garrisons in Halifax, Toronto, Montreal and elsewhere.

Even Wolseley, the regimental commander, had little warning of the call-up; in the late fall of 1861, he had been staying with his married sister in Ireland when he got an official telegram. A few days later he was in England, and on December 7, his ship, the *Magdalena*, departed for Halifax in a rough sea "running mountains high." Winter was not the best of times for a trans-Atlantic crossing, as even the iron-stomached Wolseley remarked:

I do not remember having ever been in a sea that looked more angry and, to the landsman's taste, more hateful. A few of us "old salts" had our meals as best we could, holding on with one hand as we fed ourselves with the other; but as a rule, nearly every one was sick. We lost sight of our convoy in the afternoon of the 16th, and though we fired guns by day and burnt blue lights by night, we never saw her again during the voyage.

The weather grew worse and worse, and our discomfort increased. The food was execrable, the cooking worse.[16]

In all, the miserable voyage took twenty-nine days; the ship finally landed at Halifax on January 4 or 5, 1862. For the officers on board — Pinson was not among them — it was an occasion for celebration. The night of January 5, the officers of the Sixteenth threw a lavish dinner for the officers of the *Magdalena* at the Halifax Hotel, served up by its owner, Henry Hesslein. According to the *Evening Express,* "the company sat down about seven o'clock to a splendid dinner, served up in Hesslein's best style, and those present appeared to enjoy themselves."[17]

Pinson may have surmised, quite reasonably, that his new posting on the other side of the Atlantic Ocean — which would last a minimum of four years — would spell the end of his and Adèle's one-sided affair. He was wrong. On January 15, 1862, Pinson and a fellow officer, Lieutenant Davies, arrived in Halifax, a week after the rest of the battalion. The mid-winter voyage must have been a particularly strenuous one, since it was another three months before either of the new arrivals was required to take up his official duties. Indeed, there was not much for them to do, despite the American Civil War raging to the south. Even the Trent Affair was all but resolved.

By February of 1862, the number of troops dispatched to British North America to deal with the crisis had resulted in extreme overcrowding in the various Halifax garrisons, despite the opening of the new Wellington Barracks in 1860. To make way for newly arrived soldiers, the troops of the Sixteenth were shifted from the dank and dark

Halifax Citadel (completed in 1856 and already obsolete for defence purposes) to a borrowed railway building in the north end of town. The officers of the Sixteenth fared even worse: they were housed on the cold and inexpressibly damp hulk, *Pyramus*, anchored off George's Island in Halifax Harbour.

Back in Guernsey, the sombre Adèle would gladly have traded her father's grandiose mansion for life aboard a hulk — whether or not Pinson was on it. The months passed, Adèle grew perceptibly older, and assumptions of spinsterhood began to plague her; Hugo felt a growing urgency to see his daughter settled before it was too late, for she was already well beyond the usual age for marriage. Adèle, in turn, was increasingly determined not to bend to his will.

The threat of a forced marriage had become increasingly real. Five suitors had presented themselves at Hauteville-House in the past eleven years, all of them uninvited and unwanted by Adèle. She had found them, and, at the time, marriage itself, to be distasteful in the extreme. They were amongst the most eligible men of their time, with family fortunes, noble titles, and solid reputations in literature, business and other fields. But there was nothing in their polite and flattering discourse to suggest the sort of passionate life for which Adèle yearned. She had the distinct impression that she was being sold to the highest bidder, and she would have none of it. In marrying any one of them, Adèle knew she would be serving her father's desire to unite two powerful and important families; the question of her own happiness would be only a secondary consideration.

On June 2, 1863, Adèle refused yet another marriage proposal, the second such offer from the Italian poet Tommasso de Cannizzaro, of Messina. The poet had previously proposed on May 4, after meeting Adèle in February while a guest at Hauteville-House. Her refusal, which was inexplicable to her puzzled family, strained the already oppressive atmosphere at Hauteville-House. Hugo made it clear to his daughter that his moral reputation depended upon her; she had only to do her duty and marry for her burden to be relieved. On June 3, Victor Hugo noted in his diary that François-Victor had found a disturbing sign that Adèle had some unknown project in mind: a trunk containing clothing and documents. Clearly, Adèle had made up her mind to join Pinson in Halifax, despite having not seen her reluctant lover for eighteen months. As far as she was concerned, Pinson represented her only hope for freedom and happiness; it had become painfully obvious that the solidarity of the Hugo family excluded her.

In Adèle's mind, at least, it was her father's objection which stood in the way of her marriage to Pinson. In May and June of 1863, Adèle composed a bitter, nine-page letter to Hugo in an attempt to change his mind. Pinson, she wrote, had joined the army only to have a secure income and, therefore, a means of marrying her. One of his uncles (likely Lieutenant-Colonel Albert Pinson, who had assisted Pinson in his earlier army career), she noted, was old and ill, and would leave Pinson 10,000 francs upon his death, which would almost certainly take place within a few years.

Adèle's argument was not quite true: after her initial rejection of him, Pinson had never formally courted Adèle, and he had never asked her father for permission to marry her. Yet in the letter she sounded a warning, which went unheeded until it was too late, of the lengths to which she might go to wed her lover:

> If you delay or dismiss this marriage, with the possible complication of present events, do you know to what you expose me? You are exposing me, and us, to situations which are more than painful, situations which might disturb life a hundred times more than my present marriage would do. Here I am separated, married without being married, the years will pass, this absence may last for a long while, one cannot wait for a long while at the time of life which I have reached. And I should refuse every suitor for this fiancé who is absent and far away (from absolute necessity), I should never marry another man.[18]

Adèle's brothers, who had considerably more freedom than she did, appear to have been largely unsympathetic to her plight, although they,

Adèle Hugo *(Musées de la Ville de Paris)*

too, harboured ill-concealed feelings about the confining and unsti-
mulating life they led on Guernsey. The brothers reported Adèle's
"transgressions," such as the packed trunk, straight to their father. But the
tip-off about her impending voyage proved no deterrent to the determined young woman, and on June 18, she made her long-dreamed-of
escape. She had, she felt, the spirit of her dead sister Léopoldine on her
side, and she observed in her secret diary:

> It is an incredible thing to do, for a young woman who could
> have been enslaved to the point of not being able to go out
> alone for five minutes to buy some paper, to walk over the sea,
> to fly over the sea, to pass from the old world to the new world
> to rejoin her lover. This thing I will do.

But she also intended to make her own living through her writing:

> That incredible thing, that a young woman who has no other
> means than her father's charity will have, four years from now,
> gold in both pockets, honest gold, her gold, that thing I will ac-
> complish.[19]

Ostensibly bound for Paris to rejoin her mother, Adèle departed in the
company of a fellow Guernsey resident, Madame Evans and her family.
In fact, Adèle's destination was not Paris, but Weymouth, England.[20]
She had plotted for months, and, taking along her mother's jewellery as
collateral, she had worked out an elaborate plan. She knew her ruse
would not fool her family for long, but, by the time her real destination
was discovered, it would be the August holidays. The family would be
scattered throughout France and Belgium, and it would take some time
for clear communication to be established. This, she knew, would result
in enough of a delay that she could safely arrive in Halifax and locate
Pinson. Within a few days, she expected to be married to him and place
herself beyond all reproach from her father.

She was quickly missed when she did not show up in Paris. A day later, she began spinning her well-thought-out story to François-Victor, who in turn wrote to his mother and the rest of the family:

> Dear mother, after 26 hours of mortal anxiety we have finally received a word of explanation from Adèle. This word is brief. She tells us that she had accepted an invitation from Madame Lester, living near Hampton Court and that she left without warning, to avoid the explanations which the simplest things provoke here.[21]

Adèle and François-Victor had been close as children, and her favourite brother had often interceded on her behalf in her disagreements with their father, especially when Adèle wished to accompany her mother abroad. Now, in a letter sent from England, she took François-Victor partially into her confidence. Stating that her life had become intolerable on Guernsey, she bemoaned her lack of liberty, and even criticized the annual trips with her mother — before each one of which Madame Hugo had been forced to wage a tactical battle to gain her husband's permission.

Adèle claimed that she would be joining Pinson in Malta, another phase of the deception, and asked her brother to help keep their father in the dark. François-Victor had only to explain her absence by stating that she had decided to spend five weeks with her friend Miss Lester at the invitation of her family. By that time (so she said) she would be back in England with Pinson ready to lead her down the aisle. She also ventured to write to her father; Hugo duly noted in his diary that Adèle was staying with Miss Lester, near Hampton Court — and that she intended to rejoin Pinson.

In fact, Pinson had not pledged to marry Adèle, at least not recently, nor had he invited her to England or Malta — and certainly not to Halifax. Yet Adèle was determined to break away from her old life at any cost. She stuck to her fabricated story and schemed hard to cover her tracks. Well aware that Pinson had gone to Halifax, Adèle booked passage for New York on the mammoth 25,000-tonne ship, the *Great Eastern*.

Just as Adèle had foreseen, it was not long before the family discovered what she was really up to. For one thing, the family knew full well that Pinson had gone to Halifax, since he had told them himself on his last visit in December of 1860. But it was not François-Victor who betrayed Adèle; this time, it was Mrs. Milner-Gibson, the family's long-time friend in London and the wife of a member of parliament. Mrs. Milner-Gibson, whom Adèle had also taken into her confidence, sounded the first alarm in a letter written June 30, 1863. Adèle had not gone to Malta, the woman informed the startled Hugos; she was in Halifax. Mrs. Gibson, who had connections in the War Office, would later prove a fountain of knowledge about the movements of troops in the colonies and a valuable ally in the Hugos' strategy to get Adèle back.

Hugo, predictably, was outraged. He could not fathom why his daughter was running after Pinson in such a ridiculous manner, especially after he thought he had made it clear that he would consent, although reluctantly, to the marriage. Had he not agreed to give Adèle a dowry of 50,000 francs as an advance on her inheritance? The objection to their union, Hugo now knew, had to lie with Pinson, for it certainly no longer lay with him. The memory of Pinson's comment to Charles, that he wanted to marry a fourteen-year-old girl, still rankled Hugo. "Does he have a family? a wife? a mistress? does he have children?" Hugo the father — and Hugo the philanderer — wondered. Adèle, it occurred to him, was desperate enough to do just about anything to get Pinson to marry her. He wrote to his wife:

> What would be inadmissible would be if she attempted to marry this man against his wishes. I am afraid that there may be some latent impossibility which will be revealed. Otherwise, how can one explain Adèle's incredible behaviour? I had personally agreed to and accepted everything. Isn't the resistance on the other side? Then how can Adèle . . . be so insistent as to run after him?[22]

On July 2, 1863, Madame Hugo and Charles (who had been living in Brussels since the autumn of 1861) returned to Guernsey from Paris, but there was nothing they could do. Hugo was in one of his famous rages and alienated most of his family in the process. Charles departed for the Continent on July 12, only ten days after his arrival; Madame Hugo lingered until August 13. Two days later, Hugo departed for his annual vacation with Juliette Drouet. "My father is full of indifference for Adèle," wrote François-Victor,[23] not without sympathy, for Hugo steadfastly refused to comprehend the reasons for Adèle's departure. Yet Madame Hugo had forewarned her husband many times about Adèle's despondency and confided to others about her daughter's self-sacrifice. Only she understood her daughter's motivations:

> I have shared my husband's happy days, I am sharing his glorious trial, what is simpler than that? The credit is entirely my daughter's, and it is all the greater because she does not recognize it. My dear and noble child is giving her best years to exile. . . . In an exceptional situation, God has given our dear exile an exceptional being.[24]

Desperate to escape the rigours of life on Guernsey, Adèle had, in fact, chosen a form of exile more difficult than the one her father had selected for himself and his family in 1852. At that time, her father had lamented the exile's lot; he might have been talking about his daughter:

> A man so ruined that he has nothing more than his honour, so cast off that he has nothing but his conscience, so isolated that he has nothing more than his equity, so repudiated that he has nothing more on his side than truth, thrown so far back into the shadows that he has nothing left but the sun, that is what an exile is.[25]

Victor Hugo failed to recognize that his daughter, rejected by the man she loved but determined to pursue him anyway, had, in effect, chosen the same lonely path. Adèle, unlike her father, would never know what it was like to bask in the warmth of public adulation, to have fans trek to her door to meet her, or even to enjoy the whole-hearted and unconditional support of faithful family and friends. Adèle had plunged so far into the shadows of loneliness, rejection and frustration that she had nothing left, not even the sun.

❧

1. Guille, Vol. 3, p.69.

2. Guille, Vol. 1, p.69.

3. Guille, Vol. 3, p.470.

4. Guillemin, pp.38-39.

5. Guille, Vol. 3, p.18.

6. Richardson, pp.137-38.

7. Richardson, p.146.

8. Guillemin, p.41.

9. Escholier, *Hugo, roi de son siècle*, p.262.

10. Garnet Wolseley, *The Story of a Soldier's Life* (London: Constable, 1903), Vol. 1, p.226.

11. PRO London WO 31/1111.

12. Wolseley, Vol. 1, pp.225-26.

13. Guille, Vol. 3, p.61.

14. Guille, Vol. 1, p.68.

15. Hubert Juin, *Victor Hugo*, Vol. 2, 1844-1870 (Paris: Flammarion, 1984), pp.466-67.

16. Wolseley, Vol. 2, p.105.

17. Cameron Pulsifer, *British Regiments in Halifax* (Parks Canada: unpublished report, 1980), p.86.

18. Richardson, p.177.

19. Guille, Vol. 1, p.70.

20. Juin, Vol. 2, p.497.

21. Guille, Vol. 1, p.72.

22. Richardson, p.180.

23. Boringe, p.80.

24. Richardson, p.161.

25. *Collection les géants*, p.5.

Chapter 5

A Dangerous Liaison
Halifax, 1863-1864

Subsequently the love-sick Adèle sailed to New York on the "Great Eastern," and shortly afterwards came to Halifax where she registered as "Miss Lewly" at the old Halifax Hotel on Hollis Street.

Here she met with bitter disappointment.

— *Dartmouth Free Press*[1]

*I*t was nearly the end of July, 1863. Adèle Hugo was about to disembark from the New York mail packet which had brought her to Halifax, her long-anticipated destination. The port bustled with longshoremen and stevedores loading and unloading a varied collection of ships — steamers, brigs and schooners. Stone warehouses and brightly painted wooden homes lined the streets of the rough-and-ready port city. On July 28, Adèle would celebrate her thirty-third birthday. The trip to Nova Scotia had taken nearly a month, including a stop in New York in mid-July. There, Adèle had immediately booked passage on the next Halifax-bound ship, the biweekly mail packet — and wrote to her family to divulge her deception. She could not have known that they already knew where she was and what she planned — in their opinion foolishly — to do next.

Adèle did not expect anyone, not even her brothers, to understand why she had left a comfortable home, a famous and wealthy father and an easy life for this little garrison outpost, which clung like a patch of lichen to the huge and savage land beyond. She knew that her mother would be the only one of all her family to at least try to understand her quest, for Madame Hugo also bore deep scars of impossible love inflicted during the years of secret tenderness she had shared with Charles Sainte-Beuve.

Adèle knew her father would not even attempt to understand her actions. To him, she was a traitor who had betrayed him by her desire for a life of her own with a husband of her own choosing. Francois-Victor and Charles had carved lives of their own, separate from their domineering father's influence. Adèle sought nothing more than the independence they had acquired, but she had been forced to come to Halifax to try to achieve it. After twenty months' reflection, she had come to make Pinson an offer which she felt he could not refuse. The dénouement to their relationship of nine years was about to occur. That she had lied to her family seemed inconsequential at the moment, particularly if she could accomplish her aim of winning Pinson back.

To Adèle, everything seemed perfectly logical. Her father had finally agreed, after a good deal of argument, to her marriage with Pinson. He would supply her with a generous dowry, as well as a monthly allowance which would keep herself and Pinson very comfortably. Adèle had no objection to living in remote army outposts. As far as she was concerned, the farther she could get from Guernsey the better. Adèle could easily call upon her innumerable connections to see that Pinson was received in the highest society, that he enjoyed respect, and that he would receive assistance whenever he should need it, not to mention ample cash to purchase promotions all the way to Lieutenant-Colonel, if he so desired. All she asked of Pinson in return was the freedom to write and compose and exercise her own intellect and independence, free from the sort of histrionic dominance her father routinely exercised. It seemed a simple enough bargain, designed for maximum benefit to the lieutenant's career, his pocketbook and his social standing. For Adèle, life with the man she loved, however trying the circumstances might be, was a much more pleasing prospect than anything her father might arrange for her. She overlooked one simple fact: Pinson did not love her and did not want to marry her.

Adèle's arrival in Halifax did not go unnoticed amidst the bustle. Her clothes were fashionable and expensive, neither of which Haligonians were used to seeing, and her abundant chestnut hair was swept into an elaborate chignon and crowned with a stylish bonnet. She had been so fixated on seeing Pinson again that she hadn't given any thought to where she would stay or how she would get there. Nor could she remember much of the English she had so entertainingly practised with J__ Rose back in Jersey. Her confusion was obvious to coachman Thomas O'Brien, who quickly swept her up, luggage and all, and took her to the Halifax Hotel. Although Adèle was unaccustomed to travelling alone, she might certainly have given some thought to which hotel she would stay at; the other mail packet passengers could surely have made some recommendations. But, not having made definite arrangements, Adèle found herself in Mr. O'Brien's care.

The expensive Halifax Hotel, only a few moments drive away on Hollis Street, was really the only place in town where a woman of Adèle's obvious standing in life could consider staying. In 1863, it was always full of Americans waiting out the Civil War in grand style. Adèle quickly realized that the Halifax Hotel would be too costly for her meagre budget, unless she set her plan in motion quickly. She took the precaution of registering under a fictitious name, Miss Lewly; even in this distant colonial outpost, she knew the Hugo name was likely to be recognized.

Now that she was in Halifax, Adèle had no idea how to find Pinson. Fortunately, she was able to tell her story — or at least the version she felt had a ring of truth to it — to the hotel's French-speaking manager, Henry Hesslein, a Swiss. Adèle explained that she had come to look for her cousin, an officer in the Sixteenth Regiment of Foot. At the time, the city was swollen with soldiers and officers, and accommodations, always at a premium, were strained to the breaking point. Hesslein, knowing the search could be a difficult one, directed her to Peter Lenoir, a French-speaking lawyer with an office just down the street. If

The Halifax Hotel, c.1891 *(Public Archives of Nova Scotia)*

anyone would know where to find Miss Lewly's cousin, it would be Lenoir.

Adèle took Hesslein's advice and presented herself at Lenoir's ground-floor office at 197 Hollis Street. Hesslein's hunch was right: Lenoir was quickly able to tell her where to find Pinson. The soldiers and officers of the Sixteenth, he revealed, were quartered at the new Wellington Barracks, several kilometres away in the city's north end. When Adèle proposed to set out that very day on foot, a look of horror passed over Mr. Lenoir's face. Halifax, he explained, was a seaport, and not the sort of place in which a lady could walk alone through its more dangerous streets. To get to the barracks, she would have to cross Barrack and Albermarle streets, two of the roughest in town. Adèle would not be deterred from the plan she had come so far to execute, but she could see that a compromise was in order. She decided to write to Pinson first.

Back in her room, Adèle hastily scratched a note to the man she had waited two long years to see. She also dashed off another letter to her parents, informing them that she had arrived in Halifax, accompanied by a friend, Miss Lewly. Then she waited for Pinson's reply. None came. His silence only made Adèle more determined to reach him. She despatched another letter, a long explanation of her presence in Halifax and the advantages of marriage for them both, and she repeated her everlasting love and regard for him. This time, Pinson replied; he made his position brutally clear. Not only would he not accept her terms, but he refused to marry her or have anything to do with her.

Pinson's refusal was more than a slap in the face. Adèle's continued freedom now depended, ironically, on their marriage. If Pinson would not play his part, she would have no option but to return to Hauteville-House and her father's endless reproaches. In all likelihood, she would be confined forever to the dreary island, literally under lock and key to ensure that she would not attempt to escape again. She had to convince Pinson that their union would in no way impede his freedom, that she could provide the flashy clothes of which he was so fond, keep him in ample pocket money and give him anything else he might desire.

Adèle knew she was making a fool of herself, but she had already come too far to be sent home again. She vowed to stay in Halifax until she became Madame Pinson. On August 4, 1863, she again wrote to her family to tell them she had arrived in Halifax. In the meantime, Hugo's anger had gotten the better of him, and, as he informed François-Victor, he had decided to refuse the couple permission to marry unless he received information, which the family had apparently sought for some time, about Pinson's background. This information was, of course, not forthcoming.

Unaccustomed to providing for herself and realizing that the Halifax Hotel was depleting her pocketbook too quickly, Adèle wrote to François-Victor to plead for an allowance of 400 francs a month in order to live decently. She hinted broadly that, because of the debts she had already incurred, if she did not receive at least 390 francs by the next post, the consequences could be disastrous: she had already been forced to borrow money from some people who would not hesitate to have her thrown in prison if they were not promptly repaid.[2]

It was a creative ploy; moreover, it worked. Not only did she receive a generous monthly allowance from her father of 600 francs, but she managed to find cheap lodgings as well. Her new room was in a house at 18 Granville Street, one street up from Hollis and near the Halifax Hotel. She stayed there at least until the end of September. By that time, she had devised a plan which would keep her in Halifax, for the time being.

Despite Pinson's flat refusal to wed her, Adèle wrote to her mother in September to announce that she was now Madame Pinson. Drawing on her considerable skills at fiction writing, Adèle gave her worried mother an entirely false account of her life in the New World:

September 17, 1863
My dear,

I am married, I am still under the excitement of the event and I am writing you quickly so I will not miss the mail. In the middle of our happiness, there is regret: in five days, my husband will be forced to be absent for three weeks in Canada, a necessity of his military duties. As it would be necessary to sail four times during the Equinox [when the seas are always high and often rough] if I wanted to be with him, it is better that I wait for him in Halifax until he comes back. I received the 200 francs, and recognize perfectly well the value of the . . .

Page one ends here; pages two, three and four of the letter are missing, and the missive resumes on page five:

. . . it is, therefore, very simple to say that I was married in England. Because you are very far from the [illegible], the plan is plausible. You can say that I have departed for America with my husband, where his business affairs have called him. In this manner, everything can be explained. You can address my letters to: Madame Penson (my name is written equally with an "i" or with an "e." I write my name with an "e," preferring the "e" to the "i"), 18 Granville Street, Halifax, Nova Scotia, America.

You must put "Madame" in big letters, so that your response won't go astray, and so that the word Madame will be easily read on your envelope. I don't live in the barracks or the camps where the men are; that will never happen. I have lodgings in the city like all the other wives, and our husbands always come to see us.[3]

But François-Victor was suspicious. With the best interests of his sister at heart, he told his mother, he had written to Pinson to ask for a copy of their marriage certificate. He acknowledged that Adèle had, from the moment she left home, taken her future in her own hands and that the family should respect her independence; nonetheless, he was hurt by her apparent lack of tenderness and regard for the family. He also felt compelled to note that he pitied her in her search for happiness, which had brought her, he knew, to the edge of destruction.[4]

Victor Hugo, for his part, was at a complete loss to understand his daughter's brazenness, and he was indignant that she had apparently forgotten all about him. In a letter to his wife, the patriarch complained:

The conduct of Adèle is puzzling. We consent to marriage; she sneaks away from home. All she had to do was marry with dignity, at her home, in front of her mother, her father, her brothers, her parents, her friends. She has made her marriage into an escapade. All of a sudden, she writes that she is married. This takes up three lines in her letter. The other ten pages are a demand for money. My name is never mentioned.[5]

Hugo's lament over his new role as his daughter's banker did not stop the family from announcing Adèle's marriage, on October 9, 1863, in the *Gazette de Guernesey* and the *Guernsey Star*:

> On September 17 were married in Paris, Mr. Albert Penson of the 16th Regiment of the English Infantry, and Miss Adèle Hugo, daughter of Monsieur le Vicomte Hugo, officer of the Legion of Honour, Peer of France, member of the French Academy, and Knight of the Order of Charles III of Spain, living at St-Pierre-Port, Guernsey.[6]

Adèle had discovered, in the meantime, that her lodgings on Granville Street were not to her taste. Despite the fact that the street comprised the most fashionable shopping district in the city, Adèle found the lively downtown too noisy to bear after years of quiet on Guernsey. Not wanting to risk settling in another unsuitable room, she confessed her difficulties to the Halifax Hotel's French chef, who, to her delight, said he knew just the man who could help her. Richard Saunders worked mornings as a courier for the Union Bank. In the evenings, he hired himself out as a waiter to the Halifax Hotel or some of the large households in the city which often needed extra help. So it was that the chef knew that Saunders's wife, Sarah, took in roomers. That very evening, the chef hired Richard Saunders for a banquet and took a moment to mention the young French miss in need of a new place to live.

Saunders was delighted — his wife was, at that moment, looking for just such a quiet, well-bred young woman as the chef had described. The next morning, Adèle learned the matter had been settled. She quickly packed her trunks, and, following the chef's instructions, took Mr. O'Brien's cab to 33 North Street, a square, brightly painted three-storey frame building known locally as a saltbox. Her new address was scarcely glamorous. It was, however, located in a much quieter part of town than her previous room. Perched on a steeply inclined street at the north end of town, the house overlooked the drab browns and greys of the railway yard and wharves to the sparkling harbour beyond. Adèle had familiarized herself with the city, and she knew the location had another advantage: it was only a few blocks from Wellington Barracks, where Lieutenant Pinson would be quartered until late next spring.

Having spent most of her money at the Halifax Hotel, Adèle had been reduced to living off bread and butter and chocolates for some time. When Mrs. Saunders asked her new lodger to have dinner with the family that night, Adèle gladly accepted. She did not have the slightest idea of how to prepare a meal for herself, and the mere thought of a real, home-cooked dinner made her mouth water. That evening, she met Mr. Saunders and their daughter, Grace. After just a few moments' conversation, Adèle realized that she had indeed situated herself strategically. Mr. Saunders's job as a part-time waiter allowed him to mingle unobtrusively — and eavesdrop — at most of the city's social functions, large and small, at which army officers always figured prominently. Before long, Mr. Saunders became Adèle's chief source of gossip. Soon, they established a routine. Adèle would wait up late for Mr. Saunders to return, and he would tell her everything he had seen and heard. More often than not, Pinson attended the banquets, and Adèle could barely contain her excitement when there was news of him. She wanted to know in detail what he wore, who he was with and what he said.

From time to time, Pinson even consented to visit Adèle. But the attraction was evidently not romantic, for Mrs. Saunders noticed that after each visit the heap of gold sovereigns which had accumulated in Adèle's room was gone. It was obvious to Mrs. Saunders that her lodger, who ate sparingly and was almost always penniless, was giving her money to the smart-looking young lieutenant. Mrs. Saunders had grown fond of the refined young woman who lived in her upstairs room, but she was alarmed by the young woman's thinness and her growing melancholy. Adèle kept strictly to herself and spent her days and nights writing feverishly. When she did go out, it was usually to the

British Bank of North America to cash the bank draft for her monthly allowance, or to William Gossip's book and stationery store on Granville Street for paper, which she bought by the ream. James Gossip, the proprietor's son, often waited on Adèle. She came two or three times a week, always buying her ream of paper. The store also housed an extensive military library, which Adele frequented. Pinson also spent time in the library, but their paths never crossed in the shop.

The money Adele received monthly should have allowed her to live in grand style in a small garrison town like Halifax. But Adèle was frugal and never spent money on extras if she could avoid it — not even to pay for a cab when she was out late at night. Her money, she felt, was better spent elsewhere. After a few months, Mrs. Saunders noticed that Adèle had adopted a curious habit. Dressed in a man's evening attire, she would leave the house late at night, returning several hours later. While Mrs. Saunders found this behaviour odd, she assumed that Adèle dressed as she did for her own protection. If she was taken for a man, she would have far less trouble on the streets late at night than she would dressed as a woman. In her own clothing, she could easily be taken for a streetwalker. Adèle hadn't thought up the idea of dressing in male garb all by herself. The credit belonged to George Sand, who had become a symbol of independence for Adèle. But she scarcely expected Mrs. Saunders, or anyone else in Halifax for that matter, to comprehend her methods. Besides, she found her disguise perfect for shadowing Pinson, who, she suspected, had taken another lover. She intended to find out who the woman was and reinforce her claim to Pinson.

Adèle's suspicions had been fuelled by rumours that Pinson's wife and children would join him or had joined him in Halifax. One night, she was sure her worst fears had been confirmed when Richard Saunders reported that a handsome woman whom he had heard described as Pinson's married sister had come to live in Halifax. In just a short time, she had become well-known in the city, he told Adèle. He himself had seen her out driving nearly every day in her carriage, accompanied by seven little white dogs.

Adèle still hadn't admitted to her family that she and Pinson were not married, although, in a letter to her mother, she intimated that her flight from Guernsey had more to do with freedom than passion:

> Tell yourself that my future would have been darkened and my marriage compromised by a senseless, futile delay. Just think of the situation which we should have been in if this marriage had not taken place because we had wasted time, you know yourself that what you put off is always uncertain, because though a man may be absolutely determined to get married, he cannot always answer for what life and the passing of the years may bring. . . . I might probably never have married, and then think of the situation in which we should have found ourselves! The same domestic arrangements, the same discussions about whether we could do this or that; and then, instead of knowing that I was happy, you would have seen me sad. Think of how you would have suffered! Today all this misfortune has been avoided.[7]

But soon the pressure of her double life became too much for Adèle. To make matters worse, she had no one to whom she could unburden her soul. The truth was not that difficult to discern. Mrs. Saunders had long since realized that Adèle had left home to marry the dashing Lieutenant Pinson, who was no longer in love with her, but she said nothing.

Adèle realized that the time had come to tell the truth to her family. She confessed in a letter to François-Victor that everything had not gone according to plan, and that she was not, and never had been, married; she could not bear to tell either her mother or her father the mortifying news. On November 11, François-Victor bitterly conveyed to Madame Hugo what he had suspected all along. This time, he was less sympathetic to his sister's forlorn plight:

> My dearest mother, Adèle has deceived us, as she has deceived the whole world. There was no marriage. She told me this in a

confidential letter specially addressed to me . . . she asks that I help her try to touch the heart of M. P[inson] . . . and try to convince him to consent [to the marriage]. I have written to M. P., not a supplication, as Adèle has urged, but a summary. If he does not respond, I will propose to Charles that he send him a demand for financial reparation. We will soon see.[8]

In fact, François-Victor had been forewarned by an earlier letter shown to him by Pinson's nephew-by-marriage, Monsieur Lecrosnier. The letter was written by a cousin of "this said Pinson," namely, a woman he described as being the daughter of General [actually Lieutenant-Colonel] Pinson, to Madame Lecrosnier. In it, the writer revealed that Adèle's marriage was a hoax.

François-Victor's first reaction was to accuse the Pinson family of being demented and ask why Adèle would continue to call herself Madame Pinson if the family disavowed her. But in their hearts, the Hugo family members must have known Adèle had tricked them. Almost immediately, François-Victor began to formulate a plan to get his sister, and the entire family, out of the mess in which they found themselves. He explained his plan to Madame Hugo:

> If she comes back to Europe, it will be necessary that she resign herself to living at least a year in Paris or Brussels. It will be easy to live in one of these cities without being exposed to an affront. You could join her in Brussels if she doesn't want to go to you in Paris. My father will allow you 500 francs per month for your support. This is his final word. He has decided, and, as far as I am concerned, with reason, not to receive for one year a person falsely using the name of a foreign family.
>
> This is what Adèle has reduced us to by her extravagance.[9]

Quickly and quietly, the family began to try to reassert its control of Adèle, regardless of the physical distance, and, increasingly, the emotional distance, which separated them.

Back in Halifax, Adèle remained determined not to go back to her family. She had already surmised what was happening and would have none of it. Intent on preserving her new-found independence as well as her cash flow, she repeatedly devised plans to ensure both.

Word of the false marriage had inevitably got back to Pinson via the marriage notice, which had appeared in English as well as French papers. The Hugo family's report that he had distinguished himself in the Crimea very nearly made him the laughing stock of his fellow officers. He had barely joined the army when the Crimean War ceased; it was his uncle, Lieutenant-Colonel Pinson, who had earned war honours. Pinson immediately wrote a stiff letter to François-Victor demanding to know how the family could have believed for a moment that the marriage had taken place. He had never, he stressed, asked Adèle to marry him. Only two and a half months earlier Pinson had written to tell François-Victor what he had already told his sister: that he could not marry her. Foolishly, Pinson had given the letter to Adèle to post, and she, wisely, had intercepted it.

In a December, 1863, letter to Charles, François-Victor wrote:

Today I received two letters from Halifax: one from Adèle, the other from Pinson. His letter, polite and cold, announces a firm determination not to marry her. He was strangely surprised by the news published in the newspapers, namely that the Vicomte Victor Hugo had done him the unsolicited honour of giving him his daughter. Adèle, he says, arrived in America on her own private authority.[10]

Moreover, Pinson's letter insinuated that Adèle was in some danger in Halifax and should be brought home for her own protection. If Adèle needed protection, it was not from the criminal element in Halifax. Sarah Saunders had already surmised, correctly, that the bulk of Adèle's money was going to the lieutenant. Whether he asked for the cash or not, Pinson's gambling habits had not subsided, nor had his taste for the latest fashions. While Pinson did not welcome Adèle's attention, he did welcome her money. His wily ways did not endear him to his comrades, judging from the description of a fellow officer:

> Albert Andrew Pinson came in 1861 as Lieutenant in the Second Battalion of the Sixteenth Regiment to Halifax, Nova Scotia. He was a great dandy and nicknamed by his brother officers "the Count." His father, a clergyman, was not wealthy, and "the Count" was in a chronic state of financial embarrassment. His age has always remained a secret, not even his most intimate friends knowing when he was born. He used to dye his hair and long moustache, and even to rouge his face to hide a few wrinkles.[11]

Pinson, usually the life of the party, was well-known about town, particularly for his love of horse racing, which was not an inexpensive sport for a "gentleman jockey." Lieutenant-Colonel Wolseley noted that horse racing was particularly popular among officers in British North America. Devotees used their own horses, £50 to £60 being the going price of a good mount. At least some of Adèle's money must have helped fund Pinson's hobby, and he gave little thought to his acceptance of her bribes. It was her relentless pursuit of him that he found hard to stomach, and he kept the story of her tragic fixation to himself.

Adèle was not without her supporters; certainly, Mr. and Mrs. Saunders felt great sympathy for her. In December of 1863, Mrs. Saunders saw a way she might be able to help her sad charge. Adèle had left a letter on the dining room table to be mailed. Sarah Saunders did not recognize the name of the person to whom it was addressed (which Adèle must have anticipated), but she felt sure that if she wrote to this Victor Hugo explaining the difficulties faced by Miss Lewly something good would come of it.

In her letter, Mrs. Saunders outlined her chief concern: that Adèle appeared to have no winter clothing. Winters were harsh, she explained, and the young miss would quickly freeze if she stepped outside. Her lodger was not eating properly, and Mrs. Saunders feared she was overworking herself to the point of a mental breakdown. She

noted that Adèle received no visitors except Pinson, who came very ir-
regularly, and that she paid calls only on Mrs. Gabriel across the street,
who spoke French. The letter was received by the Hugos on January 6,
1864. Victor Hugo duly noted in his diary the "sombre news from
Halifax."

It was not until the French chef of Major-General Sir Francis Hastings Charles Doyle, the Commander-in-Chief of the Halifax Garrison,
stopped by the Saunders home one day to engage Richard Saunders for
a banquet that evening that they realized the significance of their new
correspondent. Seeing a letter addressed to Monsieur le Vicomte Victor Hugo in Guernsey, the chef could scarcely believe his eyes. "Do you
know who that is?" demanded the chef. Mrs. Saunders readily admitted
she did not. Proudly, the chef informed her that Hugo was the greatest
writer in France.[12]

Mrs. Saunders's letter was answered by François-Victor, the only
member of the Hugo family who could read and write fluently in English. He responded to their letter immediately, delighted at such an
unexpected stroke of luck; henceforth it would be possible to monitor
Adèle's movements. Adèle's brother did not disclose their lodger's true
identity to the Saunderses, but urged them to buy her whatever she
needed. Upon submission of receipts, they would be swiftly reimbursed
for their expenditures. Moreover, he asked that the Saunderses stay in
touch with the Hugo family, in case there was anything else they could
do for the unfortunate young woman whom he referred to as Madame
Pinson, and whom the Saunderses knew as Miss Lewly.

Hard on the heels of Mrs. Saunders's first letter to Victor Hugo
came another missive, also received in January of 1864. It was from
Adèle, and it was most disturbing. Taking François-Victor once more
into her confidence, Adèle disclosed that Pinson intended to marry another woman in the spring. François-Victor, more understanding this
time, wrote to his mother pleading that she not blame "the poor
child," who was so obviously unbalanced. Before the month was out,
Adèle's admission sparked a stern letter from Madame Hugo to the
feckless Pinson:

My daughter, sir, left us at your provocation six months ago. She has taken herself to Halifax, where you are, believing that you would hold the engagement of marriage which, also at your provocation, you had made with her.

These things, which I leave to your conscience, are not the subject of this letter. The point is this: We want our daughter to return, as soon as possible, to take her place in her family. I be-lieve that, despite our urgings, she will stay in Halifax as long as she believes you are there. For her to return, it will be necessary for her to be convinced, by methods which you deem most ef-fective, that you are leaving for England. This thing having been done — for which I wait on you — we will not know each other any more, sir.

A.F.H.

P.S. My daughter should, you understand, be unaware of this letter.[13]

There is no way of knowing if this letter ever reached Pinson; a draft copy was found among Madame Hugo's papers.

By February 11, Victor Hugo appears to have lost patience with his recalcitrant daughter, and to a lesser degree with his wife, who did not always agree with him on what was to be done about Adèle:

In reference to Adèle, we have talked up until now of this unfor-tunate child with tenderness, but the moment approaches when, to save her, it will be necessary to speak to her firmly, perhaps even with severity. It is from you that this severity, supported by us all, must come, all the more because of the way she uses and abuses your indulgence.[14]

Hugo gave no indication of just what these new strong-arm tactics were to be, nor how they would be enforced several thousand kilome-tres away. Despite his overwhelming concern with saving face, though, he did feel some compassion for his daughter, even if he underestimated the seriousness of her fixation on Pinson and her deteriorating mental condition. On February 21 he wrote:

> There is only one thing to do and that is this: save Adèle from herself and accept as immense good luck for her the refusal of this miserable [man]. Adèle is sick. She will heal. These torments will pass. . . . At this moment, it is necessary to save Adèle's future from her present.[15]

The Saunderses, for their part, did as they had been asked. They purchased winter clothing for Adèle (she often went out without a coat in the penetrating cold and damp) and supplemented her meagre diet with eggs, sandwiches and whatever else they could. François-Victor was as good as his word, always promptly repaying their expenses. So keen was he to maintain this new arrangement that he even asked the Saunderses how he might repay them for the stamps they were putting on their letters. His elaborate care was unnecessary; they were compassionate people, and Adèle was genuinely fond of them. When they moved in the spring of 1864 to 42 Sackville Street, Adèle went with them. Adèle had said she would supply her own furnishings, but she purchased hardly anything.[16] Her room was strewn with paper, clothing and books, and "she rarely, if ever, permitted any person to enter. She lived in almost complete seclusion, neither wishing for nor having any associates."[17]

It was obvious that Adèle needed the services of Rosalie, her maid. Although her allowance was more than adequate to allow her to live well, including hiring a maid, she lived in self-imposed penury. Adèle wrote to her brother about her change of abode and, typically, asked for more money. "I still need 180 francs for the last two months. As soon as I have it (you can send it to me by the next post), I will pay my accounts and leave." Obliquely, she referred to a new plan she had hatched to force Pinson to marry her: "M. [Pinson] is starting to come around and his resistance is diminishing appreciably," she wrote. "Nevertheless, you would do well not to carry out your action before I tell you and not to write to him until I give you new information."[18]

Recently, she had seen a hypnotist perform at the Orpheus Hall in downtown Halifax. He had worked wonders, making respectable businessmen strip to their drawers and society women squawk like chickens. Adèle saw method in the madness, and after the show she had approached the hypnotist and told him her problem. The hypnotist agreed that the matter could be easily solved — for 5,000 francs. It was an enormous sum, even for Adèle, but the hypnotist had gauged his mark well. Her clothing, her bearing and the tremor of desperation in her voice assured him she would pay, and pay well, for his ministrations. Pinson's resistance would break down completely, he assured her. After being hypnotized, the lieutenant would quickly agree to marriage.

On June 26, 1864, Adèle wrote to beg her father to forward the money immediately, deducting it from her inheritance. At the same time, she vowed that she would never sail for England without Pinson. Despite the outlandishness of the idea, the Hugos did not reject Adèle's suggestion outright. Her father insisted on the presence of two witnesses and a priest at the marriage ceremony, but nowhere did he express concern over the moral implications of such a deceit.

The money for the hypnotist was never sent, and Adèle seems to have abandoned the idea. Yet the furious exchange of letters amongst members of the Hugo family continued. Plans were devised for Adèle's return and rehabilitation, but none was executed. The family's indecisiveness over what to do about their recalcitrant daughter and sister had so far given Adèle nearly a year of freedom. She had weathered her first winter in Halifax as well as might be expected, though she had found the months of darkness longer and more trying than in Jersey or Guernsey. She longed for the return of longer hours of daylight, and since March she had anticipated the budding of the flowers as she had on Guernsey. But in Halifax, snow was not unknown even in May, and the spring rains could last well into June; summer didn't really come until July.

Nothing is known of how Adèle lived during the latter part of 1864 and the first five months of 1865, but in May of that year, the officers and soldiers of the Sixteenth Regiment swapped their comfortable lodgings in Wellington Barracks for the musty quarters in the Halifax Citadel. The Seventeenth Regiment had shivered through the previous winter in the stone casemates, and the men of the Sixteenth knew from experience that they were destined to shiver no less throughout the spring and coming summer. Even in July and August, it was often necessary to keep fires burning in the dank caverns that passed for accommodations. The dearth of adequate washing facilities and the putrid lavatories only added to their misery.

Yet Adèle was delighted. Now, with her living on Sackville Street and Pinson just a few blocks away at the Citadel, the star-crossed lovers found themselves in virtually the same proximity as before. For Pinson, familiarity bred only contempt. He ceased even his sporadic visits to Adèle, having reinforced his resolve to make a complete break with her despite threats, entreaties and even the generous bribes which he had so eagerly accepted in the past. But in spite of his best efforts to eject her from his life, Adèle lingered on.

1. "For Fair One in Dartmouth Victor Hugo's Daughter Spurned," *Dartmouth Free Press* (June 2, 1955), p.80.
2. Guille, Vol. 1, p.76.
3. Laster, p.121.
4. Juin, p.501.
5. Juin, pp.501-02.
6. Guille, Vol. 1, pp.78-79.
7. Richardson, p.179.
8. Guille, Vol. 1, p.82.
9. Guille, Vol. 1, pp.82-83.
10. Guille, Vol. 1, p.84.

11. Ludwig Wudzburg, "The Romance of Victor Hugo's Daughter," *Halifax Morning Chronicle* (October 30, 1903), p.1.

12. Wudzburg, p.1.

13. Guillemin, p.122.

14. Guillemin, p.124.

15. Guillemin, p.125.

16. Guille, Vol. 1, p.120.

17. Wudzburg, p.1.

18. Guillemin, p.128.

Chapter 6

"She of Crazy Love and Folly"
Halifax, 1864-1865

The truth of the matter seems to be that Adèle was legally married to the English officer, according to the laws of England.
But since the marriage was contracted without the consent of
her parents, it was invalid in France.
— *New York Times*[1]

Through Richard Saunders's careful eavesdropping, Adèle learned
some shocking news: Pinson had become engaged to Miss Agnes
Johnstone of Dartmouth. As soon as she heard the disquieting gossip,
Adèle pledged to stop their forthcoming marriage in any way she
could. First, though, she set about confirming the truth of the rumour
by stalking the unwary couple. Many years later, *The Acadian Recorder*
gave one popular account of how Adèle went about confirming her
worst fears:

It was a warm June night, filled with the scent of roses from the
neighbouring gardens. A band was playing waltzes and other
dance music in the Commandant's residence. General Sir Francis Hastings Doyle, a gay old military bachelor, had given a ball
where the military set and the blooming belles of the city held
high revelry. One young couple had strolled across the street to
Grafton Park and seated themselves on one of the benches
under the grand elms that grew there to be more secluded in

The Lenoir Building, Hollis Street, Halifax

(Public Archives of Nova Scotia; Heritage Trust of Nova Scotia)

their love-making. They had not been there long when a man, evidently of the upper class, came, stealing from tree to tree; as if shadowing the couple on the bench. This person watched with intense interest the love-making of the benchers, who were a young officer of the garrison and the daughter of an eminent barrister and leader of the government. The person in male attire was not a man, but Adèle Hugo.[2]

Next, Adèle sought to initiate legal action to force the pair to break their engagement. She consulted Peter Lenoir, who had been helpful in finding Pinson when she first arrived in Halifax. But he would not take the case; whether this was because he did not feel he had the appropriate legal skills or because he did not believe Adèle is unknown. Instead, Lenoir referred her to Robert Motton, a prominent lawyer with a particular talent for criminal law.

Adèle wasted no time in calling on Motton (who would later become the city's stipendiary magistrate) at his Barrington Street office, where she sat fighting to maintain her composure. It had taken Motton a few minutes to calm the fiery, raven-haired French woman, whom he knew only as Miss Lewly. (Adèle had not dared tell Motton her real name for fear of discovery, nor did she give any indication of her connection with France's most famous family.) The lawyer listened intently as the young woman before him poured out her heart.

Adèle could not keep the bitterness from creeping into her voice as she told Motton the long and complex story of her involvement with Lieutenant Albert Pinson. Not only had Pinson sworn her eternal love and promised to marry her, but he had even signed a marriage contract in Guernsey. Moreover, she claimed, they had gone through a secret, although not legal, marriage ceremony which had been performed in London. Most of Adèle's explanation was fabricated, although it contained elements of truth. Despite his sympathies for the beautiful young woman before him, Motton had to admit that her case was not at all unusual. It wasn't the first time he had listened to a young lady very like herself beg for his help in putting a wayward fiancé back on the marriage track, and he told her so. The problem, he knew, was particularly prevalent among the enlisted men, who got involved in common-law, or "serial," marriages — essentially picking up a new wife in every garrison town where they were posted. Such "marriages," of course, had no official sanction, and the families which sprung from them did not receive extra rations or support from the military. Sadly, these military "wives" were frequently forced to turn to prostitution to support themselves and their children; when the regiment departed, they were more often than not left destitute. Local newspapers regularly carried stories about cases of bigamy involving soldiers.

The case was certainly a very sad one, Motton assured Adèle. Unfortunately, he was also obliged to say that aside from his writing Pinson a letter asking him to withdraw himself from the engagement, he knew of no law which would force Pinson to marry Adèle. Evidently, Motton sensed that Adèle had coloured her story for his benefit, for there were at least two other courses of action he could have pursued but did not. The first would have been to investigate Pinson for breach of promise to marry Adèle; his second course of action could have been to have Pinson charged with bigamy if it could have been proved that he was legally married to Adèle and subsequently married Agnes. Yet Motton did neither. Despite Adèle's claims, there was no evidence that any marriage existed, at least not one which would be recognized by the Nova Scotia courts, nor did there appear to have been any formal engagement. Yet Adèle refused to let the matter drop, and she returned several times to Motton's office to try to convince him to take legal action:

> Mademoiselle Hugo used to speak of her wrongs to her lawyer with burning cheek and flashing eye. Her eyes he described as being almost terrible in their fiery brightness when she was aroused. She repeatedly declared in passionate words that she was Pinsen's wife in the sight of Heaven, and that he should never marry another woman.[3]

To the superstitious Adèle, it must have seemed as though Auguste Vacquerie had finally wreaked his revenge. More than a decade before, in a fit of rage at Adèle's blatant and unrepentant infidelity with Pinson, he had sworn that "ten years from now you will be punished."[4] Now she was indeed being punished, not simply by Pinson's refusal to marry her, but by his intention to marry another. Adèle found herself in a very real and all-too-human plight. For Pinson, she had given up everything; in return, she had reaped nothing but grief.

As a musketry instructor, Pinson's talents were rarely called upon, except during annual training and field days. On those occasions, mock battles would be staged on the Halifax Commons, with the troops firing blank cartridges. At other times, the whole garrison marched, escorted by various military bands, through the streets to the north end of town, where they would conduct manoeuvres. Between June and September, Pinson helped conduct the regiment's annual training sessions at Chobham, on the Eastern Shore.

Amiable officers like Pinson were the lifeblood of remote garrison towns. Polite society looked to them for a much-needed infusion of zest into social occasions, and the officers evidently did their utmost not to disappoint the local populace. Military men were held in such esteem that their social calendars were always full. Fortunately, their professional duties were correspondingly few; officers had a particularly easy time of it and enjoyed the added benefit of servants culled from the lower ranks. In 1829, Captain William Moorsom of the Fifty-second Regiment of Foot wrote that a young officer posted to a garrison town would find himself "raised at once to a level above that accorded to the scarlet cloth at home — his society generally sought, frequently courted and himself esteemed as a personage whose opinions are regarded with no little degree of attention."[5] Wolseley noted that life for a military man in the colonies in the 1860s was far from hard: "We had very successful garrison theatre in the winter, and many were the sledge expeditions we made into the neighbouring country. Altogether, it was an elysium of bliss for young officers, the only trouble being to keep single."

This, alas, seemed to be Pinson's trouble. He was fortunate enough not to be the object of Wolseley's draconian solution to what he felt was the opportunistic preying of local women on his men. "Several impressionable young captains and subalterns had to be sent home hurriedly to save them from imprudent marriages. Although these Canadian ladies were very charming they were not richly endowed with worldly goods."[6]

In matters of the heart, Pinson was an exception amongst his peers. He was in no danger of making an "imprudent marriage"; he had cultivated an unerring sixth sense for women with money. Agnes's father, James W. Johnstone, had been a member of the Nova Scotia legislature for twenty years and had also been premier from 1857 to 1860. He continued to enjoy prestige and power now that he was a justice of the Supreme Court of Nova Scotia. Not long after his arrival in Halifax, Pinson began visiting Mount Amelia, the Johnstone's stately Dartmouth home. It was likely sometime in late 1864 or early 1865 that he declared his intentions toward Agnes and began a serious courtship. His proposal may have been hastened by Adèle's untimely arrival in Halifax, and he had the distinct impression that Judge Johnstone was less than happy about the attention he paid Agnes. Try as he might, Pinson could not escape the whispers of the town gossips which seemed to follow him everywhere. He feared that the most persistent rumours would reach Judge Johnstone's ears — that he was a bigamist, having already been married to a woman living in Halifax; that he kept a mistress, a mysterious French woman who had followed him to British North America; and that he was an inveterate gambler with staggering debts.

Pinson's behaviour did little to mitigate what was said about him. Despite his engagement to Agnes, he openly kept company with a woman whom he described as his "married sister"; he had freely accepted money from Adèle, who had indeed been his mistress; he had a reputation as a dandy; and he could hardly deny his chronic financial difficulties. Finding a vulnerable but well-off woman like Agnes once again seemed to be the answer to his problems.

Like Adèle, Agnes was considered good-looking, with a quick intelligence and a fine sense of humour. Like Adèle, Agnes was in her thirties, having avoided marriage by immersing herself in music and religion. At the age of twenty, Agnes had even had herself baptised. And, like Adèle, she lived in the shadow of her prettier, high-spirited sister, Minnie, who had a knack for getting just about anything she wanted. Agnes was in danger of becming a spinster, that is, until she met "Bertie" Pinson, who swept her off her feet.

Judge Johnstone was not pleased with Agnes's choice, nor was he alone in his low opinion of Pinson. Even Pinson's fellow officers disdained the man local women seemed to find so desirable:

> Others said that Pinson's father, although he was not rich, purchased a commission in the army for his son in order to separate him from Miss Hugo. One of his comrades confirmed that very few people in the garrision knew the story of Adèle, and that Pinson became very angry when anyone said that they had heard he was married and that his wife had followed him to Halifax.
>
> He was very sporting, and often at the race course he played at being a gentleman jockey. He was always short of money, spending it immediately for clothes and pleasures which he received. He was known, it appears, by all the money lenders in Halifax.
>
> Haligonians did not spare Pinson's feelings in their descriptions of him. They said that while he indulged in amorous conquests, he knew all too well that Adèle lived in privation because of him. He was found to be completely self-centred, insensitive, without a soul, without any ideals, and without ambition other than to easily obtain the means to lead an indolent life. He had received a good education and spoke French well.[7]

Indeed, his detractors thought that Pinson was virtually interchangeable with his more lacklustre peers in ability and personality:

He was never distinguished from the ordinary subaltern in a British regiment, except, perhaps, that he appears to have been rather more of a dandy. He was of average height, rather handsome, and decidedly stylish in appearance. He wore long mustaches, and took great pains to appear in most exquisite mode, and was essentially a ladies' man.[8]

Adèle continued trying to press her very shaky legal case against Pinson's engagement to Miss Johnstone:

It is sufficient to say that the story of her relations with Pinsen was fully unfolded, and though the case did not present many points for the consideration of a lawyer, yet Mr. Motton was so far interested in her case as to send a letter to Pinsen.[9]

Motton's letter to Pinson, needless to say, produced no results, and Adèle agreed that he should next write directly to Judge Johnstone to try to sort the matter out. Just then, Adèle dropped a bombshell: she revealed her true identity to her astonished advocate. The news that he was acting as counsel for a daughter of Victor Hugo took Motton completely by surprise. Unlike the Saunders family, Motton was well-read and quite familiar with the famous poet and his works. He knew, too, that the Hugo family was rich and influential. Motton, just a year younger than Adèle, could not fathom why Lieutenant Pinson, by all accounts a gifted opportunist, would refuse to marry the beautiful, rich and well-spoken woman before him.

Adèle then told Motton that her father had

demanded that Pinson come to Brussels and marry his daughter there. Madame Hugo agreed with this; but Adèle was infatuated, and her fiery spirit would not accept this wise paternal counsel. She insisted upon going to London at all hazards, and even in defiance of all social rules. When it was found that the impetuous girl was determined to have her way, her mother at length acquiesced so far as to accompany her to London.

On their arrival they found, to their mortification and chagrin, that Lieutenant Pinsen had sailed with his regiment for Halifax, and without leaving any message or satisfactory explanation; indeed, the circumstances gave indubitable evidence of desertion. Adèle and her mother had no other course than to return at once to Brussels.[10]

The drama of Adèle's revelation did nothing to change the facts of her case. Certainly if some contract had been signed and broken, financial reparation might be exacted, but aside from that, he regretted that he could not be of further service. Adèle left his office bitterly disappointed.

Not long afterward, Motton sent a second letter, this time to Judge Johnstone, relating the very unwelcome news. The complaint did not mention Adèle's true identity, but Motton had left little to Judge Johnstone's considerable imagination about the power and wealth of the young woman's family. His client was asking not for compensation or even an apology; indeed, she seemed to want no scandal at all over the matter. She asked only that the engagement be broken off immediately, so that her own reputation might not suffer. To Judge Johnstone, it seemed a reasonable course of action, and he lost no time in ridding himself of Pinson. He made it clear to Agnes that he considered the engagement broken — nullified by Pinson's unconscionable behaviour towards Agnes as well as to the said Miss Lewly, who had left her home and come all the way to Halifax on the strength of the rogue's marriage proposal:

> The circumstance of [Pinson's] relations with Mademoiselle Hugo becoming known to his Dartmouth friends, all social intercourse was at once terminated by the young lady and her family.[11]

Agnes's niece, Caroline Johnstone, later reported:

[Judge Johnstone] would hear of no further engagement between the young people and "Bertie" was promptly banished.
Poor Aunt Agnes felt the whole affair very keenly.[12]

Agnes was indeed heartbroken, but her father quickly devised both a
solution to the family's social embarrassment and something to occupy
his daughter for the next little while. Agnes, he decided, should go
abroad. There, she could take in the sights, study music or become involved in charitable works if she so desired. The main thing was that
she forget all about that scoundrel Pinson. Quickly, Agnes and her
trunks were packed off to England. She soon made her way to the
south of France, where she lived for the next seven years on a comfortable allowance provided by her father. In August of 1872, Judge
Johnstone, who had by then retired from the bench, joined his
daughter in France. His doctor had insisted the judge have a change of
climate to help clear up a persistent bronchial infection. But the sunny,
relaxed Mediterranean climate had little or no effect on his condition,
and, not long afterwards, Agnes and her father returned to England.
They settled in the town of Cheltenham, where the damp climate ap-
proximated that of Nova Scotia and did nothing to improve the judge's
health.

The following year, Johnstone was appointed Nova Scotia's
Lieutenant-Governor but his illness forced him to resign before he had
even been sworn in. He never returned to Nova Scotia, and on November 21, 1873, Judge Johnstone died at the age of eighty-one. After her
father's death, Agnes began working with the McAll Mission, also
known as the Mission Populaire Evangélique de la France, a Protestant
missionary group set up to try to free the French from the "more de-
pressing forms of Roman Catholicism."[13] Agnes spent the next thirty
years teaching and visiting peasants throughout the French countryside, interspersing her missionary work with trips to Madeira and
Algeria with her sister Minnie. She returned home to Nova Scotia only
once.

Like Adèle, Agnes never married, but she, too, received other proposals, including one from an old Protestant pastor in a mountain village, who had seen her speak at a meeting. Agnes, who was then approaching old age, dismissed the idea outright. She had found her life's work, and marriage, especially at her time of life, would only impede her activities — and her freedom. On December 17, 1917, Agnes died and was buried beside her father. The inscription carved on her tombstone read:

> Having loved his own, which were in the world, He loved them unto the end.
>
> *— John 13*[14]

1. "The Tragedy of Hugo's Daughter," p.20.
2. Anon., "Interesting story of the tragedy of the life of Adèle Hugo," *Acadian Recorder* (October 30, 1926), p.1.
3. J.W. Longley, "The Romance of Adèle Hugo," *Magazine of American History* (April, 1889), p.303.
4. Guille, Vol. 3, p.35.
5. Cameron Pulsifer, *The 78th Highlanders*, Vol. 2: *The Officers* (Parks Canada: unpublished report, 1985), p.88.
6. Wolseley, Vol. 1, p.106.
7. Guille, Vol. 1, p.133.
8. Longley, p.303.
9. Longley, p.302.
10. Longley, p.299.
11. Longley, p.302.
12. Caroline Biscoe Johnstone, "Annandale Johnstones Ancient and Modern," Public Archives of Nova Scotia, MG100, Vol. 170, #11: Johnstone Family, p.16.
13. Johnstone, p.16.
14. Johnstone, p.17.

Chapter 7

The Sympathy of Strangers
Halifax, 1865-1866

It is certain, at least, that she was for a time lost and that her parents caused the four quarters of the globe to be searched for her.

— *New York Times*[1]

Late in 1864, a house near the Saunders home caught fire. The event terrified Adèle, although the blaze was quickly contained and their dwelling was unharmed. Despite the best efforts of the Saunderses to calm her, Adèle was frantic over the thought that her papers might be consumed by fire or some other disaster. She attached enormous value to her papers, and following the fire she took to carrying manuscripts (some of which may have been her *Journal of Exile*, which Motton wrongly thought was her autobiography) with her whenever she left the house.

But that was not enough. Adèle found she could no longer stand to be near the burned dwelling or even to reside in the Saunders home. Although both Richard and Sarah Saunders had grown fond of her during the eighteen months she lived with them, she made up her mind to leave them and find other lodgings. Before the year was out, she had taken a room in the home of Robert and Ellen Motton, the parents of her lawyer, Robert Motton, Jr. Although she did not say as much to the Saunderses, Adèle's sudden compulsion to move house was sparked by more than her irrational fear of fire. Adèle had sensed that she was being watched, and even spied upon, by the well-meaning couple, but she did not know why. Only when she was settled into her new lodgings at 46 Cornwallis Street did Adèle feel herself free from their scrutiny.

The Saunderses had been more than a little alarmed that their charge had escaped their purview. They made a point of meeting Adèle, seemingly at random, on the streets, in the market, in the book shops and in the bank as often as they could. Whenever they met, they filled Adèle with the latest gossip, taking care to include anything they had heard about Pinson, and they solicitously inquired whether she needed anything. Despite Adèle's decampment, Mrs. Saunders continued to correspond with François-Victor, and she passed on to Adèle the clothing and other necessities shipped from Europe by François-Victor or purchased in Halifax on his behalf:

> Brussels, October 15, 1865
>
> M. Hugo presents his best compliments to Mr. and Mrs. Saunders, and begs to inform them that a box full of winter clothes is being sent through the post to Miss Lewly to be deposited in their house under the usual name of Madame Pinsen. M. Hugo has not forgotten the obliging kindness of Mr. and Mrs. Saunders, and trusts that under their good care the box will be delivered as quick as possible to the young lady.[2]

Because they maintained regular contact with Adèle, the Saunderses remained her most reliable source of local information, particularly where the Sixteenth Regiment — and Pinson — were concerned. One day, Richard Saunders told Adèle that there would be a lavish ball that very evening, and that Pinson would surely attend. The affair was to be hosted by Major-General Hastings Doyle, Commander-in-Chief of the Halifax Garrison, and Saunders himself would be there waiting tables. The Commander was especially fond of parties and loved to entertain at Bellevue, his stately mansion at the corner of Queen Street and Spring Garden Road. He was said to have a weakness for beautiful women, and he was famous for his lavish dinner parties.

That night, Bellevue was ablaze with lights. Party-goers streamed through the doors, women in elaborate ball gowns and men in their best military dress uniforms or top hats and tails. From the graveyard across the road, Adèle watched for Pinson from her customary spot. She didn't have long to wait. A few moments later, a stylish barouche drew up and out stepped Pinson and the woman who had become so well-known around town as his "married sister." Adèle had shadowed the woman for several months and had never seen the man purported to be her husband. She was distinctly inclined to think Pinson treated the woman with more affection than a sister should properly receive.

Seeing them enter the house, Adèle quickly crossed the road and strode toward the door. Placing her card on the silver salver proffered by the footman, she whispered that she did not wish to be announced, only to speak to Lieutenant Pinson on an urgent private matter. The footman obliged at once and sent a deputy off to find the lieutenant. Adèle was fully prepared to make a scene, including appealing to the Commander himself, if Pinson refused to see her; otherwise, she would simply say her piece and go away quietly.

Pinson soon appeared. Although he pretended otherwise, Pinson was considerably older than Adèle, but he still cut a fine figure in his dress uniform. He was not happy to learn that Adèle had turned up at the party and had no wish to speak to her. He could not forgive her for meddling in his engagement, and he had deliberately snubbed her time and again. This evening, though, there was no avoiding her without making a public scene. Taking Adèle by the arm, Pinson led her out of the house and along Spring Garden Road. They walked back across the street to the graveyard; there, amongst the tombstones, away from curious onlookers, he waited for Adèle to launch into a diatribe on her latest desperate proposal to win him back.

As he suspected, what Adèle wanted had not changed; again she poured our her heart to him. She told him, as he listened, patient if somewhat bored, that her only goal in life was to marry him, and that she had subverted her music, her writing and, indeed, her whole life to this dream. She would gladly give him her entire inheritance, she vowed, and would submit to whatever rigours he imposed upon her. Over and over she had proven her devotion. Had she not lived like a pauper while he spent his leisure time dancing the quadrille, acting in amateur theatrics, socializing, gambling and horse racing?

All she asked in return was that he make her his legal wife. Because of the intimacy they had shared, she was, she pointed out, already his wife morally. Adèle explained that she had acted as she did in the Johnstone affair to preserve her own self-respect and to save poor Agnes's reputation. She reminded Pinson that it was he who had promised to marry her, and she intended to see that he did.

Adèle's heartfelt plea left Pinson unmoved. Not only had any affection for his former love evaporated, but he had also abandoned the grudging tolerance he had developed for her. He could not and would not forgive her for meddling in his engagement to Agnes Johnstone, and he told her so.

The incident marked a definitive parting of the ways for them, and their meeting ended abruptly. From among the gravestones, Adèle watched Pinson's tall, slim figure retreat into the shadows, back to the gaiety of Bellevue. After a moment, she turned and walked slowly back along Grafton Street to her chilly, cheerless room.

Adèle's desire to marry Pinson never waned, but three long years of self-imposed penury, an inadequate diet, no companionship to speak off, and constant emotional turmoil had taken their toll. Agnes Johnstone had been able to channel her heartbreak over Pinson into zealous missionary work, but Adèle was unfit for any sort of occupation save her writing, to which she devoted her days and nights. She was obsessed with the idea that she would make her living from writing and be free forever from having to plead for her quarterly allowance from her father, yet she made no realistic attempt to have any of her work published. Boxes of manuscripts were piled everywhere; crumpled paper littered the floor and her unmade bed.

On most days, the once-fastidious Adèle did not even bother getting dressed or fixing her tangled hair. Nor did she eat with the Mottons, preferring, as usual, to subsist on bread, bits of meat and cheese, tea and chocolate, and gnaw on the occasional carrot or piece of turnip. Twenty-eight years later, the *Halifax Morning Chronicle* reported these oddities at length:

> Although Adèle never boarded she had not the remotest idea of housekeeping. Her meals consisted of eggs, sandwiches and chocolate, and her apartment never indicated "a place for everything and everything in its place."
>
> Her wardrobe was peculiar and diversified, consisting as it did of some very costly evening gowns which had seen better days and several good walking costumes, as well as some male apparel.[3]

Adèle rarely strayed from her chilly, damp and disordered room, not even to eat or wash. The *Morning Chronicle* was not unsympathetic to her condition, reminding its readers that "Adèle, cared for and not basely and cruelly deserted, would have taken her proper place in society. With all her marvelous eccentricities she gave evidence of marked attainments and culture, always preserving her womanly dignity and never doing anything unworthy of her sex." The paper even grappled with the touchy issue of mental illness, evincing a rather enlightened view for the time:

> Victor Hugo's brother, Eugène, was, at the former's wedding, suddenly seized with madness, the sequel of an unfortunate love affair. He died shortly afterward without recovering his reason. With a predisposition of this sort running in the family it is not to be wondered at that the terrible strain on Adèle's mind, aggravated as it was by this self-inflicted seclusion, finally culminated likewise in lunacy.[4]

While Adèle could not hide all of her eccentricities, few people suspected the full extent of her mental illness. In their first letters to François-Victor (his address had been thoughtfully provided by Mr.

and Mrs. Saunders), the Mottons stated that they had noticed nothing unusual about Adèle's behaviour, except an unusual agitation over reports that the Sixteenth Regiment might be relocated. They did not inspect her room (Adèle would not allow anyone in her quarters, not even to clean it or change the bed linen), nor did they seem to notice her eating habits or personal hygiene. In time, though, they did find Adèle's reclusiveness disturbing. She visited no one, and no one visited her. Adèle had all but ceased her nightly rambles in search of Pinson, and she went out only to collect her letters when the biweekly post arrived from abroad. As far as the Mottons could tell, only their daughter, Ellen, had been able to kindle any sort of friendship with Adèle. Together, they would sometimes play the piano and discuss music, with Adèle occasionally relating stories about some of Europe's most famous composers and musicians, whom she sometimes talked of having known.

Pinson departed with the Sixteenth for Jamaica in July of 1865; he was not to return until September. Adèle appeared unaware of his departure, since she made no move to leave the city. But by July of 1865, it was impossible to ignore the radical changes in Adèle's behaviour. She had become virtually incapable of caring for herself and was so obviously unbalanced that the Mottons wrote a frank letter to François-Victor describing her symptoms. Adèle, they said, was refusing almost all food out of sheer parsimony, would not allow a fire to be lit in her room, and bathed infrequently. She lived, they said, very nearly like an animal. Her magnificent hair, which had once hung to the floor, had become so matted, dirty, and vermin-infested that Robert Motton, Sr., had called not only a hairdresser, but a doctor as well. Nothing could be done, he reported to François-Victor, but to cut it. Even more disturbing was Adèle's recently acquired habit of pacing almost continually back and forth in her room, often talking to herself in a loud voice. More than once the Mottons endured her shouting far into the night, and their hearts went out to the troubled young woman whom they did not know how to help.

As far as the Mottons knew, François-Victor Hugo was their disturbed lodger's only true friend. He received their letter in September of 1865 and instantly realized that his sister had succumbed to the legacy of madness left by their Uncle Eugène. It was another six months before François-Victor could bring himself to divulge the contents of the letter to his father. Even then, he kept some of its more shocking details to himself. On January 21, 1866, François-Victor wrote to his father that Adèle had

> rented from them [the Mottons] for 10 shillings per week a room without a fireplace, and she bought her own food. She did not eat meat more than three times a week and the rest of the time nourished herself on tea and some vegetables. Under this regime, she was wasting away. I asked the Mottons to give her meat every day, to install a stove in her room, to give her a good fire every day, to give her a good bed instead of the pallet that she had. . . . My instructions were carried out between the end of October and the beginning of December.[5]

But it was too late. In the Mottons' next letter to François-Victor, they gratefully acknowledged receipt of the 150 francs he had sent for them to make improvements in Adèle's living conditions, but they also admitted to him that she had again moved house. Despite their entreaties for Adèle to stay on with them, the Mottons reported, she had flatly refused, saying only that her sudden decision to take a sojourn in the country had in fact been ordered by her doctor. Adèle was, so far as they knew, living on a small farm two miles from Halifax.

Adèle had promised to return to live with the Mottons, and as proof of her good intentions, she had left some of her luggage behind.[6] But she was restless and no longer capable of caring for herself. Not surprisingly, the Hugo family lost touch with Adèle entirely during the months that followed; she informed no one of her new address. Her allowance from home still reached her, however — it was sent directly to her Halifax bank, where she collected it in person.

Between January and May of 1866, Adèle lost the rest of her already tenuous grip on reality. Her late-night wanderings began again, and rumours started to circulate about the mad Frenchwoman. A dazed Adèle was reportedly seen walking about the streets in a garment made entirely from burlap salvaged from a packing crate and held together with pins, muttering incessantly to herself. She was seen out walking late at night in her male attire, alternately lurking around Bellevue, Province House, or the Masonic Lodge, all places where Pinson had been fond of dancing the night away.

Robert Motton was among those who rightly feared she had gone mad — "insane from love," as he later told a *Morning Herald* reporter. Only he and his law partner, J.W. Longley (later Judge Longley, and a member of the Nova Scotia Legislative Assembly), knew that Miss Lewly/Madame Pinsen was in fact Adèle Hugo. A quarter-century later, Longley would write an intriguing and sympathetic article for an American magazine regarding the "mysterious Frenchwoman," in which he divulged her true, and hitherto secret, identity.[7]

Adèle continued to write feverishly, but she had no idea how to go about selling her work. Several times, she offered Robert Motton parts of her manuscripts, asking him to publish them and assuring him that he would "astonish the world" by doing so. Her own father, she told the lawyer, had often said he considered her a better and more powerful writer than himself — no small praise from someone as self-absorbed as Hugo, if it were true. Motton either did not realize the value of what he was being offered or was not convinced that Adèle was rational enough to realize what she was giving away, and so he refused her offers.

Robert Motton might be forgiven if he did not see the potential value of Adèle's work. Women writers, although not unheard of, were not common at the time, and were even rarer in Halifax. Adèle, undaunted, or perhaps unaware of the difficulties she faced, continued her feverish, obsessive writing. A year later, Adèle had moved again, this time to the home of James Kerr, a customs agent. Kerr, his wife, Jane, and their three children, Emma, Frances and Clifford, lived at 38 Pleasant Street, in the city's south end. Adèle's room was at the front the house, and she spent hours watching the carriages roll up and down the street to and from Point Pleasant Park and over the Kissing Bridge. She continued to buy great quantities of writing paper, but it was now a long walk to William Gossip's stationery store on Granville Street. Regardless of the weather, Adèle would not indulge herself by spending money on a cab to Granville Street. Nor did her meagre diet leave her with great energy reserves; consequently, she was always grateful by the time she reached the Gossips' doorstep.

Back on Guernsey, Adèle had not been forgotten by her family; indeed, they often found her — unbidden — in their hearts and their dreams. In his notebook, Victor Hugo reported that on the night of December 16-17, 1865, he was awakened at dawn by a voice which sounded like Adèle's. On January 16, 1866, he wrote to his wife that when he was feeling sad, it was because he was thinking of Adèle in Halifax. The following night, he recorded another bout of insomnia; again, he had been thinking of Adèle. She was now thirty-six and nearing the end of her childbearing years. They could no longer consider her marriageable; a quiet spinsterhood could be her only future. But so long as she remained abroad, and largely forgotten, they would not have to explain her social failure.

In January of 1866, not long after the Hugo family lost touch with Adèle, François-Victor received a letter from yet another stranger purporting to have information about his sister. The man, who identified himself only as "Monsieur Penchenat," told François-Victor that Adèle had been living with Mrs. M. Cliffe at 47 Brunswick Street for nearly a month. The stranger did not reveal how he discovered Adèle's identity, nor how he knew that her family was anxious for news of her whereabouts. He opined that Adèle's absence was due to her father's anger, an observation François-Victor dismissed. François-Victor vaguely recalled having met the man on Guernsey in the spring of 1859, and he reassured his father that Monsieur Penchenat appeared ignorant of the real reason for Adèle's lonely sojourn. Despite knowing next to nothing about Penchenat, François-Victor elected to enlist his help in keeping tabs on Adèle and seeing, with money advanced by Hugo, that her landlady provided her with anything she might need. He proposed that the man might convince Adèle to return home, and even that he might accompany her to Liverpool or Crookhaven, Ireland, where François-Victor would be waiting to receive her. The plan was never executed.

Around the same time, Mrs. Saunders also wrote to François-Victor. She had heard rumours that the Sixteenth Regiment, which was overdue for a new posting, was about to be relocated to the British West Indies, where it had already done several tours of duty. The regiment had already been sent to Jamaica during the summer of 1865, followed by the Fifteenth Regiment later that year, to quell unrest. Surely Miss Lewly would not follow Lieutenant Pinson there, Mrs. Saunders reasoned, but would prefer to go home to her family. A delighted François-Victor shared Mrs. Saunders's opinion:

Guernsey, February 5th, 1866
My dear Mrs. Saunders,

I am indeed exceedingly thankful to you for your kind note. Your information has been most welcome. . . . I hope Miss Lewly will at last be induced to come home to her own family. Her mother is very anxious to get her home, and has unfortunately been prevented by a serious indisposition from crossing over to Halifax. She intends doing so as soon as spring comes. Until then, kindly keep us informed about what she plans to do.[8]

Madame Hugo never made the journey to Halifax to retrieve her lost daughter. Her health was rapidly deteriorating, and her heartache over the loss of Adèle only compounded her problems. She now spent most of her time in Paris, unable to bear life in Guernsey without her daughter. Part of the problem was Victor Hugo. His ego had grown with his fame, and he had become more unreasonable and more demanding of his children and his long-suffering wife. He constantly complained to them of their disloyalty if they disagreed with his opinions, and he accused them of abandoning him if they wished to take a holiday without him. He, on the other hand, regularly and openly vacationed *sans famille* with Juliette Drouet.

Madame Hugo no longer bore any rancour toward Juliette; in fact, she had formally acknowledged Juliette's presence and included her in the family circle. To Madame Hugo, appearances no longer mattered; by acknowledging Juliette she was only admitting to herself that for years — really since 1830 and her own affair with Sainte-Beuve — she and her husband had lived separate lives.

Adèle, too, knew a change was in the offing for the Sixteenth; the date had been fixed for May — and she began making preparations to leave. Pinson had never been back to England on leave since he came out to Halifax, and he was well overdue for a furlough; she had even heard that he was about to depart for Scotland. It was now, she reasoned, that he would be most likely to take advantage of some time off. When he did, Adèle decided, she would be with him. But leaving Halifax was not as easy as Adèle had at first supposed:

> In spite of recent occurrences, Adèle Hugo [was] determined to follow [Pinson], hoping that after he had renounced the debaucheries of the world he would honorably fulfil what she considered to be a sacred obligation, binding upon both of them. There was a possibility of the Lieutenant's obtaining leave to go home for a short time and to rejoin his regiment later in the new station, a favour generally granted to a few officers upon such an occasion.[9]

Adèle had no way of knowing that Pinson had requested leave or that his request had been inexplicably denied. She did know that Cunard Line steamers left for Liverpool, England, every eight days. There was only one way to be sure Pinson did not try to slip out of Halifax without her. Every week for the next six weeks, Adèle packed her trunks and hired coachman Thomas O'Brien to take her to Cunard's Wharf on the days Cunard liners departed for England. From early morning until the ship weighed anchor, she sat watching from the carriage for signs that Pinson was leaving town, taking care to conceal herself behind the curtains lest he spot her and change his plans at the last minute.

Meanwhile, the Hugos were unaware how close they were to getting the wayward Adèle back. Clearly, she planned to follow Pinson to England, where, she may have believed, her family and other connections could bring pressure to bear on Pinson to marry her. It was not to be:

> This precaution proved, however, quite superfluous for when the regiment eventually left the garrison [on May 11, 1866] Pinsen went with it to Barbados. Pinsen was well acquainted with all the privations this unfortunate woman had suffered on his account, but he was a thoroughly heartless and selfish man who had no soul, no ideal, no ambition beyond the desire of obtaining easily the means for an indolent life.[10]

Adèle had become little more than an unwelcome camp follower.

⚜

1. "The Tragedy of Hugo's Daughter," p.20.
2. Longley, p.302.
3. Wudzburg, p.1.
4. Wudzburg, p.1.
5. Guille, Vol. 1, pp.99-100.
6. Guille, Vol. 1, pp.99-100.
7. Longley, pp.297-304.
8. Longley, p.302.
9. Wudzburg, p.1.
10. Longley, p.304.

Chapter 8

Los Barbados

Barbados, 1866-1871

Everyone believed that she had surely suffered a great tragedy, and, little by little, it became known that there was a Captain Pinson stationed on Barbadoes and his name began to be vaguely linked to that of the pretty, mysterious woman.

— *New York Tribune*[1]

The voyage to Bridgetown was uneventful, yet it seemed endless to Adèle. Her nerves had not permitted her to enjoy the trip at all, even when the rough Atlantic had given way to the tranquil azure of the Caribbean Sea. The prevailing easterly winds had lengthened the journey somewhat, but the same phenomenon had since time immemorial provided an excellent defence for the outlying island, a hundred and sixty kilometres east of the Caribbean chain. Now she could plainly see the little coral island ringed by "los barbados," the giant bearded fig trees which gave the place its name.

The crew furled the sails as the ship prepared to drop anchor in the harbour. Adèle was already uncomfortably hot in her heavy silk dress which, with its corset and crinolines, was better suited to foggy Guernsey or chilly Halifax. It was June, and already the Barbados temperature rose above thirty degrees Celsius most days. Not until November would there be any likelihood of cooler weather. A short time later, Adèle stepped gingerly out of the launch that ferried passengers to the dockside. The small but thriving colony known as Little England depended for its prosperity upon sugar; so abundant were its cane fields that the island was called the brightest jewel in the English crown. Adèle's trunk had been heaved out of the launch after her, and for a few moments she stood trying to fit the scene before her into some sort of familiar order. Sweating stevedores swarmed around her, loading and unloading goods. Turbanned women in bright red and blue dresses carried pots and packages majestically on their heads, while small children skipped blithely along beside them under the burning sun and the waving palms.

A man shouldered her trunk, pointing it and her in the direction of a waiting horse and trap. Adèle nodded her assent and followed. This time, though, she could not afford to make the same expensive mistake she had made upon her arrival in Halifax. Adèle knew she did not have the means to stay at a hotel, not even a cheap one, and not even for one night. She asked the driver to take her to a boarding house, preferably near St. Ann's Garrison, where she surmised the officers of the Sixteenth Battalion would be quartered. As they trotted through the streets, Adèle marvelled at her new landscape. Swarms of people packed the markets lining Baxter's Road, known locally as "the street that never slept." A heady aroma of fried foods, slaughtered livestock and pungent seafood permeated the air. Sea urchins, dolphin fish, flying fish, kingfish steaks, cou-cou, spiced sweet potatoes, boiled pigs' heads and trotters, and other local dishes were offered up for sale by ample Bajan women stirring their big iron buck pots suspended over open fires. In the numerous rum shops, old men played dominoes in the semi-darkness, oblivious to the unceasing rattle of the heavily laden carts clogging the streets. After several blocks, the driver stopped on a quiet, palm-lined street, and pointed out the house of Mrs. Chadderton. Adèle again nodded her assent, fanned her flushed face with her gloves, and climbed down from the carriage. Divesting herself of some of her unwieldy, sticky garments and plunging into a cooling bath preoccupied her. Tomorrow she would begin making enquiries for Albert Pinson.

She found him easily. This garrison was not so large or so spread out as the one in Halifax. Its British officers were conspicuous and Pinson, with his legendary love of the high life, had quickly distinguished himself among them with the local people.

Despite making a promising beginning in Bridgetown, Adèle soon returned to her old habits, including her obsessive writing, her late-night restlessness — and her shadowing of Pinson. Once again, she began to call out in the night, and began neglecting her clothing and herself. Months after her arrival, she had not bothered to exchange her winter wardrobe for a more suitable tropical one, and she continued to wear her cloaks, her heavy silk dresses and even her furs in the hot climate; moreover, the garments became tattered and dirty from constant wear.

Adèle seemed oblivious not only to the heat but to the undisguised amusement of the residents. Years later, the following letter appeared in the *New York Tribune,* it was signed simply, "P":

I write from my childhood memories . . . a woman of the most noble bearing arrived on a strange island. She was tall and beautiful, with black hair, and with black eyes which frightened me. When at rest, they seemed full of melancholy, but with a very light movement of her eyelids, a strange, savage fire seemed to enflame them.

No one knew her origins. She never went out accompanied when she walked along the street, and she went out often, early in the morning and late in the evening. To see this charming woman on the streets, dressed like no other, tormented me, because she was teased by the children. I regret to say that I saw, one day, a complete lack of respect towards her, and young as I was, I felt obliged to protect her. I will never forget the polite recognition she gave me by [her] gentle look and a nod of her head. Even today I feel again the sadness which filled my young heart; a mystery so sacred redeemed her, and which to me seemed inviolable.

Her wardrobe added to the enigma; she did not wear the light robes of the tropics but heavy velours, silks and even sometimes furs. All of this was testimony to a home very far in the north, a lost home, and a spirit drowned in some strange fantasy.

She had, I remember, a room at a Madame Chadderton's, but the others who lived in the house did not know her, because she rarely talked to anyone. They said that she possessed trunks full of magnificent clothes which she never wore. She wrote constantly and had boxes full of manuscripts. After a time, she became known under the name of Madame Pinson. Everyone supposed that she was a woman of good family and an excellent education. Some people thought she was Italian and others French, because she spoke the two languages.[2]

Since earliest girlhood, Adèle had been unable to make friends easily; she had not known how to laugh at herself, and any young friends she might have made considered her too serious, too passionate and too introverted. Still, she did not lack for company. In fact, the many visitors to the Hugo's various Paris addresses — older musicians, composers, actors and writers, usually male and all friends of the family or adoring fans of Hugo — were unreservedly taken with her quiet, pious beauty. Later, in the gloomy isolation of Marine Terrace and Hauteville-House, Adèle had become accustomed to spending long periods on her own, composing, writing, and brooding. After she left home, she was alone virtually all of the time, a situation that did not change when she reached Barbados. Even the friendly openness of the Bajans did little to pry Adèle out of the protective shell of solitude she had thrown up around herself. She told no one her true identity, preferring at all costs to guard her privacy:

An exile from home, friends and country — a poor unhappy waif in a lonely and comfortless world! With her beauty, her talents, and her family connections, she might have been an ornament of European society. But that all-powerful impulse of love, which has often enough turned and overturned the lives of men and the events of history, irresistibly bore her on to a life of unspeakable misery.[3]

After her arrival in Barbados, Adèle again lost touch with her family in Guernsey. François-Victor, along with the rest of the family, waited impatiently for some communication from her. He realized that his sister could not do without her quarterly allowance, and he was anxious to send it to her. Some months passed before Adèle wrote to tell her brother where she was. Besides her allowance, she said, she was most anxious to receive new clothing, more suited to the Barbados climate. Evidently, Adèle had finally realized the shortcomings of her winter wardrobe, but she did not purchase new clothing herself, perhaps because of financial hardship.

By December of 1866, Adèle and François-Victor were once again corresponding regularly:

December, 1866
Dear Mother,

I received another letter from Adèle. She continues to do well in the favourable climate, where there is no winter. She is waiting impatiently for the trunk, which will supply her with her wardrobe. This trunk, shipped from Southampton November 2, should arrive in Barbados at any time. I have paid the freight costs which have risen to 72 francs 20 c. It is a little more expensive than Halifax, but then the distance is much farther.[4]

Not long afterwards, yet another letter came from Adèle, this time for Madame Hugo:

December 21, 1866
My dear Mother,

I received, by the last mail, a nice letter from Adèle. The dear child wrote it in enormous characters so that you could read it. ... She continues to enjoy the admirable Caribbean climate and has completely regained her health, which was altered by the icy sky of Halifax. She hopes to see you next year, and gave a seductive description of the transatlantic trip. She did not say if the money and the trunk arrived.[5]

Adèle received the long-awaited goods, including light clothing suitable to the tropics, before the month was out, and wrote immediately to thank her brother. François-Victor quickly passed the news along to an anxious Madame Hugo:

> January 2, 1867
> Dear Mother,
>
> I wanted to write you on the occasion of New Year's Day, but I decided to wait to send you my New Year's gift. This gift is good news from Adèle. I received a letter yesterday from our poor, dear child. The money and the letter had just arrived when she wrote her letter, which was at the beginning of December. Evidently, our lines of communication between Europe and Barbados are well-established.
>
> I hope that this year will make up for all of the previous years, and that we will all be reunited.[6]

François-Victor's optimism was soon shattered, for Adèle had again misled her family into believing her return was imminent. It was a cruel blow to Madame Hugo. Not only had she witnessed the disintegration of her family, beginning with Charles's departure in 1861, but she found Guernsey's isolation — and her husband's tirades — increasingly difficult to bear. Charles Baudelaire, on making the *de rigeur* pilgrimage to the Channel Islands to visit the master, wrote that Hugo "bored me and tired me very much. I should not want either his glory or his fortune, if I also had to *possess* his enormous absurdities. Madame Hugo is half crazy and his two sons are great fools. If you want to read his latest book, *I'll send it to you at once.*"[7]

In 1865, Madame Hugo and François-Victor had left Guernsey for good, leaving Hugo alone at Hauteville-House. Only Juliette Drouet stayed on at Hauteville-Fairy. Only she, it seems, was still willing to tolerate Hugo and his moods. Paul Stapfer, a French teacher at the Royal Elizabeth College on Guernsey, said neither François-Victor nor Charles visited their father once in three years.[8] Without his family to paint the picture of domesticity he so craved, and to soothe his ego, Hugo was lost. Despite his fame, polite society on Guernsey paid him little attention; most people pretended to be scandalized by his liaison with Juliette Drouet, even though his family, including Madame Hugo, had long accepted her benign presence. The local papers pointedly did not announce Hugo's arrivals and departures, an unusual step at a time when all comings and goings were noted and published.

The family's close friend and fellow exile, M. Kesler, gave Stapfer ample reason to believe that the reason for the break-up of Hugo's family was due in no small way to the poet's irascible temperament. "When he was in this state," Stapfer wrote, "Madame Drouet was the only person who had the power to restrain him. His sister-in-law [Julie Foucher Chenay] could say nothing to calm him and reason with him without him rebuking her in the most brutally rude way."[9]

Madame Hugo paid her last visit to Guernsey in January of 1867. Despite Hugo's happiness at seeing his wife, she soon returned to Paris where she underwent treatment for her eye problems. On August 27, 1868, she died in Brussels of heart failure. Her dearest wish had been to see her daughter again.

When Madame Hugo died, Adèle lost her greatest champion, and on October 13, 1869, Charles Sainte-Beuve also died. He was, perhaps, the only person other than Madame Hugo who truly understood how Adèle had suffered for love:

La Presse recalled that he had "worked day and night in a study silent and severe, all cluttered with books, which he rarely left. He died on a small monastic bed." He was buried on 18 October; a large wreath of violets was laid on his grave — a tribute, one suspects, from the emperor's cousin, Princess Mathilde. "But have you ever really loved, Monsieur Sainte-Beuve?" she

Adèle Foucher Hugo, Brussels, 1865

(Musées de la Ville de Paris)

had asked him once, in her blunt, imperial fashion. There is no doubt that he had loved. "I have had neither spring nor autumn," he had written in 1852. "I have had only a dry and parching summer . . . a summer which devoured everything."[10]

No one in the Hugo family, nor any of Victor's loyal followers, nor even Adèle's godfather ever summoned up the will to fetch her home. François-Victor was still immersed in his long and often frustrating translation of Shakespeare's works. He had a strict contract with his publisher, Pagnerre, with whom he feuded constantly over money and deadlines as well as the length and quality of the finished product. He could scarcely tear himself away from the project, in which he had already invested more than fifteen years' work, without jeopardizing the entire contract.

Victor Hugo never considered going abroad himself to bring back his daughter. He was immersed not only in his writing, which bordered on the obsessive, but with his many concurrent extramarital affairs. For her part, Adèle had been promising to return home since her departure in 1863, and had numerous times extracted large sums of money from her father for this purpose. She never made good on her promises. Perhaps she was wary of his wrath, despite his apparent willingness to accept her. She likely still sent money to Pinson in a vain attempt to win him back:

> Pinson was well known in Barbados because of his passion for horse racing, the favourite sport on the island. He had a horse which was supposed to be able to do marvels, but personally I don't think it did much. According to the gossip of the island, the master knew more tricks than his horse.
>
> After some time, we didn't see the sad woman with the savage eyes any more. One could easily forget Pinson, but never this woman. She will be always known as the unfortunate daughter of the hero-poet of the world, Victor Hugo.[11]

News of her mother's death, which came in a letter from François-Victor, may have caused Adèle to suffer a relapse of madness; not long afterwards, she took to the streets, where she made her home. She could be found wandering around Bridgetown at all hours, muttering and talking to the ever-present voices inside her head. Eventually, the Bridgetown residents connected Adèle to Pinson, who, in 1867, had finally been made a captain. He had spent nine years as a lieutenant, being unable to afford to buy his promotion; not until a non-purchasable commission became vacant could he rise up another rank.

In 1869, the Sixteenth Regiment left for Dublin, and Pinson with it. Deciding to take advantage of Pinson's new posting as an excuse to go home, Adèle wrote to François-Victor that spring, saying that she was planning to visit Guernsey in the summer. She asked for 500 francs for the voyage. François-Victor wrote to his father on April 7 with the news, but added that he had no idea if his sister was really serious about leaving Barbados. He pointed out, though, that the family could hardly allow her to continue her exile for want of money. Once again, Victor Hugo authorized the money to be sent, but this time he deducted it from her inheritance. "If she arrives," he wrote in his notebook, "I will make a present of it to her."[12] The family was disappointed, but hardly surprised, when Adèle did not appear.

Adèle Hugo and Albert Pinson never met again.

Despite his apparent neglect, Victor Hugo still thought about — and provided for — his daughter, as numerous short diary entries — chiefly dealing with the staggering sums of money he spent on her — indicate. "I think of Adèle — Adèle's trimester (for payment); draft for Adèle; 7,000 francs for Adèle";[13] "I gave to [François-]Victor, to transfer to Adèle, 945 francs, for the trimester from January 1, 1872, to April 1.[14] Hugo did not correspond directly with his daughter, preferring to let their communication pass through François-Victor. On March 27, 1870, Hugo asked his son, "Have you told Adèle that my arms are open?" and on June 11, 1870, he urged him to repeat to Adèle, "my arms are open. I am old. My happiness would be to have all of you around me." On December 2, 1870, he wrote, "I bless my daughter Adèle. I promise to watch over her. Death is the invisible presence. My soul will make her smile and protect her."[15]

One circumstance from which no one could protect Adèle was Pinson's marriage. His bride was Catherine Edith Roxburgh, the only daughter of Lieutenant-Colonel James Roxburgh. Her father had retired in late 1869 on full pay from Her Majesty's Indian Forces. The pair likely met through Pinson's uncle, Lieutenant-Colonel Albert Pinson, who, like Roxburgh, had also lived in Ireland (Roxburgh was listed as "late of The Lodge, Rostrevor") and served in India. By then, Pinson was in his forties, if not older. Despite his age, his infallible charm had worked once more to draw to him a woman of considerable status and wealth (an especially important consideration to Pinson in his retirement). On March 31, 1870, Pinson and Miss Roxburgh were married at St. John's Church, Hampstead, England, by Rev. J.G. Brewster.[16] A military friend of Pinson's, Guy Mannering, observed that Pinson's wife had an annual revenue of £15,000.

Sometime in 1869, after Pinson's regiment left Barbados, Adèle was taken in by Madame Céline Alvarez Baa, a former slave and a native of Trinidad. At the time, Adèle was destitute, wandering the streets mumbling to herself. Notably, no one from the garrison, nor any other Europeans living in Barbados, took any responsibility for Adèle, despite the persistent rumours linking her to their own Captain Pinson. The circumstances of Adèle's life at the time are unknown, but Madame Baa was evidently able to nurse her back to some semblance of health. A Dominican missionary from Trinidad related part of their story:

> It was several years ago, when the charitable creature lived in Barbadoes, where she had formerly been a slave, she met a woman who seemed to be at the time poor and mentally ill. The negress, full of pity, brought her to her own house and cared for her with the greatest devotion. After some time, she learned that the unfortunate woman was the daughter of Victor Hugo. She

had been abandoned by an officer whom she had followed to Halifax, and later to Barbadoes. Her sadness had unbalanced her. Her benefactress, when she knew who she was, wrote a letter to her father in Paris.[17]

Adèle's days of exile would soon be over, or so it seemed.

1. Anon., *New York Tribune* (May 27, 1885), n.p. Quoted by Guille, Vol. 1, pp.134-37.

2. Guille, Vol. 1, pp. 134-37

3. Longley, p.304.

4. Guille, Vol. 1, p.104.

5. Guille, Vol. 1, p.105.

6. Guille, Vol. 1, p.l05.

7. Richardson, p.188.

8. Paul Stapfer, *Victor Hugo à Guernsey: souvenirs personnels* (Paris: Société française, 1905), pp.184-85.

9. Stapfer, pp.184-85.

10. Richardson, p.208.

11. *New York Tribune*, n.p.

12. Juin, Vol. 2, p.670.

13. Guille, Vol. 1, p.108.

14. Guillemin, p.147.

15. Juin, Vol. 3, p.53.

16. Richardson, pp.183-84.

17. The letter appeared in the *Halifax Evening Mail* (May 17, 1930), reprinted from its first publication in 1885. Quoted by Guille, Vol. 1, pp.134-37.

Chapter 9

"... More Dead than the Dead"
Paris, 1872-1885

> When Victor Hugo received the wreck of his daughter, he placed her in a sanitarium at Vincennes. At first, he was pathetically hopeful for her recovery. So long as he lived, he visited her regularly once a week, and spent hours in the attempt to find in this frantic creature traces of his lost "Dédé."
>
> — *New York Times*[1]

"Sombre news from Barbados," wrote Victor Hugo in his diary on January 14, 1872.[22] The bad tidings concerned Adèle, and they had come as a complete surprise, in the form of a frank and disturbing letter from her protector, Madame Céline Alvarez Baa. Word of her pathetic physical and mental state shocked Hugo deeply. He had returned to Paris in 1870 following the overthrow of Napoléon III. It had not been difficult for Madame Baa to find his address among the reams of paper Adèle carried with her, and she promptly wrote to the poet describing Adèle's state of mind.

Hugo had already resigned himself to his daughter's peculiarities, her obsession with Pinson, and her refusal to return home. But there was little for her to return home to. Of the Hugo clan there remained only the poet himself, the terminally ill François-Victor, Charles's two children, Georges and Jeanne — Charles had died in 1871 — and Adèle. Hugo no longer made a fuss about sending Adèle's quarterly allowance and had just made arrangements to send the money a few days before receiving Madame Baa's letter. For the first time, he was apprised in no uncertain terms about the terrible and degrading circumstances in which his daughter had been living.

While François-Victor had long known of Adèle's eccentric behaviour and her self-imposed penury, he had softened the blows each time he told his father of her latest escapades. Until now, Hugo had not known the full state of his daughter's physical, mental and social breakdown. Indeed, François-Victor, ever optimistic for Adèle's return home and rehabilitation into high society, had sensed her life improving somewhat since she had gone to Barbados.

Madame Baa's letter set everyone straight. In it, she told Victor Hugo of his daughter's madness and how sharply her condition — which, in the past few years, had been perilous at best — was deteriorating. After nearly nine years, the time had come for Adèle to return from her own exile, even if she had long since ceased to call France home. Adèle apparently made no protest, or perhaps she was unable to do so, for Madame Baa informed Victor Hugo that she would personally return his daughter to him. They would arrive on January 22, 1872.

It had been a risky decision for Madame Baa to undertake Adèle's return. The venture involved a considerable sum of money — 1,000 francs for two one-way fares — which she borrowed from an acquaintance, a Mr. Werder from Martinique.[33] Her return passage would cost Madame Baa another 500 francs; she would have to depend on Victor Hugo to pay her debts and send her home again.

On January 22, the appointed day, Hugo dispatched his old friend and physician Dr. Émile Allix to meet Adèle and Madame Baa at the port of Saint-Nazaire on France's west coast. It was a considerable distance from Paris, and when he arrived, Dr. Allix was dismayed to find that the pair had not arrived; the wrong date for the ship's arrival had been given. It would not dock until February 8. Allix returned to Paris alone. In the meantime, Hugo received another letter from Barbados on January 30. This time, the news of Adèle was more optimistic; she was a little better. On February 8, Dr. Allix was again dispatched, and again he found the ship had not arrived. It was, however, expected soon, and the doctor left instructions to telegraph him in Paris the moment it docked. On February 11, the telegram came, and Dr. Allix paid a call on Hugo to tell him the news. Adèle had returned. She would be in Paris on February 12.

Finally, the day Hugo had long anticipated had dawned. Yet his diary does not reflect the joyous emotion of a man who would see his daughter for the first time in nine years. On the contrary, the terseness of the entry suggests that Hugo had mixed feelings about their reunion. "My daughter has arrived," he wrote curtly. "She will be here tomorrow."[4] In the ensuing twenty-four hours, Hugo had reconciled his feelings toward his truant daughter, and a paternal tenderness took over, far different from his earlier, egocentric reaction to Adèle's flight from home. He noted, "Adèle arrived this night at four o'clock at Dr. Allix's. He told me about her state. My poor, dear child. [François-] Victor will see her today. She did not recognize Émile Allix. The negro woman who accompanied her, Mme. Baa, is devoted to her."[5]

Not until two days after Adèle's arrival did Victor Hugo see his daughter. Promptly at five p.m., on February 13, 1872, Hugo called at Dr. Allix's, at 178, rue de Rivoli; Adèle and her father were reunited after nearly a decade apart. Hugo was not prepared for the grotesque change in the appearance and demeanour of his youngest child. His once-beautiful daughter had become little more than a derelict.

> I saw her again. She did not recognize [François-]Victor. She recognized me. I embraced her. I spoke words of tenderness and hope to her. She was calm and seemed, sometimes, to be asleep. It is just one year ago today that I left for Bordeaux with Charles, who would not return alive. Today I see Adèle again. What sorrow![6]

Hugo's first visit with his daughter had a profound effect on him. The same man who had selflessly supported and nursed his brother through several months of insanity found it almost impossible to be near his daughter. Her helplessness was almost as repugnant to him as her earlier attempts at independence. Time, poverty and illness had indeed wreaked havoc on the once-ravishing woman. Forty-two, and bearing the scars of a decade of hardship and torment, the Adèle whom Dr. Allix presented to Hugo bore little resemblance to the Adèle he remembered. Her mental condition had left her in a stupor; her gaze was fixed, and she could not even recognize her own brother, let alone close family friends like Dr. Allix. Her hair, cropped long ago because of her inability to care for it, now hung long and loose. Her once-fashionable dresses were dirty, old and worn, and her face had been lined and darkened by the tropical sun.

Even more disturbing than Adèle's appearance and demeanour were the voices she claimed to hear. Adèle imagined herself surrounded by people, one of them Léopoldine, to whom she talked continually in a strange voice. Witnesses to this behaviour described Adèle's voice at these times as being low-pitched and metallic-sounding. Hugo wasted no time in heeding the well-intentioned advice of Dr. Allix and his colleague, Dr. Axenfeld, that Adèle be placed in an asylum. At the time, mental illness in a family was highly embarrassing and so was kept quiet. Adèle's permanent committal to an asylum was felt to be the wisest course of action for all concerned.

In his diary, Hugo noted that he had secured "the best possible" sanitorium for his daughter, the "Maison de Mme Rivet," at 106, Grand'Rue in the Paris suburb of Saint-Mandé. Two days later, on February 17, Adèle was discreetly admitted. Grimly, Hugo recorded in his journal that "a door had closed, more sombre than that of the tomb."[77]

A week later, on February 22, Hugo and Dr. Allix visited Adèle in her new home. Her physical recovery from the rigours of her long period in the colonies and her voyage from Barbados had been quick; mentally, she had brightened, too, after her arrival back in Paris. The emaciated somnambulant who had disembarked at Saint-Nazaire was already beginning to regain some weight. "I saw my poor child. She seemed better," Hugo wrote fondly. But fondness was not enough to make him consider bringing Adèle home again. "I will see her as often as the doctors permit but they advise me not to make too many visits," he noted in his diary. "I left, my heart a little healed. Adèle appeared happy to see me."[8]

The upheaval of Adèle's homecoming was quickly overshadowed by other events in Hugo's life. On February 19, his play *Ruy Blas* had been revived at the Odéon theatre with great success. The Queen of Spain (a part Hugo had created in homage to his wife) was played by the sensational young actress Sarah Bernhardt. She was a spectacular hit, and after her rivetting performance, Hugo knelt to kiss her hands in appreciation. With that, the twenty-eight-year-old actress and the seventy-year-old playwright began an affair. Despite his age, Hugo was ever ready to fornicate, and even Sarah Bernhardt was not enough for him. He had yet another conquest in mind, the object of which was less famous, perhaps, but no less exotic: Céline Alvarez Baa.

On February 23, 1872, Hugo had noted without fanfare in his journal that Madame Baa was "black, nevertheless a lady in the colony."[9] The entry gave only the slightest of hints that Hugo found her desirable; nonetheless, the seduction of Madame Baa was soon accomplished. She may have been simply another notch on the poet's pen, for he wrote blandly in his diary that she was "the first negress of my life."[10] Hugo failed to note Juliette Drouet's reaction to his latest love interest, nor did he observe how willingly his latest partner engaged in bedroom romping with her geriatric debtor. Madame Baa already owed at least 1,000 francs and was dependent upon Hugo's good will if she wanted not merely to repay the money she had borrowed, but to go home again.

By March 8, Madame Baa felt confident enough in Hugo's promise of repayment that she returned Adèle's, or, rather, Madame Hugo's, jewellery. It was in sorry shape, having been carted around by Adèle during her semi-nomadic existence abroad. Most of it was scratched and broken, but Hugo was happy to have it back nonetheless. "I recovered my wife's ring," he wrote happily. In a fit of generosity, he bestowed upon Madame Baa "two gold bracelets, a brooch and golden earrings" as a memento of Adèle.[11]

Hugo and Madame Baa saw each other again on March 10 and on March 11, when she informed him she was to leave the next day for Barbados. Hugo waited until the last moment before reimbursing her for the tickets she had purchased to bring Adèle and herself to France and paying her passage back. Evidently enjoying the feeling of playing European demigod, Hugo threw in "a gold ornament" for good measure. He did not offer anything more, despite the obvious fact that Madame Baa must have suffered a considerable loss of income — whatever her means of support — in order to make the journey. Before departing, Madame Baa sent Hugo her portrait, as a final token of affection.

It was not until March 16 that Hugo again found time to visit his daughter. Whether for moral support or an additional medical opinion, he brought Dr. Allix along with him. Later, Hugo wrote in his diary:

[Adèle] is very calm and very sweet. She kissed my hands and told me, "I am happy." She is obsessed with the idea that invisible persons talk to her. My heart was broken. Poor, sweet soul! Still, since she is close to me, I do not have the anguish that I did. At least I am here. I kissed her hands in my turn and told her, "Don't fear anything, or anyone. You are close to your father and to God." She embraced me and told me, "I am happy." She refused to put on her new slippers. I told her, "My daughter, put them on." She obeyed. I had a piano brought for her. She makes a little music and writes a lot but would not show me. The doctors asked that my visits become more rare.[12]

Hugo obliged; his next visit was May 22. This time, Juliette Drouet accompanied him to Saint-Mandé, where she visited the grave of her own daughter, Claire Pradier (her child by sculptor James Pradier), who had died on June 21, 1846. Hugo wrote that Adèle "appeared content. Her fixation persists. She hears a voice that talks to her and is mean to her. I helped her with her dinner. She has a good appetite. She said she wrote to me. On the whole, she is better, but physically only. I left her with a broken heart."[13]

Hugo's visits agitated Adèle. Sometimes she refused to speak to him and remained so immobile that he wondered if she was asleep; at other times she chattered endlessly about the voices she heard. Her father, it seemed, set the ghosts of the past upon her once more. Hugo himself was plagued by the same demons as Adèle, although to a lesser degree. Adèle herself had recorded that her father "could not go to bed without a kind of dread, that he complained of waking up with a 'sacred horror' of his nightly visitations."[14] It was just as well that Hugo believed in the heightened artistic benefits of a touch of madness. He was "genuinely convinced that the creative impulse, in one way or another, has to do with chaos. The fear is often repressed, or tamed by a playful fantasy."[15] In later years, some believed that Hugo was mentally unstable, and that this was the source of his own genius — hence Jean Cocteau's quip, "Victor Hugo was a madman who thought he was Victor Hugo."[16]

On June 1, 1872, Hugo at last received some good news about Adèle from Dr. Allix. Her strange behaviour had all but ceased; she had recovered her physical health and had even begun to care for herself. "She asked to go out, dressed herself, walked for an hour, accompanied by Madame Rivet, went to a notions shop, went shopping, and lived for that hour an ordinary life. Comforting."[17] Still, her return to the world of everyday was not enough to win Adèle's release from the asylum, nor did it inspire her father to visit more frequently. After receiving news of her remarkable recovery, Hugo's visits ceased for more than a year. Once again, the poet had other things on his mind. On August 7, 1872, Hugo and Juliette, along with Alice Hugo, Charles's widow, and his two grandchildren, Georges and Jeanne, left Paris for a long stay at Hauteville-House, Guernsey. Juliette, however, had made the mistake of inviting Blanche-Marie Lanvin to accompany them. Blanche-Marie was an attractive young woman of twenty-three, the daughter of some good friends of Juliette's. Predictably, Hugo began an affair with his young guest that September.

At the time, François-Victor was terminally ill with tuberculosis of the kidneys. Yet Hugo did not postpone his trip to Guernsey. On

March 18, 1873, Hugo reported to his remaining son that Dr. Allix "has written to say you are getting better and better, and I hope that our sweet and wonderful island will soon see you; this open air is powerful, life rises up out of the sea, come and drink it in soon, as much as you can, and just see how happy you will be."[18] It was ironic, even insensitive, of Hugo to describe Guernsey so lyrically and put such unbounded faith in its power to heal mind and body. His three children had loathed what became their Channel Island prison. It was, moreover, the very place where François-Victor's fiancée had also died of tuberculosis in 1865; how could the island be a repository of fond memories for François-Victor? Not until July 31, 1873, did Hugo visit his son. On December 26, 1873, François-Victor died.

After his son's death, Hugo wrote: "Again a fracture, and a fatal one in my life. I have nothing before me but Georges and Jeanne."[19] There was no mention of Adèle, who had been reduced to a nameless obligation, one in which her father chose not to become personally involved. Hugo did not even pay the bills (amounting to 1,500 francs every quarter) directly; Dr. Allix took care of that distasteful task for him.

On August 7, 1873, Adèle received another visit from her father:

At 1:30 we went to Saint-Mandé, Juliette Drouet and I, she to see her daughter, me to see mine, in their tombs, alas! I found Adèle in the same moral state, but physically better, fattened and improved in looks. She embraced Georges and Jeanne.[20]

Hugo's next visit to Adèle was on St. Valentine's Day, 1874. He reported in his journal that she retained her obsession, but was, nonetheless, in good physical health. In May, the remains of Charles's first son, who had died in 1868 at the age of one year in Belgium, were transferred to Pére-Lachaise Cemetery in Paris, not far from Saint-Mandé. On May 13, Hugo visited both the cemetery and his daughter. The visits evidently depressed him, for he noted that Adèle was "more dead than the dead, alas."[21]

By June 5, 1874, the date of Hugo's next visit to his daughter,

Adèle's condition had improved. Yet the visit had a profound effect on Hugo. "There are emotions about which I do not want to leave a trace. My visit yesterday to my poor daughter, how overwhelming!"[22] Nine days later, Hugo visited his daughter once more, and again, the doctors recommended he not come so frequently. Ignoring their advice, he reappeared on July 12.

During this period, Adèle's mental and physical condition continued to deteriorate. Hugo described her as "always in the same state of over-excitement, augmented by fevers." This time, her condition alarmed him sufficiently that he took her doctors' advice and stayed away until May 6, 1875:

Ascension. Juliette and me at Saint-Mandé. Saw my poor child. Always the same state. She had with her a little boy of two years, the son of a house servant, whom she likes and who amuses her.[23]

Hugo's next visit took place shortly after his previous one, on June 22. Following this visit, it would be some time before he would see Adèle again. Instead, on September 9, he dispatched Julie Foucher Chenay, his sister-in-law, to Madame Rivet's. He wrote that he did not dare to go see Adèle "for fear of doing her ill and exciting her fixation." Her aunt evidently cheered Adèle, for Madame Chenay reported to Hugo that Adèle was fine, and "happy with a little blue tie which I [Hugo] sent her."[24] Not until the following year, June 19, 1876, did Hugo visit his daughter again. Adèle begged her father to take her out of the institution — whether for the day or permanently is not clear — but he refused. "Alas," a dejected Hugo wrote in his journal, "we would see what harm we do to each other."[25] Another full year passed between Hugo's visits. On June 27, 1877, Hugo wrote that he and Juliette went to see "the two tombs" (Adèle's asylum and Claire Pradier's grave). Adèle was in the grip of another long bout of schizophrenia, and Hugo noted ruefully that "the meeting between my poor child and me went badly"[26] — so badly that Hugo did not visit

Adèle again until June 18, 1878. Her condition could not have improved, for he passed no comment upon his visit.

By June 29, 1878, the intensity of Adèle's malady had finally lifted somewhat. That day, she wrote a letter to her father. Its contents are interesting because they display not only Adèle's overall lucidity, but also her determination to leave the asylum, even for a short period of time:

Maison de Santé de Madame Rivet, née Brière de Boismont
Uniquement consacré aux dames
106, Grand'Rue de Sainte-Mandé
Saturday, June 29 1878
My dear father,

I already sent you a letter asking for several things, among them that you send me the gold. I would be very happy to have prompt results which I have not had.

M. Baudoin, editor of *The National*, lost his position when the publisher changed. He desires to regain his job. You might take the situation into consideration, if it interests you, and see what you can do.

Don't forget to come and get me, also Madame Leontine and another person, and come today or as soon as possible. I insist that you take us out. Come today or tomorrow.

Don't forget, I insist. Bring us gold.

Your respectful and loving daughter,

Adèle.[27]

Adèle's first request, that her father bring her gold, likely refers to her mother's jewellery. She had cherished it for many years, never selling it despite the poverty she endured while abroad. Circumstances conspired to see that neither this wish, nor her second, that Hugo come and take her out of the asylum, was granted. On the day she wrote the letter, Hugo suffered a mild stroke or heart attack, which his doctors referred to as "congestion of the heart."

Uncertain health kept Hugo away from his daughter for another year, and once more he passed no comment on their meeting other than to record that it had taken place. However, on November 14, 1879, Hugo could report that Adèle had made substantial physical and mental improvement. "She rakes the sand on a pathway in the garden. This pleases her. She saw *Hernani* [one of Hugo's early plays]. Everything is well."[28]

Life for Adèle had settled into a familiar if tedious pattern. She had grown used to the daily routine at Madame Rivet's, and was allowed out from time to time to shop or go to the theatre (although always with a chaperon). It undoubtedly saddened Adèle that her father never saw fit to accompany her. Yet the trips to the outside world, together with daily practice at her beloved piano, seemed to satisfy her. She received few visitors, for no one — aside from her immediate family and a few of her and her father's most trusted friends (including Auguste Vacquerie and the writer Paul Meurice) — knew she was still alive.

For the most part, Adèle lived a quiet, secluded life. She had become demure and submissive, except for the occasional night-time battle with her personal demons. The desire for freedom and independence seemed to have left her; she never spoke about Albert Pinson and seemed to have forgotten all about her trying years abroad.

By now, Adèle had been formally incarcerated, with no chance of being returned to normal life. In August of 1881, there came a reminder of her years of freedom. Madame Baa once again made the trip from Barbados to see her former charge — and her former lover. She arrived on August 3, as exotic as always, bearing a bouquet of coloured bird feathers for Hugo. Once again, Hugo failed to note Juliette's reaction to Madame Baa. Perhaps she had become resigned to Hugo's conquests, for she went along with the pair on the visit to Adèle. Unfortunately, Hugo did not record whether his daughter recognized her old friend and protector, or any details of their meeting.

Hugo paid three more visits to his daughter in the course of the next year, but he was preoccupied with Juliette, who was suffering from intestinal cancer. After September 4, 1882 (the anniversary of Léopoldine's death), the aging, ill Hugo recorded no more visits in his notebooks, and Adèle was left to herself inside the walls of Madame Rivet's *maison*.

The following year, 1883, Juliette Drouet died. She had been Hugo's mistress for more than half a century and his literary secretary for thirty years. When Hugo returned to Paris in 1870, Juliette had taken an apartment below his in the Rue de Clichy; Alice Hugo, Charles's widow, who had since remarried and become Mme Edouard Lockroy, lived one floor above the poet. Juliette's death was a blow to Hugo, not only because he missed Juliette's placid companionship, but because she had painstakingly recopied all of his sloppy and often cryptic manuscripts. She had, moreover, long played the role of wife to him, if not in name, then in deeds. Juliette, like Madame Hugo before her, had put up with Hugo's continual affairs, his egotism and his temper. She accompanied him everywhere, overseeing the myriad details of his energetic life. After she died, Hugo was alone, except for his beloved grandchildren, and, of course, Adèle.

On February 25, 1885, Victor Hugo celebrated his eighty-third birthday with his grandchildren and some intimate friends. Adèle was not invited to the festivities, yet it seemed the rest of Paris participated in some way. The street outside his home, renamed Avenue Victor Hugo, was, the *New York Times* correspondent said, crowded with six thousand people. All of them had come to pay their respects to the great man. The *Pall Mall Gazette* called Hugo "the King of France"; only the *New York Times* correspondent dared to mention how Hugo's age had crept up on him:

> To a foreigner the old man seems to do most absurd things. His elaborate phrasing — which undoubtedly comes to him with facile necessity — appears frequently too pompous for the occasion.
>
> His household, for a pure republican, as that term is understood here, is singularly autocratic.[29]

Hugo would celebrate no more birthdays. Within three months, the long-lived poet would face what he had contemplated for so long: his own death. In mid-May, Hugo attended diplomat Ferdinand Lesseps's induction into the Académie français, along with Auguste Vacquerie and Paul Meurice. Despite the unseasonable cold, Hugo stood outside with his hat off for ten minutes during the ceremony. Later that night, he had difficulty breathing; the press speculated that, despite his iron constitution, he might have caught *la grippe*. Dr. Allix was sent for. Two days later, Hugo's condition had not changed, and he uncharacteristically stayed in bed. Shortly afterwards, his doctors diagnosed congestion in the lungs with complications in the region of the heart — likely pneumonia and heart disease. Concerned friends, journalists and even complete strangers flocked to his apartment. In his bombastic style, Hugo warned them, "It is the end; I feel I am going to die." He was right. On Friday, May 22, 1885, at 1:30 in the afternoon, Victor Hugo died in his Paris apartment.

Just before his death, Hugo called for his grandchildren to be near him, but he did not ask for, or mention, Adèle. When the poet's demise was announced to the world, the *New York Times*'s correspondent was among those who mistakenly believed that "all of Victor Hugo's family died before him."[30] The misstatement was close to the truth. Only Adèle, who for the past fourteen years had been "more dead than the dead," at least as far as her father was concerned, remained. To her, Hugo left 8,000 francs of his estimated seven-million-franc estate. Twelve thousand francs went to Alice Hugo Lockroy; the will had also provided for Juliette, who had died. The rest of his fortune went to his grandchildren.

In an 1883 codicil to his will, he left 50,000 francs to the poor, and he asked that he be brought in a pauper's hearse to the little cemetery in Villequier where his wife and daughter were buried. He refused a religious service, asking instead that a prayer be said for all souls. "I believe in God,"[31] he concluded. In addition to his fortune, Hugo left behind ten volumes of unpublished material, including seven from his period of exile, plus letters, notes and other documents. Juliette Drouet was to have inherited all of his papers and manuscripts; because she predeceased him, they went by default to Adèle, who became the principal owner of the copyright to her father's works. (In 1907, Adèle received $50,000 in return for granting a publishing firm the right to bring out an inexpensive edition of Hugo's writings.)

On the day Hugo died, the ever-faithful Auguste Vacquerie observed, "It was said that he was immortal, . . . and this was proven in the huge cry of sad admiration which echoed around the world. It is said that it is wonderful to be grieved for by a whole people, not just by one person."[32]

Hugo's funeral was held on June 1. Such was the adulation for Hugo that the French government decided to bury him in the Panthéon, the French version of Westminster Abbey, in contravention of his own last wishes. The outpouring of grief reached its most magnificent in Paris. The *Halifax Morning Herald* of June 2, 1885, reported that the windows of the shops and apartments all along the Champs-Élysées and the entire route of the funeral procession had been rented for the occasion. People had paid enormous sums, anything from three hundred to a thousand francs per head, in order to obtain a seat at one of these strategically situated windows.

Judged by the reporter's description of the event, the funeral might just as well have been that of a god:

> The sun shone forth brilliantly. Many chariots heaped up with the offerings of the people of France followed the hearse in procession. Enormous crowds of people line the streets that form the route of procession, while other masses of people possess intersecting streets for a great distance on either side. The buildings are black with people as is indeed every point from which may be had a view of the unparalleled spectacle.[33]

The funeral began at noon. The procession wound for nearly two hours through the streets before reaching the Arc de Triomphe. Under a sarcophagus thirty feet high, flanked by thirty-two candelabras fifteen feet tall, the funeral orations were delivered. As the coffin was removed from the catafalque, bands played a hymn to Hugo which had been written for the occasion by his good friend, composer Camille Saint-Saëns. By four o'clock, the procession had reached the Panthéon in the district of Sainte-Geneviève. During the Third Republic, the eighteenth-century church became the resting place of the country's most famous sons. In view of Hugo's refusal of the last rites and any form of religious service, the Panthéon, with its crypts full of the coffins of poets, writers and other great Frenchmen, had to be secularized for his interment. At last, Hugo's body was laid to rest alongside Voltaire and Rousseau, among others. No doubt he felt he was in fitting company.

Mme Baa's involvement in Adèle's return home did not come to light until the mysterious correspondent to the *New York Tribune* divulged his curious story. After describing the Adèle he knew as a boy, the writer noted that, when the news reached Barbados of Hugo's death, Madame Baa immediately "brought to Father Marie-Joseph a small amount of money, and begged him to say a mass for the soul of Victor Hugo. The priest was naturally astonished at her request, and asked the woman how she had known the French poet." She told her strange story to the priest, explaining the two trips she had made to France on Adèle's behalf and the promise she had made to the poet — no doubt she left out some of the finer points of their relationship. Madame Baa even recalled his final words to her as she departed Paris for the last time:

> "When you hear that I am dead, would you have three masses said for me?" And she promised to do it.
>
> As soon as she heard of the death of Victor Hugo, she cried for him and said, "What a loss! He was such a generous man, so good! God should give him peace!"[34]

But who wept for Adèle? With the death of her father, another chapter in her life came to a close. She was transferred from the care of her father to that of Auguste Vacquerie, whom Hugo had named in his will as Adèle's guardian. It is ironic that the man she had spurned so long ago would finally assume some semblance of the matrimonial role he had once yearned to fill. In accordance with the terms of her father's will, Adèle had received a staggeringly large inheritance, with annual revenues of more than 50,000 francs. Vacquerie, seeking to provide Adèle with the best care her money could buy, promptly transferred her to the Château de Suresnes, a luxurious nursing home at 10, Quai de Suresnes.

At Château de Suresnes, Adèle was delicately "tended to" rather than incarcerated. She occupied an entire pavilion complete with her own staff and a personal companion. Properly chaperoned, she could leave the premises whenever it suited her. In this rarefied world of the rich and insane, Adèle had achieved a measure of freedom she had not been able to enjoy as a young woman.

One of the clinicians trying to unravel the mysteries of mental illness, which were poorly understood at the time, was Adèle's physician, Dr. Valentin Magnin. Then an instructor at the Sainte-Anne Asylum in Paris, Dr. Magnin was renowned for his dissertations on mental illness. Adèle's niece, Jeanne Hugo, was then married to Dr. Jean Charcot (her second husband), the founder of the Suresnes institution where Adèle lived. Treatment of schizophrenia was almost nonexistent; only the relatively recent introduction of psychotropic drugs has had any real beneficial effect on sufferers. Nonetheless, at Suresnes Adèle received the best possible care. At the time of her death, the *New York Times* described her life there:

> Still Adèle lived, alternately listless and frantic, surrounded by all the aids to comfort which modern science can give a woman of great wealth — for she was a woman of great wealth.
>
> She had every luxury possible to a woman in her condition. She occupied a villa of her own within the sanitarium grounds, had a private companion whose sole duty was to attempt to amuse her, and a staff of servants in addition to the regular sanitarium attendants. She wore costly clothes, but insisted that they be made in the style fashionable at the time of her marriage. The public got occasional glimpses of her at the open-air theatre at the Pré Catalan, in the Bois de Boulogne, and in the Jardin

d'Acclimatation. But usually when she attended the play or the opera she sat with her companion in one of the baignoires, or lower loges, where she could not be seen.

She was not so totally deprived of reason as to lose all desire for personal artistic expression. During the long days at Suresnes she frequently attempted to compose an opera but her mental disease kept her from any sustained effort in this direction. She was able, however, at times to play on the piano snatches of compositions learned during her happy childhood.[35]

Another writer added:

She failed to entirely recover her reason, and after the death of her father lived a solitary existence in her villa, morose and seldom speaking. When she did consent to converse, it was never of the past.

Mlle Hugo's only appearances in public were when she went back to Paris to witness from the back of a darkened box the reproduction of one of her father's plays. Apparently she had no friends and never received visitors.[36]

Adèle's diversions remained the same as they had been during her youth: theatre and music. She occasionally went out to a matinée at le Châtelet, and, she boasted, many of the most famous operas were her own compositions.

Adèle was fortunate to be under Dr. Magnin's care. Between 1906 and 1915, Gustave Simon, who had taken over Adèle's guardianship after the deaths of Auguste Vacquerie and Paul Meurice, received letters every two weeks from one of the doctors at the Suresnes institution (more than likely written by Dr. Magnin). The letters detailed Adèle's behaviour, including the physician's observation that "her sleep is troubled each night by conversations with imaginary interlocutors," that she habitually destroyed papers and books and put the bits in her purse, and that she awoke frequently at night, called out in an unnaturally low voice, paced back and forth, and pounded the walls.[37][37]

In April 28, 1908, the writer Jules Claretie visited Adèle in her pavilion. He described her as being very neat and stylish, wearing a dowager's bonnet with long ribbons over her white hair. She talked little, but when she did, her voice had a metallic ring, and her words and tone of voice were often hostile. Critic Raymond Escholier also visited Adèle at about the same time and observed somewhat sadly that her "madness is sweet, musical, but incurable. . . . She was soon interned at Saint-Mandé, then at Suresnes (where I saw her in the spring of 1914), where she died, almost a nonagenarian, taking with her a great secret of dreams and of love."[38]

1. "The Tragedy of Hugo's Daughter," p.20.

2. Richardson, p.231.

3. Guille, Vol. 1, p.151.

4. Richardson, p.231.

5. Richardson, p.231.

6. Richardson, p.231.

7. Richardson, p.231.

8. Richardson, p.231.

9. Guillemin, p.152.

10. Guillemin, p.152.

11. Guillemin, p.152.

12. Guillemin, p.152.

13. Guillemin, p.153.

14. Victor Brombert, *Victor Hugo and the Visionary Novel* (Cambridge: Harvard University Press, 1984), p.237.

15. Brombert, p.238.

16. André Gide, *Anthologie de la poésie française* (Paris: Pléiade, 1949),

p.xxii; rpt. John Porter Houston, *Victor Hugo* (Boston: Twayne, 1974), p.2.

17. Richardson, p.231.

18. Richardson, p.231.

19. Richardson, p.231.

20. Richardson, p.231.

21. Richardson, p.231.

22. Guillemin, p.154.

23. Guillemin, p.154.

24. Richardson, p.231.

25. Richardson, p.232.

26. Guillemin, p.154.

27. Guillemin, p.155.

28. Guillemin, p.155.

29. *New York Times* (March 22, 1885), p.7.

30. *New York Times* (June 8, 1885), p.5.

31. Pol Gaillard, *Les contemplations 1856 Victor Hugo: analyse critique* (Paris: Hatier, 1981), p.71.

32. Laster, p.187.

33. "Victor Hugo's Funeral the Grandest Pageant Ever Seen in the Metropolis," *Halifax Morning Herald* (June 2, 1885), p.1.

34. *Halifax Evening Mail* (May 17, 1930).

35. "The Tragedy of Hugo's Daughter," p.20.

36. "Adele Hugo Dies at 85; Tragic Life Story of Novelist's Daughter was Never Revealed," *New York Times* (April 22, 1915), p.8.

37. Guillemin, p.156.

39. Raymond Escholier, *Hugo, roi de son siécle*, p.263.

Chapter 10

An Uneasy Death
Paris, 1915

The story of Adèle Hugo's blighted life will live as long as the
works of her illustrious father. His genius will evoke the highest
admiration, and her sorrows the deepest sympathy of mankind.
— *J.W. Longley*[1]

Adèle Hugo's time — the opulent, frenzied years of Napoléon III and
the Second Republic — had come and gone, and she hardly noticed. By
the time Napoléon III had left power, Parisians had exhausted their
frivolity and gaiety. Adèle, who had once painstakingly recorded the
artful conversations of politicians, artists and socialites, was a mute and
captive witness to the passing of an era. The serious, passionate young
woman who had so yearned to live a productive, creative and independent life had grown old and feeble.

Like Adèle herself, her literary labours were quickly lost and forgotten. The existence of the *Journal of Exile* was revealed in an 1892
article in the English journal *Athenaeum*. Just as Adèle had predicted
nearly thirty years before, the publication of her work did astonish the
world, though Adèle herself had, for all practical purposes, ceased to exist.

Few of Adèle's friends and acquaintances remained alive; fewer still
had known the tragic circumstances of her life. None of them could
have recalled first-hand the idyllic childhoods of Léopoldine and Adèle,
who had inspired their father to some of his best poetry. Still, when
Adèle died at the age of eighty-five on April 21, 1915, word of her

death made headlines in newspapers across Europe, North America, and northern Africa. The press used the occasion to reflect, not on Adèle's accomplishments, but on the greatness of her late father.

On April 22, *Le Figaro* announced her demise in a maudlin front-page article, recalling neither Adèle's achievements nor her truant years. The influential newspaper granted Adèle's funeral only a paragraph in its deaths column.[2] Other newspapers were not as respectfully reserved as *Le Figaro* about Adèle's condition. *Le Journal de Genève* bluntly noted on April 28, 1915, that Hugo, having seen one of his daughters "sink in the shipwreck at Villequier . . . saw the other sink into a shipwreck perhaps more sad, that of loss of reason."[3] The *New York Times,* in an article published May 2, 1915, revelled in Adèle's downfall: "Never, even in the somberest pages of *Les Misèrables* did Victor Hugo describe a career so tragic and so grotesquely terrible as that of Adèle, his youngest and favorite daughter, who died in a Paris sanitarium the other day."[4]

In death, as in life, the real Adèle was ignored. *Le Figaro* mourned this state of affairs but did little to correct it. In Adèle's obituary in *Le Figaro*, reporter Louis Chevreuse focused on Victor Hugo's many accomplishments and the tragedy of Léopoldine's untimely demise. Hugo *père* had been famous; indeed, his memory lingered on in almost every French town and city, where an avenue had been named in his honour. No such honours or fame accrued to Adèle in her own right; her name was known only because of her father. Then, too, World War I, the Great War, was raging across Europe, and the private tribulations of a rich French madwoman paled in comparison with the horrors contained in reporters' daily despatches from the front. *Le Figaro's* Chevreuse observed that "in Paris, where everything is erased so quickly, who knew that there existed still a child of the poet? A witness to the prestigious years of his triumphant youth, a companion of his years of exile?" Skirting the issue of Adèle's sanity, Chevreuse speculated tactfully on the reasons for her retirement from public view: "During the long years, she lived far from the world as if she doubted to display the glory of such a name."[5]

Adèle Hugo on her deathbed
(Musées de la Ville de Paris)

Adèle's funeral was held on the morning of April 25, four days after her death, in Saint-Sulpice. It was the same church where her parents had been married, and where, before that, her grandmother's funeral had been held. A few family friends attended the ten-thirty service there in the Chapel of the Virgin. Abbé Verdier said mass, and the curé of the parish, Abbé Letourneau, pronounced the absolution. Afterwards, Adèle's body was temporarily placed in the church crypt. She was buried later in the family plot at Villequier, beside her mother and sister. Jeanne Hugo Charcot and Georges Hugo, her niece and nephew, inherited her fortune.

1. Longley, p.304.
2. Louis Chevreuse, "Adéle Hugo," *Le Figaro* (April 22, 1915), p.1.
3. Quoted by Guille, Vol. 1, p.150
4. "The Tragedy of Hugo's Daughter," p.20
5. Chevreuse, p.1.

Hugo Family Tree

Joseph Léopold Sigisbert Hugo (1773-1828) m. Sophie Trébuchet
  (1772-1821)
  Three children: Abel (1798-??)
                  Eugène (1800-1837)
                  Victor (1802-1885)

Victor Hugo (1802-1885) m. Adèle Foucher (1803-1868)
  Five children: Léopold (1823)
                   Léopoldine (1824-1844)
                   Charles (1826-1871)
                   François-Victor (1828-1873)
                   Adèle (1830-1915)

Charles Hugo (1826-1871) m. Alice Lehaene (1817-1928);
  m. (1877) Edouard Lockroy
  Three children: Georges I (1867-68)
                  Georges II (1868-1925)
                  Jeanne (1869-1941)

Appendix II

The Pinsons

Albert Andrew Pinson

Albert Andrew Pinson's military service records have, unfortunately, not survived. British researcher John Dagger, utilizing records available at the Public Record Office in London, England, discovered that he joined the West Yorkshire Militia, Third Battalion, on or about November 6, 1854. He was recommended by Col. Commanding Ferrars Loftus of the Third Battalion, West Yorkshire Militia, on February 17, 1856, for a line regiment, along with three other officers. This information was found in the Commander-in-Chief's memoranda. There was no other personal information about Pinson.

Checks of several British genealogy and clerical guides did not reveal any references to the Pinsons. The absence suggests that the family was not well-to-do, and leads me to suspect that Pinson was not truthful about his family background.

Elsewhere, Lt. Albert Andrew Pinson's father was identified as "General Pinson." This is obviously a reference to his uncle, Lt.-Col. A. Pinson, the father of Lt. Albert William Pinson.

See HO 51/40; WO 31/1111; 2/16th Muster Rolls 1866/7.

Albert William Pinson

East India Register and Army Lists searched by Dagger reveal a Lt. Albert William Pinson, born in Palavaram, near Madras, on March 31, 1829, to Capt. Albert Pinson of the 46th Regiment of the Madras Native Infantry, and Sarah, his wife. He was privately baptised at Palavaram by Thomas Blenkinsop, chaplain.

Albert William Pinson was Albert Andrew Pinson's cousin; Capt. (later Lt.-Col.) Pinson was Albert Andrew's uncle. A petition from A.W. Pinson shows that he was nominated by Sir William Wilcock, director of the East India Company, and recommended by his father as a cadet for the Madras Infantry on December 10, 1845. A.W. Pinson stated that he had been educated at private schools in Jersey by Mr. Thompson and Mr. le Hardy in classics and mathematics.

Army Lists show that A.W. Pinson was an ensign in the First Madras Native Infantry in 1850. He was married at St. Paul's Cathedral, Calcutta, on June 21, 1851, to Mary Cordelia Annie Sandys. By the time his son, Thomas Harry, was born, Pinson was a lieutenant. His wife died less than four months after the baby's birth. Four months after his first wife's death, Pinson married Mary Ellis, a widow, of Serampore. A.W. Pinson's career came to a disgraceful end: he was cashiered from the Madras Army: "Albert William Pinson. Cashiered by sentence of Court Martial on charges unbecoming an officer and a gentleman in having when under close arrest offered violence to his wife and mistress Mary Pinson in the presence of the Guard posted for the safe custody of him Lt. Pinson by throwing a hammer at her which struck her violently on the leg and for having [not deciphered] made use of highly threatening and abusive and obscene language towards the Cantonment Office Captains McMahon and Walker N.I. and Lt.-Col. [not deciphered] the Officer Commanding Moulmein. Found guilty of all the charges with the exception of the word 'obscene' . . . 22 November 1854."

See PC fo.292; PC fo.290v; prov p'c 1/A; PC fo.289v; PC fo.293; PC fo.291r. prov. p'c 1/B; N/1/79; N/1/83 p.9; N/1/83 p. 298; I.O.L.: L/MIL/11/59 batch 363; prov. p'c 1/C.

Lt.-Col. Albert Pinson

Lt.-Col. Albert Pinson was born October 28, 1800. He was the son of William and Mary Pinson. On April 22, 1818, he submitted a petition to join the East India Company as an army cadet. He was nominated by John Morris, director of the East India Company, and recommended by Thomas Studdy, Esq. He stated that his mother was then a widow living in Dartmouth, England. He later joined the Bengal Army, and Army Lists show he was on leave from the 25th Bengal Native Infantry in 1853.

See L/MIL/9/130; fo. 451; fo.448; f0.448v.

Bibliography

Alleyne, Warren and Jill Sheppard. *The Barbados Garrison and its Buildings*. London: MacMillan Caribbean, 1990.

Anderson, Bonnie S., and Judith P. Zinsser. *A History of Their Own*, Vol. 2. *Women in Europe*. New York: Harper and Row, 1988.

Anon. "Adèle Hugo Dies at 85; Tragic Life Story of Novelist's Daughter was Never Revealed." *New York Times* (April 22, 1915), p.8.

Anon. *Collection les géants: Hugo*. Paris: Paris-Match, 1970.

Anon. "Local and Personal News: A Romantic Story of the Visit of Adèle, the Favorite Daughter of Victor Hugo." *Halifax Morning Herald* (May 27, 1885), p.3.

Anon. "Miss Adèle Hugo's Romance." *Halifax Morning Herald* (June 2, 1885).

Anon. "Le Monde et la Ville: Deuil." *Le Figaro* (April 25, 1915), p.8.

Anon. *New York Times* articles about Victor Hugo: (March 13, 1885), p.3; (March 15, 1885), p.7; (March 22, 1885), p.7; (June 7, 1885), p.2; (June 8, 1885), p.5; (June 10, 1885), p.4; (June 22, 1885), p.2; (May 31, 1885), p.2; (June 12, 1885), p.3; (June 23, 1885), p.2.; (June 1, 1885), p.2.

Anon. "Nineteenth-Century Romance: For Fair One in Dartmouth

Victor Hugo's Daughter Spurned." *Dartmouth Free Press* (June 2, 1955), p.7.

Anon. "Occasional Letters: Interesting Story of the Tragedy of the Life of Adèle Hugo." *Acadian Recorder* (December 19, 1925; January 16, 1926).

Anon. "The Tragedy of Hugo's Daughter." *New York Times* (May 2, 1915), Sec. 5, p.20.

Anon. "Victor Hugo's Funeral the Grandest Pageant Ever Seen in the Metropolis." *Halifax Morning Herald* (June 2, 1885), p.1.

Anon. "Victor Hugo: un génie sans frontières." *Dictionnaire de sa vie et de son oeuvre*. Paris: Larousse, 1985.

Armit, Capt. W.B. *Halifax: 1749-1906; Soldiers who Founded and Garrisoned a Famous City*. Halifax: Citadel Army Museum, n.d.

Aron, Jean-Paul. *Misérable et glorieuse: la femme du XIXe siècle*. Paris: Fayard, 1980.

Baron, Robert A. and Donn Byrne. *Social Psychology: Understanding Human Interaction*. 2nd ed. Toronto: Allyn and Bacon, 1974; rpt. 1977.

Blakeley, Phyllis. "The Mysterious Frenchwoman," *Atlantic Advocate* 54:5 (Jan. 1964), p.61.

Bernier, Olivier. *The Eighteenth-Century Woman*. New York: Doubleday, 1981.

Boringe, Bernard. "Adèle, l'autre fille de Victor Hugo." *Historia* 347 (October, 1975), pp.75-83.

Boudet, Jacques. *L'Histoire de France par image: de Louis XIV à la Révolution de 1848*. Paris: Bordas, 1982.

Brombert, Victor. *Victor Hugo and the Visionary Novel*. Cambridge: Harvard University Press, 1984.

Burke, Harry L. "Halifax Love Affair." *Halifax Mail-Star* (November 19, 1965).

Buzzi, G. *Victor Hugo*. Paris: Dargaud, 1967.

Canadian Illustrated News. 1:1 (Nov. 8, 1862); 1:2 (Nov. 22, 1862); 1:5 (Dec. 13, 1862); 2:12 (Aug. 1,1863).

Chevreuse, Louis. "Adèle Hugo." *Le Figaro* (April 22, 1915), p.1.

Deshusses, Pierre, Léon Karlson and Paulette Thornander. *Dix siècles de littérature française*. Vols. 1 and 2. Paris: Bordas, 1984.

de Mutigny, Jean. *Victor Hugo et le spiritisme*. Paris: Nathan, 1981.

Escholier, Raymond. *Un Amant de génie*. Paris: Fayard, 1953.

_____ . *Hugo, roi de son siècle*. Paris: Arthaud, 1970.

_____ . *Victor Hugo, cet inconnu*. Paris: Plon, 1951.

Farge, Arlette and Christiane Klapisch-Zuber. *Madame ou Mademoiselle? Itinéraires de la solitude féminine XVIIIe-XXe siècle*. Paris: Montalba, 1984.

Gaillard, Pol. *Les Contemplations 1856 Victor Hugo: analyse critique*. Paris: Hatier, 1981.

Galloway, Bruce. "The Life of the British Soldier in Mid-Victorian Halifax." Honours essay, April 20, 1983. Halifax: Garrison Library Collection, Citadel Hill.

Gottesman, Irving. *Schizophrenia Genesis: The Origins of Madness* (New York: Freeman, 1989).

Gregory, Richard L., ed. *The Oxford Companion to the Mind*. New York: Oxford, 1987.

Guille, Frances Vernor. *Journal d'Adèle Hugo*, Vol. 1, 1852. Paris: Minard, 1968; Vol. 2, 1853. Paris: Minard, 1971; Vol. 3, 1854. Paris: Minard, 1984.

Guillemin, Henri. *L'Engloutie: Adèle, fille de Victor Hugo, 1830-1915*. Paris: Éditions du Seuil, 1985.

Hart, H.G. *The New Annual Army List and Militia List*. London: John Murray, 1854-1870.

Harvey, Robert P. "Victor Hugo's Daughter." *The NovaScotian* (March 23, 1985), pp.19-20.

Houston, John Porter. *Victor Hugo*. Boston: Twayne, 1974.

Hugo, Adèle Foucher. *Victor Hugo raconté par un témoin de sa vie*. Paris: Ollendorf, 1911.

Hugo, Victor. "À ma fille Adèle." *Quatre Vents*, 1881.

Hugo, Victor. "Mes deux filles." *Contemplations*, 1856.

Hugo, Victor. Letter to Léonie Biard, letter #4, from the collection of the Maison de Victor Hugo (on public display).

Hutchinson, Thomas. *Hutchinson's Nova Scotia Directory*. 1864-65; 1864-5; 1866-67.

Ionesco, Eugène. *Hugoliad, or The Grotesque and Tragic Life of Victor Hugo*. New York: Grove, 1987.

Janin, Jules. *Histoire de la littérature dramatique*. Vol. 4. Paris: Lévy, 1854.

Johnstone, Caroline Biscoe. "Annandale Johnstones Ancient and Modern." Public Archives of Nova Scotia, MG100, Vol. 170, #11: Johnstone Family.

Jordan, Ruth. *George Sand*. London: Constable, 1976.

Juin, Hubert. *Victor Hugo*. Vol. 2, 1844-1870; Vol. 3, 1870-1885. Paris: Flammarion, 1984.

Laster, Arnaud. *Victor Hugo*. Paris: Pierre Belfond, 1984.

Lenoir, Fanny. "Reminiscences of a Halifax Centenarian." *Collections of the Nova Scotia Historical Society* 23 (1936).

Liebert, Robert M., Rita Wicks Poulos and Gloria Strauss Marmor. *Developmental Psychology.* 2nd ed. New Jersey: Prentice-Hall, 1974; rpt. 1977.

Longley, J.W. "The Romance of Adèle Hugo." *Magazine of American History* 21:4 (April 1889), pp.297-304.

Martin-Fugier, Anne. *La Bourgeoise: femme au temps de Paul Bourget.* Paris: Bernard Grasset, 1983.

Massin, Jean. *Victor Hugo, oeuvres complètes, édition chronologique.* Paris: Club français du livre, 1967-1970.

Maurice, Maj.-Gen. Sir F. *The 16th Foot: A History of the Bedfordshire and Hertfordshire Regiment.* London: Constable, 1931.

McAlpine, David. *McAlpine's Nova Scotia Directory.* Halifax, 1868-9.

McLeod, Carol. "The Tragedy of Adèle Hugo." *Bluenose Magazine* 3:4 (1979), pp.35-36.

Mullane, George. "Victor Hugo's Daughter." *Journal of Education* (Nova Scotia) Ser. 6, 6:1 (Dec. 1956).

Neal, Alice B. "American Female Authorship. " *Godey's Ladies Book* (January, 1850), pp.145-48.

Oliver, S.P. "Victor Hugo at Home." *Gentleman's Magazine* (1870), pp.713-25.

Peters, G.W.H. *The Bedfordshire and Hertfordshire Regiment.* London: Leo Cooper, 1970.

Pulsifer, Cameron. *British Regiments in Halifax.* Parks Canada: unpublished report, 1980.

_____ . *The 78th Highlanders*. Vol. 2, *The Officers*. Parks Canada: unpublished report, 1985.

Richardson, Joanna. *Victor Hugo*. London: Weidenfeld and Nicolson, 1976.

Sand, George. *Correspondance*. Vol. 3. Paris: Calman Lévy, 1892.

Shaw, Beatrice M. Hay. "The Love Story of Adèle Hugo." *Canadian Magazine* 60 (Nov. 1922-April 1923), pp.197-202.

Sodergard, Osten, ed. *Les Lettres de George Sand à Sainte-Beuve*. Paris: Minard, 1964.

Stapfer, Paul. *Victor Hugo à Guernsey: souvenirs personnels*. Paris: Société française, 1905.

Stocqueler, J.H. *A Familiar History of the British Army*. London: Stanford, 1871.

Truffaut, François, dir. *The Story of Adèle H.* (film). Paris, 1975.

Wolseley, Garnet. *The Story of a Soldier's Life*. Vol. 1. London: Constable, 1903.

Wudzburg, Ludwig. "The Romance of Victor Hugo's Daughter." *Halifax Morning Chronicle* (Oct. 30, 1903), p.1.

Young, Peter and J.P. Lawford, eds. *History of the British Army*. London: Arthur Barker, 1970.

Index

A

Allen, Margaret *72, 76*
Allix, Augustine *53, 84*
Allix, Émile *86, 88, 159, 160, 161, 163, 164, 165, 170*
Allix, Jules *53, 84, 85*

B

Baa, Céline Alvarez *156, 158, 159, 160, 162, 163, 168, 172*
Balzac, Honoré de *xiii, 41, 83*
Baudelaire, Charles *151*
Bernhardt, Sarah *162*
Biard, Léonie *33*
Bonaparte, Napoléon *29, 40*

C

Cannizzaro, Tommasso de *95*
Chadderton, Mrs. *147, 149*
Charcot, Jean *173*
Charcot, Jeanne, see Hugo, Jeanne (Charcot)
Chateaubriand, François Réné de *30, 46, 67*
Chenay, Julie Foucher *xvii, 152, 166*
Chevreuse, Louis *178*

Chopin, Frédéric *41*
Claretie, Jules *175*
Clésinger, Jean-Baptiste Auguste *xiii, 37, 38, 39, 75, 91*
Cocteau, Jean *164*

D

Delacroix, Eugène *45*
Delalande, Jean *xviii*
Dorval, Marie *32, 84*
Doyle, Francis Hastings Charles *117, 123, 135*
Drouet, Juliette *32, 33, 35, 36, 53, 101, 144, 151, 152, 162, 163, 164, 165, 166, 168, 169, 170*
Dudevant, Aurore Dupin, see Sand, George
Dumas, Alexandre *xiii, 59*

E

Escholier, Raymond *175*

F

Foucher, Anne-Victoire Asseline *27*
Foucher, Pierre *27*

G

Gautier, Théophile *57*
Girardin, Delphine Gay de *67, 68*
Gossip, James *112*
Gossip, William *112, 142*
Guille, Frances Vernor *xviii, xix*
Guillemin, Henri *xix*

H

Hesslein, Henry *94, 105, 106*
Hoffherr, Frederick *xviii*
Hugo, Abel *29*
Hugo, Adèle Foucher *xvii, 22, 23, 24, 25, 26, 27, 28, 30, 31, 33, 35, 44, 46, 47, 52, 53, 55, 63, 69, 73, 74, 76, 81, 84, 85, 86, 87, 88, 92, 99, 100, 101, 104, 113, 114, 117, 118, 130, 143, 144, 150, 151, 152, 162, 169*
Hugo, Adèle Foucher, *Victor Hugo raconté par un témoin de sa vie 55*
Hugo, Adèle, *Journal of Exile xvii, xviii, 47, 53, 134, 177*
Hugo, Alice (Lockroy) *164, 169, 170*
Hugo, Charles *23, 31, 36, 39, 40, 43, 44, 46, 48, 53, 55, 58, 59, 64, 68, 69, 77, 81, 82, 83, 84, 85, 88, 100, 101, 104, 114, 115, 151, 152, 158*
Hugo, Eugène *28, 29, 87, 138, 140*
Hugo, François-Victor *23, 31, 39, 40, 43, 44, 45, 46, 48, 55, 58, 68, 82, 85, 88, 95, 99, 100, 101, 104, 107, 109, 113, 114, 115, 117, 119, 135, 138, 139, 140, 142, 143, 150, 151, 152, 154, 155, 158, 159, 160, 164, 165*

Hugo, Georges *158, 164, 165, 179*
Hugo, Jeanne (Charcot) *158, 164, 165, 173, 179*
Hugo, Léopold *27, 28, 29*
Hugo, Léopold (1823) *24, 31*
Hugo, Léopoldine (Vacquerie) *23, 31, 35, 36, 37, 39, 48, 59, 63, 67, 83, 87, 92, 98, 161, 177*
Hugo, Sophie Trébuchet *27, 29*
Hugo, Victor *xiv, xv, xvi, xvii, xviii, xix, 23, 24, 25, 26, 27, 28, 29, 30, 31, 32, 33, 35, 36, 39, 40, 41, 42, 43, 44, 45, 46, 47, 52, 53, 54, 55, 56, 57, 58, 59, 60, 62, 63, 64, 67, 68, 73, 74, 82, 84, 85, 86, 87, 88, 89, 93, 95, 96, 99, 100, 101, 107, 109, 110, 115, 116, 117, 118, 130, 135, 138, 141, 142, 143, 149, 151, 152, 154, 155, 156, 158, 159, 160, 161, 162, 163, 164, 165, 166, 167, 168, 169, 170, 171, 172, 178*
Hugo, Victor, *Hernani 25, 168*
Hugo, Victor, *Les Odes et poésies diverses 27*
Hugo, Victor, *Lucrèce Borgia 30, 32*
Hugo, Victor, *Notre-Dame de Paris 82*
Hugo, Victor, *Ruy Blas 41, 162*

I

Ionesco, Eugène *33*

J

Janin, Jules *48*
Johnstone, Agnes *123, 126, 128, 129, 130, 131, 132, 133, 137*

Johnstone, Caroline *131*
Johnstone, James W. *128, 129, 130, 131, 132*

K

Kerr, James *141*
Kerr, Jane *141*
King Charles X *24, 47*
King Joseph Bonaparte *29*
King Louis XVIII *27*
King Louis-Philippe *24, 33, 40*
Kock, Paul de *59*

L

Lahorie, Victor *29*
Lamartine, Alphonse de *xiii, 24, 39, 40, 67*
Lanvin, Blanche-Marie *164*
Le Flô, Adolphe Emmanuel Charles *68*
Lenoir, Peter *105, 106, 125*
Lesseps, Ferdinand *170*
Liszt, Franz *57*
Loftus, Ferrars *90*
Loliée, Marc *xviii*
Longley, J.W. *141*

M

Magnin, Valentin *173, 174*
Messières, Réné de *xvii*
Meurice, Paul *40, 168, 170, 174*
Moorsom, William *127*
Motton, Ellen *134, 137, 139, 140*
Motton, Robert *134, 137, 139, 140*

Motton, Robert, Jr. *xv, xvi, xvii, 125, 126, 130, 131, 134, 141*
Musset, Alfred de *41*

N

Napoléon, Louis *40, 42, 44, 46, 85, 158, 177*
Nyobet, Eugénie *83*

O

O'Brien, Thomas *105, 110, 145*
Oliver, S.P. *59*

P

Paganini, Niccolo *xiii*
Pinson, Albert Andrew *xiv, xv, xvi, xix, xx, 61, 62, 66, 67, 68, 69, 70, 71, 72, 73, 74, 75, 76, 78, 81, 83, 88, 89, 90, 91, 92, 93, 94, 95, 96, 98, 99, 100, 104, 105, 106, 107, 108, 109, 110, 111, 112, 113, 114, 115, 116, 117, 118, 119, 120, 121, 123, 125, 126, 127, 128, 129, 130, 131, 132, 135, 136, 137, 139, 141, 143, 144, 145, 146, 147, 148, 154, 155, 156, 158, 168*
Pinson, Albert, Lt.-Col. *96, 114, 115, 156*
Pinson, Caroline, see Roxburgh, Caroline Edith
Planche, Gustave *32*
Pradier, Claire *163, 166*
Pradier, James *163*
Pyat, Felix *85*

R

Reményi, Ede 66
Rose, J____ 61, 62, 66, 105
Rossini, Gioacchino xiii
Roxburgh, Caroline Edith 156
Roxburgh, James 156

S

Saint-Saëns, Camille 172
Sainte-Beuve, Charles 25, 26, 30,
   32, 41, 58, 88, 104, 144, 152
Sainte-Beuve, Charles, *Livre
   d'Amour* 30
Sand, George 30, 32, 38, 40, 41,
   42, 55, 71, 83, 112
Sand, George, *Indiana* 41
Sand, Solange 38
Saunders, Grace 111
Saunders, Richard 110, 111, 112,
   117, 119, 123, 134, 135, 139
Saunders, Sarah 110, 111, 112, 113,
   115, 116, 117, 119, 134, 135, 139,
   143
Simon, Gustave 174
Stapfer, Paul 152

T

Teleki, Alexandre 68
Truffaut, François xix

V

Vacquerie, Léopoldine, see Hugo,
   Léopoldine
Vacquerie, Auguste 36, 37, 38, 39,
40, 44, 49, 51, 53, 56, 58, 59, 60,
63, 64, 67, 68, 69, 70, 71, 72, 74,
75, 76, 77, 81, 84, 127, 168, 170,
171, 172, 173, 174

Vacquerie, Charles 35, 36, 37, 59
Vacquerie, Pierre 35
Vigée-Lebrun, Elizabeth 83
Vivier, Eugène 39

W

Wolseley, Garnet 89, 90, 91, 93,
   116, 127, 128

For Porter
And in memory of my mother
Sibyl Eskew Sumner

PROLOGUE

Robin Hamilton

2013

Lessons learned are like bridges burned: you only need cross them once. Yet there are those of us who learn those lessons only after crossing our bridges over and over, retracing our footsteps as if looking for a mislaid pen or pair of glasses.

One late February evening while the wind probed and rattled the shutters of my brownstone, I read that my favorite band had filmed a documentary about the band's history. The television premiere was scheduled for that Friday night. Delighted, I called Theresa in Paris, wishing it were possible for the two of us to watch the show together. I knew that my daughter's boyfriend would be away, so I called her and asked if she would come and watch with me. I heard the grin in her voice, "I'd love to, Mom."

And then the night arrived. Was it meant to be that the producer had chosen to include film footage from the very concert I had attended that fateful night in 1977? It had been a long time since I'd thought about the night I'd met Dean Falconer. I sat in stunned reverie for a space of time, my daughter, Lark, beside me nonplussed.

All the rationalizations with which I'd built my careful house of cards shimmered before me. Could I somehow manage to pick my way back across those charred bridges for the sake of my only daughter? I wanted to tell her the truth.

Maybe it wasn't too late.

CHAPTER

1

Lark Hamilton

2013

Despite a wind that threatened to freeze my lips to my teeth, I had to grin at the thought of my mother: beneath the sophisticated surface of Robin Hamilton, New York professional, simmered the soul of a seventies rocker. Swaddled from head to toe, I plodded the last block to her home on the Upper West Side to watch a documentary about her favorite band with her. As I mounted the steps of the brownstone my grandparents had bought for a song in 1961, Mom abruptly pulled open the great door. "Lark! Did you *walk?* Are you not frozen?"

"Hi, Mom. No cabs," I said, kissing her warm cheek and tugging at the layers of scarves around my neck.

"I made a fire for us. Go get warm! I'm just opening the wine and putting a snack together." Uncommonly pretty at fifty-four, my mother, wearing a white tunic blouse and jeans, disappeared into the kitchen.

Shrugging from my coat, I extricated the laptop from my bag and made a nest in the Indian-patterned pillows tossed about the sectional. I would catch up on work while keeping one supportive eye on the TV. My phone sounded from my pocket, a pissed-off wasp against my hip. A text from Ben: "Hey, beautiful. Can't wait to see you tomorrow."

Ben. I had met Ben Holland one sultry summer night at the West Village rooftop party of one of my yoga students, Kimberly Kist. Swathed in whispering raspberry silk and sporting an armful of gold bangles, Kimberly had handed me a glass of sauvignon blanc in the kitchen and whispered breathlessly, "Lark, I have *the* man for you. Kirk invited him."

"Kimberly. You know I don't ..."

"He's *gorgeous*, Lark," she purred confidentially. "His mother was a Brazilian *model* in the sixties!" To my skeptical expression she said, "At least *meet* the man ... and talk to him."

"What does he do?" I asked grudgingly. Kimberly had fixed me up before with a Wall Street broker who, although witty and attractive, had a regrettable penchant for cocaine.

"He's a coffee buyer!" Kim said over her shoulder, fairly pulling me by the hand. I followed her onto the roof fragrant with the potted gardenia trees her husband Kirk grew.

Kirk and Ben stood under a string of industrial twinkle lights holding bottles of beer. That night I wore my long blond hair in a loose ponytail over the shoulder of a short indigo sheath embroidered with silver thread. Kirk introduced me to Ben, whose eyes, as dark as the beans he bought, lingered on mine. His teeth were very white, and the lights glinted off shiny black hair that needed cutting.

"Lark?" He tasted my name for the first time. "Like the songbird."

"It's a nickname. My name is Laurel," I said, extending my hand. "Apparently, I was a very happy baby."

Two days later, the two of us met for coffee. Ben introduced me to the art of cupping through importer samples and his milieu of green buying in verdant Latin America for Coloma Cup Coffee. An inveterate teacher, I talked of trends in twenty-first century education. Later that night, we taught each other what we liked in bed.

Ben and I had been happy in our love for more than two years. But lately, a gaggle of unsettling thoughts about our relationship had been springing up like mushrooms after days of rain. It was time to talk to him. I would do it tomorrow.

A metallic clang from the kitchen intruded on my reverie; I knew Mom was pulling out a pretty tray. Presentation was a big thing with Robin.

I noticed the program had started and called, "Mom, it's on!" I glanced from my laptop to the television screen and did an incredulous double take. I stared at the face of a girl in the swaying throng perched on the shoulders of a very happy-looking young man. *Is that my mother?* Riveted, I called, "Mom, are you coming? There's a girl who looks an *awful* lot like *you.*"

"Be right there, darling!" Her voice was light, amused.

Since she was sixteen years old, Mom had been crazy about the Eagles, who had rocked the country and chronicled the high-flying seventies. I'd cut my teeth on that music. And now that vinyl was back, it was pretty cool that Mom still had her old records. I liked the scritch-whish of the needle as it rippled over the grooves. I would swear Mom would want me to toss her original copy of *Hotel California* into her coffin before I closed its mahogany lid for the last time.

My mother rounded the corner with the tray of appetizers: quinoa crackers, our favorite truffle cheese, fresh berries, and two glasses of wine. She peered through her distinctive tortoiseshell frames at the screen and lowered the tray to the cocktail table. The Eagles strummed their guitars and tossed their rock-star tresses— young, tight-jeaned, newly minted gods. "Oh, there's concert footage too ... and from the Hotel California Tour! Lord, Lark," she breathed, fingering the chunky strands of turquoise beads at her throat, "look how *sexy!*"

"Mom. Watch the audience." I located the pause button just as the camera panned toward the girl again. "Look. *There!* The girl on the blond dude's shoulders. It *is* you, isn't it?"

Mom sank to the sofa as we stared at the close-up of the impossibly young and luminous Robin Hamilton, size six, chestnut hair falling in Farrah Fawcett waves around her face.

"Mo-om?"

She nodded almost imperceptibly. "I'm fine, Lark. Just … surprised."

"Where was this? Did you know you were being filmed? This is so cool!"

My mother clutched the stem of her glass and took a liberal gulp. "That was the DC performance," she added as if it made everything clear. I unmuted the TV.

"So who's the cute guy? Did you know him?" I asked. A prickle of concern began along the edge of my scalp, and I slipped my hand around hers. She was trembling. "Mom, what is it?" I asked softly.

Her lined eyes closed. The song "Victim of Love" spun up and out of the television. As the drummer sang, "Tell me your secrets; I'll tell you mine. This ain't no time to be cool," pain and something else, something inscrutable, settled over her face like a cloud shadow on a mountain. Beyond my grandpa Hank's andirons, the fire snickered and blazed.

After a long moment, my mother opened her eyes. She turned to me, her smile open, loving. "An old friend," she said evenly. "Someone it's time you met."

CHAPTER

2

Robin

1977

From the moment I registered at NYU, I insisted on an authentic dorm experience, with benefits: I would bump my laundry bag home once a week to Mom's squeaky-clean washing machine and enjoy some home cooking and a little pampering.

"Mom, I'm home!" I dropped my things in the foyer of the brownstone to which my parents had brought me home from the hospital as a baby and stooped to pet our capricious cairn terrier, Atticus. The little dog loved people but could be vicious with other dogs, as if to disaffiliate himself from the canine camp.

A lilting voice greeted me from the kitchen. "C'mon back, darling! I left the shop early today." Since I was ten, my mother, Olivia Hamilton (née Courtwright), from whom I'd inherited my green eyes, had managed the bookstore Speak Volumes on Fifty-Third Street for an eccentric gentleman who lived in red-velvet seclusion in a penthouse on Central Park West. With a degree in library science from Hunter College and a passion for American literature, Mom dreamed of owning the bookstore herself one day.

"What smells so *divine?*" I asked, my stomach grumbling.

"Pineapple chicken." She hugged me. Her familiar lemon-sugar smell settled around me. "It's a new recipe from *McCall's* magazine. Your dad's on his way."

"I have some news that will make his day." I grinned and opened the refrigerator to inspect its contents. Snaring a block of cheddar in a baggie, I pinched off a hunk and popped it into my mouth. My first word, rather than *Da* or *Ma* like most kids, had been *cheese* or a close approximation: I'd toddled to grasp the handle of the fridge demanding, "Deese!"

The solid slip-thunk of the front door announced my father's arrival. "Robin!" I could hear his broad grin. "Didn't expect you until *tomorrow* night. What a treat!" Chestnut hair the color of my own tumbling over his forehead, tie askew from the day, Henry Anderson Hamilton strode into the kitchen with the laundry bag I'd dropped. As he bussed my cheek I winced at the six o'clock whisker rasp against my skin. "I've missed you, sweet pea!" My dad was the happiest person I knew; his initials, HAH, fit him to a tee.

"Robin, why don't you go ahead and put your wash in while we have a drink?" Mom said, covering the rolls on top of the stove with foil. "Then we won't have to listen to the machine while we eat." She turned to my father. "Robin has news." She gave my father a big smooch. I averted my eyes as his hand cupped her backside. I loathed the thought that my parents might still be having sex.

Dad went to the wet bar in the living room and poured three glasses of Lancers. "I declared a major today ... a *double* major," I said, tipping a wink to my mother and settling into my chair. I paused a beat. "English and philosophy."

With those words, I revealed my intention to follow my father down the road paved by the great minds of his heroes Thomas Jefferson, Thurgood Marshall, and Gloria Allred (whom he admired for her savvy, chutzpah, and shapely legs). He collapsed into his chair and the throes of ecstasy. "You little minx!"

Hank Dad had eschewed the practice of litigation with its often chaotic, long hours and latent deadlines that could interfere with the positive work-life balance he craved. His residential real estate practice afforded him a comfortable living with a home-for-dinner practice. He and Mom enjoyed cooking dinner together and bantering over the evening news from the little black-and-white set in the kitchen.

"What field are you thinking?" My father was beaming so brightly you could have read by him.

"I have plenty of time to decide that, Dad," I said laughing.

As the washing machine ground through its old gears in the kitchen, Dad said, "There are two kinds of lawyers, Robin: those who make love and those who make war. If you're not the warring type, you won't enjoy litigation. Now *real estate* law, on the other hand, is a *family* practice of sorts ... with real rewards." Atticus crouched in front of Dad, his preferred human, poised to spring into his lap. Dad patted his chest with both hands, Atticus's green light, and continued, "You're dealing with mostly happy people, usually taking a step up in life." I had heard it all before but indulged my father his passion that night.

At the table Mom passed a platter of chicken, golden robed in pineapple syrup, my way. She had loosened her dark hair from the french twist she wore for work, and it moved softly about her shoulders. She asked about my most recent problem. "How goes it with Darlene?"

Being the only one from my circle of private-girls'-school friends to choose NYU, I'd applied for dorm life hoping to be assigned a compatible roommate. I'd received a letter informing me I would be rooming with Darlene Blount from Queens. On move-in day we'd met for the first time. Darlene's kohl-rimmed eyes, jet-black hair, and Ramones T-shirt were anomalies in the days when most girls resembled the silky-tressed, squeaky-clean models of the Gee, Your Hair Smells Terrific ads in *Seventeen Magazine*. I'd never met anyone like her. But it wasn't Darlene's appearance that had quelled the possibility of friendship. I found her interesting, faintly mysterious. And I knew she was smart. But as soon as our parents had left us to get settled, Darlene had been inexplicably hostile. "Keep this preppie crap on your side," she'd snarled, raising her lip like Elvis. After two weeks, I'd had my fill of her darkness and music that could inspire suicide.

"It's impossible," I said around a bite of salad. "I'm just hanging in there, trying to stay out of her way."

"I admire you for sticking it out, sweet pea," Dad said, anointing a second roll with butter. "These things build character."

Sated by the delicious meal, I gathered my clean laundry (tenderly folded by my mother). Dad walked me out into the twilight. "See you next week, counselor," he said, tipping me a two-fingered salute.

Three days later, I met Theresa Cleary at a reception the English honors college held for those who had earned the distinction of National Merit Scholar their senior year of high school. (Theresa always maintained that her test performance was a mere fluke, though a practical and self-promoting one, while I was authentically brilliant, deserving of the feather in my cap.)

A few minutes past fashionably late, I shook the soft academic hands of the honors college faculty and found the name tag table, spotting my preprinted one. Only two other tags remained, Catherine Cabot and Theresa Cleary. Nearby, a shambling bear of a professor in a flapping navy blazer clapped a bug-eyed runt of a boy in my English class heartily on the back. I feared the little dude would take a header into the punch bowl.

I stood alone sipping from a Styrofoam cup of tea and wondering what I should do with the tea bag when a slight girl slipped through the doorway. She was as boyish of figure as I was curvy with masses of Titian hair tumbling down her narrow back. I watched her move through the reception line, her manner as vibrant as her hair. This girl had what my dad called moxie. Mouth tugging into a grin, I reached for the name tag as she approached the table. "You are Theresa Cleary from Chicago, Illinois."

"I am." There was music in the two syllables as her eyes searched mine. Theresa's eyes weren't the light hue of most redheads but a rich, deep brown that made for an arresting contrast with her pale skin.

I handed her the tag and indicated my own with a forefinger. "I'm Robin Hamilton, New York, New York."

She wrapped my hand in both of hers. "Congratulations on your scholarship, my dear," she said, mimicking the faculty members.

We laughed together for the first time and soon decided to go to lunch together. In our first hour we discovered that we both liked chef salads with blue cheese dressing and cold Tab from the bottle; found sororities pretentious, catty, and exclusive; loved the band the Eagles; were terrible at math; had a taste for marijuana; were Francophiles, dreaming of living in Paris; and were miserable with our current roommate situations.

I told Theresa about Darlene, and she told me about her roommate, Donna, who sneaked guys into their room (with Theresa right across the partition dividing the small space). "Talk about awkward! She actually tried to introduce one of them to me when I walked in on them. The dude wanted to shake my hand!" she shrieked in disgust. I hooted with laughter.

The poster child for darkness was reassigned and moved out of my room three weeks later, and Theresa moved in, though she had moved into my heart much sooner. We became the sisters we had wished for as two only children, trusted confidantes. The fall of our sophomore year our parents helped us rent a down-at-the-heels but surprisingly spacious one-bedroom unit in a student apartment building. Theresa's mom cleaned out her Chicago basement and drove a U-Haul trailer filled with an assortment of odds and ends all the way to New York. The prize was a pocked but pretty antique armoire (though it never quite lost the peculiar fusty smell of Theresa's aunt Pauline) in which we installed our little TV, turntable, and speakers. My parents invited Mrs. Cleary to stay at the brownstone while in the city, and she accepted. My father made spaghetti bolognese and garlic bread for us all that Saturday night. Theresa was a near replica of her mother: Colleen Cleary was a gung ho middle-aged cheerleader, her own mop of riotous red hair threaded with gray.

In our first pad Tee, as I quickly began to call her, and I hung Eagles posters, made Chef Boyardee pizzas from the bright-yellow boxes, and watched *The Love Boat* and *Saturday Night Live* in its heyday with John Belushi and Gilda Radnor. We exercised and danced to Fleetwood Mac and Supertramp and cried with Dan Fogelberg, but the Eagles were our perennial favorite. We studied and talked late into the nights from twin beds with matching, braille-like chenille spreads.

Late one May afternoon at the end of junior year, during my turn to clean, Tee came home from an exam as I was scrubbing away at the little sink in our kitchen. She was nervous about something, drumming the fingers of her right hand against her hip, as was her way. I snapped the yellow rubber glove from my hand and turned off the faucet. "What's going on, Tee? Did the math not go well?"

She leaned against the counter and said sheepishly, "Rob, I've been waiting for the right time to tell you something." I waited as she revealed that she had applied for a study-abroad program a month before. We'd both received the same glossy brochure and letter in our mailboxes, but I'd thoughtlessly tossed mine.

"It was just a lark in the beginning. I didn't really think Mom was going to go for it, but then I got accepted." Avoiding my gaze, she began toying with the salt and pepper shakers. "And she said she could swing the extra dough." Finally she reached for my hand and peered into my crestfallen face. "It's *Paris,* Rob … What if it's my only opportunity? The only chance I ever get?"

"You're doing this then," I said. I looked at my best friend, to whom I was closer than my own parents. She bit her bottom lip and pushed the salt she'd spilled into a little pile. I opened the fridge and grabbed a beer, popped the metal tab, took a big swig, and pitched the metal tab into the sink.

"Robin, you can come visit while I'm there. You're practically fluent in French, much better than I am." I burp-hiccupped against the back of my hand. "The croissants! The Left Bank! The Louvre! French *guys*! C'mon, Rob … you *know* we'd have a blast!"

As Tee rhapsodized on about the program, I slid down the refrigerator door to sit on the scarred old linoleum. A kaleidoscope of memories of the last three years flashed before my eyes and splintered into random images: the two of us schlepping loads of stuff up the stairs of our building, breathless with laughter; a meatball slipping from my ill-advised meatball sandwich and rolling across the restaurant floor while we were on a double date;

14

us pulling all-night study sessions with Tab and bags of Oreos; me throwing up on a sexy bass player's shoes at the Bottom Line. *What will I do without my best friend? She's embarking on this adventure without me. And senior year!*

Selfishly considering the implications, tears stung my nose. "But, Tee, you butt rash, what will I do without you? I'll have to get a new roommate," I wailed.

"Maybe Darlene's still available!" Theresa said brightly. We giggled then, both sniffling, and the tension broke. Tee extended a hand to help me up. "Let's don't think about it anymore tonight. We have *plenty* of time until I have to go."

I pulled another beer from the fridge and handed it to her, a conciliatory gesture. We sat on the sofa and began to talk of the summer that shimmered ahead of us like a meadow, its fence in the far distance. With our summer jobs, we'd have more spending money. We punctuated sips of beer with talk of summer festivals, shopping in the village, parties we would throw. We spoke of summer flings. Tee and I had had our share of boyfriends, but neither of us felt we'd ever been in love. I had a chemistry experiment in mind: to find out if the spark that had leaped between our friend Nick and me would lead anywhere. Theresa had just met a foxy law student with a blue MG convertible and the improbable name of Tink. Now she flashed the mischievous grin I loved. "Let's see what trouble we can get into tonight."

CHAPTER

3

Robin

Summer 1977

"We *have* to get ourselves out of this city!" Theresa groaned and jumped to her feet. She batted ants from the seat of her white shorts. "You and I, my fine-feathered friend, are going to DC for the Hotel California concert." It was our day off from work, mine from Speak Volumes and Tee's from typing and filing in the university admissions office. We'd spent the afternoon in the park browning our legs and then reading in the shade, watching desultory games of volleyball and the inveterate joggers trudging along in the heat. Even the foliage seemed listless, the congenitally exuberant dogs dispirited.

We'd attended several good parties in June and even hosted a pretty wild one at our small place, dancing until two in the morning, Nick playing DJ with our albums and his. There was just something about Nick. He was playful and spontaneous, as un-self-conscious as a child. I found him very alluring. We had made out a little that night just before he'd told me he had taken a summer internship in his hometown of Ithaca. Theresa had learned that Tink, a.k.a. Theodore Tallent Treadwell IV, had a fiancée on whom he was industriously cheating. Almost all our other friends had left the city. It was shaping up to be one bummer of a summer.

Twining my chestnut mane up from my sweaty neck, I responded from my seat on a wedding quilt made by my grandmother Courtwright, "Well, hell *yes*, we should. How much are tickets?"

"Eh, a minor detail." Tee twitched a shoulder and helped me fold the quilt. "Don't worry; we'll pool our resources."

My mind ticked ahead to early August. "I suppose we could take the bus … but let's see if Carol Anne wants to go." Carol Anne was our one friend still in NYC with a car.

A sweaty, extraordinarily red, hairy-chested guy bounced up to us, an orangutan in blue nylon shorts and tube socks. "You ladies wanna play some volleyball?" he asked happily, bouncing on the balls of his feet.

Tee narrowed her eyes. "No. Thanks." She made a gagging face at his hirsute and quickly retreating back.

The weather in Manhattan had been sweltering, but there was another deterrent to outdoor activities. A serial killer, armed with a .44-caliber pistol, had begun stalking women with long dark hair, casting a pall over the city like a net. Incredibly, he penned letters to the newspaper about his exploits, calling himself "Son of Sam." Women thought twice about going out alone at night, some even going as far as wearing wigs or bleaching their dark hair blonde. While I maintained only a peripheral interest in the headlines, Tee read all the grisly stories about Son of Sam, engrossed in the details. "Theresa, stop reading that stuff!" I warned one morning as I discovered her on the living room floor, the paper spread around her, a black-and-white puddle of foreboding. "You'll have bad dreams."

Theresa had been a highly imaginative child. Her father had been killed in a plane crash on her eighth birthday, her mother just thirty-one years old. The morning after the funeral, little Theresa had been sent to school as usual. Colleen had showed up on time at Drs. Shapiro and Rosenblatt's dental office where she'd worked as a hygienist to improve the smiles of others. Despite Theresa's recurring dreams—her father's face framed by a window in a fiery, plummeting plane—Colleen had insisted they carry on as before. And to all outward appearances they had.

"It's *fascinating*, Rob," Theresa answered now, not looking up from the story. A newsprint smudge tipped her upturned nose.

We were psyched about the Eagles' new album, so the timing was perfect for a road trip. We had never seen the band in concert and were over the moon at the prospect. Not only was Carol Anne on board, as the pièce de résistance, she had a discreet older cousin in Baltimore who had offered to put us up for the weekend.

On the thirteenth of July, Tee and I were in for the evening. Ours was the only occupied flat in the building for the remainder of the summer. We'd stood on line for an hour that afternoon to see the movie *Star Wars* and then had picked up good, cheap takeout from Mamoun's Falafel for dinner. The phone rang about eight o'clock. I answered; it was my mother. "Hi, darling. Anita Roth just called and said there are a lot of power outages in the boroughs and into Manhattan. Is Theresa there with you?"

"Yep, she's right here, Mom." I inclined my head to peer at Tee on the floor painting her toenails a candy-apple red, white cotton balls blossoming between her toes.

"Bonjour, Madame H.," she called.

"Bonjour, Theresa," Mom sang out. "You girls stay cool and lock up. I've just taken a beautiful roast chicken out of the oven and made a cold salad, so if our power goes, at least Dad and I have something nice for dinner. Do you have candles in case you lose power? Have you eaten?"

"Yes, we've eaten, and … we have lots of candles actually." I regarded the assorted candle stubs on hodgepodge saucers placed about the room. "We're cool. See you soon, Mom. Love you."

As I replaced the receiver, Tee grinned. "Not only do we have candles, *but* … the last one of those amazing doobies Nick left us!" She tightened the cap on the bottle of polish and reached for the little carved wooden box on the trunk coffee table where we kept our stash. Wiggling her dark brows, she placed the joint across her top lip like a mustache, a flame-haired Groucho Marx. It was *Mork & Mindy* and *Three's Company* night on TV. We settled in and lit the joint, talking and giggling about the bizarre *Star Wars* characters, Tee trying to mimic the voice of C-3PO.

It was about ten thirty when everything went as dark as the inside of a boot. We had raised the living room window of our third floor flat to allow the smoke to escape but now forced open the stubborn one in the kitchen. We squinted out at the blackness; not a single pinprick of light shone from the buildings across the way. No moon lit the scene. The absence of taxi horns or haranguing sirens left an eerie vacuum of silence. "Holy shit," Theresa breathed. It was as if we were the lone survivors of some futuristic Rapture.

"I wish Nick or Gino and Ty ... or *somebody* was here tonight," I said, the prickle of chill on my flesh, and bumped toward the kitchen to grab a couple of Tabs while they were still cold. We sat, popping the bottles open with a church key, and opened a bag of Doritos. We waited by candlelight in a vague aura of apprehension. The apartment was growing warmer. The weed had made us stupid with sleep, and we dozed.

I startled awake and peered owlishly at my watch in the dimness. It was ten minutes after three, and the candles were guttering low. I had a foul taste in my mouth and a gloating headache. Theresa at the other end of the sofa woke as a terrific *ka-blam* reverberated from somewhere close by. We jerked to attention, completely sober. "What the *hell?*" we said together. Someone had kicked in the street door and was in the building. The reckless sound of battering began below.

Panicked, we realized the candles were giving a slice of light to the hallway beyond, and we crept around the room snuffing them out. "Do you think it could be Son of Sam?" Tee's voice quavered in the hot room.

21

"Oh my Lord!" I hissed, heart trip-hammering in my chest. Our eyes accustomed to the darkness, we regarded each other: the whites of Tee's eyes showed all the way around. The clamor grew louder and closer. Whoever was in the building was making his way upward.

"The chain isn't enough!" Tee seemed near hysteria.

"We'll block the door," I said, springing into action. "*Help me, Theresa!*" Pure adrenaline must have enabled us to push the unwieldy armoire in front of the door. Surely the groaning and protesting of the old piece could be heard in Far Rockaway.

Breath ragged in her throat, Tee said, "We have to hide!" A single pair of footfalls echoed from the stairwell on our floor. The only weapon in the apartment was the old baseball bat that had belonged to her father. Theresa kept it like a talisman under her bed. She moved toward it.

"The closet," I hissed. But Tee first scrabbled under her bed, fingers closing around the bat. Then she crab-crawled toward me, her lips pulling back from her teeth. I nudged her through the jungle of clothing in the closet and followed, crouching low. With shaking hands, I slid the door along its track. We were as still as flatware in a drawer for a time.

As the minutes dragged by, I began to smell my own acrid body odor. A runner of sweat made its way down my back and into the cleft of my bottom. Someone gave our apartment's outer doorknob a twist-turn-pull just as a belt slithered from the shelf above us. The buckle struck the closet door like a tuning fork. I stifled a scream and closed my eyes so tightly white spots appeared behind my lids. I became aware of the sharp, hot ammonia smell of urine. My heart contracted with sympathy for my friend, but I didn't dare speak.

The intruder must have moved on, for there was no other sound from the door but then came the tear of splintering wood and crashing from far below. We sat transfixed for perhaps another excruciating hour. Finally I slid the closet door open. Strobing blue lights from the street below illuminated the space. Theresa sat in the corner, hair plastered to her forehead, eyes dark as plums, still clutching the bat to her chest. "I think it's over," I said. I reached for my friend, gently unwrapped her hands from the bat and pulled her to her feet. We staggered rubber-legged to the front windows. In the pale yellow light of early dawn we could see cops and Tim, a campus security guard, on the sidewalk. At our screams for help they turned, craning their necks at the two of us practically hanging out the window.

Later as the punishing sun climbed high on another day, Tim told us the intruder had to have been a looter acting under the cover of the blackout. The Con Edison power system had completely failed the night before. It would be late that night before all service was restored to the city. The damage to our building indicated to police the looter had made his way upward checking to see how many people might be in the building and then had ransacked the unattended apartments on the way back down.

We guessed Son of Sam had stayed in for the night. Three weeks later, on August 10, we learned the monster had been apprehended. He had murdered his sixth victim and left seven others with injuries they would carry to their graves. Theresa and I drank a celebratory glass of champagne with my parents that night. It would be years before I would learn what the awful experience had cost my friend.

CHAPTER

4

Robin

August 1977

An early-autumn breeze heralded the morning of the road trip, and the cloudless sky was cerulean, a balm on Theresa's and my shock-worn souls. Carol Ann pulled her mother's grating Ford wagon to the curb, and Theresa and I swung our bags into the back. Snub nosed and freckled with white-blonde hair long enough to sit on, Carol Ann was one crazy, fun girl. We headed out of the city in high spirits, blasting the Eagles from the eight-track, windows down, Medusa hair whipping around our heads.

In the passenger seat I helped Carol Ann navigate, the road map as complicated to fold as an origami bird. Theresa in the backseat was rolling joints for later from the small baggie of Acapulco gold that Carol Ann had scored for the trip. "Woo-hoo!!!!" I yelled above the wind. "Are we getting fired up, girls?"

A busload of jocks passed us on the left honking and blowing kisses. Ignoring them, Carol Anne sighed, "Isn't Björn Borg gorgeous?" We spoke of Borg's Wimbledon tennis victory in July and of sexy bad-boy Burt Reynolds in the comedy hit *Smokey and the Bandit*. We talked and laughed about any and everything, the way you do in the uncensored company of close friends.

In Maryland by five o'clock, we had more than enough time to relax and primp for the concert. Tee, at the wheel as the wagon bumped into the driveway of Carol Ann's cousin Debbie's home, uttered a barely audible, "Wow." A small stone craftsman cottage was surrounded by roaring green, orange, and pink foliage and a host of gewgaws—gazing balls, gargoyles, and impish gnomes. We climbed out, stretching our limbs and gawking, to retrieve our bags. A tall, blue-eyed woman trotted out to the porch on bare feet to embrace Carol Ann, her aunt Colleen's only daughter. Her gray-blonde braids tied with yarn seemed to have a life of their own the way they bobbed and danced. "Welcome, gals, I'm Debbie!" she said. "Bathroom, refreshments, or showers first?"

If our first glimpse of Debbie wasn't enough to confirm her level of cool, our appraisal of her place instantly did. In a poster above a Victorian sofa made of carved wood and purple velvet, Janis Joplin clutched a microphone in both hands and squinted blearily down at us. A great black tomcat uncurled itself from the depths of an armchair and approached us, mewling, twining around our legs. As Tee reached to pet the cat, it leaped to the coffee table, where a tarnished octopus of a bong reached out its tentacles in welcome. Any lingering doubts we had about Debbie's discretion were dispelled like smoke. Pun intended. Debbie reappeared through a beaded curtain, bearing a tray of Tabs, chips, and dip. "Shoo!" she said to the cat and lowered the tray to the table. "That's Jimi Hendrix, Jimi for short," she said fondly.

Tee, Carol Anne, and I pulled on tight, wide-legged jeans, the hems hanging long over tall platform heels. My jeans laced sexily up the back with a brown leather cord. Carol Anne and I dressed in ruched tube tops with big shirts tied at the waist, and Theresa pulled on a low-cut long-sleeve tee, looping a fascinator around her neck. We rolled our tresses and sprayed them with Aqua Net and anointed ourselves with Debbie's patchouli oil. Merrily instructing Debbie not to wait up for us, we pranced out to the car and were on our way.

We shared a joint in the parked car at the arena giggling at the fishbowl cars around us of people doing the same, and then got out and threaded our way through the crowd. Channeled through a ticket line like minnows through a sluice, we pocketed our stubs and pressed on through the throng. Tee spotted our seats—numbers 8, 9, and 10—in the orchestra section about midway back from the stage. We settled in, buzzing with pot and anticipation. A bearded manager materialized from the depths of the darkened stage to ask if the crowd was ready for the band. On our feet in seconds, we screamed and clapped until the stage was illuminated. We squinted up at a neon image—the cover of the *Hotel California* album—at the rear of the stage. The band members strode onto the stage, hipshot and grinning. Glenn Frey, in a University of Colorado T-shirt and tight jeans, said deprecatingly, "We're the Eagles, from Los Angeles?" as if there might be a single soul in the auditorium with half a doubt. As the band led off with the eponymous song from the album, we were swept away, the bass vibrating through the soles of our shoes. The skunky-sweet, weed-infused air began to grow warmer. I peeled off my outer shirt and stuffed it into my suede hobo bag.

The low-tide crowd began its surge toward the stage. Everyone danced with abandon. Girls began scaling their boyfriends' shoulders. I felt a tug at the leather lacing of my jeans and looked for Theresa—my number one suspect—but both she and Carol Ann were clapping high above their heads. The undulating bodies were packed so closely it was difficult to turn. But when I did, I came face-to-face—more precisely, face-to-collarbone—with the best-looking guy I'd ever seen. I felt my pupils expand as the moment spun out. A spotlight that seemed to single out the two of us revealed the perfect cupid's bow of his lips, a white smile in tanned skin, clear gray eyes, a strong chin with a little cleft. His shaggy, longish hair was crayon-box maize.

Communicating to me through gestures, my mystery man offered a position astride his broad shoulders. He hoisted me up as the band launched into the encore, everyone's favorite song, "Take It Easy." My cavalier bore me closer to the stage, where the two of us were unwittingly immortalized on film our daughter would see thirty-five years later.

As the band left the stage to thunderous applause, he lowered me to my feet again. He gently held my upper arms, lowered his head, and paused, searching my eyes. The air around us felt charged somehow, full of portent. He kissed me lightly once. I ran my tongue across my top lip, tasting salt from his skin. He laughed softly. Carol Anne and Theresa appeared, both of them grinning like fools. I recovered enough to say, "I'm Robin Hamilton. These are my friends Theresa and Carol Ann."

"Dean Falconer," he said, smiling from me to my friends. "What are you ladies doing after?" He turned to a well-muscled jock and a petite brunette with an orange silk hibiscus blossom behind one ear. Dean introduced them as his friends Clay and Suzanne. They were headed to a party back in Georgetown, where they were students at Georgetown University. "You could follow us. I mean, if you'd feel more comfortable," Dean said.

Though instinctively cautious about taking off with a guy I'd literally just met, I couldn't deny the connection I'd felt with Dean Falconer. Theresa and Carol Anne were game. "There's safety in numbers," Tee murmured into my ear. "Besides, with our own car we could split anytime we want." And so we were off, chattering and reliving the concert, our wagon following Clay's stylish Cutlass Supreme through the darkness.

The main drag at GU was congested with late-night revelers who spilled from restaurants and stood on line in front of rollicking pizza joints and bars. Now I could see Dean's head in silhouette in the backseat; my stomach did a funny little flip in response. Four blocks over the Cutlass slowed in front of a brick building on the corner. There was a crowd of people in front, Styrofoam cups screwed into their hands. "This must be the place, chickies!" Carol Ann sang out.

We reapplied lip gloss, and Theresa opened a roll of peppermint Certs. "Ooh, I need one of those!" Carol Anne said.

Momentarily serious, Theresa asked me around a mint, "Do you want to be left alone with this guy, or should I stay close?"

"That remains to be seen," I said, taking a mint for myself. I raised one eyebrow at myself in the rearview mirror and inspected my mascara. "Let me talk to him for a while." Dean stepped to open our car doors. "A southern gentleman too!" I whispered.

Inside Dean's friend Dave's place, twenty or thirty people were smoking, drinking beer, and dancing to Boston's "More Than a Feeling" booming from a set of expensive speakers. Dean offered me a beer from one of the battered kegs lined up against one wall. We sat together on a blue-carpeted stair step and regarded the scene. From the loudest corner a skinny guy in a Keep on Truckin' T-shirt yelled, "Dude, quit bogarting that doobie!" Another guy in a rubber wolf mask with wild silver hair sticking up was blowing shotguns to a couple of giggly, wasted girls. Theresa and Carol Ann stood nearby, cups in hand, talking with Clay and Suzanne and another good-looking guy who was eyeing Theresa appreciatively. I sipped at my beer, hearing scraps of their conversation—good-natured arguing about which Eagles' album was the best.

"So where are you from Robin Hamilton?" Dean's eyes scanned my face as though it were a treasure map.

"My family lives in Manhattan. I'm a rising senior at NYU." I tilted my head to my friends. "Theresa's my roommate. She and Carol Ann and I drove down today for the concert." I grinned. "I know you're from the south. Where do you live?"

Dean lifted his chin and returned the grin. "Virginia. Home's just two and a half hours from here." The party was throbbing and so loud that Dean was practically shouting the last part. "Let's go outside," he said close to my ear. He stood and took my hand so naturally it was as if we were under the spell of some ancient alchemy. Theresa was dancing with the good-looking guy—who was grinning as though he couldn't believe his good fortune—at the center of a web of people. As Dean and I threaded our way to the door, I caught her eye and tipped her our okay wink.

Dean and I sat alone on a crumbling brick wall. Most of the others had drifted away or back inside. Dean told me he was a first-year grad student at GU, an aspiring architect. He loved baseball and was as big an Eagles fan as I was. As he spoke, I regarded the well-muscled forearms below his rolled-up flannel shirtsleeves, the hands with the short-clipped nails I preferred on a guy. The man was purely male, sexy as hell, but there was a gentle quality about him.

"You ready for another beer?" he asked.

"Not just yet." I was buzzing on his grin by then.

"You're a really beautiful girl, Robin. I couldn't stop looking at you at the concert."

Cheeks pinking, I bent over my cup and finished the last swallow of beer. The party was winding down, and people were beginning to leave in pairs. Tacitly Dean and I rose to move back inside. The Eagles' "Victim of Love" pulsed from the speakers. Tee and Carol Anne sat talking with Suzanne, Clay, the good-looking guy, and the dude in the Keep on Trucking T-shirt, who now wore the wolf mask, an unlit cigarette stuck between its grinning black lips. Dean poured beers for the two of us, and we took seats on a denim sofa stained with beer (and God knew what else). Though we joined the others in conversation, our eyes kept sliding to each other's faces.

When Theresa and Carol Anne were ready to leave, Dean's lips brushed my hair, and he said, "If you want to stay, I can drive you back later. I wish you would … stay."

I met his clear gray gaze, my heart pounding, and made a quick decision. "I'm going to stay on a little longer," I told the girls, trying to sound casual. "Dean can drive me back."

Carol Anne, her tongue wedged into the corner of her lips, wrote Debbie's phone number on the palm of my hand with a ballpoint pen.

Dave went upstairs with one of the giggly girls. We could all see her panties beneath her short dress as she tripped up the stairs. Clay and Suzanne and the good-looking guy, who looked decidedly morose, left for their apartments in the same building. Dean and I were alone. While he went to the bathroom, I popped a Cert and knelt in front of Dave's collection of albums. I sat back on my heels and flipped through them, looking to find something to fit my mood. As I lowered the needle on Fleetwood Mac's eponymous album, Dean reappeared. He pulled me to my feet, kissed me again, and led me in a slow dance to Christine McVie's "Warm Ways." Back on the sofa again, I slipped off my shoes and curled my feet beneath me. Much higher on Dean than on the weed and beer by that time, I pulled his face to mine. He slipped his hands into my hair, to cradle the back of my head, and kissed me, open-mouthed now. His mouth was delicious. I felt I would drown in the purest lust I'd ever experienced. We drifted between making out and talking for hours, getting up only to change records and once to eat fruit from Dave's fridge. Dean never touched me below the neck except to trace my collarbones with the pad of his thumb.

I woke and felt Dean's solid presence behind me, his breath, his chin in my hair. My lips stretched into a lazy smile. The clock on the sound system read 9:13. Unwilling to share my nasty morning mouth, I gingerly rose and stood looking down at him. The light from the window fell in stripes across his handsome face, his gold hair. Dean stirred but was still again.

I slipped into the bathroom, found a crumpled tube of Dave's Ultra Brite, and stood brushing my teeth with a finger. I had been right to trust Dean: the night could've been stamped with a PG rating. I finger-combed my hair, washed my face, and wiped the night's mascara from my eyes with a tissue. I opened the door and heard Dean in the kitchen. Suddenly shy as a geisha, I padded in. "Hi," I said and leaned against the counter.

He scored with "I knew you would still look pretty in the morning. Do you drink coffee?" At Dave's little glass-topped table we sipped coffee and ate glazed donuts from a box of Krispy Kremes we found on top of the refrigerator.

"You know, I'll be here all weekend," I said, my hands cradling a blue GU mug. "I'd *really* like to go back to Debbie's and take a shower."

When Dean went to shave and shower, I called Debbie's house from the phone on the kitchen wall. I'd neither seen nor heard any sign of Dave or the girl upstairs. I heard the drumming of Dean's shower, and spoke to Tee. "So what *happened?*" she begged. I could hear her happy-for-me smile. I told Tee Dean and I were headed out to Debbie's. "Take it easy, baby!" she said breezily.

CHAPTER

5

Dean

August 1977

The morning after the concert, Robin and I walked to my building around the corner from Dave's to pick up my Jeep. I regarded her long hair and asked, "Would you mind if I put the top down?" *Man, she was beautiful in the mellow morning light.*

From her bag Robin pulled a pair of aviator sunglasses and one of those ponytail holders with the plastic balls on it like my sister Leslie wore. "Weren't you ever a Boy Scout? *Always* be prepared," she said primly, pulling her hair back. Silver earrings hung from the sweet little ears I'd kissed the night before and held the sunlight. *I am such a schmuck.*

"Actually," I said with a grin, "I was an Eagle Scout, *am* an Eagle Scout. Once you achieve Eagle, you have it for life."

"Ah, of course you are."

"Growing up in a small town, that's what you did." I shrugged. Together, we put the top down on the Jeep. The day was going to be warm and sunny, and I had a pretty girl next to me. I aimed for Baltimore and pushed the Eagles' *On The Border* into the eight-track. Robin and I smiled at each other over the wind and the music. *Pretty as hell and an Eagles' fan to boot.*

As I swung the Jeep into Debbie's driveway, Robin invited me inside to wait. She'd told me Debbie was cool, but the bong on the woman's coffee table was a surprise. Debbie looked like a hippie past her expiration date, but she was nice. Sitting on the edge of a big ugly chair upholstered with cat hair, I chatted with Theresa and Carol Ann, liking Theresa immediately. Robin had told me that Theresa was like a sister to her and that she was torn apart about her leaving for Paris.

What the hell am I doing? I asked myself in that strange place, for about the fifth time in the last—I looked at my watch—thirteen hours. *Had it only been that long?* I was getting involved. I'd dated plenty of great girls in high school and college, but none had had such an instantaneous effect on me. I felt as if I had been struck by lightning or hit by a Mack truck or some damned thing.

I'd had an oblique view of Robin the last hour of the concert, and she had one foxy body: generous breasts, waist I could probably fit my hands around, long legs from canted hips though she wasn't tall, and one of those heart-shaped bottoms. The leather laces on the back of her jeans had taunted me. I'd known she'd be a prize astride my shoulders, and I hadn't been able to resist closing the gap between us to get her attention.

And the way she'd responded to *me*; it blew my mind. She seemed utterly fascinated by everything I said. And intelligence shone in her intense green eyes. She was classy Manhattan, private girls' school educated and headed for law school. But I had graduated magna cum laude from the University of Virginia, had a rich old man with a two-hundred-year-old horse farm, and was on my way to becoming an architect. So it wasn't her credentials that undid me.

I felt protective of this girl, as if she were one of those painted eggs my mother kept locked in a cabinet in the dining room, a Fabergé. I wanted to tuck Robin in my pocket for safekeeping. She reminded me of my youngest sister, Mary, who was fifteen and smart as hell and aspired to be an equine veterinarian. But at the same time, Robin had me so torqued up I wanted to nail her standing up. And she was clearly into me. She gazed at me as if I were a hot fudge sundae and she'd been on a diet for a year.

When she reappeared fresh and glowing from the shower, shiny hair spilling over her breasts, I swear my heart leaped. She was dressed casually in a different pair of jeans, a soft-looking mossy-green sweater, and little brown boots. Grace Slick was belting out "White Rabbit" from Debbie's speakers, which were the size of chifforobes. The imagery hit home: a potion labeled Robin Hamilton had cajoled, *"Drink me."* Damned if I wasn't falling in love.

I found myself utterly happy about the day. I wanted to take Robin to lunch at my favorite burger place, introduce her to my good friend James, show her the campus. I hadn't had a girlfriend since I'd been in DC. Robin made me realize I'd been lonely. I wanted to walk and talk with her. I wanted to spend every minute of the weekend with her.

I wanted her.

CHAPTER

6

Robin

1977

Dean and I were positively ravenous by the time we left Debbie's, so he made straight for the Tombs restaurant, a block from the historic GU campus gates. I took off my sunglasses and admired the exposed brick walls and rowing decor. My stomach rumbled loudly in response to the smell of grilling meat from the kitchen. "James is working," Dean said. He smiled and nodded in the direction of the bar. The room was noisy, packed with late-lunching students and locals as we made our way to the bar. James wore wire-rimmed glasses, his hair in a long blond ponytail. He was tall like Dean with the posture of a palace guard.

"Dude! How was the concert?" he asked, high-fiving Dean. James's grin was unaffected despite a sizable gap between his two front teeth. He noticed me then and smiled, lifting his chin in my direction. Dean introduced me. "This is Robin Hamilton from New York. We met at the concert last night." The words hung in the air like those in a cartoon bubble. Dean and I shared a look, realizing how they had sounded, and tacitly agreed to say no more. From the overhead speakers, Carly Simon's voice soared. "Nobody does it better."

James said, "Well, welcome, Robin from New York. What did you guys think about the show?" James was friendly, joking around with Dean while he filled drink orders with aplomb. We sat at a table with an unlit hurricane candle and red checked tablecloth and ordered cheeseburgers. Two more of Dean's friends came over to speak to us. I could tell he was proud to introduce me. When James had a break, he turned a chair around backward, straddled it, and asked me what I did in New York. Dean plucked two fries from the basket, dunked them in catsup, and nudged the basket toward his buddy. James was energetic and interesting; you just had to like him. We shared a chocolate brownie with ice cream and talked of the buzz of the times: President Carter's pardoning of the Vietnam draft dodgers, the *Star Wars* craze, the untimely death of Elvis Presley in Memphis.

Afterward with the Jeep's top down, the sun warm on our heads and shoulders, Dean pointed out special spots in Georgetown. He showed me the *Exorcist* steps at Prospect and Canal where scenes from *The Exorcist* had been filmed. We talked of other scary movies—we had both jumped a foot at the end of *Carrie* with Sissy Spacek, the part where the hand comes up out of the grave—and other favorite movies. We quoted lines from the movies *Jaws* and *One Flew Over the Cuckoo's Nest* and challenged each other to finish lines of dialogue, laughing in amazed pleasure.

"Do you want to see where I play baseball?" Dean asked shyly.
I could tell he really wanted to show it to me. He had been on
the baseball team in public school in Virginia but played just for
fun now, pickup games with friends. At the field, which was as
groomed and manicured as a Westminster hound, we drifted
toward the metal bleachers. "What a great day," Dean said,
looking around happily. He slipped an arm around my waist and
pulled me to him for a kiss. I smiled up at him, and he kissed me
again, lingeringly, and then a bunch of guys strode onto the field,
laughing and calling to each other.

"Tell me about your family," I said in the dappled sunlight,
twining my hair up into a ponytail again.

"Well, our home is a farm in Keswick near Charlottesville."

"You live *on a farm*?" I said, astonished.

"Yeah. It's over two hundred years old. My great-grandparents
named it Villeneuve, French for—"

"New colony or … settlement," I interrupted saucily. "I've had
seven years of French, actually."

"Ah, of course you have." Dean grinned.

"Touché. Just good ole Miss Pruitt's School training." I put my
hand on his back. "Sorry. Tell me more about Villeneuve."

"Well, it's not pretentious like it sounds," he said. "My mom
mucks around the barn in rubber boots half the time. She's
a peach, a great horsewoman. Villeneuve's a horse farm," he

explained. "My dad works as hard as the help. He loves it. He even does some of the bush hogging. There's always plenty to do on fifty acres." I interrupted to ask what in the world bush hogging was. Dean explained how they mowed the grass with a specialized cutter pulled by a tractor.

As the game on the field picked up, Dean leaned forward to watch, elbows on his knees, hands loosely clasped. "We usually have around fifteen horses, broodmares and a stallion, and there are always young foals that we sell off as weanlings or keep and train. Everybody in the family helps take care of the horses." He turned back to me with a grin. "If you ride a horse, you're expected to bathe and groom it yourself afterward, or woe be unto you."

I laughed, and he continued, "I've ridden all my life, my sisters too. We learned to ride before we learned to swim ... or ride bikes."

"I've never been on a horse in my life." I shook my head, marveling.

"*City* girl." Dean grinned. He took off his sunglasses and gazed at me. His eyes, the color of slate, dallied at my lips. He leaned in and kissed me again. The guy could kiss.

"The horses?" I reminded him with a grin.

He replaced his sunglasses. "Well, my dad and I foxhunt with our retired event horses." He began to run his hand through my hair from crown to ends. "There's a cool tradition every Thanksgiving morning called the Blessing of the Hounds. It's at a beautiful old gothic-style church right down the road from the farm." Dean's eyes behind his shades followed the baseball as it flew into foul territory.

"Shi-it, man!" the hitter, a fat guy in a Dodgers jersey yelled.

"They bless *the dogs*?" I asked.

"They do. The priest blesses the hunters, the hounds, and even the fox before the day's hunt. Hundreds of people come—it's quite the spectacle. Everybody's in full color dress."

"Do you wear one of those cute red coats?" I asked, picturing Dean looking prince-like on a horse, like in one of those hunting prints.

"They're actually called pinks."

I was fascinated. Dean's home sounded like the set of a movie. "What's the house on Villeneuve like?" I asked. I liked the taste of the pretty name Villeneuve and the images it conjured.

"It's a hundred-year-old Georgian, a two-story box. Mom has a lot of her mother's and my dad's mother's English antiques ... so it has a lot of authenticity about it."

"How far out in the country are you? Are you really ... isolated?"

"Nah, Charlottesville is only fifteen miles away. It's a college town but with a lot of history ... and culture, opportunity as they say. You know Thomas Jefferson's home Monticello is there."

"I didn't know that," I said thoughtfully.

"Folks say Charlottesville's the best of both worlds." His eyes lit up. "I'm going to have my own firm there. The countryside's beautiful—we're in the foothills of the Blue Ridge Mountains. They really do look blue—all different shades of blue—at different times of day." He fell silent again at the crack of a bat. Our eyes followed the fly ball, each of us lost in our own thoughts.

A gaggle of girls had come to watch the game (or maybe just the guys) and moved toward the bleachers. The baseball groupies, short shorts barely peeking below long jerseys, languidly flipping their hair, were making their presence known. Covertly I studied Dean's profile. The angle of the afternoon sun, more oblique now, gave it a chiseled elegance. He slipped an easy arm around me again and squeezed my shoulder. "I should have asked you what *you'd* like to do while you're in town."

"Well," I said after a moment, "there's a gallery in DC that I've always wanted to go to … if we have time." I looked up at the sun. "The Phillips Collection. But I'm not sure where it is. My favorite painting in the world is there, the most important Renoir."

Dean furrowed his brow in concentration, nodding his head. "That sounds familiar. We can find a phone booth and look up the address. Want to get some dinner in DC, too?"

"Sure! Sounds cool," I said.

Dean stood and dug into his pocket for his keys. "Let's boogie."

We found the address and headed to the museum. Dean slipped the Jeep easily through the congested afternoon traffic. I loved to watch him drive, the wind playing through his golden hair. *He is so gorgeous!* I noted a pack of gum and some crumpled receipts in the cubbyhole and a roach clip and lanyard tassel hanging from his key chain. I wanted to know everything about Dean Falconer. The song "Green-Eyed Lady" came on the radio. "Hey, it's your song," Dean said with a grin and turned it up. I laughed, pleased and knowing I'd never hear the song again without thinking of that moment. We found a spot on the street near Dupont Circle, and I fished my purse for quarters for the meter.

"This is an unexpected bonus to an already awesome day," I said as we walked down Rhode Island Street. Dean grinned and reached for my hand. We stopped to look at a *Star Wars* display in a colorful bookstore window. I told Dean about my mom and the book shop in New York.

"I'm diggin' that name. Speak Volumes," he said. "It's really creative."

"My mom suggested the name to the owner; she's clever that way."

Around the corner we found the three-story Greek Revival townhome that housed the Phillips Collection. Putting the pieces together in his mind, Dean said, "Man, now I know … I've read about the architects, Hornblower and Marshall. They began this project at the turn of the century. This was the first museum of modern art in America."

We weaved our way through the galleries of the collection. I'd never met a guy who was sophisticated enough to even pretend to enjoy a museum for my sake. I'd had dates who had taken me to the Met only to look furtively at their watches or stand jingling the coins in their pockets, but Dean really seemed to enjoy himself and discussed the art appreciatively.

"Here it is!" I breathed as we faced the painting we had come to see. "Renoir's *The Luncheon of the Boating Party*."

"Oh, *yeah*. Sure. I remember learning about this one in an art history class. It's real pretty ... the colors and the light."

"I *know*. That's the thing I love most about it. See how he used the white paint on the glasses to make them appear to shine? He was *such* a genius."

We stood soaking in the vibrant colors and the angle of the light. I wanted to run my fingers over the lifelike figure of Aline Charigot (later Madame Renoir) seated in the foreground and the brushstroked fur of her little dog perched before her on the table. Years later at the Musée D'Orsay in Paris I would gaze at a mortar bust of Madame Renoir sculpted by her husband. And Tee beside me would murmur, "Now *that's love*."

After a moment Dean spoke again. He sounded like an excited boy. "I'm going to backpack through Europe one day, see all the best museums, the ancient architecture in France and Italy ... Germany and Czechoslovakia. The buildings over there—the cathedrals, monoliths—make ours look like they were made of Tinkertoys. You know what I mean?"

I nodded, picturing the two of us holding hands across a sidewalk café table in Paris, a red beret topping my hair like a cherry.

Back outside the museum, I said, "That was *far out*, Dean. Thank you!" I did a little skip-jump up to high-five him on the sidewalk.

He smiled down at me. "I've never met a girl like you, Robin. You make me feel … just … happy … all the time. I know that sounds sappy as shit. But it's true."

"I'm pretty happy too," I said quietly, my heart pounding.

It was approaching the dinner hour. Dean had offered to take me out, but I suggested now that we pick up a bake-it-yourself pizza and take it back to his place. I didn't want to share Dean anymore. In the Jeep at the next light he turned to regard me solemnly. Moonstone eyes clear, both hands on the wheel, he asked, "Do you want to stay with me tonight, Robin?" The air around us felt effervescent.

"Yeah," the new brazen me answered.

And *that* was *that*.

Back at Dean's place, while Dean was in the bathroom, I placed a call to Debbie's house from the kitchen, which was as clean as a new paper bag except for a couple of reddish Rorschach splotches on the stove. *Did guys never wipe down stovetops or counters?* Dean returned and moved behind me. He raised my hank of hair as I ended my conversation with Carol Ann and kissed the back of my neck. He had brushed his teeth. He opened the fridge and pulled out a couple of beers. Inside I glimpsed what looked like a half case of beer, an open package of hotdogs, an egg carton, sticky condiment bottles, and little else. I was glad we'd gotten the pizza. Dean preheated the oven.

I nodded my agreement and headed to the bathroom. I thanked God Dean had an extra toothbrush. Surrounded by the masculine smells of shaving lotions and deodorant soap, I was relieved the fixtures appeared to be pretty clean. I perched on the toilet, winding tissue around my hand, and glimpsed a blue bar of soap on a rope in the shower. I grinned, thinking every guy must have an aunt who gave him soap on a rope for Christmas. I appraised a stack of green and brown towels on a shelf and the forest-green robe hanging on the back of the door.

I washed my hands and pulled the terry robe to my face to see if it smelled like Dean. Breathing the scent of him, I pretended to swoon, vamping for my reflection in the mirror. "How is this real?" I breathed aloud. Two days ago I'd had no idea that a guy named Dean Falconer existed, and already I felt I was in love with him.

The object of my desire sat cross-legged on the front room floor, thumbing through albums. "Hey, beautiful," he said and handed me a beer. "Make yourself at home."

"I really like your place," I said softly and took a measured sip. "It looks like you." Dean grinned and slid *Frampton Comes Alive* from its jacket. He dusted the album with his sleeve.

"I'm putting the pizza in, okay?" Dean asked.

"Yes, please." I sat down on the tasteful green plaid sofa and crossed my legs in a practiced fetching way. I sat my beer down on the one scarred end table lit by an attractive brass lamp and wondered if Dean's mother had helped with his decor. To my right an enormous drafting table regimented a full quadrant of the room. I smiled at a brigade of sharpened drawing pencils and white erasers lined up with perfect precision. An M. C. Escher poster I recognized, the one with the convoluted staircases, was pinned simply to the wall above. I got up and wandered over for a closer look at the lines on a large pad of paper atop the table. "Will you show me your work?" I asked.

Dean handed me up onto the stool and leaned over my shoulder, smelling like a handful of tender green leaves. He pointed to details, telling me about his current residential design project. "It's been a killer, mostly finished, all due on Tuesday. I'm glad I'll have something to keep me busy tomorrow." We looked at each other. "After you're gone I mean." Until then, we hadn't spoken of the inevitability of Sunday.

We moved to the sofa. Frampton crooned, "I'm in you, you're in me …"

"There's a reason we met each other, you know, Dean? But it's impossible for now, isn't it?" I searched his eyes.

"We seem so right together, sweetheart. We'll just … find a way to see each other as often as we can … We'll figure it out," he said firmly. As he leaned in to kiss me, the oven timer beeped. "What timing," he said.

"No pun intended." I grinned. We rose to see about dinner. I found the plates and napkins and laid them out on the coffee table.

"Do you have any candles?" I asked.

"My sister Leslie gave me one of those big scented ones ... It's around here somewhere." He scavenged through cabinets and came up with a chunky gold column. He fished a book of matches from a drawer. We sat on the carpet, legs beneath the table, to eat.

"Would you mind if I turned on the Yankees game?" he asked. "We can turn the sound off and still listen to the music." I nodded, mouth full of cheese and sauce. "They're headed for the World Series this year. I wanna see 'em win it." He grinned. I wiped a smear of sauce from his cheek with my napkin. I liked watching the man talk about the things he loved.

After dinner, he cleared the plates and insisted he would wash them the next day. He snared fresh beers for us, and we moved back to the sofa. He rolled his sleeves down and placed an arm around me. I nuzzled my head on his chest in the sweet hollow between his neck and one shoulder and listened to the music, the Doobie Brothers now. I was as content as a cat with a bowl of sweet cream. The Yankees with a comfortable lead, Dean turned the game off and grinned. "Want to get high?"

"I hoped you had some," I said. Dean swung down the hall to his bedroom and came back with a joint. He tipped it into the candle's flame, and we passed it back and forth, nodding our heads to the music. A red-and-black dartboard hung above a tiny recessed dry bar topped with an ice bucket and a few dusty UVA beer glasses. "Can we play darts? I bet I can take you."

Dean laughed. "Competitive, are we, Robin? I'll take you on." We horsed around throwing darts and laughing, and I beat him, two games to one. The games were over then.

"A hot shower with that soap on a rope I saw in there would feel great," I murmured and pushed my lips into a sexy pout.

Dean looked down at me, eyes lazy-lidded, head cocked, and smiled. "Would you like some company?"

"That might be nice," I said silkily and pulled him toward the back. We brushed our teeth again, together, and it didn't even feel awkward.

"Let me warm it up for us." Dean reached to turn on the water, unbuttoned his shirt, and pulled his arms from the long sleeves.

Oh, my. He had just the right amount of chest hair for my liking, golden like the rest of him. A curling swath of it crept low over his hard young belly, a narrow strip disappearing below the waistband of his Levi's. My heart thudded in my throat as I stood captivated, watching his every move. Dean unzipped his jeans and let them and his boxers drop in one motion, never taking his eyes from mine. He was as beautiful as Michelangelo's *David* and clearly aroused for me. He stepped into the shower and called over his shoulder, "Come on in when you're ready."

Gulping, I stripped to my bra and panties and paused and then peeled them off as well. I followed him into the steamy enclosure. Dean pivoted us so the warm water was on my back and shoulders and slid the door closed. He looked me slowly up and down. "You have a gorgeous body." My chest rose and fell heavily with my breathing. He made a big show of placing the soap on a rope around his neck, raised one dark eyebrow, and wiggled it. I laughed, a throaty laugh that sounded like Barbara Stanwyck's in the movies. Dean's skin was pure velvet under the pads of my fingers. I grew weak-kneed with desire as we began to kiss more deeply. He nibbled my bottom lip, my ears, and the hollow of my throat as the warm water cascaded over us. When I began squeezing my hair, Dean turned off the water and shepherded me out. He dried me gently with one of the green towels. I felt cosseted and smoothed, though the core of me pulsed with anticipation. He wrapped me in the big green robe, himself in a towel. "That was the hall of fame of showers," he said, his beautiful mouth, rosier from kissing, stretching into a grin.

"Indeed." I reached for his blow-dryer to give my mane a perfunctory drying. I turned off the dryer and heard the opening notes of *Hotel California*. Dean padded back to me and led me to his room.

I was dying to see his most intimate space and what it would reveal about him. I pretended not to notice the bed at once, looking pointedly to the chest of drawers. On its top was a baseball in the palm of a well-oiled leather glove, a handsome tortoiseshell box, and a small pewter tray of coins and pockety things, the coins stacked by size in orderly quarter towers and nickel and dime skyscrapers, a tiny minted city. I looked more closely at an engraved brass square atop the box that bore the initials DTF in block-style letters. "What does the *T* stand for?"

"You'll have to guess," he said.

Then I turned to the elephant in the middle of the floor—the massive bed, a water bed, the first I'd ever seen. But it was not at all sleazy looking as I'd imagined. It was tastefully framed in wood veneer. A striped spread cloaked the expanse. Stacks of books lay on the floor against the walls around its perimeter—school texts, design and architectural volumes, some classic novels, and sports magazines—no *Playboys*. About a week's worth of clothing was draped over a butler's rack in one corner, but otherwise the room was neat. I was gratified to see no dirty underwear on the floor or plates of fossilized food, as Tee and I had seen in some our friends' apartments. A goosenecked reading lamp on the headboard lit a soft, warm circle on the bed.

A box of tissues, a UVA mascot figure, and a framed picture sat on the shelf of the headboard, the picture like one of those family Christmas-card photos. I sat down on the bed and reached for the frame, giggling and righting myself as a wave rolled away from me and back again. "Your family!" I said.

Dean sat down beside me. "Yeah, that was two years ago." He pointed to the tall, blond man. "That's my dad, Tom—"

"Thomas!" I interrupted, triumphant.

"Close, but wrong." He grinned. "It's Thompson actually; I'm a junior." He indicated the striking petite, dark-haired woman. "My mom, Laurel." And indicating each of the smiling Falconer girls, he said, "My sisters, Leslie and Mary."

I looked at each of them closely. "It's a good family, a happy one I can tell. You and Leslie look like your dad."

"We do." He replaced the frame. "What's *your* full name?"

"Robin Courtwright Hamilton from head to toe," I said creamily.

"Are you on the pill, Robin Courtwright Hamilton?"

"Absolutely," she said in my voice.

Dean leaned back against the pillows, watching me speculatively. He looked thoroughly edible. Lazily he reached to untie the robe's sash, and I wriggled my shoulders to let it fall around my hips. He pulled me down and over him, to lie along his length. The robe and towel fell away like smoldering cinders. "Robin, I want you so much."

I wasn't a virgin, but I wasn't accomplished in bed. I sensed that with Dean it wouldn't matter. I met his gaze. "I want you too," I breathed. "I think I'm in love with you."

"It's crazy," he said, his hands moving the length of my back to caress my bottom, "but I feel the same way."

It began then. I was lost and found, both at the same time. We made love once, twice, and a third time that night—well, five times total if the next morning counts—the water bed rocking us like a single small craft as we moved together. We got up to change the music and drink water at intervals, holding each other at the kitchen sink. Toward morning we drifted as a chiming rain began.

A while later, Dean sat down beside me, forming a swell of wave that bumped me upward. I woke and blinked at the morning light around his head, a nimbus of gold. He had showered again and smelled of soap and coffee. He wore a freshly laundered gray GU baseball T-shirt over his jeans. He bent to kiss me. "Good morning, gorgeous."

"Let me catch up with you first," I said, ducking away and drawing on a robe. I climbed from the bed—climbing from the middle of a water bed is neither an easy nor graceful venture—to brush my teeth and shower. Dean laughed and called after me, "I'm going to go make us some eggs; they're my specialty."

Wrapped in the green robe once more, I joined Dean in the kitchen, and we ate wobbly scrambled eggs out of the pan like starved animals. "These are *delicious*," I moaned.

"Good, 'cause they're about the only thing I'm really good at."

"Oh, I could name a few other things," I said coyly.

He grinned, stretching his arms, and scratched his head. "I could use a nap already ... don't know *why* I'm so beat."

"Would you like some company?" Laughing, we moved back to the bedroom, made love, and talked quietly, limbs entwined, until it was time to go.

We were bummed then, climbing into the Jeep for the last time. We talked of the fall to come and made tentative plans for Dean to take the train to New York for a long weekend in three weeks' time. He tried on a cheerful expression for me: "We'll figure it out."

Dean came into Debbie's house to say good-bye to the others and then walked me back out onto the porch. We gravely regarded the mailbox, shaped like a Volkswagen bus, beside the front door. A rolled-up circular stuck out its back door.

"It was amazing," I said, "all of it."

We kissed and kissed, and then Dean stepped away. "We'll figure it out," he said. "I love you. See you in three weeks." I stood there hugging myself, trying not to cry, and waved until the green Jeep turned the corner and out of sight.

CHAPTER

7

Robin

1978

I spent my senior year of college hermit-like, nurturing hurt from twin betrayals: my best friend's departure and the loss of my first love. My longing was a smarting sting no ointment could assuage. Colorful postcards with excited scrawls of the things Tee had seen and done in Paris appeared regularly in the brownstone's mail slot. In the first weeks Theresa had fallen in love with the city of lights. In three months' time, she had fallen for Laurent Pelletier, a sexy painter she'd met at a café in Montmartre. Laurent was twice Theresa's age with two daughters. I wondered if Tee's upbringing sans father had drawn her to Laurent. Theresa's mother wrote to me concerned that the man would permanently tie her daughter to France. We both waited to see. Theresa transferred to a small university to finish her last quarter credits and married her Frenchman in a simple civil ceremony. *Oh, Tee.*

I had returned to live at home. My intuitive parents gave me a wide berth. I studied prodigiously. As a result, my final GPA was so stellar I applied to several law schools in the northeast, including Georgetown's prestigious school of law. I was accepted for the fall semester of 1978. I was well aware Dean might be in DC but didn't permit myself to think about him or our time together.

He had never written. He had never called.

If I saw Dean Falconer again, I didn't know how I would react.

"I think Georgetown would be a good choice," my mother innocently enthused. "The change of scenery and an exciting new city to explore will do you good. You have a wonderful life ahead of you, darling." I knew my parents had been concerned about me, but they had said little until then, their faith in my good sense and resiliency unflagging.

But I had written to Theresa, a long, tear-stained, angst-infused letter. She wrote back immediately and, like Mom, encouraged me to go to Georgetown. "If it's meant to be, you and Dean will get together again," she said. "If not, at least you'll be getting on with your life. Don't let this knock the wheels off your law-school plans."

Georgetown beckoned to me like the outstretched hand of God on the ceiling of the Sistine Chapel. There was really no choice about going. My year of self-pity had come to an end. A pragmatic plan in place, I found a one-room studio apartment in a pretty nice building near the school of law.

The Capitol Hill area of Washington, DC, where energetic young movers and shakers lived and worked was exciting. It was common to see politicians striding along Pennsylvania Avenue discussing legislation, arguing with lobbyists or reporters, staffers scurrying like tugboats in their wakes. I was in awe of the female representatives and legislative correspondents who populated the bustling lunch-hour spots. They were elegant in their tailored suits, high heels tapping briskly on to the next meeting. The superambitious shopped the same well-stocked markets on 7th Street that I did.

I walked past colorful old row houses nestled among grand early-nineteenth-century manor houses and came to know the city. Each vista seemed so expansive. It hadn't occurred to me before how vertical my New York City perspective had been. One Saturday I took the bus to Arlington Cemetery and wandered the immaculate grounds beneath great shade trees—chestnut, oak, linden. I sat before the Tomb of the Unknown Soldier amid tourists from the four corners of the world to wait for the changing-of-the-guard ceremony, the smoothed marble steps cool beneath my bottom. Stoic guards in pristine uniforms marched, rifles on their shoulders, before the tomb. Most of them didn't look old enough to shave. My dad would be pleased that I'd witnessed the moving event.

In a tangle of Asian tourists I regarded the grave of President John F. Kennedy, the poignant eternal flame. The shutter clicks of a dozen cameras punctuated the tourists' brisk conversation. And then in front I saw a flash of shaggy gold hair on a head that towered above the others. I felt as if I'd mainlined adrenaline, my heart beating crazily. I stood motionless as the figure turned from the graves. In the circle of the guy's arm was a lovely young Asian woman. They chatted softly, intent on each other, her bright face turned up to his. It was not Dean. I wound my way back down the hill to the visitor center on trembling legs.

The next afternoon some wistful internal compass guided me back to the Phillips Collection. Feeling the old familiar stab of pain, I took a deep breath and propelled myself inside. I sat alone on the padded leather bench in the gallery of *Luncheon of the Boating Party* and allowed the painting's luminous beauty to wash over me. It was a small victory in my recovery from Dean Falconer.

I met my first friend. Stepping into the elevator of my building one evening after a class, I met a girl I'd seen around the building. "Hello, I'm Robin," I said at the same time she spoke in a Cincinnati accent: "Hi. I'm Cindy." We laughed, and I complimented her on her striking outfit.

"I'm meeting some people at Feathers. I'd invite you to come," she said, regarding my nonparty clothes, jeans and loafers, "but I'm late as hell already."

"Oh, that's okay, but I'd love to go sometime," I said and realized it was true.

Thursday afternoon, Cindy, who was also a first-year law student, knocked on my door. She had been out until three that morning but looked as fresh and smoothed as rising dough. In the time I knew Cindy I never once heard her mention studying. She was tall, with a chest as flat as a boy's and legs as bowed as a career bull rider's, but she had learned how to dress and always looked terrific. Cindy's carefree attitude was what I needed to get back out again.

Dressed carefully in slinky dresses, Bare Trap platform shoes, and often a silk flower pinned behind an ear, we made the disco scene with regularity. I drank in every minute as if it were a potion for forgetfulness. One Saturday night Cindy and I pranced into Spin!, a disco as rowdy as a circus and favored by thirsty Georgetown law students. The music met us like the blast from a passing subway car. I felt the reverberating beat from KC and the Sunshine Band's "I'm Your Boogie Man" through the soles of my shoes as we waited to be seated. I knew I looked good. In the crow's nest that night was the popular DJ Felix "FM" Moore whose outrageous banter made us blush. Under the mirror balls my dress shimmered like a mermaid's tail. Aware of the pairs of male eyes tracking our movements, we ordered drinks and sat moving our shoulders to the music. "Who will the lucky ones be?" Cindy asked with a grin. Her black hair was pulled so tightly back she looked exotic, like a geisha in the dim light. A bored candy-and-cigarette girl in a spandex jumpsuit languidly threaded her way through the tables peddling Salems, Marlboros, and enough Junior Mints and Cracker Jacks to satisfy any case of the munchies.

Talk from tables drifted like the bruise-colored haze of smoke. John Giannangelo, Democratic Congressman from New York and minor celebrity, and his entourage were partying in one of the side niches. A tidal wave of Aramis made it to our table before two interchangeable guys did: Fred and Frank. I wondered who wore all the cologne, maybe both of them. In big-collared shirts, tight jeans, and platform shoes, they looked like extras for the film *Saturday Night Fever.* We hit the teeming floor to Chic's "Le

Freak" and danced two more numbers. When a slow song began, my partner, Fred, grinned and pulled me to him. I stepped away as though he had popped the top on a grenade and broke away for the ladies' room. Cindy giggled hysterically at my heels.

"You can't smell it on me, can you?" I shrieked, scrubbing at my hands and arms at the restroom sink.

"No, but I can see it! It's like a tattoo!" Cindy howled.

We slunk out hoping Fred and Frank wouldn't be waiting. A pale young man in a suit so severely conservative he was either a mortician or an earnest young aide approached. A bloody square of tissue stuck to a nick under his chin. "Hello, ladies," he said. "Congressman Giannangelo would like you to join him at his table." Cindy and I looked at each other with big eyes and then shrugged *why not?* We would at least score free drinks.

John Giannangelo was a commanding presence, powerfully built with a big-featured face, not conventionally handsome but arresting. He rose and motioned Cindy and me over. Hooded black eyes under a head of obsidian curls lingered on my face. He said he had noticed our grace and beauty on the dance floor. *Okay, he's hokey,* I thought. But the man was funny and charming, his manners unimpeachable. John spread his hands. "I can get you into any disco in DC, even the members-only clubs," he said, as though his address was 1600 Pennsylvania.

I had a hard time pretending not to see the tissue on the young aide Curtis's face and finally pointed meaningfully at my own chin. As his fingers brushed the spot, he flushed a deep plum and furtively dipped a paper napkin in his drink to dab at it. I smiled at him reassuringly. After a few minutes, his equanimity restored, he asked Cindy to dance. John moved to sit next to me. "Do you have plans for dinner tomorrow evening, Robin?" Recently divorced, he explained he needed a beautiful date for a business dinner. "It will be a nice affair at the Herald Inn on N Street. Do you know it? As a fellow New Yorker, I would be honored if you would accompany me." I knew the hurt I had suffered the last year made me vulnerable to the attention. Being made to feel special, singled out by such a powerful man, was a heady feeling. I had no intention of getting involved with a much-older man, let alone a congressman, but could I turn down such a fancy dinner date? I accepted but sidestepped giving him my address, instead suggesting we meet at the inn.

I dressed in the pearls my parents had given me for my eighteenth birthday and a soft brown wrap dress. I wound my chestnut mane into a sophisticated French twist. I splurged on a taxi and arrived just as John's elegant black limousine pulled to double-park at the door. He launched his big frame from the car, dismissed the driver with a single thump of his fist on the trunk, and joined me on the sidewalk. Exclaiming over my dress and hairstyle, he inclined his arm, and we mounted the front steps.

A large jade Buddha in a niche over a Victorian sofa greeted us just inside. Amused, I regarded the funky decor as we moved through the lobby: warm wood paneling, colonial prints, splashy French bar posters, silk flowers, marble fireplaces, and smoothed oak-planked floors. John took my wrap and handed it off to a tiny coat-check woman who blinked at him in recognition from behind enormous blue eyeglasses. "Shall we?" John said, pocketing the claim tag, his hand at the small of my back. The second-floor dining room was roped off from the eyes of curious uninvited guests with a braided gold cord like you would see in a theater. A silent waiter ushered us inside a mahogany-paneled room set about with candles and flowers on heavy Victorian sideboards and the center of a round table for twelve. Several well-heeled people were already gathered. John introduced me to his friends, one a French diplomat on my right, the first native Frenchman I'd ever met. John smiled in surprised appreciation as I conversed with the man in French over cocktails. The Frenchman had not been to America before and found it loud and brash, the food perplexing. A stout diplomat and his wife, who appeared to have been spray starched, ignored me completely. I looked around brightly, listening to the casual conversation. Apparently I wouldn't be hearing any earth-shattering political business. I talked mainly with John, on my left, about New York City. We were served a four-course meal, oysters Florentine and beef tournedos, with champagne and several expensive wine selections.

When I felt John's thigh press against mine under the table, I pushed back from my dish of bananas Foster and asked to be excused. In the powder room I chatted with the exquisitely beautiful black woman who had smiled at me a couple of times across the table. As we inspected our makeup, she introduced herself as Felicia, the date of Senator Hopkins from Maryland. The way she said it made me suspect she was a professional. I was rinsing with mouthwash from a little paper cup when Felicia asked, "Are you seeing Congressman Giannangelo?"

"Oh, no!" I almost inhaled the stuff before spitting it in the sink. "Just tonight," I added and then felt like a complete idiot. I backpedaled, dabbing at my face with a towel. "I mean …"

"Don't worry, baby," Felicia laughed softly. She pursed her mouth and reapplied red, red lipstick.

After coffee, the party moved to the dark paneled bar downstairs for brandy. I had had several glasses of wine and wanted to keep my wits about me. I eschewed the proffered brandy and asked for a glass of water. *Aha*, I thought as I glimpsed Felicia and the senator mounting a back staircase.

John murmured in my ear, his breath hot and heavy with liquor, asking if I would like to join him in his room for a nightcap. I was on my feet in a heartbeat, looking down at him. I managed a gracious smile and thanked him for the evening, claiming an early-morning class. "Okay, honey," he said and rose, swaying slightly on his feet, his big hands raised in mock surrender. "Another time." But I thought I detected a glint of anger in his black eyes.

I buckled my seatbelt in the back of the taxi and realized what a fool I'd been. I should have known that the man's motives couldn't have been pure. But flattery can be its own master, one of my grandmother's aphorisms. I was a little afraid of John now and resolved to have nothing further to do with him. Two afternoons later I turned the corner to my apartment and, burdened with grocery bags, fumbled for my key. I almost tripped over the long white box propped against my door. I sat the bags down and curiously opened the box labeled with the Georgetown Blooms branding. Nestled in tissue was a sheaf of dewy, long-stemmed yellow roses. The simple white card inside gave only the name John and a phone number. How naive I had been to believe he couldn't find my address! I crammed the box, tissue, and pungent flowers into the garbage chute, thorns tearing at my shaking hands. Fleeing to the safety of my apartment, I brushed past two neighbors coming down the hall. They stopped a heated argument about the phone bill long enough to stare at me as if I had snakes for hair.

I ventured to classes that week almost furtively, expecting to see the man around every corner, like the leering ghoul he'd become in my imagination. By the middle of the next week, I'd heard nothing further from Giannangelo and began to relax.

CHAPTER

8

Robin

1978

Despite everything, I yearned for Dean Falconer. I recalled in vivid detail the magical weekend and replayed over and over the words we had spoken to each other. No promises had been made, but nothing about Dean had given me reason to suspect he was insincere or a user. I'd been in DC for three weeks, and our paths had not crossed.

The first week of October, the air crisp and tinged with autumn, I walked to the law library to return casebooks. It was the sweater weather I loved best, the breeze intoxicating. I was wearing my favorite cobalt-and-mustard-striped sweater with a pair of denim gauchos and brown riding boots. I wandered into a small park and claimed an empty bench. I had been reading for hours and lay my head back to gaze into the arching limbs of a maple tree. Its green and gold-going-tangerine leaves swayed gently, dappling the sunlight that fell around me. I closed my eyes.

"Robin? I thought it was you," Dean said stiffly. Only he could say my name in a way that made my entire body respond. The man I'd tried to will away from my subconscious stood before me, the sun gilding his wavy hair, which was shorter now. My heart bobbed into my throat like an apple in a tub of water. Dean's face was as lean as a blade, tight with apprehension. Two guys bisected the grass, yukking it up about mustache rides. Dean scowled at them and filled the awkwardness. "How are you? Are you in law school here?" He had remembered my plans. Torn between telling him to go straight to hell and humbling myself long enough to get an explanation, I decided I wouldn't cut off my nose to spite my face. I had to know the truth. I would hear what he had to say.

"I'm at GU law, yes," I said, cool, defensive.

"Can I sit down?" he asked miserably. I moved my purse, indicating the bench with a flip of a trembling hand.

He sat heavily, his expression miserable. "I fucked it up, Robin."

"You certainly did," I said, not looking at him. "*Royally.*"

"The week after the concert last year, my dad was in an accident. He was *killed*, Robin," he said, his face like wax before a fire.

"Oh, Dean," I cried, horrified. I turned to him, my efforts to be aloof forgotten.

"He was shot ... by one of his best friends. They were out hunting. It was ... horrible. We were afraid Bill—his friend—was going to commit suicide over it." Blinded by tears, I groped to place a supportive hand on Dean's shoulder. "My uncle called me home. My mom was devastated, just lost, and the girls …"

"I'm so sorry, Dean."

He swiped at his eyes with the knuckles of one tanned hand. "I stayed home for a semester and took over Dad's work on the farm." He dragged his eyes to mine. "I was too freaked out to call you at first … holding Mom and the girls together was … the hardest thing I've ever done in my life. Then as the weeks went by, it just got … harder … and then too much time had gone by."

I looked at him.

"I know that's no excuse! But when I did call you, your number was disconnected. I figured you had … moved on," he said. My heart felt like a sponge squeezed of its water.

His eyes captured mine. "Robin, I … our time together … it was unreal."

"Yeah. It was, Dean." We watched a pair of agate-eyed pigeons—blue gray and purple speckled above, pink legs below—bob and stagger in search of crumbs. The breeze lifted and teased at our hair. I gathered my thoughts like an armful of straw. "I knew it wasn't like you to just … drop me like that. But I felt almost … buried … with hurt all this time. My senior year of college alone, Theresa in Paris." I paused, fighting a fresh onslaught of tears. "It was … so hard getting over you. I moved home with my parents. I applied to law schools, and I came here."

"I'm so sorry … what I put you through." His voice sounded as though his throat had been sanded.

We sat without words for a suspended time. Finally, I looked at him again, the corners of my lips rising into the semblance of a smile. Dean twisted on the bench to face me and sought my eyes. "Robin, will you forgive me?" he pleaded, his face naked, exposed.

After a moment, I answered gently, "I can."

Dean breathed out a titanic breath of relief. I laid my hand palm up between us on the bench. He covered it with his. We sat for a moment palms together, as if drawing strength.

"Are you seeing anyone now, Robin?" he asked then. I heard the soft edge of hope in his words.

"I'm not seeing anyone … haven't seen anyone actually since you. Since you left. Are you? Seeing someone?" A military helicopter chopped overhead, flying low, scattering the pigeons. We followed it with our eyes.

"Actually, I've been up to my neck in women," he said, a hand flat under his chin, "my mother and sisters." We laughed a little. Dean looked at his watch, the one I remembered, the one I'd seen on the tanned wrist in my dreams. "I have a class at five fifteen. May I call you sometime, Robin?"

"I hope you will," I said quietly. Hope bloomed like a mushroom cloud in my chest. I wrote my number on the back page of one of his textbooks.

The very next day, a Thursday, he did call. The beautiful patch of weather had held; the sky was cerulean. We met at the same park to study.

Dean and I spread my old patchwork quilt beneath a yellow-leaved walnut tree, its sprawling limbs a canopy. We lay back reading, balled-up-jacket pillows beneath our heads.

Dean's voice floated on the breeze; he sounded shy. "This kind of reminds me of the afternoon that weekend … at the ball field, before we went to the art gallery. Do you remember?" The wind played through the dark, dark branches of the tree overhead. A yellow leaf drifted to my chest. With Dean's proximity, red-and-blue checked shirtsleeve rolled up a brown forearm, the meter of his breath, I found I had read the same passage on constitutional law about four times. "But I was kissing you then," he said.

"I was thinking the same thing," I said. Tears pricked behind my lids. He rolled onto his elbow and gazed down at me. I looked into his clear gray eyes. Dean traced my lips with one finger. Top lip. Bottom lip. It had been so long. I twined my arms around his neck, steel to magnet. Again.

The next morning the skies were leaden, pregnant with rain, a marked contrast from the day before. Dean and I had planned to meet at my place after our classes and make plans. But he arrived at my apartment in a deluge, and history repeated itself. We spent the afternoon in my bed, Dean's shirt and pants dripping down the side of my shower curtain.

Making love with Dean was even better than before, sweeter and more intense because of the time we'd lost. As I moved above him, my hair fell around his neck and shoulders. He murmured, "My gorgeous girl ... I love you."

My throat caught, full of joy. "I love you too."

Saturday night we went dancing for the first time together, with Cindy; her new boyfriend, Kurt; Dean's friend Clay; and Clay's girlfriend, Helen. I was thrilled to be out as a couple with gorgeous Dean. We still loved rock and roll, the Eagles best, but disco music was made for dancing: the Latin influences and synthesized beat made you want to move. At Cagney's we waited fifteen minutes for a table near the dance floor. I watched Dean walk over and call something to the DJ.

"What are you up to?" I asked with a grin.

He pointed toward a mock innocent expression. "Who me?"

When the song "Fly, Robin, Fly" began, I jumped up and pulled him to the dance floor, tossing my skirt like a flamenco dancer. Later, we drifted into Spin! Frank "FM" Moore was off that night. The crowd was thinner, and we easily found a good table. We sipped drinks and enjoyed the night's more-soulful black bands, like the Gap Band. Dean and I sat close together, holding hands and kissing.

I glanced at the dance floor and did a double take at a large, well-dressed man doing a barely passable hustle with several young women. John Giannangelo was a distinctive presence, his head like that on a Roman coin. My heart in my throat, I excused myself to go to the ladies' room. I stood over the sink nauseated and trembling and allowed the cold water to pool between my wrists. Cindy came to check on me. "Robin, you okay? Dean and I were worried about you."

"I'm fine ... but Cindy! I saw John Giannangelo on the dance floor!"

"Oh no! Really?" Her head jerked to the back of the door as if the congressman would be peering in. "But surely he won't bother you tonight; you're with Dean." She handed me some paper towels. "C'mon, honey, let's go back."

As we approached the table, Dean looked up, concerned, but Cindy mouthed to him, "She's okay." No sign of the congressman.

Dean regarded me. "Where were you, sweetheart? You okay?"

"Fine." I smiled. "I was just feeling a little ... light-headed."

"Well, let's get you home and into bed," he murmured close to my ear. "I'll be just what the doctor ordered." And he was. Just.

October passed into November, the weather sharp-edged and beautiful. The trees released their tenuous hold on their leaves. The leaves drifted down, becoming a crunchy carpet for our feet. The days Dean and I spent together passed idyllically. Both our workloads ramped up, and we studied long hours together. On the nights we spent at his new apartment, this one closer to mine, Dean was often late at his drafting table, drinking coffee, a windfall of crumpled paper around his stool.

One cold night, I awoke to find him missing from bed and padded into the living room in one of his button-down shirts and a pair of black panties. Dean, in a pair of UVA boxers, was bent over his table, his beautiful shoulders knotted and hunched. I moved behind him and wrapped my arms around him. He reached to hold my forearms and asked, "Hi, sweetheart, did I wake you?"

"No, I was just chilly," I said, scrubbing my cold nose into his neck. I began to massage the knots from his shoulders. He stretched his neck like a satisfied tomcat. "Am I distracting you?" I breathed into his ear.

"You, my love, are a welcome distraction," he said and pulled me into his lap. We kissed, his mouth tasting sweet, of coffee. Greedy and impatient, I pushed our clothes aside and lowered myself to him.

Dean clicked off the gooseneck lamp clipped to the table. I slipped into the bathroom. My cheeks were flushed and rosy in the mirror. I grinned at myself and padded to the bedroom for seconds.

Dean was everything I dreamed he would be in a boyfriend. I began to think more about our future. I knew I wanted to marry him someday, but we talked of the future only in nebulous terms. As the Thanksgiving holidays approached, we made separate travel plans.

Dean was needed in Virginia. Mrs. Falconer had not made the progress the family had hoped, and Dean needed to check on his sisters. His aunt Martha and uncle John had been godsends— Martha cooking and ferrying the girls and John running the farm.

74

But John was barely managing to keep up with his own work and responsibilities.

I wanted to meet Dean's family but understood it wasn't the right time. And I missed my parents. We would have a lovely Thanksgiving in New York. Mom always invited neighbors, friends, and acquaintances that had no family gathering to attend to come to the sumptuous dinner my parents worked days to prepare. I pictured the brownstone decorated in an explosion of fall color—lime, Kelly green, orange, persimmon—with gourds, pumpkins, chrysanthemums, and fall foliage, with yet more pumpkins on the front steps. Good wine would be plentiful, the conversation lively and interesting. There would be other Thanksgivings to spend with Dean.

Dean and I returned the Saturday after Thanksgiving to a blustery, frigid Georgetown. He reported that his mother had been depressed and distant, his sisters troubled. But as they were young and resilient, he prayed they would adjust. Spending time with Dean had been good for them. I knew it was difficult for him to focus on his course work with family concerns. But I also knew our love was to him the safe and warm place it was for me.

CHAPTER

9

Robin

Christmas 1978

The streets of Georgetown rang with the sights and sounds of Christmas. A light snow fell overnight, a dusting of confectioner's sugar. Exams were over. Dean and I were ready to party hardy with our friends. I slipped into a scarlet dress and silver wedge-heeled shoes and brushed a shimmery shadow onto my lids. While waiting for Dean's knock, I put on the fluffy brown-and-white rabbit coat that had been a gift from my parents, tied its leather belt, and appraised myself in the mirror.

We stopped first at a party at James's apartment that was rock-and-roll rowdy with students blowing off steam. Helen took a picture of Dean and me, Dean laughing and handsome in a dark-green pullover, his arm encircling my waist. We didn't have a picture of the two of us yet, and I hoped the photo would turn out well. James had some great weed. He invited Dean, Clay, Helen, and me up to his room for a smoke.

We piled into a taxi for Spin! and arrived at the club laughing. We toasted each other at a table so far in the back of the room the couples on the dance floor looked like gyrating pygmies. When the Bee Gees' "How Deep Is Your Love" began, Dean and I grinned at each other and made the journey to the roiling floor.

Back at the table, Clay told us they'd learned a group of Arab sheikhs were partying in the club that night. Apparently they were in one of the side rooms blowing cocaine. Helen grabbed my hand. "Less go take a lil peek at the sshheikhs," she slurred. Among suit-clad businessmen in the second alcove sat four saturnine, bearded men in white head wraps. We regarded them from about ten feet away. Their silky robes were the color of fresh butter, elaborately embellished with embroidered trim. The men were drinking and flirting with well-dressed women, but we saw nothing illicit about their movements.

Then jolted, as if struck with a cattle prod, I recognized John Giannangelo in their midst. I stood mesmerized, breath held. I followed his dark curls as he bent over a small mirror on the table. Helen elbowed me. "They'rrre doin' coke!"

"Shhhhhh, it's Giannangelo!" I whispered, my heart racing.

Helen's dark brows furrowed. "Who'sss that?"

The congressman couldn't possibly have heard, but he raised his head and looked directly into my face. His eyes glittered crazily. A flare of recognition appeared to register in his big-featured face. I did an abrupt turnabout, propelling Helen forward, and made for our table as if the hounds of hell were at our heels. Dean and Clay

78

stood talking with two guys at the next table. I had a moment to compose myself and clutched a glass of water. Dean turned to me and grinned. "Did you get a good look at your sheikhs?"

"Their robes were prettier than our dresses," Helen said. She twined her hard arms around Clay's neck. I sipped demurely at my water, willing myself to appear calm. When the beginning beats of Marvin Gaye's "Got to Give It Up" reverberated through the club, we all bounded up to dance.

Dean and I were about to head for our own celebration at his place when heads began turning toward some activity behind us. The group of sheikhs, exotic as giraffes, drifted toward the door.

John Giannangelo appeared at my side. My heart plummeted toward my stomach. He said in his deep, cultured voice, "Merry Christmas, Robin." He squeezed my elbow lightly and moved on with his group, nodding and smiling into the crowd as he made his way to the door.

Dean turned to gape at me. "Who the hell was that?" he growled.

"It's a long story," I said.

"I'd like to hear it, Robin." The others tensed, the back of the night broken.

The four of us were subdued on the ride back, Helen nodding off on Clay's shoulder with her mouth open slightly. Dean had been deathly quiet. The taxi took us as far as Clay's apartment. The temperature had dropped significantly, and few people were on the streets. As Dean and I started down the sidewalk, he said, "You have something to tell me, Robin?"

"Dean, in September ... we were broken up. I had just moved here ... I felt really lonely. And I guess it made me vulnerable. Cindy and I met that man at Spin! one night. His name is John Giannangelo. He's a congressman from New York."

Dean stopped to look at me, nonplussed.

"He was very charming," I continued. "He asked me to a fancy dinner at the Herald Inn."

"My God, Robin. Did you sleep with him?"

"No!" I shouted. "It was all respectable ... but I know, have known, it was stupid and impulsive to go."

We started walking again; my feet were freezing. "Why would you go out with a smarmy old bastard like that ... and a congressman, Robin! I can't believe this. You lied when you said you hadn't been seeing anyone!" he ranted.

"I wasn't *seeing* him, Dean; it was just the one night. But there's more," I said miserably. Dean stopped again, glaring at me under a streetlamp. A huge tinsel candy cane thwacked against the metal in the wind. "I met him at the inn that night ... took a taxi. I didn't tell him where I lived ... but two days later when I got home from school, there were flowers at my door."

Dean's hands were deep in his pockets, his shoulders hunched in his coat as if to ward off a blow. "What happened then?"

"I never heard from him or saw him again. Until tonight."

"Robin, I thought I knew you. I just didn't think you would do something like that." He shook his head as if to clear it.

"You do know me!"

We were in front of his building then. "I'll drive you home," Dean said shortly. I began to cry. "I need to think about this," he said.

He handed me into the Jeep, his face shuttered. He flipped the heat on and blew into his cupped hands. Slowly the two blocks of ice at the end of my legs began to thaw. Dean never took his eyes from the road. I was anguished. He walked me into my building and kissed my forehead briefly. "I'll call you later."

I climbed the stairs to my apartment like an old woman. I brushed my teeth; stripped, my clothes littering a path; and put on a long cotton gown. I drank a huge glass of water and drew the curtain. I looked dismally out at the twisting snowflakes that had begun to fall.

I missed Theresa desperately. I wanted to pour it all out to her, to cry on her shoulder; a letter wouldn't suffice. I did cry then, great hiccupping sobs; hot salt tears and mascara ran down the front of my white gown. After a space of time, I calmed and sat down on my upholstered chair in silence. I laid my head back, scrubbing my cheek against the fabric, and nodded off.

I jerked awake to a knock at my door. I was on my feet, heart thudding, disoriented. My bedside light was on. The little silver clock on the nightstand read 1:19. The knocking came again. I called, "Who is it?"

"It's Dean." My apprehension was replaced with a rush of sweet hope.

I unchained the door and opened it, my heart thudding. Dean began first. "Robin, I'm sorry. About that Giannangelo guy … I went a little nuts. I felt betrayed … concerned, and damned jealous at the same time. I've been driving around and sitting out front in the Jeep. It's cold out there."

"Come in, Dean," I said gently. I held my arms out to him, stained nightgown, red swollen eyes, and all. Dean came into them and embraced me tightly. "Let's just get some sleep," I said into his chest. I reached to extinguish the lamp. We lay on my bed and slept like stones until nine o'clock the next morning.

We woke hungry and bundled up to go to brunch, a woolly toboggan over my wild hair. We ate like starving refugees at our favorite diner—eggs, pancakes with butter and syrup, bacon, and hash browns. But our conversation was subdued. The swags of tinsel, waxy flakes of fake snow, and "Holly Jolly Christmas" on the jukebox didn't dispel the tension that stretched between us like hot wire. But Dean asked if I wanted to go to the movie *Superman* starring Christopher Reeve and Gene Hackman the next night. We went our separate ways to do errands and our laundry.

The next morning Cindy called me, breathless. "Robin! Have you seen the news?" Her ominous tone told me it couldn't be good.

"No. What's going on?"

As she gave me the scoop, my flesh crept with chill. A high buzz began in my ears. The *Washington Post* and television networks were reporting that New York congressman John Giannangelo had been indicted in a scandal they were calling Operation Abscam. Giannangelo had accepted a bribe from an FBI agent posing as an Arab sheikh. He had been offered money in exchange for helping the Arabs overcome certain immigration laws. "Oh my God!" I said. "Dean and I saw him in Spin! Friday night with some sheikhs ... some Arab men!"

I had to talk to Dean, to tell him about Giannangelo in person. Had he already heard the news?

I spent an anxious afternoon nauseated and shaky. Dean knocked at the door twenty minutes before I expected him. I was wearing only my underwear, my hair wrapped in a towel. I draped the damp towel around my torso and opened the door. "Dean, you're way early." I managed a warm smile. *How I love this man; everything has to be okay.*

"I wanted to talk before we went to the movies," he said.

He knows. But he's calm. A measure of relief rang in my chest as I pulled on my bathrobe.

We sat down on the bed, and Dean said, "Robin, I've been really messed up about this Giannangelo thing ... You've heard the news today?"

"Yes," I replied quietly, waiting.

"What if you had gotten more involved with this man?"

"I know," I said wretchedly. "But I wouldn't have!"

"Look, I've done some stupid things in my life too. I'm sorry I overreacted. I love you, Robin. I do know you, and I want to be with you. Forever."

My eyes filled, tears sliding down my cheeks. Dean leaned over to kiss me. "Don't cry, sweetheart," he said. He took the towel, dabbed at my tears, and began squeezing at my hair.

"Make love to me, Dean?"

"I think I could manage that," he said with a flicker of the adorable grin I hadn't seen for a couple of days. He raised his hand to pull at the robe's sash. Neither of us ever saw *Superman* at the theater. Years later, catching it on cable TV, I would recall poignantly the night Dean and I made up after our first fight.

Christmas was just around the corner. We planned an intimate celebration before leaving for our homes as we had at Thanksgiving. I wanted to take Dean to New York with me. There was no place like New York City at Christmastime. It was decorated so festively with the towering blaze of the Rockefeller Center tree, the enchanting department store windows, the fairylike twinkling lights, and the brightly festooned horses and hansom cabs in Central Park.

And I was dying to introduce Dean to my parents. But as before, I understood the responsibility he felt toward his family. I truly admired him for his loyalty. I packed my bag, making sure I had stationary and a pen in my purse. I would write Theresa a nice long letter on the train to New York.

I met Helen for a quick lunch at the diner. She shook her head in disbelief as I explained the "Giannangelo debacle"—as I would always remember it—to her over club sandwiches and cold Tabs. "Thank God it had a happy ending," she said. Helen had had her film developed and handed me the picture of Dean and me from the party at James's place. She'd had double prints made so I had a copy to give to Dean. I grinned at the photos and carefully tucked them into my purse as if they were treasure. Helen was headed to Maryland for the Christmas break. I hugged her good-bye, and we wished each other Merry Christmas. I would never see Helen again.

My mind ticked ahead to the evening; excitement rippled through my midsection. I was cooking my first meal for Dean. I hummed Christmas tunes and smiled at people on the street. I went to the market for the dinner ingredients, a pair of elegant red tapers, inexpensive champagne flutes, and a small bouquet of spicy white carnations for the table. Dean was splurging on a celebratory bottle of champagne.

I'd helped in the kitchen and certainly watched my parents cook often enough, but I had never prepared an entire meal. I called my mom at Speak Volumes to ask how she would cook a roast the butcher said was the right size for two people. A roasting pan had come with my tiny furnished kitchen, and I tugged it noisily from the oven drawer. I plopped the roast into the pan and nestled chopped carrots, potatoes, and onion quarters around it. I sprinkled it with onion soup mix and water and covered it with a tenting of aluminum foil before sliding it into the oven. I made a green salad and then began to prepare the most challenging dish: my mother's famous scalloped potatoes. I peeled and sliced

85

the potatoes—very thin, Mom had cautioned—and made a white sauce of butter, flour, and milk, next stirring cheddar cheese, salt, pepper, and a pinch of nutmeg into it. I poured the sauce over the potatoes—slopping a good bit of it over the sides of the dish—and sprinkled it with more cheese and breadcrumbs I'd made from my morning toast. Then I set it on top of the stove until the roast was done. It was quarter to five, and Dean was due at six. I had to clean up, set the little table, shower, and dress. As I showered, I thought about the first shower Dean and I had taken together and giggled to myself. "An-tic-ipation, an-tic-i-pa-a-tion is making me wait," I sang, my voice reverberating against the tile.

I wore a silky green dress I had found at a consignment shop. It accentuated my green eyes, and I knew Dean would love it. He arrived promptly wearing a white shirt and red pullover sweater and jeans, his suitcase in one hand and the paper-bagged champagne in the other. "You look good enough to eat," he said, shucking out of his coat. "It's not the finest," he said, brandishing the bottle, "but I got us an extra surprise." He grinned and pulled a joint from his pocket. "Your table looks great," he said, moving into the little dining alcove. "Is that roast beef? Man, that smells *good*!"

"It will be ready in about an hour," I said. Then I confessed I'd called my mom three times that afternoon. As we laughed together, I placed the champagne into the refrigerator. Then I remembered the photograph. "Oh! Guess what I have!" We regarded ourselves in the picture. The camera had captured our happiness, the love between us.

Dean slipped his copy into his suitcase to take home with him. "I'll show it to my mom. She'll have a fit over how pretty you are."

Dean lit the joint and raised the window just a bit—the wind outside was positively glacial—and we sat leaning against my large floor pillows, laughing and talking, the Eagles' *One of These Nights* on the stereo. Dean pinched the joint at midpoint and smiled shyly. He looked completely adorable. "I have something for you, sweetheart." From his shirt pocket he withdrew a tiny white cardboard box.

"Dean ..." I murmured as he held the box out to me. On a bed of cotton inside was a delicate pair of silver earrings. As I laid them in my palm, I saw they were little birds.

"I decided they were robins," he said.

"I love them. Thank you, sweetheart! I'm putting them on." Jumping up, I moved to stand in front of my mirrored dresser and worked the wires through my lobes. Dean came to stand behind me. We stood gazing at our reflection. He pulled my hair aside and bent to kiss an ear and then my neck. Entranced, I watched his gilded head and the hand he raised to slip into the V-neck of my dress. "Not so fast, Mister," I giggled. "I have a gift for you too."

"You *know* what *I* want," he said lasciviously, drawing my earlobe between his teeth.

Squirming from his grasp, I went to my bedside table and took out a small red box cinched with green ribbon. "Merry Christmas, Dean," I said. He opened the box and lifted the silver medal up by its slender chain. "It's Saint Thomas," I said, "the patron saint of architects."

"It's great, Robin," he said sincerely and then grinned. "I didn't know architects had their very own saint."

"Turn it over," I urged. I'd had the jewelry store engrave the back with "Forever, Robin."

"Put it on me," he said, turning his back. I clasped the chain around his neck, and we kissed and wished each other merry Christmas again.

I went back into the kitchen, threw my apron on, took the roast out of the oven to rest, and put the potatoes in. I lit the candles while he opened the champagne. "I've never done this before," he said, "but the dude at the package store told me how." He pulled the wire hood, grimaced, and popped the cork, spattering the carpet and the front of his jeans. We sat down to the meal hooting with laughter.

"This is delicious, sweetheart," he said, sliding his fork under a second bite of potatoes. "You can cook for me *anytime*."

"Guess who's doing the dishes?" I grinned.

In the end, we washed them together and left them to dry on the drain board. We flipped on a radio station playing Christmas music and slow danced, sipping our champagne in the glow of the candles.

After a while Dean said huskily, "As good as you look in that dress, I'm about ready to get naked." That was all it took for me. We carried the candles into the bathroom and placed them on the back of the toilet. We showered by candlelight, making love there, the water eddying around us. "Merry Christmas!" we shouted, laughing like loons as we finished.

Later in bed Dean raised himself on his elbows, regarding me intently. "You are so beautiful, sweetheart. The earrings look just like I knew they would."

I reached for the medal that dangled from his neck and brought it to my lips. I whispered, "I hope you'll wear this always, especially while we're apart."

"Robin … you're the best … thing in my life," he said, his voice husky with emotion.

"I love you, Dean," I whispered, my eyes filling again. *I seem to cry so easily these days.* Twin tears slid into my ears as my lids closed in rapture. *Must be what love does to you.* We spent the rest of that wonderful night together, cuddling and making plans for our New Year's Eve celebration. The next morning we bundled up against the cold, got our bags together, and were off to Union Station in Dean's Jeep. My train was called first, and I boarded.

From my window seat, I watched Dean on the platform. As the train lurched away, he waved, and then he plunged his hands deep into his coat pockets and bounced on the balls of his sneakers. He hadn't bothered to shave that morning; his face was shadowy and pink with chill. I leaned my head against the window, fingering one of the new earrings, and gazed at my love until his figure grew smaller and smaller and then disappeared entirely.

My heart swelled with excitement when I saw the familiar street decorations in Manhattan. My parents met my train, and we rode home in my father's black BMW. Mom was full of the plans they had made for my time at home. They had bought tickets to see the Rockettes at Radio City Music Hall, as was our annual tradition, and this year we were going to see the newest Broadway play, *The Importance of Being Earnest*. Another night we were going to a dinner party at the Roths' and to *The Nutcracker* at Lincoln Center. Dad piped up, "I also want to take my girls for cocktails atop the Empire Hotel."

I had told my mother about Dean. She asked me careful questions about him on the way home. I gushed about how wonderful he was until my dad rolled his eyes at me in the rearview mirror. Dad sat quietly behind the wheel, but he hung on every word. Both of them were shocked and sympathetic about Dean's dad's death and family situation.

Mom had decorated beautifully: small boxwood wreaths with red velvet bows and a larger wreath for the great front door graced the house. (Dad brought the door wreath in at bedtime each night to keep it from being stolen; after all, it *was* New York City.) Garlands of fresh white pine crested the bannister and mantle. The beloved needlepoint stockings stitched with our names—Hank, Olivia, and Robin—that our friend Anita had made for us when I was a baby hung from the mantle. The regiment of nutcracker soldiers we had had since my early childhood stood guard along the front windowsills. An enormous tree glimmering with gold and silver orbs spread its limbs to preside over the living room. Even Atticus looked festive in his red-and-green jester collar with tiny red bells, but the little dog wore a pissed-off expression and planted himself often to scratch at the collar with a back foot.

In my room a small, fresh arrangement of crimson-berried holly sprigs and white spider mums greeted me on my bedside table. I smiled and sat down on the double bed to take off my shoes, rubbing my cold toes. On my pillow were a few of my favorite little chocolates. *My sweet mom.*

My thoughts turned to Dean; I wondered what was happening in Virginia. *Dean.* I reached for a decorative pillow on my bed and hugged it to my chest. I hoped things were going well with his family and they would be able to enjoy this Christmas. *Next year Dean and I will spend Christmas together,* I thought. I would bring him home with me to New York. *Or maybe we will go to Virginia,* I thought with a swell of excitement.

The air redolent with the smell of Hamilton Christmases drew me downstairs. Mom had made a simple crab quiche and salad. I knew she had probably been on her feet all day at Speak Volumes, helping frantic last-minute Christmas shoppers. Impulsively, I kissed her cheek. The three of us had a quiet dinner with wine, and they caught me up on the latest news. The Rosenblums next door had installed a hot tub in their garden, and my parents were pretty sure they got in it naked at night. And down the block, the Capellis's son was "on dope." I felt my face redden at that last remark and studied my salad, painstakingly loading the perfect bite of lettuce, celery, tomato, and carrot on my fork.

One of our family traditions was to read Truman Capote's bittersweet memoir of a particular childhood Christmas, *A Christmas Memory.* "Let's start it tonight," I said. We moved into the living room; Dad banked the fire and ousted Atticus from the center of the sofa. Mom reached for her reading glasses, but I said, "Let me read tonight, Mom."

"Okay, Rob!" She smiled, propping her feet atop the veteran ottoman I had lain across on my tummy to watch *Captain Kangaroo*. Atticus, minus the festive collar he had managed to remove, jumped onto my chair. He turned three times before settling against my hip. I'd read just two chapters when Dad nodded off on the sofa. Mom looked at him with fond indulgence. She whispered, "Let's finish it tomorrow night." She reached for a throw with Santa and his eight tiny reindeer on it and smoothed it over his big torso. I rose and checked the fire, poking at the orange-blue embers until they were settled. Mom and I turned out the lamps and ascended the stairs quietly. I could hear the ticking of the old mantle clock that had been a wedding gift to my Courtwright grandparents.

"Do you think Dean's the one, darling?" Mom asked.

"Mom, we're too young to get married. I've just started law school, and Dean has another year in his program … but I am *crazy* in love, Mom, and he loves me too."

"It's lovely to see you so happy, darling. I can't wait to meet this fellow. Night, night, sleep tight; see you in the morning's light."

While Mom worked the final day before the holiday, Dad and I set out for a little shopping and lunch. He wanted to know all about the classes I had taken that semester. We enjoyed the time together, completing our shopping lists, and then collected his car and drove to pick Mom up and take her to dinner. We went to her favorite restaurant, Gabriella's, for Italian, where I stuffed myself with spaghetti carbonara and a luscious, fluffy tiramisu. I had probably gained a couple of pounds already. *I'll dance them off when I get back to DC,* I thought complacently.

The days were passing quickly. The shows we went to were terrific, but we had differing opinions about the casting of *The Importance of Being Earnest* and argued heatedly about it on the way home. "Wilde would never have casted a woman in that role," my father had said.

"That's just sexist. You're impossibly conservative." I said from the backseat. I'd reached the point in the visit where my parents were starting to get on my nerves.

On Christmas morning we awoke like incredulous children to a lovely eleven-inch blanket of snow, the first white Christmas in six years. We didn't poke a toe out, instead reading and lazing by the fire most of the day. I ate most of the box of the Russell Stover Rosebud Mints that Dad unfailingly placed in my stocking every year. (Inveterately, I nibbled the pastel mint parts from around the icing rosebuds first before sucking the rosebuds until they dissolved on my tongue.) We dressed warmly and walked the glittering blocks to St. Michael's for the annual candlelight service. We spoke to the Roths and the Capellis seated behind us. Jeff Capelli did look a little stoned, and I grinned to myself. On the way back, our arms linked, we called "Merry Christmas!" to neighbors and strangers alike. We stamped the snow from our boots on the stoop, and Mom said, "Why don't you call Theresa? For a Christmas treat."

"*Allo?*" Tee answered, sounding very French. It was so good to hear her happy voice.

"*Joyeux Noel,* Madame Pelletier!" I caroled across the ocean that separated us. The sibilant long-distance tone even sounded like the scrubbing of shells across sand.

"*Zut alors,* Rob! How are you? Merry Christmas, *cherie!*"

"I'm fine," I laughed. "Merry Christmas! How are you and Laurent?"

"We're fine. Tabby and Michelle are here with their husbands. Tabby told us she's pregnant, and we've actually had fun with them for a change. But me a grandmother! Are you kidding me?" She laughed, chagrined.

"Only by marriage," I said.

"*Tu est* ... you are in New York?"

"I'm at home. I don't have much time, but there's so much I want to tell you. I am so in love! But, Tee! Dean and I almost broke up a couple of weeks ago." I told of the Giannangelo debacle with Tee asserting "Oh no!" and "*Pauvre bebe!*" in the pauses. "But man, Dean and I had fun getting back together!"

"Rob. I'm so happy for you!"

"So what's it like sleeping with an old guy like Laurent?" I teased. Tee had sent a photo of her husband. He was striking—tall, dark, and handsome at forty-four.

"Rob, you have *no idea!*" She was whispering now, afraid of being overheard. "The boys I went to bed with in New York knew nothing about a woman's geography. Laurent had a vasectomy when his girls were small, so we don't have to worry about using anything. And maybe it's because he's French, but ... *si fantastique!*" she sighed. Tee told me she had taken a position as a copy editor for a publishing company and would begin working right after New Year's. She was excited about starting a career.

We knew the long distance was costing my parents a fortune, so Tee said she could call me back on New Year's Day. We wished each other Merry Christmas once more, and I hung up the extension in my parents' room. I lay back on the bed for a few minutes, wishing for the hundredth time that Theresa didn't have to live so far away.

I would be going back to DC in two days and spent them taking long walks and reading a novel by the fire, Atticus often curled into my side. One day I had lunch with my best friend from high school who was in town, Beth. Beth had graduated from Davidson College in North Carolina and was engaged to her college sweetheart, Kent.

The last night my parents hosted their annual holiday dinner party. Mom had been working on the menu and cooking for days. She took great pleasure in entertaining, and it was fun to hang out in the kitchen with her. We dressed to the nines for the party. I greeted the guests at the door and hung up their coats while Dad served the hors d'oeuvres. We enjoyed expensive wine and talked and laughed with old family friends—the Roths, Hicks, LeVacas, Boucks, and Gibbs. The meal was superb—stuffed crown pork roast, (my now special) scalloped potatoes, lemon green bean bundles, yeast rolls, and a rich chocolate-mocha cheesecake. I cleaned up the kitchen afterward and went to bed early.

I awoke refreshed and felt excited butterflies in my tummy as I remembered, *Today I see my love!* Then I sat bolt upright, suffused with nausea, and ran to the bathroom, my mouth streaming saliva into the toilet. I retched, but my stomach was empty. I grabbed a washcloth from the shelf, ran it under cold water, and held its coolness against my jaw the way my mother had when I was a little girl. When the feeling subsided, I showered and packed and joined my parents downstairs. I refused breakfast. "I think I might have a bug," I said.

"Well, at least take a banana," my mother said. I snagged one from the pottery bowl on the counter for the train. I hugged my parents at the station, told them I loved them, and thanked them for the wonderful Christmas. I couldn't wait to get back for New Year's in DC.

My train was late. Hours later I turned the key in my apartment lock. I looked about my cozy one-room home and noticed the carnations on the table. The white flowers were dead. The petals lay on the tablecloth like litter on snow. I turned to pick up my suitcase and noticed a folded piece of notebook paper just inside the door.

Dean has already been here! As I read the note, my hand lifted involuntarily to press against my mouth. I read it again … and a third time. I sat down on my bed in grief and disbelief.

Dear Robin,

Uncle John and I drove his truck down today just long enough to pick up my things. I'd hoped you would be back so I could tell you all of this in person.

My mom had a breakdown, and we've hospitalized her. The girls are a mess. I may have to stay at home for another semester to help. I can't believe this. I can't believe I have to leave you again. I'm so sorry, sweetheart. But at least this time, you'll know where I am.

My address and phone number at Villeneuve are on the back. I hope you had a good Christmas with your folks. I'm sorry about New Year's. I can't believe I'm writing this. I'm wearing my medal and thinking of you.

Love forever,

Dean

I lurched back into the bathroom, looked at the red candles sat on the tank, and threw up again. I crumpled and sat on the cold porcelain tile. Like an oscillating fan, my thoughts turned back and forth between pity for Dean and his family and the tyranny of our circumstances. *Dear God, why can't things work out for us?*

I had Dean's number but was afraid I might call at a bad time. Of course he had mine too. He would call soon. Exhausted, I clicked off my lamp and fell onto the bed in my clothes. Sometime during the night, I slipped out of them and beneath the covers. I slept fitfully, waking at the slam of my neighbor's door. Remembrance of the night rose as if it had been submerged in deep water. When it did, I boohooed for a while and then rose to go to the bathroom.

The nausea hit me again. I barely made it before I vomited. Standing shakily, the truth swamped me like white water. I scrabbled through my unpacked travel case for the pink sleeve of birth control pills and counted back the punched-out plastic bubbles. I had missed three pills (three!) somehow in the last month. "Oh my Lord," I said aloud. My period had not come over Christmas. I counted the pills again. I was six days late. In the street a fire engine blasted by, the cacophonous siren intruding on my disbelief. I showered, tried to wash away the growing certainty, and stepped out before the mirror. I wiped the condensation from the surface with a trembling hand and inspected myself. My breasts were fuller, my pink nipples a darker mauve, and the veins across my chest darker and more prominent. Hands against my flat stomach, I said to the pale, green-eyed woman in the mirror, "You're pregnant."

CHAPTER

10

Robin

1979

I spent a few virtually sleepless nights, limbs leaden as though I had slogged through a field of sucking mud. I wrote a letter to Dean in support of his decision: "You did what you had to do, what a good son would do. My thoughts and prayers are with your family."

Dean called on a Saturday morning, sounding loving and preoccupied. He thanked me for being patient and understanding and said he missed me badly. He had told his aunt and uncle about me and showed them our picture. They were sympathetic and encouraged him to make time to come and see me.

My classes would resume in five days. I called the university health center and made an appointment. The rumpled young doctor was kind as he confirmed the pregnancy. "Forgetting pills especially at the beginning or end of your pack can increase the rate of pregnancy. Now, if you have this baby, you can expect him or her to be born about August fifth." He pushed his John Lennon glasses up his nose and regarded me solemnly. I had been pregnant the whole month of December then. I couldn't articulate a single response. "Have you thought about what you want to do, Miss Hamilton?"

I had thought of nothing but.

I didn't have the heart to burden Dean with this front-page headline. On the other hand, I needed him to help make the decision. We had both tangoed. The timing was as poor to enter into marriage as it was to have an abortion. Either scenario would be difficult. My Catholic parents would never support an abortion. Utterly consumed with Dean, I'd given no thought to any conceivable (no pun intended) negative consequences. I had been on the pill! This speck of life, just a blastocyst of cells at four weeks the doctor said, was a life nevertheless, a life conceived in love. Part Hamilton and part Falconer. My parents—I loathed the thought of telling them. And Dean's mother—what would the news do to her?

And so I waited.

I received a letter from Dean and read it a dozen times, keeping it in my pocket, fingering it often, as though it were a talisman. I mailed him cheery little thinking-of-you cards, the words light, and once a deeply emotional love letter. On New Year's Eve, Dean called again, the news grim. The eldest sister, Leslie, eighteen and the more sensitive of the two, had essentially stopped eating when her father had been killed. Their aunt Martha had forced a hostile Leslie to mount the scales. At five feet seven, Leslie had weighed in at 104 pounds. An excellent student and bookworm since childhood, Leslie had dropped out of her first semester at UVA as if leaving a shop she'd been browsing. She had begun seeing a boy with a reputation for trouble and was breaking curfew and coming home smelling of booze and cigarettes.

Sixteen-year-old Mary had become fearful and skittish. Though she'd been looking forward to getting her driver's license for months, she refused to discuss it now. Mary went about her after-school chores, taking care of the animals, but did so dispassionately, as though folding laundry. Dean was deeply concerned about his sisters, especially Mary, with whom he was closest.

Laurel Falconer sat in the psychiatric wing of Martha Jefferson Hospital, her head like a wilted balloon flower on her slender stem of a neck. Both girls wanted to be with their mother, now their only parent, but faced with her silent stares, they found their time with her gut-wrenching. Often Leslie wept all the way back to the farm, Mary holding her sister's hand and gazing dry-eyed out the window. Dean, the eldest at twenty-four, was the head of the family whether he liked it or not. Exhausted, he said, "I wish I could teleport myself to you for the night. Beam me up, Robin!"

"Me too." I covered the receiver and stifled a sob.

"I'm going to ask Aunt Martha to stay with the girls for a weekend—a whole weekend," Dean said, his voice muffled. I pictured him stretching his long frame across the bed, scrubbing his face back and forth into a pillow, as was his habit. "I need to see you. I need to be in your arms." My stomach flipped, and I pressed a hand against my mouth. I wanted to tell him so badly then.

In the next days I became aware of my decision the way your eyes get used to the dark. Plunged into blackness, your pupils contract, and silhouetted edges begin to appear. One by one shapes begin to bloom—a counter, a chair, the floor, a door—until you can navigate. Dean and I were in love. Though our time together had been short, a season, it was the real thing. I could not end the life of this baby.

But I could not tell Dean now.

With hindsight a smug and sure twenty-twenty, I could have found a way around it, a way to tell him without compounding his problems, but I was barely twenty-two years old. I did what I thought was right at the time.

On the first day of classes, I went to the dean's office and withdrew from law school. I was going home.

I stepped from the train at Penn Station in New York City, my heart as heavy as the two suitcases of necessities I carried. The rest of my things would just have to be sent for later. The streets were bleak with detritus, gray snow piled at the curbs, but the sky was clear and bright as I plodded to the subway.

I let myself into the house knowing neither of my parents would be home from work. Atticus met me in the foyer, enraptured. *You're back already?* I fed him and, hoping we didn't meet another dog, took him for a quick spin down the block. The familiar smell of our house—beeswax, lemon, Atticus's kibble, nutmeg, and fresh laundry—smoothed my jangled nerves. As I wandered the well-loved and tended rooms, it struck me that the house had become a niche for two—two place mats on the kitchen table, two rumpled chair cushions, two pairs of shoes by the back door. I knew my parents had grown accustomed to their empty nest. My stay would be as brief as I could manage.

"What in the world? Robin!" Mom cried, entering the foyer ahead of Dad. "What a happy surprise!"

"Hello, sweet pea! What are you doing back?" Dad boomed.

I rose to greet them and let them smother me with hugs. Mom noticed the suitcases by the stairs and looked from them to my face. "Are you all right, darling?" she asked, her face tight with apprehension.

"Yes, I'm all right," I said and moved to a chair by the fireplace. "May we sit down and talk?"

I told them everything. As my mother wept for me, I moved to sit at her feet. She stroked my hair. My father said all the things I had known he would: "You were right to come home. We will take care of you. It will all work out."

But in the following long winter days, each of them asked if I would reconsider telling Dean about the baby. They felt keenly that Dean deserved to know. But I was adamant. Not then, not yet.

I couldn't visualize myself as a mother, that I would be holding a child of my own in eight months. My Madame Alexander dolls still looked down from their places on my bedroom bookshelves, and my bulletin board held high school invitations, tickets, photographs. Resolutely, I made an adult nest of my room, boxing my childhood belongings for the basement.

I knew my parents' hearts ached for me. They had never considered that I wouldn't finish college and marry before making them grandparents. They kept up brave faces for me, and if they cried as they held each other in the night, I never heard them.

Of course I called Tee. Though she listened and cried with me over the literal sea of distance, it was not the same. She vowed to come and be with me when the baby was born.

I was not ready to think that far ahead. I couldn't think beyond the next week when Mom would go with me to my first obstetrician's appointment. It was some small measure of consolation that proficient and jovial Doctor Taliaferro had delivered me when I was born. In my coat and boots I walked for miles. I thought of little but Dean. My love and desire for him was undiminished, as present and familiar as the scent of my hair blowing around my face. I remained suspended in the present, like the wintry slate clouds above the city.

CHAPTER

11

Robin

1979–1980

Awaiting the baby that winter and spring, my father and I sat up late one night in his study talking softly. It was my dear dad, in his cozy cinnamon Mr. Rogers sweater with the elbow patches, Atticus snoring like a human at his side, who helped me find my plan B.

"Rob, what do you think about doing paralegal work? You'd have more time to spend with the baby." He nipped at a short tumbler of scotch. "You'd still be making a contribution to the profession. Most lawyers rely heavily on their paralegals."

"I don't know what to do, Dad." I blew across the surface of my chamomile tea, peering into the steaming cup as if an answer might be found there. I knew my baby deserved a mother who would be there to make breakfast, pick him or her up from school, and spend time with him or her in the evenings. I owed my child … everything. While I'd cut my teeth on the law, I couldn't continue the path I'd begun at Georgetown.

"I've been asking around, sweet pea. *Hypothetically*," he added quickly at my raised brows. "You know I'm connected. Pace College has a respected paralegal certificate program. With the credits you've already earned and your diligence, you could complete it in five or six months."

I sipped my tea pondering. "Dad, I hope you know how grateful I am to you guys for supporting me and taking this whole thing on," I said, indicating my small swell of belly. "But I want to be independent as soon as I can."

He patted my hand. "Well, the paralegal program would certainly help you do that. By this time next year you'd be able to take a job. Earning the certificate would give you a leg up on paralegal candidates who *don't* have it." We heard water running through the old pipes in the master bath. Dad looked toward the door. "You should know your mom has been kicking around leaving the shop to take care of the baby for you."

"Oh no! Dad!" I reacted, spilling my tea a little. "I would *never* ask her to do that! She *loves* her work!"

"Are you kidding, Rob? You know your mother. She loves *you* more, and she can't wait to get her hands on the baby." He grinned. "It will be like having a little *you* around here again. Mom can always go back to the shop later on."

"Well, you guys are too much," I said around a lump in my throat. I rose to give him a hug. "I'll talk to Mom in the morning, and I will think about it."

* * * * *

Tucking my unwieldy form into a college desk was a surreal experience. I did my best to ignore the covert stares from other students. Much to my chagrin, my center of gravity compromised, I'd begun to waddle. That I was carrying an actual child just didn't seem real. One day in the middle of contracts class, everything changed. Winter was hanging on with the persistence of a badger, and the humming of the radiators in the old classrooms made me drowsy. Dr. Napolitano was droning on about illusory contracts when I felt a stirring, like the flick of a goldfish tail just above my pubic bone. Rapt, I sat as still as a stare. I felt it again. An incredulous smile stretched itself across my lips. I dropped my pen to my notebook and cradled my lower belly. I felt the sensation again and then once more. Fathoms deep from the less-than-desirable circumstances, this inchoate life was making itself known. The baby was real, part of me forever.

My parents noticed the change. At dinner that evening, Dad said, "Sweet pea, I believe you are glowing as they say."

Mom had been late at the shop, supervising inventory, and had been distracted since she'd gotten home. She stopped and studied me now and put her fork down. "Oh, darling, you really are."

I studiously cut my meat into uniform little pieces. It still felt awkward talking about being pregnant with my parents, even though they had been nothing but loving and natural with me. "I felt the baby move for the first time today. In class," I said, still averting my eyes.

"Robin, how *wonderful*," she breathed. "I *still* remember the first time I felt you. I was sitting on a bus in Chinatown."

I smiled and wiped my mouth, replacing the napkin over my lap. I watched as it rose like an ocean swell. Mom followed my gaze and asked, "Is she moving now?"

I nodded.

"May I?" her eyes asked. She rose and stooped beside my chair, placing her hand over my belly. The obedient baby rolled again. Mom grinned as if she'd won the church raffle.

"Dad, do we still have my baby cradle in the basement?" I asked.

"Of course we do," he answered, "and all your other baby things."

Mom was starting the coffee in the kitchen. "Wouldn't you like to have some new things especially for this baby?"

"I'd like to use my old things; no sense spending money on things we already have."

Dad grinned at my pragmatism and winked at me over a last sip of wine.

* * * * *

For the first time since I found out I was pregnant, I began
to think more about the baby than about Dean. I was beginning
to get excited about the sweet little outfits and blankets we were
making ready for the baby. Anita Roth and the parish ladies had
showered me with a layette. I doodled names for boys and girls
in the margins of my notebooks. Usually I wrote the surname
Hamilton and a few times Falconer. By mid-July my belly was the
size and tautness of one of the soccer balls I'd played with at Miss
Pruitt's School.

One day in the library I saw a guy that looked incredibly like
Dean from the back. I froze, heart trip-hammering until he turned
around, his face hawk-like and pitted with acne scars. I found that
my hands had moved to cover my stomach as if to protect the baby.
I wondered what unexamined subconscious notion had prompted
such a reflex.

And though I willed myself not to, I dreamed about Dean
again at night, about us making love, Dean curling around my
belly, stroking my breasts. Waking from those illusions, tears
drying on my face, I wondered what Dean would think if he could
see me. In the space of a single week I picked up the phone to call
him twice, but frustrated with my convoluted thoughts, I replaced
the receiver before dialing.

I finished my first semester of classwork on July 15 and
attended Lamaze technique classes at the hospital with Mom. I
wasn't the youngest mother-to-be, but I was the only without a
wedding ring. I felt the others speculated about me, and not one of

them spoke to me the entire course. At my eighth-month checkup, Dr. Taliaferro had suggested a new pain-blocking procedure for labor called an epidural. But when he'd described how they would (simply!) thread a needle into the spaces of my spine, I'd shuddered. I wanted to have the baby naturally. I didn't want to wake when it was all over the way my mom had when I was born. It seemed anticlimactic, like showing up at the end of a surprise party, having missed the best part, the big moment when the guests shout surprise.

On August 3, a cloyingly humid night only a fern could love, Mom knocked on my door. I lay on top of the covers in my lightest gown, my belly a small heaving mountain. "Do you feel like talking, darling?" she said.

I laid aside an old, worn copy of Dr. Spock. "Sure, Mom, come on in." I scooted my girth over for her to sit down and winced. "Ooooh, I think she's playing soccer tonight." A little monkey foot jabbed against my lowest rib again.

"May I feel?" Mom asked. She placed her hand over my abdomen. I hated it when strangers touched me without asking but welcomed my mother's touch. "Do you think it's a girl?"

"I do think she's a girl," I said. I'd sensed it for a while but hadn't articulated it before that moment.

"I dreamed it was a girl," she said. After a moment she grew solemn. "Robin, I want to talk to you. About Dean again."

Oh, shit, here it comes. I waited, knowing what she would say.

"Robin, your dad can't imagine not having known about you and missing being there when you were born. Dean has already missed the entire pregnancy. It's his child too."

"You're right, Mom," I replied shortly.

"You haven't contacted him, have you?" she asked, beginning to stroke my hand as you would an animal that might bite you.

"No."

"Well," she said and gave my hand a final pat, "if you change your mind, or if a times comes that you want us to call him, I am prepared to do so." She placed her palms together as in prayer and pressed her fingers against her lips. She was quiet for a while, and then she said, "You're an adult now, Robin, almost a mother yourself, and we will respect your wishes. But will you pack Dean's phone number in your suitcase just in case?"

"Okay, okay, I will," I groaned, rolling my eyes to the ceiling. "But keep away from that suitcase!" She stood and sighed. I felt churlish then and contrite and put my hand on her arm. "Mom, I'm sorry. I love you. I feel really bitchy tonight."

"I understand." She stood again and smoothed my brow. "I felt like tucking you in tonight. It could be the last night you go to sleep as *my* little girl. You have that look about you."

"Do I? Well, I'm past ready to get this show on the road." My eyes fell on the bag in the corner that awaited the trip to the hospital. I had packed my things and two of the doll-sized gowns I'd received from Anita, the soft yellow one with Peter Rabbit hand-embroidered on a tiny pocket and a pink smocked one with tiny rosebuds. I was dying to know which one of them would be worn home from the hospital and who would be wearing it. I wanted so much to see the baby's face.

"Night, night, sleep tight; see you in the morning's light," Mom called softly, closing the door behind her.

Her intuition was right. I woke at four thirty with a dull, deep, deep backache. The baby was very still. I changed positions and tried to drift again, but the sensation returned a few minutes later. I got up to pee. My belly had dropped low, low into my pelvis, and for a week I'd had to hold it up off my bladder to go. I crawled back between my sheets and pushed a pillow behind my back. Minutes later a searing pain banded my abdomen. I gasped and sat to turn on the lamp. I looked down at my belly as if expecting to see the Triple Creek Ranch logo burned into my nightgown. Tremulous and gasping, I called, "Mom! Can you come?" My voice rang high in my ears. There was no mistaking this punishing pain.

Mom padded in wide-eyed, hands fumbling to cinch the sash of her robe. I was on my feet beside the bed. I followed her eyes toward my feet where three drops of blood spattered the cream wool rug. More spots crept across my white gown. "Ohhh, Mom, I'm bleeding! Is that supposed to happen?" I cried and then doubled over again as a new surge of agony traveled the equator of my belly.

"It's normal to spot a little. You're okay," she said, hurrying to my bathroom and returning with a towel. She pressed it tightly against me. "Can you get dressed?" She yelled, "Hank! Please get the car; Robin's in labor."

Down the hall, Dad bumped around and then poked his head in the door, his hair wild. "Showtime, sweet pea?" Seeing the blood, he blanched. "Hang in there; I'll have the car down in front in a minute."

I gasped as another pain swamped me and panted to my mother, "This is happening really fast, isn't it?"

"It seems to be. I need to time the pains now. Try to remember the breathing, deep and slow." In a big shirt now, I pulled on panties over the towel and maternity jeans and stuffed my feet into sneakers. Mom bent to tie the laces for me as she had when I was four years old. How very far we'd come.

Rain was falling in great sheets. Dad had double-parked at the curb and sprinted from the sedan with a large umbrella. Cringing at a spraying squall, I gingerly stepped into the backseat, Mom close behind. A cabbie momentarily delayed honked and hurled curses at us through the rain. We caromed away as another contraction rounded home plate. Mom said, "That was six and a half minutes. We were right to head to the hospital. Breathe, Robin. That's right ... that's it."

At the hospital, the nurses had their way with me, stripping me of my clothes and any notion of modesty I'd ever known. Comfortable for the moment, I lay tucked into the starch-sheeted hospital bed. My parents sat as stiffly as ventriloquist's dummies on the room's plastic sofa. Dr. Taliaferro strode into the room, hair sticking up in the back as though he had bolted from a cot, to confirm the labor. It was six-thirty by then; just a sliver of sun peeked through the blinds at the window.

"Mr. Hamilton, do you want to go get a cup of coffee while I check Robin's progress?" Dr. Taliaferro asked.

Dad paled, uncrossed his legs, and sprang to his feet. "I'll be right outside."

Mom's grin flickered for a moment. "He's so cute."

I changed positions and felt a hot whoosh of liquid as forceful as that from a garden hose rushing from my body. I shouted, losing control, "I'm hemorrhaging! Help me! Oh, God ..." I began shaking violently. Mom pressed her hands against her heart. I was counting on her to keep her composure as she always had.

Dr. Taliaferro quickly assessed me. "Relax now, Robin ... You're not bleeding; your water just broke." He smiled reassuringly. "That means you're a keeper—this baby's coming soon." In my pain and panic I had forgotten about the water-breaking part. "I'll see you shortly."

The stout nurse who looked sort of like Ethel on *I Love Lucy* briskly rearranged my coverings and gave me a sip of water through a bendy straw. "Not too much now; we'll get you a big cup of whatever you want after the baby comes." Mom came to stand on the other side of the bed and breathed with me again.

And then one of the best surprises I could have hoped for showed up: Theresa Cleary Pelletier perfunctorily rapped on the big wooden door and breezed into the room. Her molten hair was cropped short. Elegantly dressed in layers of dark knit and black high-heeled boots, every inch the Parisian, she grinned her familiar grin. "Tee?" I breathed. "Oh, Tee! I can't believe it!" My eyes flooded as she approached the bed and kissed me on both damp cheeks.

"I *told* you I would come. How are you? I see I barely made it in time. She and Mom exchanged hugs and greetings, apparently coconspirators. Theresa had shown up at the house and, finding no one at home, headed to the hospital. Dr. Taliaferro came in again to check my progress. As another contraction came, Theresa sat down on the sofa, twisting the straps of her purse, her eyes practically out on stems. Neither she nor I had ever even been around anything like that.

"Let's get her to the OR," Dr. T. said to Ethel, and then to me he said, "Are you ready to meet your baby? It shouldn't be long now. When you go into labor, you don't mess around."

I smiled up at him gratefully and then raised my head to feast my eyes on my friend again. *Theresa.* Dad loped back in. I was glad Tee would be there to wait with him. Now I had almost all those I loved best in the world with me. Almost.

In the operating room minutes later, fear leapt like a trout in my chest. I remembered the epidural and pleaded for it as if asking a judge to spare my life. "The window of opportunity for that has closed, my dear. You were blessed with one of those record-short labors. This baby is coming now," Dr. Taliaferro said. "Mrs.

Hamilton, breathe with her through these last contractions? Fast, hard puffs now. That's the girl."

As I breathed and gripped my mother's hands, I closed my eyes. Unwittingly Dean's face materialized behind my lids. The sun played in his hair. He was grinning at me, his gorgeous face open and relaxed. *Oh, Dean. Oh my. Dean. Oh …* "Dean," I groaned aloud, wanting him terribly. I could smell the leafy scent of his hair, feel his hands reaching for me.

"Do you want me to call Dean, darling?" Mom loomed over me, her dark eyes anxiously searching mine.

"No, Mom," I moaned. Then the worst agony yet seemed to rip me in two. I let out a throat-scouring yowl. I sounded like a wounded animal in a trap, my misery complete.

"Okay, Robin, I want you to push, bear down now … That's it. And one more time. Your baby's head is coming. One more time …" said the doctor. I was squeezing Mom's hand so tightly our hands seemed to have melded. She was breathing hard and crooning to me at the same time.

And then I felt the most tremendous flood of relief as my body expelled the baby. "*She's* here … She's just fine," Dr. T. announced.

"She!" Mom and I said at the same time and burst into tears of joy.

A new nurse bustled around making the baby ready and presented her to me bundled in one of those pink-and-blue-bunny blankets in every hospital in America. A little pink cap framed her face. "You have a very healthy and *beautiful* baby girl," the nurse said.

Finally, her face. I devoured it gratefully. Petal-soft, pudgy cheeks. Fine artist's- brush sweep of dark brows. Itty-bitty round nose. How could nostrils be so tiny? Her darkish, gray-green eyes were alert and seemed focused on mine. I touched the tiny comma of cleft in her chin. She was unmistakably her father's daughter. "She's amazing," I whispered with the greatest rapture I would ever experience.

My mother looked from the baby's face to mine. "Darling, I'm so proud of you. She's perfectly healthy and so lovely. You're a mother. God has blessed you."

"Oh, Mom," I sobbed, "I didn't know I'd be so happy." We were quiet for a moment. "She looks like *him*. The best of him."

Mom pressed her lips together and nodded twice in acceptance. "She looks like you too, I think. Like you did when you were born," she said.

Kind Dr. Taliaferro, who we'd virtually forgotten—though he'd been busily finishing up at the business end—said, "Let's get you back to your room so the others can see this perfect specimen. She's almost as pretty as you were when you came squalling into my hands."

"Thank you so much, Dr. Taliaferro," I said, suffused with gratitude. As the nurse took the baby to weigh and measure her, my girl began to cry for the first time. "Oh, listen to her!" I said amazed. The nurse said the baby was six pounds, nine ounces, and twenty inches long.

"She's a *long* sip of water," Mom said with a grin. A bolus-like lump formed in my throat. *She'll be tall like her father*, I realized. *Oh, Dean.* I reclined, peering down at my own bloomy Renoir. I brushed the downy fuzz along her jawline, like that of the white peaches I'd loved as a child. An orderly wheeled us back to my private room where Dad and Theresa waited. They stood and exclaimed over the baby and me. My father kissed my forehead, his eyes filling. "What do we call this divine dumpling, sweet pea?"

For weeks I'd thought of many pretty girl names, of the most popular names of the day, and of classmates' names from Miss Pruitt's School that I'd admired. Now I announced the name I had decided the most fitting. "Her name is Laurel Olivia Hamilton." I paused. "After both her grandmothers."

Mom swallowed, her lips turning up into a smile. "There's a nice symmetry to that, darling. I'm honored." But her eyes told me she was thinking of the three-hundred-pound gorilla in the room: Dean, his mother, and their unwitting role in the event. I passed Laurel to Dad. The three of them took turns holding the baby as gingerly as if they were inspecting antique porcelain.

The nurse returned and handed me a little paper cup with a pain pill in it. I drank deeply from an icy cup of Sprite, my thirst unquenchable. I marveled at the relative flat feel of my belly and breathed deeply into the tug of the stitches I was beginning to feel, though they seemed to be at a great distance. I was drowsy, as content as a grazing cow. A skinny nurse who introduced herself as Laurette—"How good of you to name your baby after me!" she cackled—came to take Laurel to the nursery. I told Tee I couldn't wait to talk and talk and talk with her. They all left then, insisting I sleep and closing the door softly behind them. I plunged into a layered velvet sleep.

I awoke disoriented, the room fully dark. With a rush of sweetness accompanied by a pulsing throb between my legs, I remembered. I heard a nurse making her way down the hall, opening and closing the doors of the other patients. The clock on the wall said it was five after seven in the evening. I scrabbled under the blankets for the call button and asked a nurse to bring me the baby and another pain pill. Impatient, I called home from the phone beside the bed and was surprised when Anita Roth answered. "Robin, I'm so thrilled for you, dear! I hear baby Laurel is beautiful!" Anita said the family was on their way back to the hospital. She had brought a tray of sandwiches to the house and started a load of laundry for us.

"I can't *wait* for you to see Laurel. You're such a good friend, Nita. I know they'll appreciate your help." I hung up as a new nurse, Kathleen, came into the room with my swaddled little love. When I saw Laurel's face again, my breasts ached in response. Kathleen gave me an injection that would dry up my milk. I was so entranced with the baby I scarcely felt the needle's prick. Kathleen showed me how to tickle the baby's cheek to get her started sucking on a plastic bottle of formula. My daughter was a natural. I chuckled when she burped like a gunshot over my shoulder after drinking only a few ounces. I thought of Dean again, of how we would have laughed together.

119

When Kathleen left, I propped the baby against my knees and gently unwrapped the swaddling to examine her. She was a petit four of a baby, delicately pink and white. She had my mom's and my finely shaped hands; the fingers seemed carved by a clever miniaturist. But her little feet were Dean's. *Genetics don't lie, unlike me.* Dean's narrow heels, the crescent-moon sliver of toenail on his pinkie toes. "That little piggy nail will be a pain to polish one day," I said to her. Laurel's skin was soft and butter sweet. I couldn't believe that inside her were tiny little ovaries, a womb of her own. I rewrapped the blanket and held my daughter's face level with mine. Enigmatic gray-green eyes regarded me solemnly. "Guess it's you and me, my darling. I promise to do the best I can." I wondered if her eyes would be gray like Dean's or become the green of my own. Laurel closed her eyes as I planted little kisses over her face. I laughed when she fussed in earnest for the first time, fists the size of cherry tomatoes flailing. I reached for the bottle again. "Here you are, my darling." She squeaked and grunted, a greedy piglet.

Room 3512 became a verdant, fragrant paradise. My parents' friends sent glossy green-leafed plants and lavish arrangements of pink-and-white flowers: peonies, lady's slipper orchids, roses, snapdragons, and sweetly curled tulips. Pink and white balloons tethered by ribbons floated above serene-faced stuffed animals and dolls.

The following morning a woman who introduced herself as Genny from hospital records came to collect information for the birth certificate. Laurel was in my arms sucking noisily on another bottle. "What a little beauty!" Genny exclaimed. "She's sure to grow up as pretty as her mother." She smiled, pen poised, and recorded my full name on the form. "And her father's name?"

120

"Dean Thompson Falconer, F-a-l-c-o-n-e-r," I stated without hesitation.

"And what's the little angel's name?" she continued.

"Laurel Olivia Hamilton. L-a-u-r-e-l," I said.

"The baby's last name will be Hamilton?"

"Yes, Hamilton," I said firmly, just making the decision. "Her father is not in my life."

A day later, I was home again, feeling wonderful, totally enamored with the baby who slept in my old cradle next to my bed. I was thrilled to have Tee with me again. As I rested and healed, Tee and I lay on my bed with Laurel between us, holding her dimpled doll fingers and gazing at her as she slept. We talked for hours every day, catching-up talk, the sort that wasn't possible during long-distance calls or letters.

Neither Theresa nor I had ever even been around a newborn baby. Everything she did amazed us. "Rob, you're somebody's *mother*," Tee marveled again and again. I knew it would be awful when she had to leave, but for the present we were old roomies, best friends in the world. "I'm bummed I didn't get to see you walking around *plus grande* ... big and fat!" Tee said.

Of course we talked of Dean and our untenable circumstances. I told Theresa I still intended to contact him but wanted to wait until it felt right to me. "Don't I have the right to decide?" I said.

"I guess, Rob," she said.

I made Theresa change a dirty diaper just for the experience. I gleefully watched her clean Laurel's bottom with a cloth, grimacing, swearing in French, and exaggeratedly averting her nose. The last day of Tee's stay, we took the baby to Bryant Park in the new carriage my parents had given us. Her first time al fresco, the baby lay wide-eyed, entranced by the trees, the expanse of blue sky, the cotton ball clouds. "She's so alert," Tee said. "I can tell she's going to be smart like you, Rob. And not unlike a wise little Yoda she does look." I hooted and swatted at Tee in mock horror.

As Laurel grew older, she would accompany me to Chicago while Theresa was in the city. Laurel loved her cosmopolitan and exotic "Tante Tee," who, without children of her own, spoke French endearments and doted on Lark. And Tee would send little presents from afar—charming anachronistic toys and puppets at first, then little treasure boxes, and later intricate flea market baubles.

Dad and I drove Theresa to the airport, leaving Laurel home in her grandmother's arms; it would have been hard to say who was more contented. I walked Theresa to her gate. It had been a wonderful reunion, but it was always hard for us to say good-bye.

With her cropped hair, Tee's eyes were enormous. "Robin, I hope you're doing the right thing—about Dean, I mean. You know I want what's best for you—and for Laurel."

"Tee," I said, brushing aside her comment as I would a fly, "it meant the whole world to me that you came all that way and were here for Laurel's birth." We hugged again. "Will you and Laurent be her godparents?"

She placed both hands over her heart. "Awwww, Rob," she said. "I know I speak for Laurent; we would be honored."

"I love you, Tee," I said, wiping aside a tear. "Hey, I just this minute realized the L-a-u connection … Laurent and Laurel."

Tee laughed. "And I love you. Now mind you stay healthy, or else I may come back and whisk that little darling away." We smiled at each other for a last moment as her flight was called a second time. "May the force be with you *and my goddaughter*," she said with her old grin and bent to pick up her carry-on bag. My throat clogging with tears, I watched her red head bob down the Jetway until it disappeared.

* * * * *

At two months of age, Laurel chuckled aloud. The house rang with her musical peeps and trills. One Sunday afternoon, she lay on her tummy on a floor pallet in a pink-and-orange-striped sleeper. She waved her arms and legs, as though dog-paddling, her taffy-blonde head held above the water. Atticus cocked his head with interest from his perch on the ottoman. The dog had been surprisingly tolerant with Laurel. He seemed to regard with fascination her noisy, miniature humanity. Dad stretched out beside Laurel and made goofy faces and a general fool of himself. Mom and I looked on indulgently from our chairs as we read. Laurel crowed, bobbing her head, the taffy hair whorling neatly at the crown. "This baby is as happy as a lark!" Dad said. She truly was. And at that moment she was Lark.

I was astonished and humbled by the fierce bond between my daughter and me. The love of my child had eclipsed my yearning for Dean.

CHAPTER

12

Robin

1980–1981

Lark was ten months old and the apple of our eyes. I would change, feed, and dress her in one of her cute doll-sized outfits in the mornings before I went to class, and then I'd hand her off to Mom. In the afternoons, Lark greeted me with exuberant squeals and grins that showed off her top and bottom Chiclet teeth. The new recipient of the Courtwright women's thighs, Lark was chubby. She was not yet trying to stand but content to crawl and scoot from room to room in her walker.

The weather was warm in May with the promise of summer. I took Lark to the park often. Though I was a single mother, I knew I was incredibly fortunate to have my parents to help take care of Lark. Many women did not. And how Mom and Dad loved their grandchild. By that time I was a week away from earning my legal-assistant certification.

One Wednesday evening, I attended a group study session at the library and afterward got stuck on the train for forty-five minutes. I found my parents and Lark already at the dinner table when I got home. Lark industriously smeared applesauce across the tray of my old high chair. As the phone rang, I snagged the receiver from the wall phone. "Hello?" I answered, inclining my head to give Lark exaggerated air kisses.

The long-distance operator's voice captured my attention at once. "Allo?" she said around clicks and cracklings. "Is this Miss Robin Hamilton?" *Theresa!*

"Yes," I said happily.

"Go ahead, Monsieur."

Monsieur? "Robin, Laurent Pelletier here … from Paris." Like most Parisians, Laurent spoke flawless English.

"Hello, Laurent. How are you? Is everything all right?"

"Robin, I'm calling about Theresa." His voice was grave. A chill began to creep along my arms.

"What is it, Laurent?" The harvest-gold phone cord was long enough that I could move to a kitchen chair. I sat down heavily. My parents studied me, Dad spooning applesauce into Lark's open baby-bird mouth.

"Ma-ma!" Lark said.

"Theresa is experiencing panic attacks," Laurent said. "She … hasn't left the apartment voluntarily in more than a month. She has taken a sabbatical from her work. She is sleeping now. You see, she was *mugged* one evening on her way home. She was physically unhurt, but *le connard* held a knife to her throat as he stripped her of her handbag."

Oh, Theresa. I listened with mounting concern as Laurent described taking a reluctant and silent Tee to a psychologist who had diagnosed her condition as post-traumatic stress disorder. Theresa had managed to subjugate a shrouded fear stemming from as far back as her father's death and including the blackout episode in college. Apparently the recent event had brought the terror back, had triggered it, he said.

"Robin, I've done everything I can to help her … I'm calling to ask if you could come. I feel badly asking … I know you have your little baby to care for—"

I interrupted without hesitation, "I will come. I can arrange things with my parents." Both my parents were nodding their heads in confirmation. My mind ticked to the days ahead. I could arrange to take my finals early; I was ready for them. Laurent would make my travel arrangements.

"Please give Tee my love and tell her I'll be with her soon," I said. I hung up the phone, plucked my cherub from the high chair, and told my parents the grim news.

Twisting my long hair in her sticky little fingers, Lark regarded me soberly. "I don't know how I can do without this monkey," I said, putting her over my shoulder and holding her close. I'd never spent a night apart from Lark. But I would do anything for Tee.

In the luxe first-class seat Laurent had booked, I pushed the window shade up to study the vivid early sky over the wing and pensively sipped at a cup of tea. I had risen at four in the morning, and it would be evening before I arrived in Paris. With no annoyingly chatty seatmate, I was free to reflect.

Theresa had become a moderately successful journalist for the political magazine in Paris. We'd not spoken in three months, I realized. Tee had been consumed with the busyness of her career, with playing hostess at Laurent's gallery, and with the myriad issues of her demanding stepdaughters.

Why had the traumatic night we'd suffered three years ago affected Theresa this way? Why her and not me? *The mind is incredibly complex.* Theresa's doctor and Laurent believed that because I'd been with Tee the night of the blackout, I could help her talk through it and begin purging the fear from her mind.

A horse-faced stewardess offered me more tea, a pair of disposable slippers, and a blanket. I accepted all gratefully, slipped from my heels into the slippers, and pulled the light blanket over me. With a thumb, I slid the snapshot of Lark from my wallet and peered at her precious face. "Absence makes the heart grow fonder," my grandmother Courtwright had said, but I knew I couldn't love my child more.

My old Judas thoughts turned to Dean. How right I had been to keep our baby! What if I hadn't? Would Dean love her as I did?

He would if he could see her and hold her in his arms. His arms. I turned toward the window as tears oozed. Watching Lark grow the last months, I'd considered calling Dean again. I was reclaiming the grace and courage I had lacked during the pregnancy and Lark's infancy. When I returned from France, I would serve the ball into Dean's court and see how he played it. The stewardess brought warm towels around. I bathed my face and hands as the breakfast trays were served. I nibbled on a buttery croissant, a ham-and-cheese omelette, cheese, and fruit. Eventually the roar of the engine lulled me to sleep.

Hours later, Laurent Pelletier, whom I recognized from his picture, met me at Charles de Gaulle Airport's bustling baggage claim. He kissed both my cheeks in greeting. His photograph had not done him justice. I could see how Theresa had fallen for him so quickly. Laurent was warm and gracious, but his dark eyes were rimmed with sadness. I spotted my voluminous bag, and Laurent carried it to the trunk of his black Mercedes.

I couldn't help but feel excited about seeing Paris for the first time. On the dusky drive to the Pelletiers' boulevard Saint-Germain apartment, Laurent pointed out the lights of Notre Dame on the right bank of the Seine. The lights reflected off the rippling night water like a casting of gold coins. Through the moonroof of the car the gray-blue evening sky deepened. I lowered my window, and a fresh, cool, faintly salt-scented breeze teased my face and hair. Seeing Notre Dame brought Dean to mind again. I hoped he would see it one day. Maybe he already had. I shook myself, willing away torturous thoughts.

"Are you chilled, Robin?" Laurent's accent was silken. He reached toward the heat dial.

"No, no, I'm fine; the air feels wonderful." I managed a smile.

The Eiffel Tower wasn't visible from the route, but Laurent promised to show me the sights another day. My thoughts turned to Theresa. Laurent began to detail the therapy her doctor had proposed. The three of us would meet with Madame Desrosiers the following morning. Tonight I would shower my friend with love.

A sturdy and florid female domestic opened the door of the apartment and greeted us in lilting French. "Bonsoir, Monsieur Laurent, Madamoiselle Hamilton." I realized she must have been briefed on me. The French were formal and apparently as thorough as their neighbors to the east.

Laurent said to the woman in French, "Madame Heloise, may I present Mademoiselle Hamilton?" And to me he said, "Robin, this is our devoted Madame Heloise; we couldn't do without her. Know that she speaks little English." He smiled. "She can't be bothered to learn." He asked Heloise to show me to my room.

"Oui, monsieur," Heloise piped briskly. She lifted my weighty bag as though it were made of straw and led me toward a long hall lined with more art.

"I'll tell Theresa you've arrived," Laurent called after us.

The spacious apartment was elegant and bright and decorated with clean contemporary pieces. Stark white walls provided the perfect backdrop for Laurent's vibrant paintings. I loved his still-life work—eclectic arrangements of fruit and flowers and found objects—and the life-sized portrait of Theresa, hair aflame, wearing a plum dress and sapphires, over the mantle in the living room. My room echoed the rest of the apartment, spare except for a brightly hued rug in the middle of the floor. An antique sleigh bed beckoned, the linens crisp and turned invitingly down. And on the expanse of wall above it was a series of three of Laurent's botanical studies.

Theresa had told me that Laurent's family money had allowed him to paint until he had established a place for himself in the community of commissioned artists. I realized his work must fetch large sums. I unpacked and freshened up a bit and then ventured out to find Theresa. The apartment was redolent with what smelled like roast lamb. My stomach grumbled in anticipation. I hadn't eaten in six hours. Theresa sat at the edge of one of the white leather living room sofas. I saw her before she saw me, and my heart stabbed as I registered her thinness, her haunted eyes. Theresa stood and burst into tears. "Rob!" she said and held her arms out to me. As we embraced, I noticed her hair lacked its former luster. It didn't smell fresh. Tee's wraithlike appearance contrasted sharply with the vivid portrait behind her on the wall.

"Darling, Tee, everything will be okay. We're going to get to the bottom of this thing, I promise," I said as if soothing a frightened child.

"Je suis désolé ... You came all this way and without Lark." She clutched her hands nervously. I realized we had our work cut out for us.

The three of us sat down to dinner in the dining room. Madame Heloise's succulent lamb chops and fresh vegetable risotto, followed by piquant goat cheese and fresh, crisp salad greens, was incomparably delicious. I ate every morsel of my chocolate profiterole dessert, while Tee only picked at her plate.

Laurent was clearly crazy about his young wife. After coffee in the living room, he kissed her good night, murmured something into her ear, and retired to his own room. I went to bathe away the day of travel. As I filled the luxuriously appointed bath, I regarded my first bidet with amusement.

Refreshed and comfy, I padded to Theresa's room, where she was reclining on a great gilded bed, her pretty face as pale as the linens behind her. Though shattered, this was still my best friend in the world. I grinned and jumped onto the bed. I told Tee about Lark and how fast she was growing, spreading the sheath of photographs I had brought with me across the duvet. Theresa exclaimed over the baby, her face lighting for the first time. *"L'ange! Tu est belle!"*

Madame Heloise knocked to ask if we would like a nightcap. Wide-eyed, I accepted a heavy crystal tumbler of scotch. "Tee, you live like a queen!"

"I realize that," she said simply. "Too bad money can't buy peace of mind. But I feel better just having you here, Rob, I do! But I feel terribly guilty about taking you away from Lark."

Looking intently into the face I loved, I said, "I don't want to hear you say that again, darling. I am here because I want to be."

Theresa closed her eyes and nodded, a single tear coasting down one wan cheek. And then jet lag began to claim me. "Rest well," I said, kissing Tee's forehead. I closed the door softly behind me.

As Theresa, Laurent, and I pulled away from the apartment the next morning, Theresa's mouth trembled below large, dark sunglasses. She pulled a large silk scarf closely around her shoulders. She said little in the car as Laurent and I chatted brightly. Laurent held the wheel with his left hand; his right firmly held Theresa's.

Handsome with cherry paneling, fresh flowers, and overstuffed chintz chairs, Madame Desrosiers's office could almost lull you into believing you were there to have tea with royalty. Indeed the doctor's carriage was regal, but her open manner put me at ease immediately. For ninety minutes (in which a silent, blue- eyed woman brought a tray of tea and coffee) I spoke until my throat was scratchy of Theresa's obsession with the Son of Sam story and described the night of the blackout, tasting words I hadn't spoken in years.

As details emerged, the doctor would interrupt and ask Theresa's perspective. For the first time Laurent learned the whole story. Madame Desrosiers concluded the session and asked if she could speak to Laurent alone. Tee and I waited in the exit room. Laurent later told me the doctor felt the session had been productive and an integral part of Tee's recovery.

I attended the next three sessions with Tee. Laurent would drop us off and drive to his studio. I had been nowhere except the doctor's office and the apartment since I had arrived. On the third day Theresa said as casually as if commenting on the weather, "Let's go *out* to lunch today."

In the backseat my heart leaped. Laurent turned to stare at his wife. The hope in his eyes was so naked I had to look away. And then he asked with a tremulous smile, "Where to, cherie?"

"I'd like to go to Bistro Beaubourg," Tee said evenly. "Robin will like it, and it's nice enough to sit outside."

We were seated at a quiet corner table in the sunny courtyard under a red umbrella. Theresa ate from her plate of perch with fennel, tomatoes, and wine and a potato galette. But she looked as if she should be stamped with a "Fragile" sticker. The three of us shared a nice bottle of white wine, a Vouvray from the Loire Valley.

Each night when I went to bed, I prayed for Tee and for my baby at home. I missed Lark terribly and couldn't wait to hold her again, to kiss her cheeks, and to smell my favorite spots beneath her chin and at the tender nape of her neck.

Theresa and I participated in two more sessions together, and after each the three of us lunched at Tee's favorite spots. Laurent drove me to see the Eiffel Tower and the Arc de Triomphe and down the historic Champs-Élysées. He parked near Ladurée and returned with a beautiful assortment of airy, pastel macaroons.

One afternoon in a spot rowdy and clotted with tourists, Theresa had a panic attack, the first I'd seen. "My heart, Laurent!" she gasped. She held her chest and trembled. Laurent's arms tightly around her, Tee closed her eyes. I saw her lips move with the calming mantras Madame Desrosiers had taught her. She breathed slowly and deeply, fighting the panic. I stroked her hair. "That's it. You're so brave, Tee."

Each day my friend's face regained color. Madame Heloise prepared all her favorite meals to tempt her appetite. We enjoyed them with robust glasses of good French wine. At last the lines around Theresa's eyes and mouth began to smooth, her cheeks to take on the former curves.

On Saturday, though the clouds were pregnant with rain, we went to the world's largest flea market, Les Puces de Saint-Ouen. I loved the funkiness of it—the antique luggage, jewelry, architectural pieces, books, and garden pots. I bought a pretty antique alphabet poster for Lark's room and a handsome antique wooden box for my parents. The air rang with of the sounds of hawking vendors and twitters from the tall cages of parrots and parakeets as flashy as a marching band. Theresa laughed easily that day, though she continued to cling to Laurent's hand or arm.

On Sunday the three of us headed south into the quiet countryside. We passed through quaint villages, farms with vivid fields of lavender and poppies. We stopped at a small family market for a fresh baguette, a sampler of cheeses and sausages, fruit and bottled water, and two bottles of wine—a dry white Sancerre and light red Beaujolais. Laurent was enjoying teaching me about wine.

The sun high, we spread our picnic in a grove of trees. We laughed a great deal. Tee lay gazing at clouds, her mass of Titian hair like a ring of fire on the grass. "Wouldn't a joint be perfect about now, Rob?" she said. Laurent shook his head with an indulgent smirk. He said recreational drugs had never appealed to him.

"I guess those days are behind us, Madame Pelletier." I hadn't smoked in over two years. It was a tranquil, healing afternoon for us all.

An easy alliance had sprung between Laurent and me. I was coming to love him, to think of him as I would a brother-in-law. His love for my truest friend was strong and lasting. This simple fact filled me with gratitude for his solid presence.

The next week Madame Desrosiers asked that Theresa attend her sessions alone. Those mornings I drove Tee to the doctor's office, parked the sedan, and wandered into a different café each day for a decadent, flaky chocolate croissant or crepe and a café crème. I was surprised to hear so many different tongues in the conversations around me—German, Chinese, Dutch, and once what I thought must be Portuguese. The last day of appointments as I enjoyed the last of my rich coffee, the woman at the next table whom I'd seen before, with the Brillo Pad hair and nostrils so elongated you could have inserted a couple of nickels into them, moved on, leaving a French tabloid on her table. I picked it up, amused at the universal love of gossip.

I glanced at this or that overweight, stretch-marked cinema star in a bikini and then did a double take at a photograph on the second page. It was the Eagles. I read the article with interest and learned the band had broken up. The paper reported that the band members had developed a conflict of interests and that collaboration on the last album had been miserable. I was shocked and wanted to confirm the story from another source. I couldn't wait to tell Tee about it when I picked her up.

Tuesday afternoon Theresa and I walked to the Musée D'Orsay in a cool, slanting rain. She explained I would see more of the impressionist work I loved there, rather than the Louvre. I savored the Renoir masterworks and told Tee the stories of the two very different experiences I had had at the Phillips Collection in DC. In a gallery of late-nineteenth-century sculpture, we found the bust of Madame Renoir in a case. Her husband, then almost crippled from unrelenting rheumatism in his hands, had created the piece shortly after her death. "Now that's love," Theresa murmured, her eyes shining.

On Wednesday afternoon Tee took me to her favorite place in Paris, the Luxembourg Gardens. "Robin," she said, taking my arm as we strolled through the old iron gates, "I can't believe I was trapped in that ... shell ... of my own fear for so long." Madame Desrosiers had said that fear was at the root of Theresa's problem. The sessions were helping my friend to excise the fear like a rotten tooth. "And I have missed this place. Isn't it beautiful?" she said, gesturing with a sweep of one small, expressive hand. "I used to come here once a week to write."

"It is spectacular! Now you can do that again," I said, smiling at my friend. We stood at the edge of a round, shallow pool dotted with jaunty wooden sailboats of yellow and blue. Young children industriously prodded the boats along with long sticks. I wished for Lark as we watched little boys in short pants and T-strap shoes at play. Artists perched at easels around the perimeter of the promenade painted vistas of the park in the light. Wide, old stone stairs, their steps worn into silky troughs by millions of feet, were flanked with columns topped with centuries-old statuary. Weatherworn cherubs held aloft urns filled with riotous flowers and trailing vines. The steps led to upper terraces and paths surrounded by dense green foliage. Tee and I could have been extras in a movie as we sat in a pair of painted metal chairs, a row of nodding summer flowers at our feet, Marie de Medici's former palace magnificent behind us.

I had waited to bring up the subject of Theresa's therapy, but the moment felt tranquil, ripe for disclosure. "Tee," I said carefully, "I wish I'd known how deeply that night in New York affected you. And I've wondered if there was … something I could have done … but you seemed fine after those first few days."

"I compartmentalized it, Robin. That's how my mind copes with fear. My pattern has been to bury shit … trauma … deep within myself. I'm afraid my mother encouraged that. After I was mugged, the new fear was too much to add to what was already there. It was like … you know when you try to cram too much into a suitcase? You can force the lid down, but when you let go, it pops back up; the contents are too full to compress. Does that make sense?"

"It makes perfect sense," I said, watching her face. A rubber ball rolled toward us, chased by a darling little boy. I bent down and caught the ball in one hand and grinned at him. "Voilà," I said, offering it to him. He took it in both pudgy hands, smiling shyly, and ran away on sturdy legs.

Theresa's eyes followed him. "I have to deal with the fear head on … fight it from now on, now that I can see it for what it is. It's real, and it can feel … just crushing, but it's just fear. It will get easier with time." She looked at me again.

"Tee, I'm so proud of you. It has taken a lot of courage to do what you've done." I leaned over to hug her thin shoulders.

"Thank you, my friend." She smiled. "I know I couldn't have done it without you. I'm going to continue to see Madame Desrosiers. And I'll have Laurent—he's been amazing—and *you*, you've been *incredible*, Robin! You'll be pulling for me from across the ocean, right?"

"You can count on it, baby." We smiled at each other in the sunlight.

That evening, my last in Paris, Laurent drove us through a fine mist to the elegant old restaurant Lasserre on avenue Franklin D. Roosevelt. The street was still, the streetlamps haloed in mist, as Theresa and I walked beneath Laurent's huge black umbrella. I regarded with awe the Louis XVI furnishings, the brocaded walls, and the tables set with fine porcelain and crystal glasses edged in gold. And the ceiling! Painted with clouds and an azure sky, it could be retracted in fair weather to allow moonlight or sunlight to pour into the room.

My mouth twisted as the steward ceremoniously decanted our wine into a silver pitcher. Laurent smiled at me as if I were Marie Antoinette, laughing and feasting on Belon oysters, fillets of sole with asparagus cream sauce, and a salad of truffles. After a soufflé

Grand Marnier, I was practically woozy from the decadent excess. I couldn't imagine *l'addition* in the leather binder Laurent held. I sensed the extravagance was his final way of thanking me for coming to Paris.

The last night Theresa and I sat up in her bed again talking of the future. I told her I was determined to tell Dean the truth about Lark. Her eyes fervent with passion, she said, "It's time, Robin. You owe it to Dean. To Lark. And even to yourself, although you may not yet realize it."

Early the next morning we left for the airport. Both Pelletiers embraced me. Theresa promised to call me with updates on her progress. Laurent said simply, "Thank you, Robin," his throat constricted with emotion.

"Give *mon alouette* a kiss from Tante Tee!" Theresa called as I moved down the Jetway.

* * * * *

I was grateful Lark hadn't taken her first steps without me. It had been only twelve days, but it seemed a month since I'd seen her. The child seemed to have grown an inch. I put her in bed with me the first night. Snuggling with her, I tumbled into a miles-deep sleep. My mother tiptoed in and plucked the baby from the bed without waking me the next morning. I slept for ten straight hours.

My excellent grades and certificate in paralegal studies arrived in the next afternoon's mail. Mentally I checked off another benchmark toward my independence. It was time to draft my first résumé and begin to search for a job. Once again for a time, I forgot my commitment to call Dean.

I knew Dad's contacts in the legal community would be invaluable. We discussed the fields of law again, and I spent several mornings in the library pouring over information about the fields that interested me. In the end I decided to apply with a firm specializing in trusts and estates. That lawyers in these fields usually built long-standing personal relationships with their clients appealed to me. An acquaintance of Dad's, Stephen Adams (who looked like Gary Cooper) of the firm of Wickersham, Collins, and Adams, was adding a paralegal to their growing practice. At my interview I found Mr. Adams a thoroughly nice man, and he hired me on the spot. I had my first job.

My parents and I agreed Lark and I should stay with them until I was on my financial feet. Mom and I shopped for business attire. She bought me two tailored suits and three blouses. I dug in at the firm, working prodigiously, but at the end of the day the sight of my child always reinvigorated me. I loved giving Lark her bath and snuggling as we read *Pat the Bunny* or *Goodnight Moon* at bedtime. She babbled and drooled and patted the books, completely absorbed in them. "Night, night, sleep tight; see you in the morning's light," I would say as I put her down.

Lark would be a year old in a few days and looked more like Dean than ever. The early taffy tuft of hair had become Dean's darker gold. She was beginning to use real words now—Ma-ma, Gam-ma, Gam-pa, bye-bye, quack, moo, and Ack-cus. After dinner one evening she pulled herself to a standing position at the old ottoman. We laughed at her astonished face.

It was time to call her father. It took me two days to make the call after I'd made the decision. On a Saturday afternoon, Lark down for a nap and my parents out of the house, I dialed the number, my heart thudding with anticipation. I heard the phone ringing in Virginia, my palm slick with sweat on the receiver. "Hello?" an out-of-breath, feminine voice answered on the sixth ring.

"Hello," I responded in my best Miss Pruitt's School voice and a bravado I didn't feel. "This is Robin Hamilton calling. With whom am I speaking please?"

"This is Laurel Falconer." Her voice was friendly. "Robin." She paused, searching her memory. "Hello, my dear, I'm glad that you called. Dean's not here right now." She paused again, and I felt a prickling disquiet. "Robin ... Dean tried for months to find you." My heart flipped in my chest as she added, "He was very much in love with you, but ... I'm afraid I was quite ill at the time and needed my son. Dean was wonderful to take the family in hand. It has taken me ... a long time to pull myself together after my husband's death."

I managed to murmur something that sounded like "I'm-so-sorry-but-pleased-to-hear-you-have-recovered" while my thoughts spiraled crazily.

"Dean is engaged to be married in June," she said quietly. Eight words and my legs threatened to fold like a battered lawn chair. I sat heavily on the floor, a death grip on the receiver in my fist. "I hope this news isn't painful for you." Only like a rusty hatchet in my sternum. But this kind, southern-voiced woman, Dean's mother, was only the unfortunate messenger. "Would you like me to have him call you?"

I collected myself with effort. "No, thank you, Mrs. Falconer. And please, will you keep this conversation between the two of us? Please. I don't want to interfere."

"Well … yes, of course, if you want me to," she said slowly. "I understand. I'm sorry I won't get to know you, Robin," she continued gently. "If Dean loved you, I know you are a special woman."

I couldn't remain on the line another second. "Thank you. Good-bye, Mrs. Falconer." I sat looking at the receiver until a shrill tone began. Then I walked ponderously up the stairs to my room where Dean's beautiful, rosy-cheeked baby lay sleeping peacefully, a yellow cloth duck peeping from beneath one plump arm. I sat beside the crib and watched her in a void of stillness until the room grew shadowy and she woke. "Hi, sweet Lark," I said. She grinned from ear to ear, her face flushed, sheet creased, so vulnerable. She pulled up to stand, her chubby tummy pushing against the rail of the crib and held her arms up to me, "Ma-ma!" I picked her up and held her against me, closing my eyes. Her diaper was wet and heavy. She squirmed to be changed. I took care of my daughter's needs.

I would not be undone by this. Not again. I had Lark, and she was enough. I headed down the stairs again, my blissfully oblivious child chattering happily on my hip, to the kitchen to start dinner.

CHAPTER

13

Dean

1980–1982

Missing Robin like hell, I wrote her two mushy letters I knew she'd like—just days apart. Within ten days, both of them reappeared in the mailbox at Villeneuve. Someone had scrawled "No longer at this address" across both of them. Bush-hogging all afternoon, I thought, *Why would she move?*

I took a long, hot shower, my muscles tired and sore, and stretched out across my bed. At least hard work kept me from thinking too much about sex. I reached for the phone and scrap of paper with Robin's number. The phone rang once in DC, and then, following three shrill tones, an automated voice said, "The number that you have dialed is no longer in service." I hung up, nonplussed, checked the number again, and redialed with the same result. *What is going on?*

The next morning I called directory assistance and got the number for the law school registrar's office. "I'm sorry, sir; I'm not allowed to give out personal student information," a woman said.

"Please. I have to find her. I'm … concerned about her."

"I'm sorry, sir." But then her voiced softened. "Actually, I see here that Miss Hamilton withdrew from school … at semester."

What? Robin quit law school? "Is there a forwarding address?" I asked the woman.

"I really am sorry. I can't provide that information." I thanked the woman and held the receiver to my chest for several minutes. *What now?*

I worked hard the next few days replacing sections of fence, hoping to hear from Robin. But as another week went by, there was no word. If she had quit school, something was very wrong. Maybe she had gone home to New York. I called directory assistance for the Hamiltons' number. I remembered her father's name was Hank. I tried Hank, and there was no listing. Then I tried Henry. The operator told me that Henry A. Hamilton's number was an unlisted one. I had no idea what the name of his firm was.

I'd been a fool not to get Robin's New York number. I knew her parents lived in an old brownstone on the Upper West Side, but what was I supposed to do? Go knock on a hundred doors? I had about as much chance of finding Robin as I did of signing a free agent contract with the Yankees.

Friday night I waited up for Leslie to come in. I'd spent the evening watching TV and playing backgammon with Mary. My little sister had finally lost the wide-eyed, perpetually startled look she had developed after Dad had died. Tonight she had laughed aloud at my corniest jokes. But I had sent Mary to bed at midnight. I felt like an indignant father sitting there fuming about Leslie until two thirty, wishing I had a joint to smoke.

Leslie crept in then, and I asked from the shadows, "Where the hell have *you* been?" startling her. In the lamplight I saw my sister had a kissing chin and messed-up hair. She waved her hand in dismissal. "I've been at a party, with Tony, at the place of some friends' of his." Tony Childs, no doubt.

"Listen, Leslie, I don't like having to act like a parent, but it's not safe out driving around this late."

"You are not Dad!" she spat, venom in her gray eyes.

"Well, I'm the closest thing you've got to it right now. Get upstairs!" I growled, rising from the chair as if to do something we would both regret.

"Gladly, Mr. Prison Warden!" she yelled, but I detected a prickle of fear in her eyes.

"We'll talk about this in the morning," I said through clenched teeth, breathing hard. Leslie stormed up the stairs and slammed her door. I hated myself then for scaring her. Wearily, I moved to the liquor cabinet, poured myself a hefty scotch, and took it upstairs. I lay back against the pillows on my bed, sipping from the glass and thinking about Robin, how much I wanted and needed her. *Where the hell is she?* I thought for the hundredth time.

On a whim one Saturday I drove to Georgetown. It had been a long time. I realized I had no idea how I would find or contact any of Robin's friends there, but I went to the apartment building and knocked on door 129 with a lump in my throat. A tall—Amazonian-tall—girl with oily black hair answered the door and scowled at me. She said yes, it was she who had gotten my letters and put them back into the mail chute. She knew nothing of Robin. Looking past the girl, I glimpsed the apartment where Robin and I had loved each other, and a flood of memories just about took me down. With effort, I thanked the girl and walked away.

I went by the Tombs and found James in. "It's great to see you, buddy!" I said, squeezing his shoulder. "How've you been?"

"Dean, I've missed you, man! How is your mom?" I sat and ordered a beer, and James and I caught up with each other. I told him I was looking for Robin. "Dude, I'm sorry," he said. "I never saw her again after that night at my party."

Two beers later, I rose to pay my tab. James waved my open wallet away. "It's on me, Dean. Good luck, man. I hope you find her; girls like Robin don't come along every day."

"No, they don't," I said, my throat constricted. "Later, man." I had to get out of there before I started bawling. I climbed in my Jeep and aimed it for the farm. The only girl I had really loved had disappeared like the sweet smoke from a doobie. All I could do was pray and hope that Robin would get back in touch with me.

By summer there was still no word or trace. The situation was like a ball game that had gone into extra innings, tied at zero inning after inning, and finally called because of rain or dark or who knows what … but in the end it didn't count.

The farm and helping with the girls consumed all my time. I had the barn help, Harry and Justin, to take care of the horses but still could use more manpower. Uncle John helped me on weekends, but I carried the bulk of the load myself.

I *had* to get back to school. With just a few more courses in my master's program, I knew I could finish it at UVA in no time. What I really needed was a farm manager, to fill Dad's shoes.

My mother had made nice progress. The doctor had started her on a new medication that seemed to be making the difference. Mom was more animated and spoke of coming home to us, of the farm and her animals. The attending physician planned to release her in two weeks' time, when the antidepressant had reached its full effectiveness. He said she would need to stay on the medication for at least six months.

The girls were guardedly excited about the homecoming. Mom's depression had frightened and confused them. Both of them had been happier since I'd come home, although the truce between Leslie and me had been strained since the night of our fight. But Leslie's clothes no longer hung on her tall frame. Her cheeks were gently rounded again. I took her fishing one Saturday as our dad had done. On the pond we had learned to swim in as children, the opportunity to talk presented itself. Leslie spoke of her eating problem. I listened casually but was duct-taped to every word. I alternately baited our hooks with crickets and cast my line.

"I know about anorexia, Dean; I've read the magazine stories and seen all those movies." A huge catfish jumped from the water across the lake, making a loud clattering smack as it plunged again below the surface. Her gray eyes on the rippling water, Leslie continued, "When Dad died, I just couldn't eat, and then when Mom went off the deep end, I felt like the only thing I could control in my life was what I put in my body. It was just like the girls you hear about on TV. But it's very ... I don't know ... seductive ... when you're in the middle of it."

I looked at my sister. Her lashes were dark with unshed tears. "You were lucky to be able to see it, Les, and ... stop it before it killed you. There are people who don't, and they *die*. This has been ... a total nightmare for everybody, but you're better now. We all are ... and life will go on." We watched our floats drift and bob silently with the boat's wake, the only sounds the drone of horseflies and the water lapping lazily at the sides of the aluminum boat.

"Oh, and yeah," Leslie said, startling me from a reverie, "you'll be happy to know, big brother, that wild Tony Childs has headed west, left for Colorado last week, to work on a cattle ranch. His old man laid down the law." Leslie watched me from the corner of her eyes, gauging my reaction. I just nodded my head. "He wasn't my type anyway," she added a minute later, wrinkling her nose and sniffing. She reeled in her line, swatting at a horsefly, and cast again. "I got one!" she called excitedly as her cork plunged beneath the surface. I cheered her on as she reeled in a thrashing bream as big as my hand.

"Nice one! Way to go, Sis." I grinned. We caught a nice mess of fish that afternoon and gave them to Justin, who took them home for his wife, Stacey, to fry for supper. The trip had been a success.

I also spent time with Mary, driving her to and from school every day until summer vacation started. I quizzed her for tests on the morning drives, and some afternoons we'd get frozen slushies for the ride home. We fed the horses early in the mornings when the barn was cool. One afternoon we took the three hunting hounds out into the fields to run. I almost crapped my pants when she asked me out of the blue, "Does everybody have oral sex, Dean?"

My thoughts ricocheted like bats in a box. "What do you mean, honey?" I asked, buying time.

"I hear people talking about it at school, and I just … wondered if it's something that you *have* to do when you have sex."

"Are you having sex, honey?" I asked, a pain beginning behind my right eye.

"Dean! No! I don't even have a boyfriend!"

I wracked my brain trying to come up with a decent answer for my sweet little sister. "Well, when you make love … with … someone you truly love … you do what you feel comfortable doing." The dogs came bounding back, weaving through the tall grass, hassling, great tongues lolling, Buddy with the ball. I wrestled it from his mouth, wound up like Catfish Hunter, and threw the ball again.

"Okay," Mary said studiously, rubbing at a scratch on her boot with a thumb.

"And if you think about having sex before you're married … and I hope you don't … only do what makes you feel respected. And make sure you are protected. Do you know what I mean by that?" That was all I could stand to say.

"Yeah." She looked up at me again and punched me in the bicep.

"Oww! Damn, you pack a punch!" I said, holding my arm. Mary grinned and took off after the dogs. While she had floored me, I was humbled to know how much she trusted me, that she would ask her brother about something of that nature rather than Leslie.

One morning in the barn as I squeezed a sponge over Tartan's broad haunches, I heard Mary talking to her horse Missy as she tended to a sore spot on the mare's leg. Missy was all stillness … completely captivated by Mary's tone. It was the intro I had been looking for. "Hey, little sister, how 'bout I call Dr. Doss, to see if he could use a teenage helper this summer?" I knew the clinical experience would be good for Mary, and she would be terrific with the animals, a win-win situation.

"I guess so. Are you trying to get rid of me?"

I laid my thumb across the hose nozzle and sprayed water up and over the stall wall between us.

"Crap, Dean, you got my hair wet! I'll get you back double."

"I'll get you back triple." I grinned at our old routine.

Mary loved riding in my Jeep with the top down. One afternoon the first week of June, the two of us were driving home from the farm supply store together. I pulled into the drive from the main road and stopped the Jeep. "I've got a charley horse," I said, reaching down to rub my calf. "You drive us to the house."

"Dean, I can't drive!" Mary said, looking at me as if a third nostril had spontaneously appeared in my face.

"The gas is on the right, the brake in the middle, and the clutch is on the left. If you can use the pedals on the piano, you can work the pedals in a car. Then, little sister, all you have to do is steer."

"I don't know, Dean. I'm scared. What if I wreck us?" There were two hectic spots of color on her cheeks.

"Do you think I would let you drive *my Jeep* if I was worried?" I said, tipping her a wink. I got out and strolled around to her side of the car and then made her scoot across the console and into the driver's seat.

Mary did drive that day—after a lot of jerking and bucking and grinding of my gears—all around our property, and loved it. I took her out every afternoon that week. And when she was comfortable, bordering on cocky, I took her to some parking lots in town to practice parking. We picked up a driver's manual from the DMV, and Mary studied for the Virginia driver's test.

Majestic Oak Hill, the next farm over, was home to the Babbitt family. Mr. and Mrs. Babbitt had socialized quite a bit with my parents through the years. They were generationally wealthy but good, down-to-earth folks. I had grown up with their kids, Billy and Victoria. Billy and I were the same age and had gone through junior high and high school together. We'd played on the baseball team in high school, he the shortstop and me the first baseman. Billy had been a helluva hitter, the star player. An all-around good guy, he had been voted by our senior class Most Friendly *and* Most Sportsmanlike. Billy had been headed for the University of North Carolina, handpicked by selective recruiters for a scholarship, but the summer before we were to leave for college he'd wrapped his truck around a hundred-year-old oak tree one night on the way home from a party. Suffering two compound fractures and slight brain damage from a concussion, Billy hadn't been able to go to college after all. I knew Billy worked for a homebuilder in Charlottesville now. Though he had regained most of the short-term memory function he had lost, the limp that remained after a year of intense physical therapy would be with him until the day they closed his coffin.

I had Billy in mind for the position of farm manager. If he was interested, I knew he would do a good job and earn more money than he was at present. I was counting on Mom to go back to keeping the books when she got home and was strong again. On the tractor one Thursday afternoon in July, the sun biting my neck as if it had teeth, a baby-blue Mercedes Benz 500SL rolled up the gravel drive, its tires gathering dust and scattering it into the air. *Shit, I just washed my Jeep,* I thought. It was Victoria Babbitt's car.

Victoria was thirteen months younger than Billy and me and had gone through junior high with us. Before ninth grade she'd transferred from public school to the swanky girls' school in Ivy. I hadn't seen her much after that, though she'd asked me to take her to a school dance once when she had been in eleventh grade. I'd known she had a crush on me; Billy had told me so. I'd taken her to the dance and had even made out with her a little in the driveway when I'd taken her home that night. She'd looked hungrily at me all that evening and had asked me to call her, but shortly after, I'd met Katie Sumner, a petite blonde and a talented violinist with a dry wit. Katie and I had dated until she'd gone off to study at Indiana University's prestigious school of music. After that, I'd never seen her again.

Sweating like a pig, I climbed down from the tractor and walked across the grass to greet Victoria. "Dean Falconer!" she said, smiling and stepping out of her car in a pink Sweet Briar College T-shirt, coltish legs in Daisy Duke cutoffs. "I heard you were home." She took off her sunglasses. "I'm so sorry about your father; He was a sweet man," she added kindly.

"Thank you, Victoria. How are you?" I said, pulling a bandana from my back pocket and wiping my face streaming under a UVA baseball cap.

"Well, I'm just fine, Dean. I'm home this summer and wondered if you wanted to take me out to dinner," she said with a toss of her blonde head and a saucy smile. I knew Victoria had studied for a semester in Italy and then earned her master's in teaching at Sweet Briar. Victoria's quiet, dark-eyed beauty had ripened since I'd seen her last.

I smiled at her. "A dinner out would be pretty nice actually. I've done nothing but work and crash every night since I've been home."

"Well, how 'bout tomorrow night?" Victoria suggested. "There's a new Italian place downtown that's supposed to be fantastic."

"It would be my pleasure … on one condition," I said.

She laughed, tossing her hair again. "And what's that, Dean Falconer?"

"That you let me drive that sweet car." I gestured to the sleek coupe. It was mighty sweet, the sun glinting off its blue paint and immaculate chrome.

"Well, okay, but I have a condition too," she said, opening the car door and stepping in. "That you smell a little better than you do right now." *Shit.* Victoria laughed at me, put her sunglasses on again, and started the engine. She spurted away, kicking up the dust again, and called out the window, "Pick you up at seven."

I went inside to cool off, thinking about what had just happened. I stood over the kitchen sink, drinking water and looking east toward the Babbitt place. I'd unwittingly stumbled into a date with the girl next door.

A week later my mother finally came home to Villeneuve. The girls had cleaned the house thoroughly, putting crisp sheets on Mom's bed and armloads of fresh-cut summer flowers in her room. Aunt Martha had cooked all afternoon, Mom's pot roast recipe. She and Uncle John would stay for dinner with us. Before her breakdown and with Martha's help, Mom had stoically and silently boxed all of Dad's clothes and taken them to Goodwill. (When she gave me Dad's watch, I almost started bawling.) We were all a little nervous about how Mom would reacclimate, my father's ghost in every room.

Uncle John and I drove Mom home from the hospital. She was timid and seemed fragile at first in the hubbub of hugs and greetings, but by the time we sat down to the big oak table, the girls chattering like magpies at her elbows, Mom was laughing at all of our news.

When Uncle John asked the blessing, we all echoed, "Amen." Then Mom cleared her throat and surprised us with a little speech that I thought was pretty eloquent. "I want to thank you all so much for your love … for being so … strong, giving me the time I needed to recover. I know it couldn't have been easy around here, without … your father *and* without your mother." She looked around the table at each one of us, her eyes bright with tears, though she kept her composure. "I am so proud of you … the way you have rallied together and kept Villeneuve going. Your father would be very proud." She looked back at me. "Dean, I am beyond proud of the man you have become. I know about all you've done," she said and winked at Martha. "You've sacrificed a great deal for your family. I want you to know that I intend to make it up to you."

"No, Mom. I did what I did because it was the right thing to do. It's what Dad would have expected." I reached across the table for her hand. "I love you very much. We all do. We're proud of your courage, Mom."

Smiling broadly, Uncle John lifted his glass of red wine. "To Laurel Falconer … and to family."

"To Laurel Falconer and to family," we all responded.

The evening was a success, a benediction to the last two and a half years of pain, of fear and uncertainty. I couldn't help breathing a huge sigh of relief as I climbed the stairs to my room that night. I felt like a grand piano had been lifted from my twenty-five-year-old shoulders. My mother had made a damned miraculous recovery, and I was free to get on with my life.

But as I crawled into bed that night, the sheets cool on my body, my thoughts turned to Robin again. I reached for the book I'd been reading, Ayn Rand's *The Fountainhead*, and slid out the fingerprinted photo of Robin and me at James's Christmas party. I stared at the picture for a long time, running my finger over Robin's face. She was so beautiful in that red dress; she actually glowed. With love for *me*. It seemed like such a long time ago.

Taking Victoria out felt strange at first, as though I were cheating on Robin, and then it was as if I was on automatic pilot: hold the door for her, smile, look interested when she's talking about girl stuff, pull out her chair. But Victoria was a nice girl. She arrived like a breath of cool air on that sultry summer night, wearing a pretty white sundress and sandals that contrasted with her golden summer tan. And that sweet ride: the coupe hugged the curves of the country roads like a lover. James Taylor's *JT* spilled from her in-dash cassette player. I couldn't have stood it if Victoria had been a big Eagles' fan.

I ceremoniously parked the Benz a block away from the pedestrian mall for the benefit of a clump of frat boys who were gaping like fools at the car. Victoria and I entered the restaurant, my hand automatically at the small of her back. We placed our wine order, and I regarded Victoria across the table. I liked the combination of Virginia drawl, intelligence, and dark eyes you don't usually see in blondes. We took our time getting reacquainted over spaghetti carbonara, salad, and crusty bread. After dinner we walked out onto the outdoor mall where musicians were playing outside the shops, their guitar cases strewn with dollar bills. I was curious about Victoria's experience in Italy and what she had seen. She told me about it as we strolled.

And that night as I pulled up in front of my house again, she leaned over and gave me one light, sweet kiss on the lips. After she'd caromed away again, I stood listening to the haranguing cicadas in the trees. What I didn't feel was real chemistry with Victoria. What I felt was relief. I would be safe with this girl. I wouldn't lose my heart and soul to her.

* * * * *

Mary was champing at the bit like her spirited mare Missy, like any happy teenager, to get her driver's license. Mom and I decided to surprise her with a Jeep for her seventeenth birthday. I drove her to the DMV on her birthday, and she passed the test. She came out acting all cool and asked for the keys to my Jeep. She drove home, a shit-eating grin splitting her face the whole way.

We crunched down the drive at Villeneuve and rounded the curve to the house. The family and barn help were gathered around a shiny blue Jeep. Leslie had decorated the windshield with a huge white bow. Mary hopped down, her mouth an astonished O, to cries of, "Congratulations!"

"Really?" she said over and over, walking around the car and shaking her head in thrilled astonishment. The next Monday morning my little sister started work at the veterinary clinic.

Mom had wholeheartedly agreed with my choice of Billy Babbitt as farm manager. I took him to lunch in town and offered him the job with a good salary. Surprised by the offer, Billy asked if I was sure he could handle the job. I reassured my old friend I had faith in him and knew he would do a good job. "How about a six-month trial run?" I said. Billy accepted gratefully and began work at Villeneuve two weeks later.

Leslie, in the meantime, had applied to the University of Virginia for the fall semester and had bought her books and a bunch of new clothes. She was fired up about going to college and living in the dorm with a roommate from Richmond whom she had met and liked. Hope shone in her eyes again.

I would finally be going to grad school myself and took an apartment in town where I could work on projects and plans in peace. I left Villeneuve in late August. Victoria and I went out three more times, to the movies and to the wedding of one of her friends from Sweet Briar. By then everyone had begun to think of us as a couple. I guess it was inevitable. Victoria helped me move into my new apartment and decorated it for me. She came over to cook dinner for me a couple of nights a week. Victoria loved and got on well with my family, and I took her to Villeneuve on Sundays for Mom's big noon meal.

I kissed and hugged Victoria affectionately the way a boyfriend would, but I still didn't feel the heat ... the passion ... I'd felt for Robin. *Robin.* I wanted to get married and have a family. I didn't have my first choice of woman—maybe someone like Robin was a once-in-a-lifetime shot. But Victoria was a good catch; the blending of our families would be a good one. I couldn't go on living in the shadows of the things that might have been. I slipped out of the man that belonged to Robin like a snake shedding its skin.

In my bedroom at Villeneuve on Thanksgiving night, I reached behind my neck and released the clasp on the St. Thomas medal. It was warm in my palm from lying against my heart. For a moment I pictured Robin's face again, seeing her as she'd looked as she'd given it to me. My heart squeezed with a long-familiar pang. I went through my chest of drawers and found the things I was looking for. I put them in a shoe box and taped around it with masking tape. With a Magic Marker I labeled it DEAN's and slipped out to hide it in my secret boyhood cubbyhole in the barn.

At Christmastime, Leslie helped me pick out a sparkly half-carat diamond ring, and I asked Victoria Babbitt to marry me.

CHAPTER

14

Robin

1980–1988

Lark had her first messy cold and spiked a fever. I took her to the pediatrician hoping to get a prescription, but the doctor said the cold was a virus; it was best to let it run its course. The fever was productive, she explained, helping Lark's body fight the virus. *Easy for you to say, when I'm the one walking the floor with her at night.* I was irritable and exhausted in the mornings but grateful I had my mom to take care of Lark at home while I worked, unlike many mothers who had to schlepp their kids out to day care.

We were two birds together, a robin and a lark, certain now that Dean would never share our nest. I tried not to show my sadness around Lark. She was a preternaturally perceptive child; her little face mirrored mine when I was feeling blue. One of our favorite books to read in those days was *Are You My Mother?* The mother bird in the story leaves an egg in the nest and goes in search of food. While she is away, the baby bird hatches, and because it cannot fly, it walks to find its mother. It encounters a kitten, a hen, a dog, a cow, a boat, a plane, and finally a power shovel and asks each, "Are you my mother?" The power shovel eventually drops the baby bird back in its nest, and mother and baby are reunited. Lark wanted to read the story again and again. I taught her to say "Mama Robin and Baby Lark" as we looked in the mirror. At thirteen months Lark was ready to walk, wander, and explore, as curious as *The Poky Little Puppy*. Grandpa Hank quickly went about childproofing the house with gates and locks.

I did the family grocery shopping on Saturday mornings, Lark in the cart in front of me. People were drawn to her rosy prettiness and bright chatter. Each time, I bought her a little red-and-yellow box of Barnum's Animal Crackers. Lark would ask for them as soon as we entered the store, so I always headed for aisle eight first. She would eat a cookie or two from a gummy fist and mimic the animal sounds. "Ooh, ooh!" she'd cry as she pulled out a monkey, or "Gurrrr!" for a tiger.

In those days Mom would say to Lark, "How did you get to be so smart?" She taught Lark to answer, "I was born that way!" The best part was that as Lark parroted the phrase, she'd stick out a dimpled arm and point her finger, *that way*. We made her say it over and over.

At eighteen months Lark loved to go out to the front steps of the brownstone to sit and talk. "'Teps and talk, Mama," she'd say, pulling me by the hand. One day on the steps she looked at me, her face astonished. "I've got fingernails on my toes, Mama!"

Though Theresa and I wrote to each other regularly, I missed her more than ever. I felt an ineffable sadness about our likely lifetime separation. And then one drizzly April Sunday night she called from Paris. She was coming to Chicago for two weeks to visit her mother. Overjoyed, I arranged to make a weekend trip with twenty-two-month-old Lark in tow. I was dying for Tee to see the baby again. Theresa sounded strong and happy, scoured clean of fear. She would be starting a new job, a nice promotion, when she returned to France, as a staff writer for the magazine.

I took a personal day the next Friday. Lark and I excitedly boarded the train for Chicago. Theresa met us at the station wearing a broad grin and a knitted black beret over her flaming hair, longer again. It thrilled her when Lark greeted her with "Tante Tee!" as I had taught her.

"Rob, your *alouette*! She is so beautiful!" Tee took Lark from me to hug and kiss her. She looked wistful and then gazed at Lark's face. "And looks … exactly like her father," she added quietly.

"I know. I think about it all the time. She even has some of his expressions. But I'm okay, Tee. I really am. I'm over him. I'm getting on with my life."

"*Bonne fille*," Theresa said, nodding once firmly and taking my arm. We began to walk. "Let's take this little angel to meet her grandma Cleary." I spotted an idling taxi, and we headed for Colleen's new apartment in the old Gold Coast section of the city.

On Saturday night, Colleen, who was clearly enamored with Lark, urged Tee and me to go out and leave the baby in her care.

Theresa and I jumped at the chance. Lark had developed a degree of stranger anxiety at home, and I worried about leaving her, but as we slipped out, she was busily smearing Colleen's caramel custard across the tray of the high chair we'd unearthed from the basement, crowing and kicking her legs with delight. Tee and I set out to find a neighborhood happy hour. Though we'd been through a great deal of adult drama in the last two years, we felt very young that night in jumpsuits and geometric jewelry. At the Tavern on Rush, we might have been two college girls. The music was good and loud, the place packed. We sipped scotch and waters and enjoyed the appreciative looks from men, although no one bothered us. Later, we walked just down the street to Bistro Zinc for dinner. We studied the menu on the glass, Theresa twitching a shoulder, pouting, and looking very French. "Let's see if they know how to prepare authentic French cuisine," she said over her shoulder as we entered. We ordered a bottle of wine, and Theresa ordered cassoulet with white beans, sausage, and duck confit in flawless French. I moaned over a plate of Norwegian wolffish with glazed mushrooms and potato-leek ragout. We savored just one bite each of warm clafoutis. Thoroughly sated, Tee leaned back and sipped a café crème. She sighed and conceded to the waiter, *"Mes felicitations au chef."*

We strolled ponderously back to Colleen's, stopping at a package store for a bottle of Scotch. I was happy to see my cherub sleeping surrounded by pillows on Theresa's bed. We said good night to Colleen, who was ready for bed. "I'd forgotten how exhausting it is keeping up with a toddler," she marveled. Tee and I took two glasses of scotch upstairs. As before, we sat on the bed talking with Lark between us. Apparently Theresa's stepdaughter

Tabby wouldn't allow Tee to babysit for her new baby, Jacque Charles. "He's so cute! But Tabby doesn't trust me, the little bitch."

"Give her time. She'll come around." I smiled and regarded my best friend. It was preposterous to think of Tee as a grandmother at twenty-four. "Do you ever wish you could have a baby? Have Laurent's child?" I asked and pulled at a strand of my hair wedged between my melting ice cubes.

"You know, I really don't," she said pensively. After a moment, she said, "I used to say that we could always adopt a baby someday. Laurent would if I wanted it. But our life is pretty perfect the way it is. I don't feel the need for a baby of my own to complete me. Maybe I'm not the maternal type." She looked at me for confirmation. "Everyone doesn't have to be, right?"

"Of course," I answered. "I didn't get much of a chance to decide whether I was or not." I gazed down at Lark. "But now I can't imagine not having her, a life without her. Life's funny, isn't it, Tee?"

"Stranger than fiction, my friend," Tee said with a wry smile. She raised her glass to clink against mine. "Have you thought about dating, Rob?"

"You know, I honestly haven't," I said, amazed. "I'm so busy with this little monkey." I smoothed Lark's damp hair. She was too warm for the sleeper Colleen had put her in. I took the blanket off her and unsnapped the sleeper's legs. "And with work. I'm so exhausted I fall asleep when my head hits the pillow." I sipped again at my drink. "I don't really *go* anywhere to meet men, just back and forth from home and work." I grinned. "There is one guy at work, Porter, who's attractive … but you know dating work associates is ill-advised.

When the phone rang, we both jumped. The baby fussed at the shrill sound, scrubbing her nose into the mattress, and was still again. Theresa reached for it, cringing in Lark's direction, and then she whispered, full of joy, *"Allo, cherie!"*

"Bonsoir, Laurent. I miss you!" I stage-whispered toward the receiver. I went to wash my face and brush my teeth while Tee was on the phone. When I came out in my pajamas, Theresa was standing in a pair of aqua panties, rummaging through her suitcase. She pulled out a matching aqua nightgown and pulled it over her head. *French women and their fancy, sexy lingerie,* I thought, fleetingly envious, and then rushed to say, "I'm glad you and Laurent are so happy, darling. You're wonderful together."

Tee appraised me. "You're a beautiful woman, Rob. You look even better than you did in college. You should meet someone. You deserve some romantic … tending."

"I know you're right," I said, readjusting the pillows behind my back. "But I'm *constantly* busy." I sipped at my drink. "There *are* times I feel lonesome. But you know, Tee, I don't pine after Dean the way I used to," I said and realized I spoke the truth.

"I cannot *believe* he's married," she sighed, closing her eyes and shaking her head.

"I know. Yet another tragic development in the Robin-and-Dean saga." We drank in silence for a few minutes. "I don't think

I'm ready … to *date* yet. But I *am* fired up about moving into my own place." I smiled. "Don't get me wrong; my parents have loved having us there, and they've been completely wonderful, but it's time for me to fly on my own."

"What about sex, Rob! Don't you miss it?" Tee insisted, frowning.

I smiled a little half smile, remembering for a moment. "I sure miss it with Dean. But with things the way they are right now, I guess every sexual impulse has just been purged out of me."

"Well, promise me you'll at least start looking at men again," Tee said. She yawned hugely.

"Okay, okay! I promise." I laughed and yawned at the same time. "Ha-ha-ahh-hahhh." I stuck a finger into Lark's diaper. It could wait till morning. Tee and I turned out the lamps and tumbled through sleep on either side of my daughter.

Sunday morning we went to brunch with Colleen and Tee's aunt Bridey—possibly the world's loudest-talking human in this teeny-tiny Chanel suit—and they drove us to the train station. Theresa had brought Lark a Madeleine doll from Paris, dressed in a bright-blue coat and yellow straw hat. Lark clutched the doll in one chubby fist and waved it. "Bye-bye, Tante-Tee!" she piped at my prompting.

"Bye-bye, *mon petit alouette*!" Theresa said, her eyes filling.

"Thanks for everything, Colleen," I said warmly. "Write soon, Tee!" Missing her already, I swayed on the platform, Lark on one hip, my diaper bag and purse slung over a shoulder, and my heavy suitcase in one hand. "Bye-bye!" We all smiled and waved.

For Lark's second birthday, a few of the neighbors came to the brownstone for cake and ice cream. Even Atticus tolerated the pointy paper party hat Lark placed on his head, one of his ears comically crimped by the elastic band. Dad captured on camera the moment the birthday girl sang "Happy Birthday" to herself along with us and then planted a hand into her grandmother's buttercream icing.

Through his generous real estate contacts, my dad helped me find a decent apartment just four blocks from the brownstone. It was a two-bedroom, second-floor walk-up, badly in need of airing and fresh paint. It came complete with a dead mouse in a kitchen corner. The tiny bathroom had no shower, but a surprisingly luxurious claw-foot tub separated the bedrooms. I wanted to do the work myself. It would be my first adult home, and I was thrilled with it.

The October late nights I peeled, scraped, scrubbed, and painted were some of the best nights I'd had in a long time. I brought my little cassette player over, sat it on the kitchen counter, and listened to Hall and Oates, Journey, and the Eagles while I worked. I could finally listen to the Eagles without drowning in a puddle of tears and self-pity. With the apartment's four windows open wide, I listened to the sounds of my new neighborhood as I slapped the paintbrush up and down the walls. Someone in the next building played a record of Puccini's *La Bohème* at the same time every night. *That should be soothing for my new little New York native*, I thought with a grin.

I worked at the office all day, went to Mom and Dad's for dinner to see Lark, and then headed back to the apartment to paint. We would move over Thanksgiving weekend. I took Lark to the new apartment when I had finished the work to show her where we would live. I flipped on the light. The paint job was strictly amateurish, but it was a soft, sunny yellow that pleased me, and "yeh-yoh" was Lark's favorite color. Lark looked around curiously, her little brow furrowed. "Why is dare no tunniter?" she asked.

"Oh, darling," I laughed, "we'll bring the furniture *with us* when we move."

Dad contracted for a moving truck and two men to help us move. As an early Christmas present, Mom bought us a pretty yellow-and-blue floral sofa bed and a chair in a blue companion fabric. I shopped at a thrift store for other things. Anita Roth, who luckily for me was on yet another of her redecorating binges, gave me a pair of matching chairs for my bedroom and a soft blue rug for the front room.

The movers showed up two hours late and dropped and broke my little kitchen table. I shrieked as one of the wooden legs rolled into oncoming traffic. Dad hurt his back moving the sofa. A nasty neighbor popped in demanding to know if I had noisy children. The toilet refused to flush. I discovered a pair of big nasty roaches frantically mating—at least somebody was having sex—in one of my freshly papered kitchen drawers. When Lark arrived with my mother late that afternoon, her little pink suitcase in one hand, she promptly vomited across Anita's rug. The poor baby had a stomach bug and cried and cried to "go home." After everyone had left, I put Lark in the claw-foot tub with me, shampooing her golden hair and soothing her with spills of warm water. We spent the next couple of hours in the rocking chair in her little bedroom until she finally fell asleep. We were home.

Just before her fourth birthday, I enrolled Lark in a preschool near my office. I was concerned about how she would fit in with other children as an only child and the epicenter of a tight-knit clan of adults. I walked her into the sunny classroom with some trepidation. In a crisp jumper and red Mary Jane shoes, her bright pigtails tied with blue ribbons, my daughter marched over to a tangle of kids at a sand-and-water table and never looked back. I slipped out gratefully but hovered over the telephone on my desk all day, afraid to take a lunch break. But Lark took to school like an intrepid little spelunker in a treasure-filled cave. She loved her playmates, especially a little boy named Christopher, and they tumbled like puppies. She came home chattering happily each afternoon with scraped knees, an empty lunchbox, and new ideas. By November she was sounding out and recognizing printed words. Her much-loved teacher Miss Sally, who never made me feel awkward seated in a parent-teacher conference alone, told me that Lark was one of the smartest children in the class, the best reader. *Oh, Dean.*

Grandma Olivia's transition back to work was a seamless and productive one. The gratified owner, thrilled by her return, immediately increased her salary by a third and then offered to sell the shop to her for a fair price. My parents were considering it. Grandpa Hank was so crazy about Lark he often dropped by the school on his lunch hour. Since Lark and I had moved into our own place, it had been our habit to walk back for late lunch at the brownstone after Sunday mass. A couple of times a month we had my parents over for dinner at our tiny place. And one night a week, Lark and I took our laundry over and visited with them while the clothes washed and tumbled dry.

Determined that Lark wouldn't be a picky eater, I devoted myself to learning to cook well. I pored over *The Joy of Cooking* until the pages were smudged with chocolate fingerprints, splotched with oil and tomato sauce. Lark's favorite meal was croque monsieur with a flavorful ham—the owner of the corner deli loved giving her samples—and Gruyère cheese. She ate spears of fresh asparagus like french fries.

One apple crisp of a fall afternoon when Lark was in first grade, my little girl, swinging her Care Bears lunchbox and kicking at acorns, rooted me in my tracks on the sidewalk. "Why don't I have a daddy?"

"Oh, sweetie, well ..." She'd rendered me effectually speechless. My thoughts made concentric circles around the question. *Oh shit. Why didn't I prepare myself for this?* I dug deep for a casual tone and willed my legs to walk on. "You do have a dad, darling."

"Well, who is it? Where is he?" She looked up at me, her light brow furrowed, one red ribbon trailing from a pigtail.

Stalling for time, I looked for a place to sit down. There were a couple of benches around the corner in the pocket park close to our apartment that Lark had named the Little Park.

"Let's go sit in the Little Park. It's such a pretty afternoon," I said brightly. A woman with an enormous blue Great Dane whom we recognized approached and diverted Lark for the moment. Lark stopped and spoke, eye to eye, to smoky, silk-coated Wellington.

Lark was aware that a couple of her school friends didn't live with their fathers, so I thought she might be able to understand our lifestyle. Reaching the park, we settled ourselves on a bench in the slanting sun. I retied the ribbon and kissed her soundly on the head. "Lark, darling," I said carefully, "you do have a father. Everyone has a father. But you know sometimes fathers don't live with their families. Rebecca's father lives in Connecticut, right?"

The child looked at me from Dean's clear gray eyes. "Why not, Mama?" she asked.

"Well, sometimes mamas and daddies decide not to live together, and sometimes mamas and their little girls or little boys live together."

She seemed to chew on my words for a minute. "Who *is* my daddy, Mama?" my God-sweet girl asked again.

"Your daddy," I said, plowing ahead with a sangfroid I didn't feel, "is a wonderful man named Dean Falconer. He … lives in Virginia." I paused, remembering I had read not to give a child more information of a delicate nature than what she asked.

"Can he come see us?" she asked as a squirrel jumped to the seat of the bench across from us. Bristled tail twitching, it stood on its hind legs and begged for a treat. We laughed, and I took my daughter's hands in mine.

My throat felt clogged with grief. "Well, darling …" I looked into her eyes. "I haven't seen your daddy since we were in college together. But we loved each other very much then." Lark swung her legs back and forth at the edge of the bench, scuffing at uneven brick with the toes of her sneakers.

"Does Dean love me?"

My heart on the verge of imploding, I looked across the park at the traffic, the tourists in yellow taxis, the cars with families inside. I struggled to compose myself and a careful answer. "I'm sure he does, sweetheart, but he has another family now. And we have a family too, Grandma and Grandpa, who love us more than anything in the whole world. Right, Lark Bird?"

"Right, Mama Robin." She smiled a little smile and snuggled against my side.

Holding her close, I offered a silent prayer of thanks. The conversation seemed to have gone well and appeased Lark. *At least for now*, I reminded myself. I wondered how long she would be content with my answers.

It was getting chilly. "Let's go see about some dinner," I said as Lark picked up three acorns and put them in the pocket of her denim jacket.

I unlocked our door, dropped my keys on the table, and opened the electric bill with a thumbnail. Lark scooted off to feed her pet goldfish, Georgie. I smiled at an airmail envelope and set it aside. I would savor that one later with a glass of scotch. And I had to call my mom and tell her what had happened with Lark.

175

As I turned on the lamps, I thought about how much I loved our little home. Since that first hectic year, I'd papered the kitchen in a cheerful yellow geometric pattern and put up crisp white café curtains. I'd had the old, worn green kitchen linoleum ripped up and replaced with a classic black-and-white square pattern. I stuck my finger in the soil of the glossy jade that spilled like a weeping willow on the table by the front window. It needed water. "Lark, please come water the jade." I opened the pantry, thinking about what to make for dinner. Lark chattered to the plant as she watered it with the little brass can. "You have such a green thumb," I said with a smile and pulled out a can of tomatoes.

She looked at her hand. "A green thumb! That's hilarious, Mama."

I laughed at her vocabulary and wistfully thought about how not that long ago she had said "fumb." I explained the idiom as Lark set the table with our pretty, old, mismatched dishes, the ones that had spoken to me in a village thrift shop. I displayed a few special ones on a wooden shelf on the wall. I liked to wonder about the families who had eaten from them. "Who did the pink one belong to?" I asked Lark now.

She traced the flowers on the plate with a finger. "I think it belonged to a little girl. Named Rosie … with curly black hair and a little dog named Tippy."

Later that night, Lark and I snuggled in her bed to read. We took turns reading pages. As Lark read, I regarded her sweet room. The alphabet poster I'd bought in Paris hung above the bed. We'd found a dusty old gumball machine at a junk shop for six dollars.

I'd had it made into a bedside lamp with a smart paper shade
and had filled it with gumballs. On Saturdays, I allowed Lark to
insert coins from her allowance for a special treat. An impressive
dollhouse that Grandpa Hank had constructed from a kit squatted
in one corner, little dolls strewn around it like confetti. "Mama, it's
your turn!" Lark said.

I took my turn, and then, as she read again, I glanced at
Georgie swimming back and forth in his bowl on the bookcase,
where books competed for space on the narrow shelves. Often they
spilled to the floor with a slither or thump and annoyed Lark.
One day, I'd heard her utter, "Dammit!" I'd been shocked but
tickled. I reminded myself where she'd heard the word in the first
place. I was happy that books were Lark's favorite belongings, her
treasures.

"Time to say your prayers, love," I said, marking the place as we
finished a chapter. Lark blessed the two of us, her grandparents,
Georgie and Atticus, Christopher and another friend Lindsay, and
her teacher Mrs. Parker.

"Close the closet door, Mama," Lark reminded me. The
apartment had only one closet (in my room), so I'd found a small,
pretty armoire for Lark's room. One Sunday afternoon we had
painted it with birds—highly stylized robins and larks—fat-petaled
flowers, and one orange fish in honor of Georgie.

"What's the magic word?" I said.

"Please!"

I kissed her good night, her butter-soft skin and fragrant hair filling my senses, closed the closet door, and turned out the light.

Unbuttoning my blouse, I padded to my room, my oasis. A blue-and-white ceramic lamp softly lit the blue-and-white bedspread and crisp white sheets that welcomed my tired body each night. Stacks of my favorite books sat alongside found objects on bookshelves I had constructed from hardware store two-by-eights and white bricks. With my last raise I'd bought myself a small stereo system with a cassette player. I contemplated the blue-and-yellow braided rug that covered the stained old carpet our chintzy landlady, Mrs. Ratcliff (whom I dubbed Nurse Ratchett), refused to replace. It needed vacuuming. But not tonight.

Lately before sleep took me under its wing, a lusty yearning had begun to bloom in my chest, like an orchid with an open throat. I needed another dimension to my life. I was lonely … for the touch of a man, someone to love and romantically tend me. I had found myself noticing and appraising men on the streets again as I'd promised Tee. And a new awareness had emerged: Dean Falconer had spoiled me for anyone else. Who could possibly be as fine and beautiful and wonderful and sexy and gentle as he?

* * * * *

The firm of Wickersham, Collins, and Adams was growing. The partners hired two junior associates and another paralegal, a young woman just a year older than me, Lindy Corcoran. I hadn't had a girlfriend in New York since Theresa left for Paris. Working closely, our desks adjacent, Lindy and I got to know each other quickly. Lindy was living with her parents in Brooklyn and working to pay off college loans before going to law school. She was tall, with permed brown hair and unremarkable brown eyes, but Lindy was conscientious and quick, with a dry wit that kept me giggling all day. Her high school sweetheart, Michael, was a big macho fireman. Michael, in his uniform as crisp as new currency, grinned at me every day from the photograph on Lindy's desk and reminded me of my aloneness. Lindy and I went to lunch together a couple of days a week. One Thursday, she asked me to go to happy hour with her after work. My parents had urged me to go out, and they were always happy to babysit. I called Mom at Speak Volumes and asked if they were available that night.

Lindy and I were wearing our work suits and heels, but I could slip off my jacket and look nice in my navy-and-red foulard blouse and navy skirt. I unclasped my hair from an updo to fall over my shoulders. The bar was dark and smoky, wall-to-wall with young working people drinking, laughing, and calling to each other across tables and over the music. Lindy ordered a gin and tonic and I my usual scotch and water. Michael came in and sneaked up behind Lindy, grabbing her around the waist. His photograph hadn't prepared me for the sheer size of the guy. He was at least six three and 220 pounds. What a hunk! But Michael wasn't my type. As I looked about the bar, I didn't see many guys who were.

I hopped down from a stool to go to the ladies' room and bumped smack into a guy, spilling my drink down the front of the red tie he'd loosened at his throat. I apologized into his starched shirtfront and dabbed furiously at the tie with my napkin. He took my wrist gently. "It's really okay," he laughed. He introduced himself as Stuart Eskew. When I came out of the restroom, he was waiting for me by the bar, a fresh drink in either hand for both of us. Stuart's softly curling brown hair, smug grin, and sherry-colored eyes were appealing. I invited him back to our table, where Lindy and Michael sat gazing at each other with the concentration of brain surgeons.

Stuart was a tax accountant and three years older than me. He was polite and attentive and told me a couple of truly funny stories. When Lindy and Michael were ready to leave, Stuart gave me a business card, with his home number on the back, and asked me to call him. He was staying on at the bar to meet friends.

I walked out with Lindy and Michael, the cool night refreshing after the smoky bar. "Cute guy, Stuart," Lindy said. "I've seen him around. He's been in there every time we have … right, Mike?"

Two weeks later, I regarded Stuart's card taped to the refrigerator next to Lark's current painting of a dappled cow chewing on vibrant green grass and got up the nerve to call him. First I cleaned the kitchen, the little radio playing softly in its spot next to the toaster, and supervised Lark as she completed her math problems and spelling practice at the kitchen table. "What's AIDS, Mama?"

"Where did you hear about that?"

"On the *radio*; they *just* said it," she said as if I were one marker short of a box.

"Well … it's a disease, a sickness that a few people get where their bodies can't fight off infection like healthy people. It's very rare."

"Oh," she said, satisfied.

We moved to the front room and curled up on the sofa to watch *Family Ties* on TV. Later when Lark was asleep, I poured a Scotch—Dutch courage as Dad called it—and dialed the number on Stuart's card.

"Hello, Stuart? It's Robin Hamilton."

"Robin! Great to hear from you!" I could hear the smile on his face. He asked if I'd like to have dinner with him that Friday night, at PJ Clarke's on Third. I told him I would meet him at the restaurant.

Mom and Dad were babysitting, so I hurried straight home from work that afternoon for a fresh bath. The weather was hot for early June in Manhattan. I pulled on nice jeans and a sleeveless asymmetrical top. I slipped wedged espadrilles on my feet and a gold bracelet on my slender wrist. I stood and took a deep breath before the mirror. *My first date in eight years. How is that possible?*

I entered the rowdy, packed restaurant and found Stuart inside. "Beautiful!" he said. His breath was beery, his color hectic, as he lurched from his seat at the historic bar and tried to pull me into a huge embrace. He had been there awhile.

I planted a hand in the middle of his chest and pushed him gently away. "Are you ready for dinner?" I asked brightly. This guy needed to get some food in his stomach. We ordered draft beers, and I asked for water as well. I suggested we order an appetizer. "I'm famished," I lied. We nibbled on parmesan tater tots, and Stuart seemed to sober up a little. But after smacking down five tots, he downed his beer and signaled the waitress for another. He was talking in an embarrassingly loud voice by then and elbowed his silverware onto the tiled floor with a series of metallic clanks and tings. The southern tourists at the next table, as red as a flock of cardinals in their Arkansas Razorback T-shirts, were staring openly. When Stuart remarked what a brick house I was, I'd had enough.

I was on my feet and dropped my napkin to the table. "I should call my babysitter." Stuart looked at me quizzically. "Yes," I said, "I have a seven-year-old daughter at home." In the bar, I slipped into the battered phone booth Ray Milland had used in the movie *The Lost Weekend. How ironic,* I thought, pissed and disappointed I'd wasted the evening on a loser. I called Mom and told her I was on my way. I stalked back to the table and stood looking down at the buffoon. "I have to go."

Stuart was midway through his next beer. "Do you wanna try this again tomorrow night?" he asked, oblivious and slurring his words.

"Definitely not," I said and poured the rest of my water into his lap. I left him sitting there staring at the widening spot on his crotch, his big mouth agape.

I met Bill Simon one rainy Friday afternoon at the diner around the corner from the office. I had finished a contract and dashed over for a late lunch. It was gross and humid out, so I'd left my suit jacket at the office. I twisted my damp hair up into a topknot. My pink sleeveless blouse clung to my back and torso like spider silk. I ordered a chef's salad and wiped my neck and arms with a paper napkin. As I drank deeply from my glass of iced water, I noticed a man being seated in the next booth.

We looked up from our lunches and looked directly at each other. After the second time he smiled at me, after the third I returned his smile, and after the fourth we laughed together. "This is pretty awkward," he said. "May I join you?"

Surprising myself, I said, "Sure, but I have to be back at work"—I consulted my watch—"in fifteen minutes."

Bill's deep, pansy-blue eyes lit up when he smiled. He was in the neighborhood of truly handsome but a couple of blocks away. I appraised his dark-blue suit. *A banker,* I thought. Bill was indeed an investment banker and articulate and intelligent. He asked how often I came to the diner. We figured out that it was equidistant from our offices, and I agreed to meet him there again on Monday at twelve thirty.

Over the weekend I was determined not to get optimistic. At least I was sure Bill wouldn't get sloppy drunk at lunchtime. On Monday, he was waiting outside the diner smiling broadly. But as we walked through the door together, I noticed he was short. With me in my three-inch pumps, he wasn't as tall as I. Tee and I liked tall guys. *What difference does that make?* I asked myself, annoyed. *He's a nice guy.* And Bill was as impressive as he was the first time. *Two for two,* I thought. I told Bill about Lark. Bill was thirty-one and divorced, with a nine-year-old daughter of his own. *Hmmm ... that could be neat,* I thought. He asked me to go to the movies with him the next night.

My thoughts returned to Bill the next day at work, and I looked forward to the date. We stood in line to see a movie with Goldie Hawn and Chevy Chase. "You look beautiful tonight," Bill said. It had been so long since I'd heard those words from a guy. And I could tell he wasn't just coming on to me. The movie was good; we laughed at Chase's pratfalls and shared a box of popcorn. But as I watched the screen, I felt Bill's eyes on my profile.

"What is it?" I asked, finally turning to him. "Aren't you watching the movie?"

"I'd rather watch you," he said dreamily. It was a bit off-putting. Bill stared at me at intervals throughout the movie. "You have the perfect profile," he murmured, "the perfect nose." The staring was getting creepy.

After the show, I let him convince me to walk to a piano bar a couple of doors down for a drink. Afterward when he walked with me to hail a taxi, he leaned in to kiss me. But as his lips touched mine, I couldn't stand the intimacy. An old checker cab was trundling slowly down the block. I stuck my hand up as if someone had asked for volunteers to accompany Mel Gibson on a cruise. "Thank you for the evening," I said as the taxi screeched to the curb, and I jumped into the backseat.

Undaunted, Bill called as we sped away, "I'll be in touch!"

I stared ahead at the battered partition, the cracks in the glass mended with tape and pressed my fingers to my lips. No one had kissed them since Dean had. *Dean's lips. His lovely kiss.* I closed my eyes and almost managed to suppress a great gulping sob. "You okay, miss?" the driver asked in dubious English. The bloodshot eyes that appraised me from the rearview mirror had seen their share of misery.

I looked dully out at the rain that had begun to fall and wash the grime from the streets. "Fine."

Bill called me for another date, but I made excuses, saying I would call him another time. There would be no other time.

A month later, I was shopping at Macy's with Lark for new school clothes. Her pants and skirts were getting too short. *She'll be tall like her father,* I thought. Lark was getting opinionated about what she would wear. It was maddening but funny to see her becoming a person with her own ideas. It was my lucky day, though, and we found several cute outfits that pleased us both.

"Mama, I'm going to be in third grade!" Lark exclaimed, bouncing up and down on her toes as we headed down the escalator to lunch. Her birthday was a little over a week away. She was having her first party with friends at my parents' house, so that the kids could spread out and into the back garden.

"I know, darling." I smiled and squeezed her hand. We had a special squeeze: one of us would squeeze the other's hand three times, I—love—you, and the other would squeeze back four times, I—love—you—too. Grinning up at me, Lark squeezed back.

I smiled and glanced to my left. On the up escalator I saw a familiar face and recognized my old college friend Nick. Almost at the top, he must have felt my gaze and looked back at me. "Robin Hamilton!" he called. "I'll be right down; stay there!"

"Who is *that*, Mama?" Lark asked.

"It's an old friend … who went to college with Tante Tee and me. His name is Nick."

As he stepped off the escalator, I said, "Nick! How are you?"

"Fine! How are you? It's been a while!" We stepped forward to hug. Nick had the same easy grin and rangy, loose-limbed way of moving—a man entirely comfortable in his own skin. "Nick, this is my daughter, Lark," I said smiling. Wide-eyed, he stuck out a long-fingered hand to shake hers.

Lark said, "How do you do, Nick?"

He grinned, enchanted with her precocious manners. "It's nice to meet you, Lark. You're a *doll*, and I like your name."

"My whole name is Laurel Olivia Hamilton," she said.

Nick and I chatted for a few minutes. He had stayed in New York City and worked in advertising. He lived in a Soho loft not far from NYU.

"So you're a married lady, Robin."

"Uh … no."

Lark tugged at my hand and said, "Excuse me, Mama, but I'm soooo hungry. Can we go eat now, please?" Nick laughed softly.

I said to Nick, "Will you call me? I'd *love* to catch up." I pulled a pen from my purse and scratched my number and the words "I'm single" on Nick's paper shopping bag. We parted ways.

The next Friday, Nick called. "I would've called you sooner, but I couldn't find that damned bag. I had to paw to the bottom of the trash can like a raccoon to find it." I laughed at him.

We planned to meet for lunch the next day. I couldn't wait to see Nick, to catch up and talk about old times. My mother said they would be happy to have Lark spend the day with them. She and Dad were going to take her to the park. I dressed in a floral sundress and sandals, my hair loose and flowing.

Nick and I met at Gatsby's, where the owner placed a fresh white daisy in a vase on each table—a charming nod to Jay's girl—and were seated at a corner table. I regarded my friend across the table. Nick was more appealing now than ever. He reminded me a little of Jackson Browne with glasses, his shiny brown hair shorter but still shaggy. That day he wore jeans, a gray NYU T-shirt, and running shoes. "Robin, you're as good lookin' as ever," he said. "I can't believe you're a mother." We ordered lunch, and I told him the story of my time at Georgetown, the Eagles concert, and Dean … the whole thing. Nick listened sympathetically. He had dated a girl for four years and wanted to marry her, but she had broken up with him a scant three months ago. Finishing the meal, I asked Nick if he wanted to walk awhile. We still had seven years to catch up on.

It was a beautiful late-August afternoon, the back of the summer broken. We strolled down Bleecker Street and around campus. We stopped to get ice cream cones and wandered over to Washington Square Park, where we found an empty bench in the shade. We talked about Theresa. I told Nick the story of the blackout. "That's right," he said. "I was in Ithaca that summer. Man, I can't believe what you guys went through." I told him I remembered wishing he were there that dreadful night. "I wish I had been, honey." Nick reached over and wiped ice cream from my chin with a thumb. "How is Theresa now?" I told him about my trip to help Tee and Laurent in Paris and then about how Theresa had traveled to surprise me when Lark was born.

Then Nick told me he couldn't believe I had never contacted Dean. He pushed up his glasses, the lenses very clear, and looked into my eyes. "Robin, I can't imagine having a daughter … and not knowing it. She'd be … well … family."

As though by cinematographic trick Nick's face seemed to become Dean's, just for an instant. I heard the words he had spoken again, in Dean's voice. I felt my face drain of color. The skirts had been lifted from my careful house-of-cards defenses for keeping my daughter a secret, brutally exposed. I sat staring at Nick. My parents had never approved of how I'd handled the truth, nor had Theresa. Hearing the opinion of a trusted friend, his male point of view, I saw other implications with clarity: not only had I deprived Dean of his child, but I'd also deprived Dean's mother of her grandchild, and my child of the other half of her family.

"Rob, are you okay, honey?" Nick was concerned. Suddenly it was vitally important to make someone understand why I'd never told Dean the truth.

"Nick, I want you to know that I've struggled with this thing … this huge *dilemma* … ever since I found out I was pregnant."

A gaggle of NYU students, an orientation group, passed through, the giddy teens playful, noisy. I saw that the afternoon light had changed and thought to look at my watch. It was ten minutes after five. I needed to call my mother. "Let's go to my place, Robin. We can talk there," Nick said. He put a comforting arm around my shoulders. "C'mon, you can call your mother and check on Lark."

Stopping at a crosswalk, I gathered my tumultuous thoughts and looked up at Nick. "Things like this happen in families all the time, don't they?" I asked, yet another juicy rationalization from the Robin Hamilton collection.

He looked at me and said simply, "They do."

We stepped off the curb, and I looked at him again. "Nick, I *will* do it. I'll find the right time to tell Dean. I will." We turned a corner and stepped around a legless man on a grate. I began to cry.

"Shhh, honey, it's okay; we're almost home." We were at Nick's building. He shepherded me inside and toward the elevator.

"Nick," I began again. But an older couple entered the building and followed us into the battered old elevator talking about their good-for-nothing son. Inside the apartment Nick led me to his sofa. I was still sniffling. "Do you judge me for what I've done, Nick?" I asked plaintively.

"I don't judge you," he said kindly. "You know the right thing to do. The timing will come to you." He held me then, rocking me back and forth until my tears were spent.

"Nick, what have I done without you all these years?" I said against his tear-wet T-shirt.

"All will be well, Robin." And after a moment, he asked, "Are you hungry? There's a good Chinese place on Prince that delivers."

"That sounds good. I haven't had Chinese in forever. Maybe a little later?"

"Sure. Do you want to call your mother now?"

I picked up the phone on the end table and dialed my parents' number. Nick went to the refrigerator and pulled out a bottle of white wine. He held it aloft, questioning me with his eyes. As my mother answered, I gave him a big thumbs-up.

"Are you enjoying yourself, darling? Tell Nick hello. Everything is fine here. We're playing a game of Clue. Lark called Miss Scarlett as usual. And Dad's going to grill hamburgers in a little while." She was quiet for a moment. "Robin, why don't you take the night for yourself and pick Lark up in the morning? We'd love to have her spend the night with us."

Nick had left the room, and I could hear water running. "Okay, Mom, I might do that. Thank you. I'll call you in the morning. Love you."

"I love you too, darling."

And I hung up. When Nick appeared, I excused myself to freshen up as well.

When I returned, Nick had moved back to the sofa, his lanky arms spread across the back, two big glasses of wine on an iron-and-glass table in front of it. "What kind of music are you into these days, Robin?"

"Surprise me," I said. Nick had a super-nice sound system. He put on a Sting CD. "I love Sting!" I said, pleased. "And aren't CDs cool? They're like little doll records." Nick laughed.

"Do you still have your old albums?" I asked.

"What do you think?" He smirked. "Me, part with my albums?"

I picked up my glass and wandered around looking at the loft. Nick had done well for himself. Really just one big room, the place suited him. Like him, it was spare and comfortable. Movie and music posters, some like ones we had in college but now handsomely framed, were artfully arranged on one huge wall. I complimented Nick on his decor. He explained that his former girlfriend Natalie was a decorator. The kitchen area boasted a massive, rustic and knotty, polished wood counter. "This counter is fantastic, Nick; the wood is *beautiful*. What is it?" I asked, running my hand along its length.

"Cypress. You know it's the wood Noah used to build the ark." He grinned. "I cleaned up. I hoped you would come over."

I sat in a chair near the sofa and smiled at a lush brown bearskin rug. Nick and I talked about our album collections and the way technology had changed the music world. I told Nick that I had been in Paris when I'd learned that the Eagles had broken up. He had been bummed about it too. Then he asked, "Robin, do you still get high? I mean, I know you're a mother now and everything."

"I haven't since I found out I was pregnant with Lark," I said thoughtfully and then grinned.

"Well, I still do occasionally, *and* I just *happen* to have a couple of nice joints right now," he said with a wolfish leer. "Can I corrupt you tonight and sully your perfect record?"

"I'm going for it." I grinned again, feeling young and excited and cool.

I'd forgotten how good it felt to drift and find everything absolutely hilarious. And then we were hungry. Nick called to have the food delivered and poured the last of the bottle into our glasses. I was glad I didn't have to go and pick up Lark. In fact, this night was kind of a "lark." It was crazy and pretty wonderful.

We ate shrimp with snow peas and sesame chicken, ferrying bites between the container and our mouths with wooden chopsticks, talking and laughing. I told Nick about my apartment. Nick talked of the traveling he'd done. Then he put on another CD, an old one, Steely Dan's *Aja*.

I told him I didn't have to go and pick up Lark, and he replied, "Well, all right! Let's open another bottle of wine. The night is young, and so are we!" There was a singular sweetness to Nick's smile as he said, "I can't believe you're really here!" He spoke then of Natalie and their breakup, and I told him about the two guys I'd dated, making him laugh some more. The incidents were funny in retrospect.

We were on the sofa now at either end. Nick slipped off my sandals and began to rub my feet. I actually began to purr; it had been so long since I'd had that kind of attention from a man. I drifted in a tranquil bubble. The revelation that afternoon had been cathartic for me. I felt especially close to Nick now, grateful for his support and for how he hadn't judged me. I felt sexy, as I hadn't in a very long time. I righted myself and slid down the couch and next to him. I took off his glasses. Nick was perfectly still. "Robin?" he whispered. I leaned over and planted a light kiss on each of his eyelids. "Robin?" he said again. "What are you doing, honey?"

I looked into his sweet eyes and slowly said, "Nick, I haven't had sex in eight years. Can't you tell when a girl wants to get laid?"

"Are you sure?" I thought he trembled a little. I placed a hand on his thigh. "I'll be right back," he said. He was back in a flash with protection. I pulled him down to the rug. As Steely Dan sang, "Aja, when all my dime dancin' is through, I run to you," we kissed and undressed each other slowly. The rug felt exotic and warm against my skin. Even as toasted as I was, it was curious seeing Nick naked after all this time. He was even rangier that he looked in clothes. But Nick was extraordinarily pleased with *my* body. "I can't believe this is happening. Robin Hamilton in the raw," he breathed. "Gorgeous … you're so gorgeous." I giggled some more and trailed my fingers down his concave belly.

It was a sweet joining, light and playful. When it was over, Nick reached for a throw, covering us lightly, and we slept there until morning. When I awoke, the scent of fresh coffee in my nostrils, Nick was in the kitchen. I crawled around picking up my clothes, slipped into them, and padded to the kitchen. He stood, eating last night's rice from a container, in jeans and a clean white T-shirt. He hugged me and kissed my forehead, a brotherly kiss.

"Thank you, Nick," I said warmly. "It was a wonderful night … all of it."

He looked at me for a long moment. "It won't happen again, will it, Robin?" he said. It was not a question.

"I don't think so," I said slowly, peering up at him. "But can we be best friends?"

"Absolutely." He nodded firmly. "I make a mean cup of joe. Want some?"

My head was beginning to ache. I moved over to sit at the counter, grimacing. "Please, and a couple of aspirins if you have them."

Nick walked me downstairs and to the street. "Let's sit with this awhile and then get together again … as friends," I said, smiling at him in the early sun. "I would like for Lark to spend some time with a really good man."

"She's a doll. I would love that," he said. And with that I left to go and retrieve my daughter.

Lark loved every minute of her birthday. Five friends from school attended, bringing bright, pretty packages. Atticus retreated to safety under my parents' bed, only the tip of his broad carrot tail sticking out from under the dust ruffle. The Roths and a couple of other neighbors joined us. Lindy popped in to meet Lark and my family and brought Lark the first of the Barbie dolls she would collect. Lindy's fireman had presented her with a small diamond ring, and they were getting married at Christmastime. There were balloons and party hats, and the children played vintage games like pin the tail on the donkey and musical chairs with little prizes. We had refreshments and cake and ice cream at a pretty table Mom had arranged in the garden. Lark was adorable, a polite and gracious hostess. I stood at the periphery, grateful for the new video camera that hid my face. The tears I blinked back tasted bittersweet. I was proud of my child and knew Dean would have been too. Lark was eight years old. It had been almost nine years since Dean and I had been together. I was nearly thirty years old. Dad put his arm around my shoulders and asked, "You okay, sweet pea?"

"I'm okay, Dad," I answered, squeezing him in return. And I knew that I was.

CHAPTER

15

Lark

1996–1998

My mother was making me crazy. At sixteen I knew everything, and she knew nothing. And she was constantly on my case.

My clothes: "Lark, that dress is cute, but it's way too short."

My diet: "Lark, all those Pringles will make your face break out."

My time: "Lark, your curfew is eleven o'clock. It is now eleven oh three!"

My music: "Lark, that grungy Nirvana business *again*? Please turn it *down*!"

My friends: "Lark, is Jeanne smoking cigarettes? I thought I smelled smoke on her yesterday." Or "I don't want you riding with Christopher until he has more driving experience."

Ad nauseam. The things she said made me itch to respond like a hornet. At least I wore a uniform to school—a tartan skirt and vest—and didn't have to argue with her every morning about what I put on my body. When I started ninth grade, my grandfather offered to send me to the school my mom went to, Miss Pruitt's. Mom was making more money by then as well, and we'd moved to a larger apartment closer to the school. I missed the cozy place we'd lived in since I was two, but the new place was really nice. We finally had our own washer and dryer and an elevator. The building even had a doorman, an old Hispanic guy named Romeo. He was cool and always joked around with me, calling me his Juliet. It was neat that I could walk to and from school by myself and not have to have a watchdog, although Mom would have probably preferred that I did. I made straight As, and my friends were perfectly nice girls and guys, so why the constant scrutiny? If Robin and my father were together, there might be a kind of buffer or mediator between the two of us. Maybe Mom wouldn't have to hyperfocus on me all the time. She didn't even have a boyfriend.

My friends were always saying how beautiful my mother was. She was certainly prettier than the other mothers; a few of them were strictly Hagsville. And she didn't try to dress and talk like a teenager; I had to give her points for that.

I asked her once when I was younger if I looked like my father. She had turned to me, her mouth a surprised O, and then gotten this faraway look in her eyes. "You have his gold hair, the angles

of his face, and his beautiful gray eyes." She smiled, but the smile
never reached her eyes. "And his narrow feet … with that little
sliver of baby toenail." I hated my pinky toenails. They were a bitch
to paint and always looked crappy. But at least I had Mom's figure.
My friends said I had the best boobs and tiny waist of anyone.

It was *obvious* that my mother had had sex with my father
without being married ("No shit, Lark," said Jeanne), so why was it
such a big deal for me to be guarded like some paragon of virtue? I
babysat for a family in the neighborhood, and who was to know if
my latest boy toy Asher came over after I put the kids to bed?

"You will not make the same mistakes I did!" Mom said
adamantly, raising her voice during one of our fights.

"So I was a mistake?" I yelled, outraged. That had been a bad
one. Even as I ran to my room in tears and slammed the door so
that it rocked on its hinges, I knew better. I heard Mom crying
through the vent in the floor but was too mad to go to her. I knew
she adored me, and I adored her right back. Why did it have to be
so hard?

Once at my grandparents' I eavesdropped on her and Grandma
Liv in the kitchen. I'd been watching an old movie in the study
with Grandpa Hank and his new puppy Blondie, the dog curled
like a skein of yarn in my lap. Poor arthritic old Atticus had died
two years before. "Grandpa," I had said when I'd held the new
puppy for the first time, "you can't name her *Blondie*; that was
Hitler's dog's name." But as the dog had grown, she'd become
blonder, almost white atop her fluffy head, and the name fit her.
She was a sweet dog, more even-tempered than Atticus had been.

Grandpa had said he was naming her after some old comic strip character anyway.

I went downstairs in my sock feet to get a soda but stopped short and tucked into the alcove by the kitchen door when I heard the conversation.

Mom: "I don't know, Mother." She sounded exasperated.

Grandma: "Robin, Dean has a right to know. Have you considered his legal rights?"

Mom: "But after thirteen years? There are statutes of limitations on those things."

Grandma: "If only you had let him know before she was born …"

Mom: *"Mother!* We've been over this a hundred times. You know I was only trying to *protect* Dean. He was going through hell at the time."

Grandma: "I know. I'm sorry, darling. You can't worry about the timing now. But if you get in touch with—"

At that moment Blondie came up behind me, licked the back of my knee, and scared the shit out of me. I jumped two feet and stumbled against a planter with a loud ka-clunk. The talk stopped. The silly dog's tail was wagging three-quarter time, her version of a delighted smile. I scooped the dog up and breezed into the kitchen. "Oww, I stubbed my toe," I said, limping toward the refrigerator. My heart beat like a wild thing.

I poured my soda and obliquely saw them exchange a look, and then Grandma asked me what Grandpa wanted to do about dinner. They didn't seem to suspect anything, and Mom never said anything to me about it. But I was freaking out. *My father doesn't know about me? Is that what they meant?* I could hardly sleep for a couple of nights, no off switch for the thoughts that spiraled through the darkness. I knew my father's name was Dean, but I couldn't remember the last name. And he lived in Virginia … I thought that was right. I had snooped around trying to find my birth certificate before, but Mom must have locked it away. Could I find him myself? How could I without a last name? Did Mom intend to tell me at some point?

For a while I asked myself if it really mattered. I had a family who loved me, but still … it was there. I felt confused, hurt, and betrayed. But by whom? Mom? Or my father? Or both of them? It was something I would wrestle with for a long time.

My uncle Nick taught me to drive a car when I was sixteen. He wasn't really my uncle but my mom's good friend from college. He was a cool guy, with a hip loft in Soho and a bangin' car, a red Porsche 911. Nick took me to the movies and ice-skating a lot when I was younger. Like Mom, Nick had never married. The two of them were close. He came to our holiday gatherings, even at my grandparents' house.

With my August birthday, I'd just turned seventeen when I began my senior year of high school. My friends and I were totally amped and called ourselves the seniors of '97 in seventh heaven. My boyfriend of six months Louis' school and mine were in a consortium, so we went to dances together and saw each other during the school days sometimes too. Jeanne and I had been best friends for five years and still slept over at each other's apartments. Good grades came pretty effortlessly to me, but Jeanne had to study. When we started looking at colleges, we agreed we wanted to go away for school and room together. My Tante Tee and Mom had been roommates, and they were still tight even though Tee lived in Paris.

Louis was set on Columbia and begged me to stay in New York. I felt bad about leaving him behind, but Jeanne said, "Look, you wanna do Guiltapalooza, fine, but I'm done with the high school scene." Jeanne had no qualms about dropping her boyfriend, Jason.

So we applied to Boston University, American and Georgetown in DC, and Duke down south in North Carolina. We also applied at NYU, even though we really didn't want to stay in New York.

In the end we were both accepted at BU. Mom was excited and happy for me, but I knew how much she would miss me. I told Jeanne I bet Mom had breathed a sigh of relief that I wouldn't be going to Georgetown—probably too much history for her there.

Our senior prom was the first Saturday in May and hosted by a Miss Pruitt's board member out on Long Island at a mansion with a name, Emerald Point. Louis, Jeanne, Jason, and I were going together. Robin was spazzing about me riding out there and back late at night with Jason at the wheel. "Darling, we can rent a car to take you all," she said.

"Mom, chill! We'll be fine. Jason's a good driver. I promise I'll be home in time for curfew." She had halfheartedly extended my curfew until one o'clock for the special events.

Mom went with Jeanne and me to shop for dresses. At Bergdorf's I chose a sleeveless coral chiffon dress with a scoop neck. I liked the way the wispy chiffon layers swished against my ankles when I walked. "You look very elegant, Lark," Mom said, smiling. Jeanne found an aqua taffeta with a ruched, fitted bodice and big, puffy sleeves. It looked really pretty with her blue eyes.

"You two will be the belles of the ball." Mom grinned the evening of the prom as we dressed at my apartment.

"Thanks, Mom," I said. I felt like a fairy princess in that ethereal dress, but it was too embarrassing to say out loud.

My mother extended a palm to me. In it was her pair of diamond stud earrings. "Would you like to wear these on your special night?" She smiled her loving smile.

"Mom … *thank* you!" I hugged her. As I pushed the posts through my lobes, Romeo buzzed the apartment.

When the guys came up, Mom took pictures and hovered anxiously in the doorway as we left, calling, "Have fun and be careful!" I felt kind of sorry for her standing there all by herself.

It was super dark in the burbs, but when we found the address, the magnificence of the place blew us away. Jason drove through towering iron gates emblazoned with the gold initials EP. The place, lit by a dozen floodlights, was enormous, rising astonishingly from the hill on which it was planted. "It's the freaking Emerald *City!*" Jeanne breathed. I had to agree. We entered the vast foyer and were greeted by our headmistress, Mrs. Prudhon, and some board members and teachers. My French teacher, Madame Quinn, exclaimed over my dress, "*Tu est belle, Alouette,*" and hugged me. About twenty couples were there, stunned and blinking in the golden light of elaborate chandeliers: five- and six-foot stalagmites in formal wear.

At the end of the great hall, a rock band was warming up with the Goo Goo Dolls' "Eyes Wide Open." We hit the dance floor before finding a table. My beautiful dress moved alluringly as Louis and I danced. As he held me during the slow songs, I liked the feel of his starched tux shirt against my chest. Long tables were laden with flowers, crystal punch bowls, and tiers of an amazing array of refreshments: my favorite petit fours, cookies with the school seal piped on top, nuts and candies, sandwich rolls with ham and roast beef, glazed meatballs in chafing dishes, vegetables and dip, and enough fruit and cheese to feed an African village. We found our table and attacked the food on our plates during the band break.

The party was over at midnight. We thanked our hosts and moved down the sweep of drive, Jeanne and I still dancing and singing the Stone Temple Pilots' "Big Bang Baby." We felt like Cinderellas leaving the ball before our coach (Jason's dad's Peugeot) turned into a pumpkin. The car hugged the curves of the road as if it was on rails through a rising, swirling fog.

"Slow down, Jase," Jeanne said tightly from the passenger seat. She clutched the overhead passenger strap in her right hand.

"I'm doing the speed limit, babe." Jason leaned over the wheel, straining to see the lines on the road.

Louis and I had been fooling around a little in the back. I felt one of Mom's earrings slip down the front of my dress and bounce into my lap. Reaching around Louis's arm for it, I knocked it to the floorboard. "Wait, my mom's earring." I released the buckle of my seat belt to reach for it on the floor, my fingertips blindly grazing the mat. I pinched the solitaire between two fingers. "Got it!"

That was the precise moment a majestic buck materialized from the mist directly in front of the car. The others screamed as Jason stomped the brake and swerved to avoid the deer, hitting the edge of a culvert. My eyes shut tightly with the impact, and I felt myself catapulted up and over. The lark was flying.

I awoke in stages. Once, I opened my eyes but, feeling the sting of bright light, closed them again. Then hazy images shimmered as though I peered through the gauzy fabric of my skirt. My mouth and throat felt as parched as July pavement. I tried to speak but only swallowed painfully and closed my heavy lids again. Another time, my vision clearer, I could make out people in the periphery. *Mom? Grandma? Uncle Nick?* But my head didn't seem to want to move. I heard my mother's stricken voice. "Lark darling, can you hear me? Lark?" A cool, soft hand smoothed my forehead, and I drifted some more.

Another time, Grandpa said, "Lark, you're all right now, sweet pea. Will you wake up for me?" I opened my eyes against a dreadful pounding in my head.

"Where is it?" I croaked disoriented, my throat ravaged. "What happened?"

"You were in an accident, darling … on the way home from the prom, but you're all right now," my mom said. *Mama.* She was crying.

"My head … my head hurts so *bad*," I moaned. I tried to look around me. I was in a hospital room. Grandma and Grandpa were there. I saw Nick and Mrs. Roth behind them. Everybody looked like hell, Mom a shell of herself, oily hair in a ponytail. I'd never seen my mother with dirty hair my whole life. "Jeanne?" I asked, suddenly frightened.

"Jeanne and Louis and Jason are just fine, darling," Grandma Liv said.

"Your head hit the windshield. You've been asleep for three days, Lark," Grandpa Hank said and gently kissed my right eyebrow. "Good thing you have a hard head."

"Asleep for three days," I parroted, incredulous. "My head?" I tried to raise my arm, but it felt as if it was pinned beneath a heavy object. Grandpa told me my head had broken the windshield. I had lost so much blood before the ambulance had arrived that I'd needed a transfusion in the ER. That freaked me out. I didn't want to know any more.

On the room's long windowsill three balloons floated above a flower arrangement flanked on either side by a host of greeting cards, my grandmother's favorite handbag, and my grandfather's gray rain hat. "Just lie still and rest, darling. Just rest now," Mom soothed. She smiled, but her eyes looked wrecked.

When I awoke again, it was late afternoon, the sun through the blinds striping one wall that held a painting of Jesus and children. Jesus's face was luminous. Mom and Grandpa sat talking quietly on the sofa, one of those ugly plastic hospital ones. "What day is it?" I asked.

Mom bounded to my side. "It's Wednesday, baby. How do you feel? Are you hungry?"

"Yes," I said and realized I was starving. "I want a cheeseburger."

Grandpa laughed his big froggy laugh. "A cheeseburger you shall have. Fries? I'll be back in a flash." He moved toward the door.

"Grandpa, have I told you how much I love you?" I managed.

"And I you, sweet pea," he said smiling. The door snicked closed softly behind him.

A nurse named Carla came in, bringing me an icy cup of Sprite and another pain pill. She deftly changed the bag on my IV. Carla, who was really skinny and pretty like Ally McBeal on TV, said brightly, "The doctor says you should be able to go home the day after tomorrow." She nodded at Mom and slipped out again, shoes squeaking on the waxed floor.

"Oh, Mama …" I hadn't called her Mama in a very long time. "I'm so sorry about all this."

"Darling, we are just very thankful you're going to be all right. It could have been so much worse. God has a plan for your life," she said and took my hand.

"I love you, Mama Robin," I whispered as another nurse strode in to check my vitals. Mom squeezed my hand three times. I squeezed back four.

The next afternoon after school was out, Jeanne, Louis, and Jason came to visit. Louis was shaken and pale and bearing a chocolate milkshake. Jason's left arm was in a cast. Jeanne's face was bruised, a bandage on her chin. We all cried a little bit as we spoke of the accident. I sipped the shake, the best I've tasted to this day, while they took turns reading the funny get-well-soon cards to me.

I ended up taking my final exams from home but was able to attend graduation with the others a week later. I was awarded both the senior English and French awards. As I moved the tassel on my mortarboard at the ceremony, I thought, *I'm going to college!* In the audience Mom's and my grandparents' faces were suffused with pride. With them were Dr. and Mrs. Roth, Uncle Nick, Tante Tee, and Uncle Laurent, who my friends all thought looked like a movie star. After the ceremony my family went to lunch at Tavern on the Green. My mother presented me with a small pair of diamond stud earrings of my own. I opened an envelope, a gift from the Pelletiers. Inside was a round-trip ticket to Paris and a check for $5,000—"To save for a rainy day," Tante Tee said with a wink.

CHAPTER

16

Robin

1998–2012

The days surrounding Lark's accident were the absolute worst of my life as a parent. I received the call from the state police at 2:20 that ghastly early morning after the prom. My child, critically injured, had been taken to the hospital; there were no further details at the moment. Almost literally blinded with fear and anguish, I called my father and asked him to meet me there. He insisted on picking me up. I was pacing up and down in front of the building, a raincoat over my pajamas, a pair of slip-ons on my feet. A miserable Romeo attempted to calm me and bring me inside to wait. *Why is he staring at my feet?* I thought at one point. I looked down and saw the shoes were not from a matched pair. Dad drove breaking every NYC traffic law, jaw tightly clenched, one hand a death grip on the wheel, the other atop my hand.

The young emergency room doctor who smelled of Clearasil would not let me in to see Lark. Dad almost had to physically restrain me from blasting past security and into the room. My daughter could not, would not die. Mom arrived by taxi, and the three of us spent agonizing minutes praying and pacing until the doctor approached. He removed the mask from his acne-scarred face. "Mrs. Hamilton," he said, "your daughter has sustained a significant head injury. She lost just enough blood at the scene that we need an immediate transfusion. Do—"

"Take mine," I blurted. *What is Lark's blood type? I knew it when she was born.* Then I remembered with a flash of lucidity. "No, wait, my daughter's blood type is B negative and I'm B positive."

"What is your husband's type? Is he here?" The doctor appraised our group.

Dean. Why isn't he here? Why do I have to do this by myself? I thought with an irrational flare of anger. "Her father is not in my life," I said evenly.

Dad spoke up, a placating hand on my arm. "Her grandmother is B negative."

At the same time Mom, her face a bone-colored oval framed by messy hair, stepped forward, her hand raised as if she were about to take an oath. "Yes. Let me do it," she said.

The staff took Mom back immediately. Dad and I were left to wait again. "If Lark dies, I will die myself," I said to him at one point.

"Lark will not die, at least not now, and neither will you," he said sternly. "We are going to hang on for the next minute

210

and then the next hour … as long as it takes … until we know something."

"I should notify her father … but under these circumstances? After all this time? What have I done?" I asked him, practically wringing my hands. I began to sob. His face blasted, he patted me absentmindedly.

Another hour went by. Mom reappeared. "Any word?" she asked, looking anxiously from Dad to me.

"Not yet," Dad said shortly.

Mom was pressing cotton batting to the inside of one elbow and sipping from a small plastic cup of orange juice. I moved to embrace her. "Oh, Mama, thank you. Are you okay?" *Mama. When's the last time I called her that?*

"I'm fine, darling, and Lark will be too." She smiled briefly.

Another hour passed as the three of us sat slumped and hollow-eyed on a bench covered in hideous orange vinyl. The doctor walked toward us again. I was on my feet at once and searching his eyes. "Your daughter is stable and resting comfortably but still unconscious. We're running more tests now. Lark's a strong, healthy young woman, and I expect her to be all right," he said. "We'll give you another update as soon as we can."

"Thank you, Doctor," the three of us breathed in unison.

All through the interminable day we waited. I called Theresa in Paris, catching her as she was leaving her office. I told her not

to come, that I would keep her abreast. At 3:20 we received word
that the brain scans had predicted no permanent damage. It was
just a matter of time before Lark reawakened. She was moved to
a private room and monitored closely. Nick joined me when Mom
and Dad went home to rest, but I would not leave the chair beside
Lark's bed. He sat silently and did paperwork, a solid and soothing
presence. From time to time I drifted off, jerking awake when my
head fell to one side or the other. Nick tucked a pillow behind my
head, and I slept for two hours.

As Lark began coming around the second day, we all
maintained a bedside vigil. When at last she spoke, I begin to cry
scalding tears, my knees almost buckling with relief and gratitude.

In the following months it was clear that my daughter had
moved beyond her disdainful teenage years and become a loving
and gracious young woman. She spent ten days in Paris with
Tee and Laurent and came back enriched, with a palpable new
maturity. Lark and I spent a great deal of time together before we
made the drive to Boston, enjoying shopping for clothes and dorm
items together. We were two birds of a feather once more, our
relationship renewed and stronger than before.

Driving back to New York alone three days later, I was forced
to reevaluate my life. I had achieved my goal of making myself
indispensable to the team at work, and I enjoyed my collegial
relationships with Lindy and the partners, but the work no longer
provided the challenge I needed now that Lark had flown the nest.

My nights were long, with no one to share my home. And I
was uncherished, lonelier than when I had been young and without

a man's arms to hold me. Nick had been a faithful friend to me and to Lark, and I was grateful for his agreeable company, but I needed a romantic relationship. Often Dean Falconer, who hadn't aged beyond twenty-five in my mind, made cameo appearances in my dreams.

I fantasized about the life he must lead. I decided to place the call.

One evening after work, I sorted through the mail—my credit card bill, a decorating magazine, and a glossy postcard addressed to Lark that of course I read—and poured myself a glass of wine. I thoughtfully regarded my solitary apartment. I slipped my new iPhone from my purse and sat down with it at the kitchen table. I smoothed a lone place mat with the flat of my hand and, once again, called the number in Virginia.

A woman answered, the cadence of her voice Hispanic, "Falconer residence."

"May I speak with Dean Falconer, please?" I asked. My heart threatened to choke off my air supply.

"Mr. Falconer is not here at the moment. Would you like to leave a message?"

"I'm an old friend … Robin," I said inanely, as if anyone would know me. "With whom am I speaking, please?"

"I'm Rosa," the woman answered kindly, "Mrs. Falconer's caregiver." *His wife was ill.* "Would you like to leave a message?" Rosa asked.

213

"No … No. I'm sorry." I tried to corral my wild-mustang thoughts. "There's no message. I'll call another time. Thank you," I said dully and pushed the end button.

I began to cry … for Dean, for his wife. Were there children? For myself. For Lark. For all that had been lost for such a terribly long time. As a slogging fatigue crept over me, I laid my head on folded arms. When I awoke, the kitchen was fully dark. My neck stiff, I felt as though I had been pummeled. I put my glass in the dishwasher and walked through the house and up the stairs to my bed. I was weary to the bone of thinking about my responsibility for the truth. My efforts to try and square things had met with nothing but a series of emotionally charged obstacles. Maybe later. I fell asleep in my clothes on top of my covers and slept for ten hours.

A week later I met Greg Faircloth at a dinner party at the home of one of the partners. He was a very tall, handsome radio show host, and his deep velvet voice and crooked smile left me weak-kneed. Greg was thoughtful and intelligent and, after the third date, a skillful lover. He always had tickets to the best shows and sporting events. We had fun together, but after almost a year, he made it clear that he was not a fan of commitment. When I found out he was still hung up on his first love, a woman from Tennessee named Debbie, Greg and I went our separate ways amicably and without rancor. I moved on.

I wanted to be married, to share my life with someone. I became restless and bored and abhorred that in myself. Then one day it came to me; I could return to law school. It wasn't too late. Once again I talked it over with Dad. It would be two more years of hard work, but Dad was keen on the idea and insisted on paying my tuition. "We would have paid for it the first time, and we'll do it now. Besides," he said with a grin, "my motives are entirely selfish. I want to bring you on board with John and me."

With the money I'd saved through the years, I could afford to work only part-time. Stephen Adams agreed to allow me to stay on in that capacity, sharing the position with a new paralegal named Khaled. It was settled almost too easily. Lark and Tee were excited for me and became my cheerleaders from afar. We e-mailed often. And via Skype sessions, Tee and I were able to "see" each other frequently after more than thirty years of letters and brief phone calls.

A few months into my studies, I noticed my mother repeating herself in conversation. One day she called me Lark and not in the way you do when your mind is busy and full of the people in your life, where you correct yourself with a laugh and "Where is my mind?" Another time, I asked where she and Dad had had dinner the night before. "I don't know," she said, a perplexed look on her face.

A few days later I called Dad at his office and asked if he had noticed anything amiss with Mom.

"Rob, we need to talk," he said with a fifty-pound sigh. We met the next afternoon for coffee. He reported similar anecdotes and voiced his growing concern. We agreed to wait and watch.

But Mom's short-term memory continued to deteriorate. She was often confused, her eyes wide, fearful. Scattered around the house was a collection of sticky notes scrawled with the things Mom wanted to remember—the types of birds in her garden, how to use the microwave, Lark's name and Boston University. Mom's once lovely, round penmanship became jagged, her sentence structure like that of a third grader. With burgeoning dread we suspected Alzheimer's disease. Then the owner of Speak Volumes called my father. Things had been slipping through the cracks at the shop, and Mom's sweet and loyal assistants had been covering for her. Dad gently convinced Mom to take some time off from work and rest. She would not be going back.

Dad took her for a neurological evaluation; the report was grim. The doctor confirmed that Mom was in the early-mid stages of the disease. A devastated Dad insisted that Mom not be told the result. "Why would you want to know?" he asked me, his eyes agonized and red rimmed. "I don't want your mother to spend the time she has left with that terrible knowledge." I agreed wholeheartedly. And so we kept it from her. It was a suspended time. Again we watched and waited to see where the dread road would lead.

And then one day coming home from the market just down the street, where Mom had shopped for twenty years, she got lost. Miraculously, Anita Roth was walking home and saw her standing as motionless as a fire hydrant on a busy corner, hordes of people brushing past her in both directions. Anita took her old friend's hand and walked her home. She stayed with her until Dad came home from the office.

Fearing for Mom's safety, Dad and I quickly looked for someone to stay with her during the day. Uncommonly kind

Sharron, a friend of Lindy's who had lost her husband and was looking for work, agreed to take the job and became part of the family. We introduced Sharron to Mom, and the two hit it off right away. Sharron was a godsend. I don't know what Dad and I would've done without her equanimity, humor, and affection for my mother.

When Lark came home for the holidays that year, she could hardly bear to be in her grandmother's presence. "It hurts so much, Mom. I'm afraid I'll burst into tears." We carried the ache inside us like a malignancy.

The arrangement with Sharron worked for almost a year, and then Mom needed more than help with bathing and dressing. She was no longer able to climb the stairs to her bedroom and became increasingly agitated and on occasion even combative with Sharron and Dad. She forgot my name and one day introduced me to Anita as her sister. Other relationships grayed and blurred in her mind. She no longer remembered anything about my life, not even my childhood, and that hurt me to the marrow of my bones.

I had read that it was most difficult for the spouse of an Alzheimer's victim to face the hurdle of placing him or her in a nursing home, and I struggled to help Dad see beyond the denial he felt. We found a facility that specialized in the care of Alzheimer's patients and took Mom there on a Monday morning. I decorated her room with a few of her special things—an Asian lamp, a pretty mirrored tray on which she kept her toiletries, and a few botanical prints on the wall—while an attendant took her on a tour. Mom was placidly sitting in front of a bingo board when we slipped out, though her hands remained like a pair of oven mitts in her lap. In the empty brownstone afterward, I held my father as he wept. "How can I live here after all these years without your mother?" he sobbed.

Dad visited Mom every evening, and Anita and I each went two days a week. The staff reported that Mom had adjusted well. Her contentment was the most important thing to us. For a time we lived in a shell of quiescence.

Then Mom became incontinent and was put into adult diapers. She loathed the papery feel against her skin. Next she lost her appetite, and her weight plummeted. And then my lovely genteel mother began to curse and snipe at other residents. She was placed on medication that helped with the hostility but left her with a flat affect and unable to sustain a conversation.

It was one of the worst times of my life. I dreaded going to the nursing home. I spaced my visits farther apart and limited the time that I spent with my mother. The guilt I felt threatened to consume me. One Saturday afternoon, I walked into her room with a vase of her favorite white peonies, a smile pasted across my face, and a stench hit me with the force of a tsunami. Mom had been nattering at the hated diaper again, and trying to hide the unspeakable evidence, she had smeared it around the room. There were unholy brown stripes of shit across her bedsheet and the little French chair and swaths of it down one wall—like a mad decorator trying out paint samples. Transfixed, I saw that the dark stuff was lodged beneath her too-long fingernails. I dropped the bouquet and fled, sour acid rising in my throat, and pushed through the double doors to take in great breaths of fresh air. The nurses had seen my exodus; I knew they would follow up on Mom. And so, God help me, it was the last time I saw my mother.

I stayed away a week, two, unable to face going back. And then it was too late. Dad received the call about three o'clock one morning and promptly called me. Olivia Courtwright Hamilton had passed away in her sleep. I knew she was already in heaven. The next days were blessed with an outpouring of affection from friends who had loved her. The good women of St. Michael's Parish kept us hugged and fed. It was a terrible relief.

At my most vulnerable following my mother's death, lonesome to the point of floor-walking insomnia, I astonished Nick one cold, cold night after we'd been to a movie by inviting him to my bed. He had begun seeing an editor named Tonya, and I'm afraid I derailed that relationship in my need for succor. Nick's and my lovemaking was as it had been years before, as freeing as slipping into a happy childhood dream. We both knew the affair was temporary, and we got it out of our systems after a month. Although I wanted to be, I wasn't in love with Nick.

A year later, I graduated from law school with my doctor of jurisprudence degree, eighteen years after I had first begun. I jumped on the bar exam and passed with a comfortable margin. I was an attorney with all rights and privileges. My father and John Hicks took me to the Four Seasons for an exquisite dinner and fine champagne. They offered me a partnership with the firm. We were Hamilton, Hicks, and Hamilton. I relished the new role and began working with my own clients excited about buying their first homes.

Shortly thereafter, Lark graduated with honors from Boston University with a master's degree in education. Teaching was the noblest of professions in my mind, and I was so proud of Lark and all she had accomplished. She would make a wonderful teacher. Lark returned to New York and lived with me for a couple of fun months before finding a plum first position in a charter school for the arts and moving into an apartment with another new teacher at her school.

The bottom fell out of John Hicks's world. Our elegant and conservative friend was devastated when his wife, Linda, in love with another man, told him she was leaving after forty years of marriage. John's humiliation was complete when he learned that not only was the man much younger than Linda but also an ex-con, a professional poker-playing stud who wore gold chains around his neck.

Two years later, Dad blew all of our minds by announcing his plan to retire and move to the Outer Banks of North Carolina. One of his clients was selling her summer home there. He hadn't even discussed it with me. "My bones are tired of the New York winters," he said over lunch one day. As I looked at my father, I saw that he was thin. He looked tired and old for seventy-five. He asked if I would take the brownstone. "I would love for the house to stay in the family. And your mother would be happy with that."

The full circle feel of the idea compelled me. An excited and grateful Lark took my apartment. All the pieces came together smoothly, as though orchestrated by Shostakovich. The evening before the movers arrived, I helped my father pack the things he would carry by car. Blondie, restless and confused, paced and sniffed at boxes. I poured a couple of neat scotches, and we sat down at the dining table Dad would take to the beach. *What wonderful times we had with Mom around this table,* I thought.

My dad was concerned about me. He scooped Blondie up, stroking her fur. "Robin, I worry about you being alone here and lonely. Would you get married if the right guy came along?"

"I do get lonely, Dad," I said, propping a foot on a box. "My life is pretty full again, but if I met the right man, I'd definitely consider it. Funny the way life turns out, huh? I never dreamed I would be an old maid."

He laughed. "If you could only see from my perspective how young you still are. It's all relative, sweet pea. Your mother and I were so happy ... We always wanted you to be as happy in love as we were. It's so sad the way things turned out between you and Dean." He pulled pensively at his scotch. "And Lark. She and Ben have been together for what? Three years? I wish they'd hurry up and tie the knot. What are they waiting for?"

"I know. It must be Ben's travel. They love each other, but I'm not sure Lark wants a part-time mate." Blondie nudged me with her leathery black nose. I reached to scratch behind her ears. "I'm going to miss this mutt."

My thoughts crept to Dean again. "You know, Dad, sometimes I think over the years Dean became ... an abstraction for me. An idea. A symbol of love. Maybe that made it easier for me to live the lie."

"I guess so, Rob." We sipped at our drinks in silence.

"What a morose pair we are! Let's talk about your new house!" I said, brightening for my father. "I can't wait to see it. You'll be walking on the beach every morning while I'm slaving away at the firm."

"But I'll be thinking of you," he said and rose to kiss my forehead. "And I want you to get your first visit on your calendar."

Five years Dad's junior, John Hicks stayed on at the firm. We hired another attorney, a young whippersnapper named Morgan Jordan whom we lured away from a helter-skelter two-year stint with the DA's office. Morgan became an integral part of the practice. Her superior technology skills helped take the firm into the twenty-first century.

Dad's contemporary home in North Carolina with walls of glass and sweeping view of the Atlantic was breathtaking. Dad relished being able to sit on his deck and watch Blondie run the beach, darting and barking at the leaping and slapping surf. The timeless sea helped to heal his grief. He met Nancy Bronson, a Carolina native who was close to his age, and they clicked immediately. Nancy loved to dance—ballroom, salsa and samba, and even the Carolina shag—and taught Dad to enjoy it. He lost the haggard look, his life revitalized. I liked Nancy and was grateful for her vivacious presence in my father's life. The Outer Banks became the perfect getaway for Lark and me on long weekends. Lark enjoyed extended school vacations there. Theresa even came from France and stayed with us there for a month one happy, lazy summer.

And then there was the sanctuary of my home in New York City. I padded about the uneven, old wood flooring and imagined my bare feet as the roots that anchored me to the place where I had been born and reared, laughed and cried, where I had loved and been loved. I kept many of Mom's old special pieces, hoping that Lark would want them for herself one day. Combining them with the pieces I'd collected over the years, I created a charming, eclectic space.

The only new things I purchased were a large, comfy sectional and heavy, antique dining table that had once graced the dining room of a monastery. Charmed by its history, I loved running my palm across the indentations near the edges worn by a century of elbows and forearms. I kept the top of the treasure shining and fragrant with lavender polish. Sleeping in the master bedroom had taken some getting used to. The room was steeped in memories of my mother. I spent the first nights downstairs on the sofa. But I had the room freshly painted and decorated it much as I had my bedroom in Lark's and my first little place, a restful blue and white, with white cutwork linens and matelassé spread. The space soon became my own. I cut back the garden foliage that, as if mourning for my mother's gentle care, had grown scraggly, almost obscuring the kitchen window. Abundant sunlight made the room inviting and cheerful again. I felt my mother's spirit as I cooked.

One late February evening while the wind probed and rattled the shutters of the brownstone, I read online that the Eagles had produced *The History of the Eagles* in two parts. The premiere would be on cable that Friday night. Excited, I called Tee, wishing we could watch it together. I called Lark and asked if she would come and watch it with me. We hadn't had a mother-daughter night in a while.

I worked until six on Friday and took a taxi home. The weather was so damned cold. I took off my skirt and pumps and pulled on a pair of jeans. I had bought our favorite truffle cheese and a couple of bottles of wine that Lark and I both liked. With Ben out of town I might persuade Lark to spend the night. It would be fun, a slumber party.

Lark rang the bell at a quarter to seven. I couldn't believe she had walked over in the cold. She got herself settled while I pulled the snacks together. I was still in the kitchen when the show began. Lark called me to come and look at a girl she said looked like me. I laughed to myself: we girls all looked alike in those days-- the hairstyle, the outfits we wore. But as I ferried the tray to the coffee table I was thunderstruck. The producer had included footage from the Hotel California tour. The scenes looked eerily as though they'd been filmed at the DC concert.

And then I saw myself. And *Dean*. My heart slammed against my ribcage.

I sat in stunned reverie, Lark beside me suddenly looking so much like her father my heart squeezed with ineffable sadness, with regret. All the rationalizations with which I'd built my careful house of cards shimmered before me.

I wanted to tell Lark. Now. Maybe it wasn't too late for Lark and Dean. It was time to embrace the truth.

Damn the consequences.

CHAPTER

17

Lark

2013

My stomach clenched like a fist. Convinced my mother had some big revelation to make, I asked again, "Who?" I sounded like a petulant owl. I saw that I still clutched the remote and pressed the mute button.

"My darling daughter, that is your *father*, Dean Thompson Falconer," she said evenly, at once altering the course of our lives.

I looked back at the screen and saw that it was true. I stared at the young man frozen in time. *So much younger than I am now,* I mused, and a range of emotions washed over me. I watched him smile and sway to the music. Hot, salt tears began to flow down my cheeks, tears of loss, of grief, but through them I smiled and uttered little laughs of amazement. A spark of hope ignited in me like good, dry tinder.

The expression on the young Robin Hamilton's motionless face was a look I'd never seen before. I found that I had moved closer to the television on my knees and turned back.

At last the words came past my teeth. "Why, Mom? What happened to you two?" My mother turned and pulled a couple of afghans from the sofa. She moved to sit with me, and we faced each other before the hearth. As she told me the story, her gaze was clear and direct. Occasionally she prodded at the snickering logs with Grandpa Hank's iron poker.

She told me about the night she'd met Dean Falconer at the concert she and Tee had attended in DC. Mercifully, she gave me what had to have been a PG version of the first weekend they had spent together. She spoke of falling in love with Dean at first sight, and he with her. As the old Courtwright clock ticked away the hours from the mantle, she told me the whole of it, the glorious and tragic story leading to my birth. As she looked from my face to the fire, I saw the pain she'd suffered again and again. She had wanted to tell Dean about me many times, but revelations had stopped her like road-closed signs on desolate highways. When she'd learned that Dean was getting married, it had been as though she'd suffered a small death. And finally as she told me again how much I meant to her, all the pieces of our lives came together. I thought I should feel betrayed. I thought I should feel anger. But woman-to-woman, I found I understood my mother, the bittersweet choices she had made. All I felt was a gessoed peace. By tacit agreement we hauled the afghans over us and slept.

"How do you want us to go about this?" Mom asked the next morning with a smile. She blew across the surface of a nutty

Peruvian coffee Ben had brought from his last trip. We sat in the kitchen nibbling toast, the photograph of her and Dean Falconer, the only one she ever had, on the table before us. I regarded the two again. They looked as if they'd just won the New York State lottery.

"Will you call him, Mom?" I asked. "It should be you. And I want to know every word he says. Promise."

"Every word, darling, I promise." She flashed a grin over the "Best Mom" mug I had given her in seventh grade. "I'll take notes."

CHAPTER
18

Robin

2013

I cleaned up the kitchen and gathered the afghans and pillows from the living room floor where they lay tangled from the night before. I thought about all that had transpired and summoned courage. I had no sense of what Dean would say when I called him, but something told me that unlike my former ill-fated attempts, this time Dean himself would answer the phone.

I sat at the monks' table with my cell and the dog-eared notebook paper with the address and number penned in Dean's hand so many years ago. I'd kept his letters along with the single photograph of us and Lark's birth certificate folded and tucked into the false bottom of my jewelry box.

Taking a last deep breath, I dialed the number. Dean's unmistakable voice, though deeper and more resonant with maturity, answered, "Hello?" on the second ring. How many hundred times had I heard that voice in my fantasies?

"Dean, this is Robin Hamilton calling from New York City," I said in my best lawyer's voice.

I heard a sharp intake of breath and then silence. Then he said, "*Robin?* What … Are … you all right?"

"I'm fine, Dean. It's just time … I got in touch with you." The words drifted like mail through a slot onto a carpet runner.

Finally he said, "After … thirty-four *years?*"

"Dean, it's best that I speak with you in private. Do you need to call me back another time?" I heard the scraping of chair legs on a floor. *Yes, I guess you'd better sit down*, I thought.

"No. Yes. I mean it's okay; I'm alone," he said. And then after a moment, he said, "I was married. But my wife … Victoria … died of ovarian cancer in 1985. We were married just five years."

"I'm so sorry, Dean," I replied, meaning it. My thoughts did a 180: *What about the caregiver I spoke to, what, four years ago now?* "I actually tried to call you several years ago. I spoke with a woman who said she was Mrs. Falconer's caregiver. I assumed she was there for your wife. Was it your mother?" I asked quietly. I heard a dog barking on his end and tried to picture Dean in the house at Villeneuve.

"Oh, that must have been when Mom fell off her horse and broke her leg. She's fine, by the way. Strong and healthy. She made a complete recovery from the breakdown when … after my father died."

"I'm so glad, Dean. That's wonderful."

"Victoria … my wife … was four months pregnant when they found the cancer. She lost the baby … a girl … and Victoria died just three months later."

"Oh, Dean," I said, tears scalding the back of my throat. I rose to get a Kleenex and sat heavily back down. "And you never remarried?"

"No," he said shortly. "I just never had the … impulse again."

"Oh," I said lamely and softly blew my nose.

"It's surreal talking with you," he said then. "What about you, are you married?"

I checked my emotions and swallowed. "No. I *never* married." The pivotal moment was at hand; my segue had come. "But I have a daughter … an incredible daughter." I paused and took a deep breath. "She's thirty-three years old."

"*Thirty-three!* Incredible. Robin Hamilton with a thirty-three-year-old kid," he marveled. I waited while Dean did the math. And then he knew. "Is she … *mine?*" he asked, his voice rising on the last word.

I realized I'd been holding my breath and let it out slowly. "She is." I clung to the answer as if it were a life preserver. Dean's choking sobs sounded as though from far below the surface of deep water. I would wait; I would give him time.

He cleared his throat, his voice husky, raw. "Good God! Why, Robin? Why didn't you tell me?"

I closed my eyes and grasped for the words to explain the last three and a half decades. I'd rehearsed them a dozen times, but they seemed to have flown from my head like birds from a shaken tree. Then with sudden clarity I saw myself in my little studio apartment in DC, heartsick, morning sick, and frightened. I began to speak as that Robin. I described the first days after I found his letter under the door when I had drifted in a transitory bubble of shock and disbelief. I explained how through the years I'd waited until I thought it was the right time and how it never seemed to be.

Dean listened in deafening silence. Finally, he heaved a ponderous sigh. "Robin, I'm sorry. This is just too much. Too much of a shock to deal with right now. I don't …" I heard the scrape of the chair again. "I can't … I have to go." And he hung up the phone.

I stared at my phone until the screen went to black, anguished I had hurt him so profoundly and swamped with uncertainty. I'd been foolish not to expect a visceral reaction from Dean. Had all the years that I'd held the secret close to me in the dark desensitized me? *Of course* Dean would need time. *Of course* he would need to absorb the shock, wrap his head around it.

I rose heavily to my feet to shower and dress. I called Lark to see if she wanted to meet for lunch. An hour later we shrugged from our coats at Cappomaggi's, where the comfort food was rich and substantial. In a quiet corner booth over hearty bowls of minestrone and buttery garlic bread, I relayed the conversation I'd had with her father. Lark's face was very still. "Darling, I just know," I said, placing my hands over my heart, "that Dean … your father … is a thoroughly good man. He's had a *terrible* shock today, but I *know* he'll come around."

"I hope so, Mom," Lark sighed, hands cradling a cup of hot tea. She tried on a little smile for me, but her clear gray eyes were replete with unspoken questions.

"My number's on his caller ID now." I winked at my daughter. "That will be our juju."

CHAPTER

19

Lark

2013

I found myself standing in the market before a plundered display of Valentine cards with no memory of walking the familiar route. Thoughts of my father and of Ben whirled and tumbled like socks in a dryer that would have to be sorted. Poor Dean. Not only had he lost his first love, my mother, without a trace, but then his young wife had died. I knew enough psychology from the two years of sessions with Dr. Rike—ironically therapy I'd needed from growing up fatherless and believing he didn't know of my existence—to realize how profoundly the news that had come out of the blue must have affected *him*. I plucked a loaf of Ezekiel bread from the rack.

Someone had said, "The truth will set you free, but first it will make you miserable." The revelation had been difficult for all three of us. But would it prove ultimately freeing? Organic apples and bananas and Greek yogurt fell into my basket. If only Dean and I had met when I was a little girl. Was it possible to forge a relationship now? Would we want to? I wanted so much to know this man from whom I'd inherited my gray eyes, my pinky toes, and the planes of my face. What sort of man *was he*? To hear Mom tell it, when he was twenty-four, Dean was God's gift to the planet—friendly, loving, talented, loyal—an *actual* Eagle Scout. But Mom hadn't seen the man in more than three decades. How might life have changed him?

And then there was Ben. Just two days ago I'd been consumed with thoughts of our relationship. Ben traveled constantly. We had talked of a life spent together only in nebulous terms. But I knew I wanted to have at least one baby before my eggs began waving microscopic white flags. Absently, I swept brown rice and quinoa from the shelf.

I didn't want my children placing moist and sticky kisses on a framed photograph of their father at bedtime, Ben in South America, in Manizales or Cuzco. I wanted a real home, one like my mother's, a home filled with carefully chosen, well-loved pieces, a home that rang with the music and clutter of family. While my little place on West Eighty-Sixth could be generously described by an ambitious real estate agent as "cozy," Ben's apartment was no more suitable, a studio impersonally furnished by IKEA, a functional place to crash.

Two days ago, I'd made the decision to talk with Ben about my feelings this weekend, perhaps even issuing him an ultimatum. But as I squeezed avocados as unyielding as river rocks, I thought about what I taught my students: we must study the past in order to inform the future. Perhaps my root system should be exposed and inspected before I could wholly cultivate my future.

Queuing up at the register, a litany of questions eddied about my head like a vortex. What about Dean and my mother? Could a thirty-five-year-old love be rekindled? Since the big revelation, there had been a new look in my mother's eyes, a different rhythm to her breathing. Had the hope of love come to roost in her heart? What would it do to her gentle soul if it didn't work out this time?

On the sidewalk, a text alert sounded. I fumbled with my bags. Mom: "I've heard back from Dean. He's calling me at 8:00 tonight. Love you, darling."

It was time to rock and roll.

CHAPTER

20

Robin

2013

A bee in my bonnet, I pulled out an Eagles' album, dusted it with a sleeve, and put it on to play as I cleaned my house from top to bottom. It had been a long time since I'd listened to albums, but they connected me with the past, and the Eagles felt like good karma today. I would never erase from my phone the voice mail I'd received while at mass that morning: "Robin, this is Dean. I'm sorry about last night. I'm ready to talk now. I will try you tonight after eight. Until then."

I popped a frozen entrée in the microwave and picked at it from a tray before the fire, watching the news as though the anchor spoke in some unknown tongue. At 7:50, I turned off a Cary Grant and Irene Dunne movie and peered out the front shutters at the street. The warm front had shown up, and a chiming rain had begun to fall. I stoked the fire and sat on the sofa, surprised by the balloon of calm in which I seemed to float. At 8:05 the phone rang in my lap: the 434 area code. *Here goes everything.* "Hel-lo?" I answered brightly.

"Robin? It's Dean. Listen, I'm sorry about yesterday. You … pulled the rug out from under me to put it mildly. I needed some time. Time to try to get my head around this thing."

"Dean, it is okay. Really. I totally understand," I said.

"I've had one day to take this in … while you've had the thirty-year home-field advantage." He was calm, his voice more like the old Dean's. "I've had some … I guess righteous indignation going … I had a right to know, Robin. No matter what was going on in my life back then, you should have told me."

"I know," I said miserably. "I was so young. I thought I was protecting you. When I look back on it, it's easier to see what I should've done … the times I could've told you." We were silent again.

"All this time I had a daughter … I still can't believe it," he marveled. Then as if it were just occurring to him he said, "I don't even know her name."

"Her name is Lark," I said, warmth pouring over me like spilled honey. "It's her nickname. I named her Laurel Olivia, after your mother and mine." A jagged sigh from Dean was followed by the liquid sound of tears. I continued, "She was such a happy baby that one day my father said she was as happy as a lark, and the name just stuck."

Dean sniffed deeply and cleared his throat. "Lark." The name was a sonnet on his lips. "I like it. Did you ... does she have my last name?" he asked expectantly. I told Dean his name was listed on the birth certificate as the father but that her legal name was Hamilton.

"So you lived with your parents?" Dean asked. I told him about how I had come back to my parents' home in the beginning.

"I'm just so damned sorry for us both, Robin." His words were suffused with disappointment. I heard him crying softly again. "For it all ... for all that we missed. I don't ..." His voice caught, and I heard the devastation he felt. "After thirty years ... my whole adult life ... it shouldn't matter, but it does. I'm ... stunned by how hurt I feel."

"I know."

"I loved you, Robin," he said evenly. "If only I had known about the baby then ... I would've asked you to marry me right away."

"You don't regret your marriage, Dean?"

"No. I don't know ... It was a long time ago. She was my next-door neighbor. My years with Victoria were good. We had a nice life. I feel disloyal to her memory ... telling you ... that things between her and me were never like they were between you and me ... but it's true. Maybe you only get to love that way once ... with that ... passion." My heart soared and shimmered above his words.

Now a youthful and energetic seventy-nine, Dean's mother enjoyed a full life and lived alone in the main house. Dean had designed and built a new house for himself on the property. He worked as an architect with an office in Charlottesville, designing homes for clients in the central Virginia area.

And then it was my turn. "I worked as a paralegal after I dropped out of law school ... for *years*. Then, believe it or not, I went back to law school ten years ago."

"That's fantastic. Congratulations." he said warmly.

I spoke of my mother's illness and death, of becoming partners with my dad, and of his move to North Carolina. Dean talked of his sisters and how well their lives had turned out. We were quiet then, each of us lost in our own thoughts. And then he said, "Robin, I was thinking last night about when I left you that first time ... after my father died, after that first weekend we were together. The Eagles' concert weekend. Remember?"

"Of course I do. I was devastated. But do you remember that I forgave you?"

"Yeah. You did. And those months in DC were ..." He fell silent.

"Yeah, they were." Those memories were drawn in indelible ink. I wondered if Dean was seeing as I was the two of us in each other's arms.

"Dean," I said very slowly, "I need to ask you to forgive me now. For keeping the knowledge of Lark from you."

Everything depended on his answer. My fingers gripped the phone like a life preserver. Finally he sighed again. "I do. I forgive you, Robin. It must have been very difficult for you. I know that."

"But I got a wonderful daughter out of the deal," I said smiling into the phone. "I want you to know her too, Dean." My eyes slid to Lark's picture on the mantle. "She belongs to you as much as me. I realize that now."

"Ah, Rob. It seems we were both so caught up in emotions ... we made some irreparable ... misjudgments ... didn't we?" He paused. "It's terrible doing this over the phone," he said, echoing my thoughts. "I want to see you." My heart leaped again. "I want to meet our daughter. There's so much more I need to know. Do you think you could catch me up on the last thirty-five years?"

"I'll give it the old college try." I laughed a little. "No pun intended." Then I added, "Can we take a break? I really need to pee."

Dean laughed his old laugh. "So do I. So call you back in ten?"

"Okay, my cell's almost dead. I'll plug it in. Bye." I snared my power cord from my briefcase and plugged it in behind the sofa, smiling tremulously to myself. Before the phone rang, I put another log on the fire and poured myself a glass of Pinot Gris.

I took a deep breath and answered on the third ring. I heard the clinking of ice in a glass on Dean's end. "What are *you* drinking?"

"Scotch," he laughed.

"I'm a scotch drinker too. But I opened a nice wine for this ... for tonight."

I told Dean about his daughter. "Lark's a third-grade schoolteacher *and* a yoga instructor. She's not married but has a boyfriend of three years, Ben Holland. He's a terrific guy; you'd like him."

Before I knew it, the old clock was striking one, the wine at low tide in the bottle. I eased myself down to lie on the sofa and pulled an afghan over me. I tried to picture Dean doing the same on his end. "Robin, we have to make this happen. There's an AIA, American Institute of Architects, Convention in New York next month, late March. Would that be a good time to see you both?"

"Yes, of course," I said, scanning my mind's calendar. *That's only four weeks away!*

"I haven't asked ... but does *she* want to meet *me*?" He sounded diffident now.

I smiled. "She's *dying* to meet you. She made me promise to tell her everything you said tonight." And then incredibly, I began to yawn. The emotion had exhausted me.

"Could you and I meet first? I'd like to take you to dinner. We could talk face-to-face ... before I meet Lark."

"Of course, Dean. I'd love that." *That's the understatement of my adult life.*

"I think I'm feeling like a nervous father-to-be," he added with a small chuckle.

"I can only imagine how you must feel. I have to say you've taken this really well."

"It's all a big act. You should have seen me when you called yesterday. I was literally shaking. I've been a wreck ever since." He mused, "There's so much I want to know … I don't know where to start." He was quiet a moment and then pragmatic. "I'll call you the day before I get there. It's been a long time, Robin." His voice thickened. "I'm looking forward to seeing you."

"Me too. Talk to you soon. Good night."

I spent the next weeks in a tempest of fevered excitement. I willed myself to compartmentalize the visit so I could focus on work. I talked with my support circle—Tee, my dad, and Nick—asking for their thoughts, advice, and affirmation.

Tee said, "*C'est pas vrai*, Rob, you talked to him? My God, I can't believe you finally did it! What did he say?" And when I had told her the whole of it, she said, "I'm proud of you, Rob. You deserve to be happy. And you deserve a second chance at a life with Dean. The stars just may align for you two after all." I gulped, loving her. Then she burst out, "What are you going to *wear*?" and I snorted with laughter.

My dad said, "I couldn't be happier, sweet pea. It's not too late for Lark to benefit from a relationship with her father. And as for you and Dean, this could be a second chance at a life together. I hope to finally meet this young man."

Nick said, "That's *fantastic*! I'm sure Lark's jumping out of her skin. Dean's a *helluva* lucky guy. Just wait till he sees how gorgeous you still are. The guy will be on his knees. Just be you, and the rest will take care of itself." Nick was happy in those days. He was engaged at last to his girlfriend of the past year, a boho-chic designer named Dakota. I had had dinner with the two of them twice and liked Dakota.

Of course I was wildly curious about what Dean looked like. I tried to envision his face through the lens of one of those age-progression photos on missing-children posters. Then one morning in the office, I remembered the professional networking database LinkedIn. Morgan had created a slick new website for the firm and had shown John and me how to create profiles on LinkedIn. I had done little with my account. Did Dean have one?

I fidgeted, drumming my fingers on my desk, and typed in the password I used for everything, Eagles!77. I logged into the site, navigated to the search box, and typed in Dean Falconer. There was a maddening delay as the page loaded, and then there he was! Dean T. Falconer. My tummy did a funny little flip. I leaned forward in my chair and studied the thumbnail image. First I noticed the wavy gold hair was missing in action. He must have begun to lose his hair and buzzed it short. I could imagine Dean doing that and gave him respect points for it. The only thing worse than a man with a comb-over was a man in a toupee.

But Dean's face! His face and neck had broadened, but his gray eyes were still clear and beautiful even in the tiny photo. Although he smiled a closed-mouth professional smile, I could still see the sexy shape of his lips. The sum of his features amounted to a man who was still very attractive. *Okay, Dean Falconer!* I grinned and glanced furtively up at my open office door. I had a meeting in fifteen minutes.

I navigated to *my* LinkedIn page. What if Dean had looked me up too? What would he think of how *I'd* aged? My coworkers' and my LinkedIn profile pictures had been taken by the photographer who had helped design our website, so the photographs were of good quality, well lit and flattering. At least you couldn't see the full extent of my middle-aged voluptuousness in the headshot. My hair was expensively colored and highlighted. The silk scarf I had worn around my throat for the photo session hid the changes that gravity had wrought there. My color was vibrant, the green of my eyes prominent. *Not too bad overall, old girl.*

I called Theresa. It was six hours later in Paris, but Tee was working late. She asked me to hold as she got up to close her office door. The time difference between us had *always* been annoying and damned inconvenient, so we had long been used to planning our calls. And unlike the early years of the scratchy sound of overseas long distance, we could hear each other as clearly as if we were in the same room.

I told Tee what I'd seen on LinkedIn, about Dean's picture. I waited while she shuffled papers and navigated to the website for her own assessment. *"Mais il est vraiment bel homme.* He's aged well, Rob."

"I know! I'm so excited."

Theresa was quiet for a moment and then said, "Do you see how much Lark looks like him?"

I had been so busy evaluating Dean's appearance I hadn't thought about that. "Wow. Yeah. The eyes ... and planes of their cheeks," I said. And then I asked, "But, Theresa, what about me? I weighed about a hundred and twenty pounds the last time Dean saw me!" To my chagrin I was now a size twelve.

"Robin," she said chastising me, "with that hourglass figure of yours?"

"Yeah, but the glass has ... expanded. The sands are ... passing through and settling in the bottom at an alarming rate," I said ruefully, looking down at the generous hips and thighs in my suit skirt. With my big boobs, I was as curvy as a bag of apples.

"C'mon, Robin. You see the way men look at you," Theresa said. "You know damned well you still look great. And with all the walking you do, you're pretty fit. I'm assuming you don't have halitosis?" I hooted with laughter, and she said, "You have *nothing* to worry about."

Reflecting on our conversation as I stood before the mirror before bed, I thought that on the main Tee had to be right. I had taken scrupulous care of my skin, slathering on moisturizer and sunscreen through all seasons. If the jeans I wore now had a high percentage of spandex in them, it was my secret.

"Mom, come to class tomorrow night," Lark urged the next day. She had been trying to get me to start practicing yoga. "You'll feel so good. Look at my yoga body. Lean thighs are nothing to sneeze at."

"I also have twenty-two years on you, darling daughter," I said archly. But Dean's visit was the impetus I needed to follow her advice. Lark's studio offered beginner-level classes two evenings a week. I began that week and immediately felt better in my own skin.

The evenings also provided a great diversion from long nights of waiting and wondering. I hadn't come right out and told Lark I was still interested in Dean, but she sensed it, and I often caught her smiling an indulgent three-cornered kitten's smile at me. I told her Dean and I planned to have dinner alone the first night, while she was at the studio. "That's probably a good idea," she only said.

Dean would be there in less than two weeks. Lark and I planned for the evening as if it were a state dinner. She and I would cook the simple meal, roast chicken, quinoa, and spring vegetables and a salad dressed with my homemade shallot vinaigrette. For dessert Lark would prepare a strawberry shortcake trifle. I would light a fire in the fireplace if the evening was chilly, and we'd have drinks in the living room before dinner. I splurged on an extra-nice bottle of scotch for Dean and two special wines for chilling, a rich white Burgundy and a Chardonnay from the Jura Mountains of France. My liquor-store guy smiled and waggled his caterpillar eyebrows at the extravagance of my purchase.

Dean called me the night before to give me the name of his hotel, the Hotel Lucerne, which was in walking distance of my home. I thought that my favorite Italian restaurant, Crispo in

Chelsea, would be the perfect place to have dinner. I made a reservation and gave Dean the address, and we agreed to meet there the next night at seven.

And then it was D-day. Dean day. The day we would breach the foreign soil of the future. I took the day off and hit the spa. After a massage, facial, manicure, and pedicure, my skin glowed like a string of cultured pearls. Damn the brown spots on my face and hands—but they were what they were. The week before I had found a little black dress whose price tag didn't make me shudder, with a V-neck and wrap waist in a knit that gently skimmed my curves. My muscles felt more toned and supple from the yoga, and I knew I'd feel good in the dress.

I'd never told my hairdresser Rhonda—a true romantic and single mother herself who was so adept at styling she could simply run her fingers through my hair, gently tugging at this or that strand, and it would look amazing—the story of my past. But today as she applied my base color and shimmery highlights, I regaled her with the whole of it. When I asked for my check, she stunned me. "No charge today. Just all the best, Robin."

At home I brought in the mail, flipped on the foyer lamp, and fairly skimmed up the stairs with my shopping bag. I bathed and slipped into my robe and padded downstairs to pour myself a big glass of wine. I put in a sultry Diana Krall CD that matched my mood and rested for a few minutes.

Finally I appraised myself in the new dress. I felt satisfied. I texted Lark for luck. She was dashing out to the studio. "Love you,

Mom. Have a wonderful evening!" *In twenty-four hours my sweet girl will be with her father for the first time in her life.*

As my heels clicked down my front steps, I noticed a taxi trolling slowly down the block. I hailed it so abruptly I looked as if I were doing the Hitler salute. The driver pulled to the curb right in front of the house. Good omen number one.

But the traffic was heavy, and I arrived at Crispo five minutes late. Stuffing bills to the driver, I stepped out of the cab and stumbled a little in my heels at the curb. Looking up again, I became aware of a tall figure, hands in pockets, silhouetted against the bright facade of the building. Heart pounding, I stepped forward. The figure took a step in my direction and into the light. "Hello, Robin Hamilton," he said in the voice of my dreams.

"Hello, Dean," I said, staring. He was even better looking than I'd thought he would be. In the half light I saw the familiar relief map of his high-planed face, a little broader, the cleft in his chin not as deep as before. Dean's darkened gray eyes locked on mine. His short hair was still blonde, but bristles of gray-white shimmered among the gold. We extended our right hands, but then he grinned and put both arms out to hug me. I stepped into the light embrace of man and memory.

Light-headed as we stepped apart, I heard Dean say, "Ready?" He opened the restaurant door. I remembered his southern gentleman's manners. As we stood together at the hostess stand, our eyes kept sliding to each other's faces. We smiled together again, and I suddenly felt shy. Dean looked handsome and broad shouldered in a dark-navy blazer—the first I'd ever seen him in—over a blue checked button-down shirt, crisp khaki slacks, and tasseled cordovan loafers. The ruddy complexion and deep creases at the corner of his eyes testified to a lifetime of outdoor work and of frequent smiles. He said, "Robin, you look beautiful. I knew you would." My chest filled with a rush of warmth.

"You look wonderful too," I said softly. Dean pulled out my chair for me at the table, and I draped my wrap over the back of my chair. I pulled my hair forward to frame my face and flow over my collarbones. Dean looked around at the warm brick walls studded at intervals with flickering votive candles.

"Nice place," he said.

"This is some of the best Northern Italian food in New York City," I said, tilting my head back to peer at the menu through my bifocals. "I love the pasta with truffle butter, peas, and parmesan," I said, pointing it out to him, "and we *have* to start with the grilled parmesan-crusted asparagus appetizer."

"Do you always wear glasses, Robin?"

"I do. I like them. I started wearing them for distance in my twenties, and now I need them for reading."

"They look very attractive on you."

"Thank you." I smiled, acknowledging the compliment, and then laughed as Dean slipped a hand into his breast pocket and withdrew a pair of tortoise readers of his own. He unfolded them, cleared his throat, and made a big deal out of putting them on. "Would you like to choose a wine for us?" I asked. A large woman at a nearby table shrieked with laughter as her companion loudly described her class reunion. An unobtrusive black-clad young man arrived to pour water into our glasses.

"Sure, let's see ... a nice red?" Dean scanned the wine list. He looked sexy in the dark plastic frames. He selected a bottle of Montepulciano d'Abruzzo with black cherry notes and a dry finish that would complement the pasta dishes. I sipped my water and watched him. His beard was heavier than it had been back then, and the darker shadow spread over his jawline. This older version of Dean appeared effortlessly elegant and self-assured.

We ordered roasted kale salads and I the black truffle ricotta ravioli special, Dean the pappardelle and duck ragu. Taking the first sip of wine, I complimented Dean on his choice. He smiled and leaned back in his chair. "I don't know where to start," he said. "There's so much more I want to know. Does Lark look like you? Is she pretty?"

I grinned and said, "She's beautiful. She has my mouth and nose ... hands and ... figure." I blushed. "But she has your eyes, the planes of your face, your gold hair ... and your feet." Dean laughed, rubbing a hand over his scalp, and then slid one loafered foot from under the table, looking down at it for a moment. "She looked so much like you when she was a baby. It haunted me for years," I said, looking into middle distance.

I slipped my cell from my purse and thumbed to find a recent picture of Lark. I handed the phone to Dean. He peered at the photo through his readers. As he studied the face of his daughter for the first time, his throat worked with emotion. Finally he said,

"You're right: she's beautiful." He took a big sip of wine. "Do you have more?" I showed him all I had on the camera roll. He studied the pictures as if he had been handed Jefferson's blueprints for Monticello. "She also looks a lot like my sister Leslie."

"Really?" I said, interested.

He raised his head and smiled at me again. "I can't believe I'm going to meet my daughter, *our* daughter tomorrow night. I hope I sleep. I didn't do so well last night. Are we still having dinner at your house?"

"Walk over about six thirty for a drink? Does that give you enough time after your sessions?"

"Yes, perfect. I should be finished by four." Dean took my hand and squeezed it. Our salads arrived, and we declined the proffered hot bread and olive oil.

"Do you remember the last meal we had together?" I asked him shyly, sipping at my wine.

"Of course," he said right away. "The first big meal you ever cooked." He smiled at the memory. "Roast beef and potatoes. It was delicious, and you looked … gorgeous … in a green dress," he added triumphantly and speared a cherry tomato.

"Wow, very good." I couldn't believe he remembered the dress. The look on his face told me we were both remembering the rest of that night. I flushed and changed the subject. "Do you cook, Dean?"

He refilled our wineglasses. "I've lived alone for twenty-eight years remember, so yes, and I'm pretty good at it actually. My mother taught me a lot, and I watch the Food Network. I like to grill and smoke meat and fish too. I make killer smoked salmon. I use pecan for the wood chips and add a beer to the water. Speaking of smoking," he said, lowering his voice and grinning, "do you ever smoke weed anymore?"

I laughed and said, "Not since I did with you." Then I remembered the night with Nick years ago. "Actually, I did once with a friend from NYU, Nick, who's still a close friend." Dean looked up at me, the unspoken question in his eyes, and I felt compelled to add, "Just a friend. Nick. Actually, he's been a godsend for both Lark and me. He spent time with Lark when she was young; she loves him."

Dean put his elbows on the table, laced his fingers together, and lowered his head to rub his lips across his knuckles. I saw his jaw muscles clench and unclench. I wondered what I had unleashed and sipped at my wine, waiting. After several minutes he said quietly, "I should say I'm glad that Lark's had your friend as a father figure, but I'm surprised by how I feel like I've just been impaled with a fence post." He swore under his breath and then looked at me in apology. I pressed my lips together and nodded, trying to beam understanding from my eyes. "I should have been the one spending time with her," he said.

The server approached smiling cautiously. "Your dinner will be here shortly."

"Thank you," I answered. Dean ordered another bottle of wine. Tipping the rest of the first bottle into our glasses, he asked, "And Lark is close to your father?"

"Oh yes. She and her Grandpa Hank have always been close. Dad is my rock. I couldn't have made it all those years as a single mother without him and Mother."

"I'm so sorry, Robin," he said, his eyes suffused with sadness. "I'd give anything if I could have been there for ... both of you."

"I know," I managed and squeezed his arm. The waiter arrived with our entrées then, and we tucked into them in silence, reflecting on the devastating events that had passed through our lives like a natural disaster.

Dean ate several bites of his pasta and moaned with pleasure at the flavor of the duck. "This is seriously good," he said and smiled again. A group of women passed our table on their way out of the restaurant, and I noted two of them noticing Dean. Without a doubt the man was stare worthy.

A mother and teenaged son in a Rolling Stones T-shirt with the big red lips and tongue were being seated at the next table. Regarding them for a moment, Dean said, "I meant to tell you ... I told my mother about your call and about Lark. She boo-hooed, Robin, especially when I said that you had named the baby after her."

"Awww, Dean." My eyes stung with tears. "I'm glad she was touched. I would love to meet your mom. I know that she must feel terribly hurt too, about being separated from her grandchild."

"She told me about the time you called when I was engaged to Victoria. I know you tried to tell me about Lark then … but I can see that you wouldn't have felt right telling Mom about Lark without telling me about her first." I nodded sadly in acknowledgement. We returned to our plates and shared a bite of each other's dishes.

I put my hand over Dean's on the white tablecloth. His skin was very warm. He put down his fork and looked at me. I asked, "Can we agree to try not to beat ourselves up anymore about the past? About what we can't change?"

He put his other hand on top of mine. "Yeah," he sighed. When he leaned to kiss my cheek, my head reeled. We had connected emotionally, and the feel of his lips on my skin left me dizzy.

Mopping up sauce from his plate with a last piece of pasta and savoring it for a moment, Dean looked at me again. "Do you date much?" I told him about my few bad dating experiences and about Greg.

"What about you?" I asked. Dean told me that he had dated a few years after Victoria's death and then again recently but hadn't found anyone he wanted to spend his life with. My heart swelled with hope. The waiter appeared then to clear away our plates, and we declined his offer of coffee and dessert. We sipped the last of the wine.

"Thank you, Dean. I enjoyed that so much," I said as he paid the bill.

As we rose to leave, Dean took the wrap from the back of my chair and dropped it over my shoulders like a blessing. As I pulled my hair from under it, he said, "Your hair still looks the same." My mind's eye flashed back to leaning over Dean in my bed, my hair spilling around us. I had to steel myself to walk through the restaurant gracefully.

Outside, I asked casually, "Want to share a cab?" We waited for one to appear, each lost in our own thoughts again, Dean's hands in his pockets. The early spring night had cooled. I pulled my pashmina closer. In the cab, Dean's solid thigh pressed against mine, and electricity leaped between us like lightning between clouds. But we talked of inconsequential things, New York City versus life in a small college town.

I asked Dean to come in for a nightcap. He said he had to get up early to prepare for a presentation the next morning but looked forward to seeing my home the next evening. "Thank you for having dinner with me," he said. "It was terrific."

He leaned in, his eyes on my mouth, but froze there. His eyes moved up to meet mine. Mesmerized, I answered the unspoken question and inclined my face slightly. I closed my eyes as he kissed my lips, a searching kiss. I noticed his scent that I thought I'd forgotten, and another rush of memory rolled over me like so much surf. My hands clung to Dean's elbows as he held my face in his hands. Then he released me and stepped back, nodding once. "See you tomorrow night, Robin Hamilton," he said.

As I turned the key in the lock, I was breathing as heavily as if I'd run back from the restaurant. Dean waved once and moved off down the sidewalk toward his hotel.

I spent the next day at the office preparing contracts, meeting with two young couples closing on their new homes, and watching the clock on my computer as if I were afraid it would steal something from my desk. I left the office at four to join Lark at my house. She had shopped for the ingredients for our meal and was already preparing the chicken for the oven. She looked young and lovely in one of my aprons over a heather-colored sweater and jeans, her hair pulled back from her face in a half ponytail. Excited myself, I hugged her and hurried upstairs to freshen up. I pulled on jeans and chose an emerald-green silk blouse that I knew accentuated my eyes and a creamy cardigan. *This is Lark's night, Robin,* I reminded myself.

Downstairs I helped Lark prepare the salad. The chicken was in the oven, and Lark had chopped the vegetables. I whisked together my special dressing, put it into the refrigerator to chill, and tore radicchio and romaine for the salad. Walking back into the living room, I saw that Lark had set the dining table with a bright blue-and-yellow Provencal tablecloth and napkins. "Where did *those* come from?" I asked, smiling my approval.

"Impulse buy." She grinned. "I saw them in the window at Williams-Sonoma on Fifty-Ninth and couldn't resist. I thought they would look nice for our French meal." She regarded the table. "Doesn't it look spectacular?"

"It looks wonderful." I admired the flowers she had placed in my French white soup tureen. "And what a good idea to pair daisies and lavender. You have a great eye, darling." We set three places with my plain white plates over natural rattan chargers, and Lark added my cobalt water goblets and casual stainless flatware. We stood back admiring our work with the scrutiny of art appraisers.

"My ... father ... is going to be sitting right there," Lark said, her gray eyes large and dark. "Mom, he'll like me, right?" She sounded as she had when she was twelve.

"Oh, Lark, how could he not?" I said hugging her. I looked over her shoulder at the old clock on the mantle. "And he'll be here in precisely nineteen minutes." That sent her scurrying back to the kitchen. The night had turned chilly, so I lit the fire I had laid just in case. I put the bottle of scotch, three glasses, and a plate of the pâté and crackers that Lark had bought on a black tole tray, carried it to the coffee table, and plumped the cushions. I tried to picture Dean in my home. I pushed play on the CD player, and the French soundtrack from the movie *Something's Gotta Give* spilled from the speakers like blown kisses.

The doorbell rang at exactly six thirty, as Lark was pouring water into the goblets. She took a deep breath and whipped off the apron, drying her hands on it. I smiled at her reassuringly. "Do you want me to get the door?" I asked.

"Yes, please!" she said. I opened the door to the handsome, smiling man holding a sheaf of yellow-and-red parrot tulips, as riotous as a parade.

"How beautiful! Thank you."

He stepped inside, smiling nervously, and then noticed Lark standing by the table. "You're Lark," he said evenly and walked toward her. The three of us stood together for a moment, smiling, frozen like a tableau in the Museum of Natural History: *A Family*.

I said simply, "Lark, this is Dean Falconer."

She had been holding her breath and let it out. "Hello, Dean, it's nice to finally meet you."

Dean's eyes were the same polished gray as his daughter's. He extended his hand to her. She extended hers, but instead of shaking it, Dean took it between both of his for a moment, looking down at it and then into her face. Choked with emotion, he said, "My daughter." They stood smiling shyly at each other, looking so much alike that I burst into happy tears. We all laughed in relief, and I swiped at my cheeks. I invited Dean to help himself to a drink and slipped into the kitchen to put the tulips in water. I stood, my back against the counter, hugged myself around the shoulders, and bowed my head. *Thank you, God.*

Dean and Lark were sitting on one section of the sofa, spreading crackers with the pâté. Remarking on their beauty again, I placed the flowers on the coffee table next to the appetizers and settled into the sofa to study Dean. More casual this evening, he was wearing a tweedy brown blazer over a denim shirt. He leaned forward, forearms on his knees, hands clasped loosely together—a posture I still recognized. The swell of belly that pushed against the shirt above his belt heartened me. The few little imperfections

I'd noticed only served to make him more attractive. Lustful thoughts were springing up again like spring jonquils. I took off my sweater and laid it over the arm of the sofa.

"Wow, what a nice bottle of scotch," said Dean.

"Well, I splurged … for tonight." I grinned.

"Lucky for me." He poured some of the golden liquid into each glass. We all took a sip, agreeing it was excellent. Dean asked Lark about her work. I excused myself, popped a cracker into my mouth, and returned to the kitchen to put the quinoa on to boil and the vegetables into the oven. When I returned, Dean was telling Lark about his career as an architect as Eartha Kitt belted out "C'est Si Bon." Indeed. It was very good.

When the oven timer signaled the chicken ready, Lark rose to go to the kitchen. Dean and I were alone for the first time. Eyes glistening, he said, "Robin, she's a beauty. So intelligent and poised."

"Yes, she is," I agreed happily.

"Thank you," he said simply, shaking his head in amazement, "for the … incredible job you did raising her." He pulled a monogrammed white handkerchief from his pocket. "I can't imagine … I know how hard you must have worked." He blew his nose quietly and pocketed the handkerchief.

"It was all worth it," I said as Lark reappeared with the platter of golden chicken and placed it on the table. Dean and I watched her movements, deft and economical, graceful. I hopped up to help bring the other dishes to the table, and we sat down to dinner.

"Dean, will you pour the wine?" I asked.

"I'd like to ask a blessing first if I may," he said humbly, looking from Lark to me. We smiled and nodded, touched. Dean bowed his head and began, "Dear Lord, thank you for this delicious meal and the hands that prepared it. Thank you … for this wonderful young woman, the daughter you gave us, and for bringing us all together. Amen."

"Amen," Lark and I said together.

Dean sniffed, took the wine bottle, and filled our glasses. Raising his glass, he said, "To Robin and Lark." Lark and I smiled, and we all clinked glasses.

Then Lark surprised me by raising her glass again. She added solemnly, "To family."

"To family," Dean and I echoed, eyes bright with tears again.

Louis Armstrong's distinctive falsetto filled the room with "La Vie en Rose" as we began to eat. The simple meal was delicious, Lark's chicken moist and tender. The conversation flowed comfortably, allaying my worries about awkward pauses. I mostly listened quietly, letting Dean and Lark initiate the majority of the conversation, delighting in watching them together. Lark told her father about the accident she had been in senior year of high school and then about her college days. Dean talked about his family. "You have a grandmother and aunts, you know, Lark." He sipped his wine thoughtfully and suddenly said, "I have a great idea." He wiped his mouth with his napkin. "What do you think about coming to Virginia this summer for a couple of weeks? I know you have summers off from teaching, Lark. Could you take some time off, Robin?"

Lark and I looked at each other. She said, "Sure … I would love that actually. I could probably block out my schedule at the studio too."

I took a bite of chicken and chewed it thoughtfully, planning ahead, and then took a sip of water. "I think I could make that work too. I suppose we could hire a temp, an interim paralegal to help John and Morgan. And God knows I have vacation time I haven't taken."

Lark excused herself to fetch the dessert and returned brandishing the prettily presented trifle dish. "That's impressive," Dean said appreciatively. Lark spooned the dessert into my little Italian dessert dishes as Dean continued, "I can't wait for you both to meet my mother and sisters … and see Villeneuve. There are so many things to do and see around Charlottesville too. I can take you to the Shenandoah National Forest—it's gorgeous—and to some world-class vineyards. Believe it or not, there are over fifty in the area." He waggled his glass.

"Really?" I asked, astonished.

"People in Virginia are *serious* about their wines. They say Napa is for auto parts." Lark and I laughed.

"We have wonderful restaurants and all the shopping you could want."

Lark and I sipped at our wine, listening with enjoyment. I winked at her across the table.

"I built my house and a two-bedroom guesthouse behind it. It would be comfortable and private for you. It's nice," he said, sounding like a kid talking about Disneyland.

"Sold," Lark said, spooning berries into her mouth.

"I guess that pretty much settles it," I said.

"What month would you want us? Late August is out for me because of in-service and back-to-school stuff. But June or July would work," Lark said.

Dean had a dab of whipped cream in one corner of his mouth, and I wanted to blot it with my napkin ... or lick it off.

"We could come the second week in June," Lark said. "That would give me time to button everything up at school and then get packed. Mom? Would you be able to work it out then?"

I was astonished at how casually we were planning it all. "I'll talk to John this week about it." I was as excited as they were. That was only about ten weeks away. "This was superb by the way, Lark Bird," I said, taking another bite of my dessert.

Dean grinned, cocking his head at the expression. "Lark Bird?" Lark told him about the nicknames we had given each other when she was a little girl. He was leaning back in his chair enjoying himself. "I love it," he said.

He finished his dessert, scraping at the last of the whipped cream with his spoon. "Yum. Well, between now and June, may I call you both?"

"Sure, and we could Skype," Lark said. "Do you know about Skype, Dean?"

"I know about it but haven't done it. I'm a pretty quick learner though." He grinned.

"I could call you from school and have my kids meet you. They would love it," she said, the idea exciting her. "And you could even tell them what it's like to live on a farm. Most of my kids have never been out of the city."

"Cool. That sounds like fun. Let's do it," Dean said enthusiastically.

I sipped the last of my wine, my heart full again as I watched them. I rose and carried the dishes into the kitchen and spooned some decaf into the French press. Then I carried the pot and three cups into the living room. We talked for a while, enjoying the coffee, and then Dean leaned forward, his hands on his knees and said he had an early flight the next morning and should get going. Lark and I walked him to the door, and as he turned to her, she held out her arms to him. He smiled tremulously, and they embraced for the first time.

"Call you soon, Robin?" he asked me then.

"I'll look forward to it," I said.

"Thank you, for one of the most wonderful evenings I've ever had," Dean said, looking from me to Lark. "The food and drink were superb and the company first rate." As I moved to open the door, he turned to me and pulled me into a brief hug. "Talk to you soon," he said to Lark. He looked at me again and mouthed a silent, "Thank you."

CHAPTER

21

Robin

2013

Lark and I had sat aboard the suffocating commuter jet on the runway for almost an hour, but we got excited all over again as the plane finally lifted off. Lark was in a doubly celebratory mood; school was out, her faculty checkout list complete. "I think a glass of champagne is in order," she said, fanning her face with an airsickness bag.

My partner John (who was completely supportive of my journey) and I had hired Morgan's friend Cory, an NYU law student, as a summer intern who would help handle the workload while I was away. I would follow John's parting advice and not worry about a thing. A flight attendant who looked as if she had a terminal case of jet lag served us tepid champagne in plastic cups. "To Villeneuve," Lark said, grinning as she touched her rim to mine. We grimaced around our first sips of the cheap airline stuff and wrinkled our noses at each other. *Oh well.*

Lark leaned her seat back and opened a fat, juicy *InStyle* magazine, thumbing pleasurably through pages of a periodical that for a change weren't related to education. I grinned as I watched her begin reading at the back. I always read a magazine from back to front too. I leaned back and breathed deeply, thinking about Dean and the weeks to come. Was this thing completely insane? Six months ago it would have been inconceivable. From time to time I looked over at the glossy pages of stick-figure celebrities in red-carpet attire.

Lark looked up, interrupting my reverie, and caught me off guard. "Dean is attractive for his age, don't you think?" I feigned an offended face at the age remark. "You know what I mean," she said. "You two *have* been flirting, haven't you?"

Indeed, we had been "flirting." Dean and I had talked many times the past few weeks. The last conversation had lasted into the wee hours and had left me loose-boned and wriggling with pleasure under my covers. In physical science, the law of conservation of energy states that energy can never be created or destroyed but is conserved over *time*. The inherent magnetic field that had encompassed Dean and me in 1977 was still powerful. How I loved his southern baritone curling into my ear again.

"Ye-ess, you could say that," I answered Lark with a small smile.

She laughed and squeezed my hand on the armrest. "I'm glad, Mom."

I slipped my earbuds in and queued up my playlist. The attraction wasn't *entirely* physical; Dean and I truly liked one another. As before, we never ran out of things to talk about. We talked of historical events, cultural trends, music, and life events from the three decades we hadn't shared together. Some of those talks were bittersweet, tinged with sadness. Of course now we could talk about Lark. That I would have the pleasure of telling him the story of her childhood—a narration that could literally take the rest of our years—was a small semblance of recompense for all we'd forfeited. My stomach gave a fishlike leap: I would be with him again in a couple of hours. I pushed the play button on the Eagles' latest, *Long Road out of Eden*. At Richmond, Lark and I would rent a car and drive an hour west to Keswick and on to Villeneuve. If the drive was smooth, we should arrive at the farm around four o'clock, in time to freshen up before dinner. Mrs. "Please call me Laurel" Falconer had invited us for dinner at the main house. Dean's sisters and their husbands, who lived in Charlottesville, were driving out to join us. I felt a little nervous at the prospect of their scrutiny, but Dean assured me they would be supportive.

Lark dozed, her mouth slack, and her head fell to my shoulder. *My precious girl.* I reflected on what Lark had told me of her conversations with her father. Getting to know one another, they'd found that some of her affinities reflected Dean's. It brought to mind studies of twins who were separated at birth and met later in life to learn they had taken similar paths. Dean's genes had contributed to Lark's interests and attitudes in seemingly random ways: they had strong aversions to the scent of rosemary and of turmeric, were gifted spellers (each had won a spelling bee in their sixth-grade years), threw up if they saw someone else getting sick, and made an almost identical funny sound when they sneezed.

Lark and Dean had executed the Skype session with her third graders the last week of school. Dean had worked up a special PowerPoint presentation for the children with photographs, painting a picture for them of life on a horse farm. The Q&A period at the end had been lively and funny. Dean had loved it and had been as proud as a gamecock to be introduced as Lark's father. The children had made construction-paper thank-you cards, with drawings of horses and dogs on them, and Lark had mailed them to her father.

Everything I'd witnessed between the two of them had convinced me that Dean would have been the father I'd dreamed. I began to think about the future and what Dean would be like as grandfather to Lark's children. Without a doubt I now knew he would want to be involved in their lives. I closed my eyes and pictured Dean leading a delighted child around on horseback in the sunshine, Lark looking on with contentment from beneath the shade of a great tree, Ben's arm around her waist. A baby a few rows behind us began to shriek, and I laughed to myself. But where did I fit in this fantasy of mine? Would I be there as well? And in what capacity? Lark woke abruptly and stretched, her limbs as supple as a lizard's. "What time is it?" she asked, crinkling her nose and yawning deeply. "Did I really sleep?"

I peered at my watch. "We should be landing in … twenty-five, no, twenty-seven minutes." I was wearing black leggings, a tunic, my double-strand turquoise necklace, and black flats. Lark was pretty in black shorts, an Indian cotton print blouse, red chandelier earrings, and silver sandals. Dean had asked us to stay until after the Fourth of July celebration, and we had packed accordingly. The airline had zinged us for an extra hundred bucks for overweight bags. Dean had a pool, so Lark had bought a sleek new red suit before we'd left the city. I loathed the thought of making an appearance in a bathing suit, especially in front of Dean. I didn't even own one.

As the plane touched down, Lark and I groped underneath and above, gathering our belongings and grinning like fools with excitement. We headed to baggage claim only to spend fifteen frustrating minutes in line at an understaffed rental car desk. Finally we schlepped our bags in the June heat to a particularly hideous beige Dodge Avenger. So much for arriving in style.

The Central Virginia countryside was beautiful, pastoral: rolling hills and valleys dotted with contented black-and-white cows and sleek horses. The sunlight was more luminous here. It dappled the forest floor through white bark and evergreens. We turned off Richmond Road at Keswick and, according to our GPS device, onto the road that would take us to Villeneuve. Lark and I were enchanted by stately old houses on beautiful farms with a romantic lexicon of names that conjured images of the earth, soil, and trees of the region: Tall Pines, Willow Brook Farm, Fox's Earth. We passed two vineyards, antique shop fronts, and a great old stone church. And at last ... among split rail fences and weather-smoothed rock walls was our destination. A small, white oval sign made of wood and rimmed in gold swung gently from an iron post: Villeneuve, established 1877.

Lark swung the car onto the gray graveled drive bordered by white fences and sprawling oak trees. *So this is Dean's world!* My stomach flipped again. To our left and right as the car crunched along were manicured paddocks of green, green grass bisected at intervals by dark wooden horse jumps. I lowered my window to breathe it in. "Wonder where the horses are," I murmured to Lark. Until then, neither of us had spoken, as if fearing to break some alchemy. We climbed a gentle mound, and there settled elegantly atop the rise was the main house, a gracious and modest old Georgian with twin chimneys. "How lovely!" I breathed.

Lark braked and stared. "*Wow*, right?" The butter-yellow stucco with multipaned windows and black shutters seemed to preen for us in the late-afternoon sun. A columned portico topped with a Chinese Chippendale railing sheltered the small front porch and drew the eye to the glossy black front door flanked by red geraniums in concrete urns. And all around, massive oaks with twisty, gnarled limbs shaded the house. Their leaves shimmered faintly in the summer breeze as Lark veered smoothly around the circular drive and came to a stop. Tandem dogs appeared from around the house. We looked to the door and around but saw no one about. We giggled, debating whether or not the dogs would find a couple of New Yorkers too tough for an afternoon treat.

Then a figure stepped from beneath one of the oaks, raising a hand in greeting, and called to the dogs. My heart inched up my throat as I recognized Dean's face under a University of Virginia ball cap. He was in faded jeans and a T-shirt. From the deep shadows I saw a broad smile stretch itself across his tanned face. Lark and I opened our doors and stepped onto the drive, the jagged gravel as big as eggs. This was not a place for heels. "Welcome to Villeneuve, ladies!" Dean said.

"Dad!" Lark called. Never in her life until that moment had I heard my daughter say the word. The endearment on her lips was palpable and tinged with promise. My nose stung with tears. Dean stepped toward her, and they embraced. The dogs circled, sniffing us out and wagging their broad tails.

"Robin, you're here," Dean said, moving to hug me too. As our bodies touched, I was suffused with the feeling of coming home and something exotic and unexplored at the same time. I felt Lark's eyes on us behind her big Kate Spade sunglasses.

"I know … I can't believe it." I grinned. "The farm is spectacular, Dean."

"Just wait; Villeneuve's pretty seductive. It will get into your blood." He grinned. My stomach rippled again at the word *seductive*. "These savage beasts are Charlotte," he said, indicating the smaller of the dogs, a chocolate Labrador retriever, "and Hudson." Hearing his name, the great glossy black Lab seemed to grin himself and nudged Dean's leg for a petting.

"Hello, sweeties," I said, bending to pet Charlotte. She bathed my hand with her pink tongue.

Dean said, "Careful, her breath could knock a buzzard off a dead skunk." Lark and I hooted. "Come on in, girls. We'll get your bags to the guesthouse later. Mom can't wait to meet you." We were still giggling as we entered a small, stately foyer hung with colonial-era portraits. Just ahead were stairs of gleaming old wood, a graceful curving bannister. To the right a small dining room seemed stuffed with a great cherry table and chairs, more oils, and handsome English antiques. And to the left was a living room or parlor with deep, comfortable chairs, a great fireplace, and many shelves lined with books that had been read.

From the rear of the house a woman approached. Petite, sturdy, and smiling, with a cap of lustrous gray curls, she said in a cultured southern voice, "Welcome. I'm Laurel Falconer."

Dean said, "Mother, I'd like you to meet Robin Hamilton."

Laurel took my hands in between hers and leaned to kiss my cheek. "Hello, Robin."

"And this is Lark." Dean was grinning like Howdy Doody.

Laurel turned to Lark and held out both arms. "Lark, my beautiful granddaughter. At last." She pulled Lark into a warm embrace and then stood back again and gazed at her, tears darkening her lashes. "You are the image of your aunt Leslie."

"You really are," Dean said happily.

"Really?" Lark replied, pleased.

"You'll meet her tonight ... *and* the rest of the family," Laurel said. "Come on, Robin, Lark, you must be parched."

Dean inclined his arm toward the kitchen and then followed me down the hall.

The kitchen was the heart of the old house. Gleaming copper pots and sheaves of dried herbs and flowers hung above a large central island, and everywhere were touches of vibrant color— plaid curtains, art, and family photographs. In the breakfast area a wooden church pew bracketed one wall and served as seating for the rustic farm table, a copse of mismatched wooden chairs on the other side. A pair of comfortable old wing chairs dressed down in a neutral duck fabric sat in one corner. The table between them was scattered with mail, reading glasses, a leather journal, books, and pens, telling me this was where the lady of the house spent most of her time. The large modern windows afforded her a generous view of the rear of the farm. "What a wonderful, cozy room," I said.

Lark and I perched on stools at the island as Laurel pulled a metal pitcher of iced tea from the stainless steel refrigerator. While Lark talked with Laurel about her teaching career, I watched Dean repair his mother's leaky sink sprayer as if he were performing Macbeth in the nude. I downed a second glass of iced tea. Laurel followed my gaze. "Dean's so busy; I have to snare him when I can." She winked at me.

We chatted about the home and its history. Dean told us the house had originally been built in 1877 and had been remodeled three times, twice in the forty years the Falconers had owned it. A powder room and laundry/mudroom had been added off the kitchen, and other structural reinforcements and improvements had been made through the years, all without compromising the integrity of the original house. Dean had designed the flagstone terraces in the backyard for entertaining. Laurel told us that a few of the enormous post oaks around the house were reputed to be at least 270 years old, around since the time "Mr. Jefferson" had been president. "The name of Thomas Jefferson is always spoken with reverence in the Charlottesville area," she said with a grin. "You may know that his home is here. Monticello."

"I'd love to see Monticello," I said.

"I would too," Lark said.

"Dean's a great tour guide," she said smiling at her son. "Now if you girls would like to rest and unpack, we'll have dinner here about seven," Laurel said.

"Thank you, I think we would." I looked to Lark, who nodded her agreement. "We're looking forward to dinner and meeting everyone. Thanks so much for your hospitality, Laurel," I said.

"It is *our* pleasure; we are just thrilled to have you here," she said. "Dean will take you back to the guesthouse. Please let me know if there's anything you need during your stay." Her eyes glistened again as she looked from me to Lark. "I'm looking forward to a nice long visit."

"Another Jeep," I commented to Dean as we walked out to the driveway.

"It's the only make of car I've ever driven; they're good cars. Ride with me, Robin?" Unlike the basic green one I remembered, this model was tricked out with leather, heated seats, a sunroof, and all the extras. Lark followed us in our rental car around the back of the house, and we saw the barn for the first time.

"Where are all the horses?" I asked.

"In the heat of the day they're in the barn, but the help will be turning them out in a few minutes to graze the paddocks. We'll go meet the horses in the morning. My plan is to *ease* you into the saddle." He grinned. About fifty yards back, Dean's home, also Georgian in style, nestled into the landscape of oak and towering pine. "I designed and built my place twenty years ago. I hope you like it," he said shyly.

"Dean," I said, full of pride for him, "you're an architect." Then I felt like a fool. "I mean … you know what I mean." He laughed softly, and I said, "I'm happy that you have the career you wanted and are obviously successful. I knew you had a gift."

"I knew what you meant." He smiled. "Thank you. That means a lot to me." He drove around the side of the house to a parking pad. Lark nosed the awful rental car in next to his Jeep. A large pool surrounded by a black iron fence shimmered in the sunlight between his house and the guesthouse, a low-slung one-story bungalow.

"This is fabulous," I said.

"I'm … so happy you're here," he said, turning to look into my eyes. I wanted so much to kiss him then, but Lark was waiting. Dean opened the door of the guesthouse. One large room, a kitchen/sitting area, was flanked on either side by a bedroom and bath. The space was well appointed but spare.

"This is so nice," Lark said. "We'll be really comfy here."

He left us then, and I watched him walk back to his house. He stopped and appeared to fish something from the pool and then disappeared through french doors at the back of his house. I loved the way the man moved.

Lark was already staking a claim on a room. Each room had a queen-sized bed, a chest of drawers, and a roomy closet with padded hangers. The bathrooms had glassed showers and deep soaking tubs. In the well-stocked kitchen, I discovered that someone had filled the refrigerator with cold wine, beer, bottled water, and fresh fruit. What luxury! It was as welcoming as a four-star bed-and-breakfast cottage.

Lark snared a bottle of water and said she was going to do a half hour of yoga practice. "C'mon, Mom, we've been sitting all day. You'll feel great." Consulting my watch, I saw that she was right. I'd still have an hour afterward to take a soak and dress for the evening.

Freshly stretched, relaxed, and bathed, Lark and I walked to Dean's. "This pool is fab!" Lark said as we skirted it. The gunite bottom was as dark as a deep, still pond, the decking formed of natural stone. It seemed to belong somewhere in the French countryside. I wouldn't have been surprised to find topless sunbathers reclining languidly at its perimeter. We knocked on Dean's back door. He appeared wiping his hands on a bar towel.

"Come in, come in," he said heartily. Most of the downstairs was occupied by one huge living space with a fireplace—large enough to roast a pig in—a group of chairs and sofas at one end, and a long open kitchen at the other. Lark and I exclaimed over the house and Dean's special pieces as we drifted through. Foxhunt prints on the walls and animal-patterned fabrics on the furniture reflected his interests and lifestyle. Dean had striped the white ceilings with dark wood beams.

Glass shelves above a well-equipped wet bar held jewel-toned glassware that Dean had collected during his travels. "What can I get you to drink, ladies?" he asked. I chose a glass of cold sauvignon blanc, and Lark, a craft beer. Lark and Dean talked about the breweries in the area and the one Dean wanted to take her to first. "Let's sit down," he said, indicating a grouping of comfy chairs. "So you're about to meet the sisters." Dean grinned. He prepared us. Interestingly, neither sister had had children. Lark was Laurel's first and only grandchild.

A few minutes before seven we walked the gravel drive and a path through a copse of fragrant pine and cypress to the main house. The dogs barked, announcing the arrival of the others. So Lark and I were introduced to Mary, Leslie, and their husbands, Robert and Warren, in the driveway for the first time. I immediately noticed the uncanny resemblance between Leslie and Lark. "Lark, it's like looking in the mirror ... *twenty years ago,*" Leslie marveled. Although Leslie colored her hair now, she said that Lark's shade was close to her and Dean's natural color. Leslie's eyes were large and, like Lark's, as gray as moonstones. Both sisters gave us hugs and told us they were happy to finally meet us. Amid the chatter we entered Laurel's house through the back door, and our noses sprang to attention at the spicy smell of meat sauce (sans rosemary for Dean and Lark) and garlic bread.

"Wait till you taste Mom's meat lasagna," Mary said with a grin. "It will make you happy to be alive." Mary was lean and willowy, green-eyed like her mother, with luxuriant red hair, a few shades lighter than Tee's. "Mom, where's the wine?" she called to Laurel, scanning the refrigerator without success.

"It's iced down with the beer in tubs in the mudroom. Y'all help yourselves!" Laurel called, bustling around and sliding on blue gingham oven mitts to take the lasagna out of the oven. "Leslie, dress that salad, please?"

Unaccustomed to large family gatherings and the booming voices of the hearty, back-slapping husbands, Lark seemed a little overwhelmed, as I was. When we assembled at the dining room table, Dean asked a sweet blessing, and everyone tucked into the meal. The conversation was easy, comfortable—if the Falconers were assessing us, it didn't feel that way. We learned that Mary had earned her veterinary degree years before but now worked exclusively with the Falconer animals. Both she and Leslie were responsible for training the horses, readying them to compete in what they termed "three-day events." Several times a year they took the horses to compete in regional and national competitions.

After coffee, everyone helped clear the table and stack the dishwasher and then drifted out to the back terrace. Robert and Dean carried the tub of beer out between them. Warren consulted his Weather Channel app. "Man, it's going to be ninety tomorrow." Dean suggested they all come swimming midafternoon. Warren and Mary said they would bring meat and "fixin's" and grill burgers.

I had been drained by journey and emotion, and my head felt too heavy to hold up, my neck a hollow dandelion stem. "I think I'd like to turn in for the night," I announced.

Dean set his beer can down and was on his feet. "I'll walk you back." His mother and sisters exchanged meaningful looks. Lark said she would stay and visit a while longer.

"Good night then, everyone," I said.

Dean and I walked off down the drive, a voluptuous moon lighting our path. The dogs ambled in our wake. As we reached the tree-lined path again, we were surrounded by fireflies— lightning bugs, Dean called them—their brief flickering like those of match strikes. "We used to catch 'em in jars when we were kids." Dean grinned at my puzzled look. "We used 'em for night-lights, city girl."

Hoots of laughter echoed from the main house. I recognized Lark's musical lilt and smiled thinking of her in the midst of her new family. After a moment Dean said, "They're all pulling for the two of us, you know. If I know my family, there's probably a bet going."

"Oh no!" I said, embarrassed but pleased. Our arms brushed as we walked the uneven ground. When Dean reached for my hand, my arms shivered with contentment. With the country sounds— the drone of cicadas, the wind through the trees, the occasional snort from the barn—I felt I might succumb to a sensory overdose. Sleep would sandbag me soon.

We had come to the pool between Dean's house and the guesthouse. "I'm looking forward to tomorrow," Dean murmured.

"I feel the same way."

"It feels like … a dream. I can't believe you're really here at Villeneuve." At last he bent his head down to mine. The pads of his fingers were warm on my upper arms as he kissed my lips, once, twice, and again. "Sleep well, Robin Hamilton."

My head had begun to swim. "Yes," I said.

"I'll make breakfast for you and Lark … about eight?"

"Night, Dean," I mumbled, turning the knob on the guesthouse door.

My last conscious thought when I'd slipped between cool sheets in my underwear was of Dean's kiss. The way our lips fit seamlessly together. The way their fusion seemed to glow like filament wire.

It was not until six o'clock that I woke again to the sounds of Lark—the inveterate early bird—moving about the kitchen, making coffee. I rose refreshed to join my daughter. She'd had fun learning more about the Falconers and was full of information and funny family anecdotes over coffee. She said that Dean had returned to the group after walking me back. "He was actually humming," Lark said grinning. Apparently he had looked sheepish as talk had abruptly died away and the family had regarded him. "Should I speculate about what's happening between the two of you," she asked, "or am I on a need-to-know basis?"

"*I* don't even know what's happening between the two of us," I said, drawing my shoulders up in a high shrug. Then I looked into my daughter's eyes. "But I *can* tell you, my darling, that I am unequivocally in love with Dean. Part of me may have never stopped loving him."

"Oh, Mom, I knew it."

"But I don't know what my loving him will mean … for the future. And I don't know what his feelings for *me* are now, other than …" I took a sip of coffee, fumbling for the word. "Lust." I blushed. "I know you and I don't talk this way … but after all … you *are* thirty-four."

"It's okay, Mom; you're entitled to lust," she said, topping up our mugs from the steaming carafe. "For the record I know that you slept with Nick on occasion too." She grinned.

"Laurel Olivia Hamilton! How did you know *that*?" I asked, truly shocked.

"It wasn't hard to miss the signs," she laughed.

"Well … *that's* certainly in the past. But, Lark, there's something else. I want you to know I've been feeling guilty."

"*Guilty*?" She raised her dark brows.

"Because this summer was supposed to be about you and your father."

"But I'm getting to know the family too at the same time." She smiled. "It … takes the pressure off feeling like I have to forge"— she rotated her hand in the air—"this … perfect relationship with Dad. It feels more *natural* in the context of other family. And

Mom," she said, covering my hand with hers, "I'm glad you love him."

I pulled her into a hug then, my heart brimful, until her phone chimed with a text. "It's Dean," she said with a grin. "Are we hungry?"

"Tell him we'll be right over."

Dean's formerly scrambled-egg breakfast repertoire now included bacon and homemade biscuits with Laurel's strawberry jam. *A man who makes homemade biscuits!* Lark and I ate with gusto, heaping praise on Dean's fuzzy head.

We trooped to the barn. The baying of hounds as we approached made the back of my neck prickle. "Those are just the foxhunting hounds," Dean said. "They're penned behind the barn. They're just *annoying* as hell, the way they howl, but completely harmless." The horses had been let out at dawn and were already back doing their thing in the barn.

"Exactly how *early* do you get up, Dean?" I asked.

He laughed shortly, "Early." The barn's interior was cool and dim, painted a dark green. The first stall was labeled King George. Dean leaned a brown arm on the bottom half of the dutch door. A blowing and snorting began as the horse left off eating hay to plod toward the door. "On the weekends, my barn manager, Billy, and I let them out about six, so we can clean the stalls, but the other days the help are here early. Billy lives in the apartment upstairs," he said, pointing to the ceiling. "You'll meet him next week—he's on vacation right now. Billy's in charge of the whole operation:

the horses, the dogs, and the physical property. We have a small crew that maintains the property. There's Justin, who's been with us since before Dad died, Dillon, and Andi. Dad always gave the help the weekends off, so I've carried on that tradition. They do an awesome job for us."

"*Here's* King George," he said as a large brown head with black mane poked curiously over the door, nostrils quivering in a nicker of greeting.

"He's a beauty. May I pet him?" Lark asked, holding out a tentative hand.

"Pet him up here on the nose, but hold your palm out … flat … and let him smell you first. *Then* you can scratch back here on his neck or high up here on the withers. You *like that*, don't you, George?" he said, stroking the horse. "He needs to get to know your smell."

As we petted King George, I blurted, "I love the way they smell … the whole barn smell. It's so … organic and leathery. Like a *really* expensive handbag." Dean laughed and touched my nose with a finger.

Lark moved toward the next stall. "Kirby," she called, reading the nameplate.

"George and Kirby are my foxhunters, the retired event horses. And across the hall here is one of our older mares, Trolley. She's the one I have in mind for *you* to ride."

"Well, hello, Trolley," I said, turning to regard a pretty chestnut mare with a lighter mane. "She's the one for you to get started on. Trolley's pretty unflappable, what we call a bombproof horse."

"*Bomb*proof?" I said. "That's too funny."

"Her color has always reminded me of your hair color," he said, reaching to slip a hand into my hair. "I've never forgotten it." Then he froze, embarrassed. Lark moved on to the next stall.

Dean stroked my neck with a thumb. Trolley nickered softly to be noticed again. I grinned and reached to let her smell my palm once more, rubbing her nose. I was charmed with the beautiful creature, though her size was a little overwhelming. "When's the first lesson?" I asked.

"Tomorrow morning. Lark!" he called to her down the barn. "The first lesson's tomorrow morning."

"I'm ready," she called. "Are you in, Mom?"

"I'm in if you're in." A great swollen gray tabby stalked into the barn, twitching her tail.

"And who's *this*?" Lark asked, squatting to stroke the length of her back.

"That's Sassy. She's about to have a new litter of kittens. The barn cats keep the vermin at bay. Let's see, there's Sassy … Voltaire, and Penelope now. You'll see 'em around."

We moved on to the other horses: the resident studs, three-year-old stallions Cavalier and Frankly My Dear; a graceful palomino, Lady; four more chestnut broodmares, Martha, Pandora, Magnolia, and Missy, who was Mary's thirty-four-year-old mare; and a half dozen darling yearlings and untrained young foals. They were all so beautiful I couldn't decide which one I liked best. Mary and Leslie were working with the yearlings, teaching them "manners"—to lead quietly, wait, and stand tied. We stopped to watch awhile. "Which horse will I ride?" Lark asked Dean.

"I'm going to put you on Lady. You'll be a natural … It's in your blood after all," he said grinning and slipped an easy arm around her shoulders as we walked back to the house. Lark's look of transparent pleasure made me so happy.

Later that afternoon, the gang arrived for the pool party. Lark, looking lithe and strong in her new red suit, draped a towel over a chaise and sat to rub sunscreen into her fair skin. Wearing a short black A-line linen dress and wide-brimmed straw hat against the sun, I sat down on the side of the pool and plunged my feet into the cool water. The Falconer women wore summery floral sundresses or shorts over printed swimsuits. In my black, I was a crow in a field of summer flowers. *An albino crow,* I thought wryly, peering down at my arms and legs.

Dean and the other men were in the pool talking and drinking from cans of beer. Dean swam to the deep end and took my ankles. He floated and squinted lazily up at me against the sun. He wore a pair of aqua trunks, his shoulders slightly sunburned, his chest and the tender underside of his throat pale. "Where's your suit, pretty lady?" he asked.

289

"Bring me a beer, Sister!" Leslie yelled to Mary, who was bending over the ice chest. "It's hotter than the hinges of hell!"

"I didn't bring a suit. The only time I appear in one is on the private beach at my dad's," I said prissily. Then I heard myself. "I just don't feel comfortable in one."

He smiled a lazy-lidded smile. "You're kidding me; your body was made for a bathing suit." His gaze moved over me like oil, settling into my curves.

He still hasn't seen my body, I thought, dubious. Still holding my ankles, he pulled his body closer. He was aroused.

"Dean!" I gasped, quickly scanning the pool to see if anybody was watching. Lark had disappeared into the little pool-house bathroom. The husbands were busy planning a cannonball contest. Laurel and Leslie watched them, smirks on their tanned faces, shaking their heads in a "boys will be boys" way.

"Let's play some volleyball!" Mary called from the pool steps, hands planted on the hips of a vibrant Lilly Pulitzer suit that contrasted with her tan and her big white sunglasses. Dean turned to the group at her words, and the spell broke. Warren and Leslie stretched a net across the expanse of the pool. I saw that Lark was going to play too and rose to take her chair, a better vantage point to watch the game. Laurel pulled up a chair to sit beside me.

"Hi, Laurel," I said. "What a wonderful place you all have here."

"*Are* you having fun? I want you to like it here."

"I am. This is so relaxing." I smiled warmly at her.

"You have beautiful skin; you've been smart to stay out of the sun," she said. Her crinkly skin, brown as a berry, was patchy all over with dark spots. We talked quietly amid sprays of water and shouts from the pool. Laurel expressed regret for the years that we all had lost but told me she was grateful that Lark and I had come back into their lives. I retrieved an errant ball and threw it back to Rob. Then I looked at Dean's mother and saw something of his face in hers. It seemed the right time to say what was on my heart. "Laurel, I hope you'll forgive me for not telling you about Lark all those years ago."

She patted my hand. "I learned a long time ago not to dwell on the past. It's a dangerous preoccupation," she mused, gazing across the apron to her granddaughter in the pool. "I live in the present now." She grinned at me then and tipped me a wink. "It looks pretty good from where I sit." We regarded Lark and Dean standing next to each other in the water. They gave each other an exultant high five, laughing. "I don't know when I've seen Dean happier," Laurel said. And after a moment, she said, "Thank you, Robin." I smiled, not trusting my voice, my throat working against tears. Then she put her hands on her leathery knees and pushed herself to her feet. "Would you like a soda or a beer?" I asked for a beer, and she went to the ice chest to retrieve beers for both of us.

The game over, Leslie yelled to her husband, "Warren! We need more beer!" Mary, Dean, and Lark padded over to us laughing and shaking their limbs like big wet dogs.

291

"That was fun," said Mary, drying her sunglasses on a towel. "Lark, you play well."

"I played a little in high school." Lark smiled, squeezing out her ponytail with both hands.

Hudson and Charlotte had begun barking at something. An elegant Range Rover crunched around the side of Dean's house, nosed into the parking pad next to the Avenger, and beeped its horn twice in greeting. Dean looked up. "James is here!" And to me he said, "He's my partner. You remember my friend James from Georgetown."

"*He's* your *partner?*" I was astonished. I did remember James. The last party Dean and I had attended together—the night our only photograph together had been taken—had been at James's apartment.

"Yep." Dean smiled, looking toward the gate. "I lured him away from the big city fifteen years ago when business took off. He and his wife, Jill, moved down here from DC. James is one talented architect." Dean stood, removing his sunglasses, to greet the couple as they stepped inside amid calls of "James!" and "Jilly!" from the others.

Dean kissed Jill's cheek and ushered the couple over to meet me. "Robin Hamilton, I'd like you to meet Jill Culpepper. And you remember James." We exchanged greetings.

James remembered me and said, "You're just as good lookin' as you were thirty years ago." He hadn't done anything about the quirky gap between his teeth, but it still suited him. The shoulder-length hair I remembered was almost as short as Dean's now.

Jill was plump with masses of blonde hair and a beauty queen smile, and Laurel said, "Jill was a contestant in the Miss Virginia pageant back in the day."

"*Way* back in the day," Jill laughed. I liked her immediately. "Robin, it's nice to know you. I've been hearing about you for the last month. We want to have you and Dean over for dinner."

Across the pool Lark and Leslie were lying on chaises again, deep in conversation, another beer screwed into Leslie's fist. "Lark, come meet my partner and his wife," Dean called.

Jill and James got into the water. I admired Jill's skirted swimsuit. Maybe I could get one like that. Leslie called, "We need music, peeps!" and sashayed, dripping, into the pool house. Dean sat next to me on the side, our feet in the water. Momentarily "Hotel California" began to tumble from the speakers. Leslie reappeared and saucily announced, "Some mood music for Robin and Dean! We *all* know how they met." Leslie abruptly crumpled and fell hard on her bottom, her eyes wide.

"My sister's had one too many," Dean murmured. "Don't pay her any attention." I felt the eyes of the others on us as Laurel swam over.

"Robin, we have to get you a bathing suit. Aren't you burning up?" she asked. I was grateful to her for running interference.

Mary climbed the ladder from the shallow end. "Let's go get the burgers and fixin's," she said, pulling her blushing sister to her feet. "I'm positively ravenous."

Soon the air was infused with the smell of grilling meat. The dogs appeared at the fence hoping to find a soft touch among the guests. Laurel, in a white terry cover-up, flip-flopped to the fence. "Now you pups have already had your dinner. Yes you have," she said to them in baby talk. Dean and I walked over to help with the spread. Mary had made huge dishes of baked potato salad and slaw and a large pan of baked beans. We sat casually around the deck, eating and talking. *It would be fun being part of a big family like this,* I thought and then realized I already was, at least by proxy.

The next morning, my phone chimed with a text message at seven o'clock. I was barely awake. It was Dean. "Morning, sleeping beauty," it read. "Ready for the riding lesson? Would have let you sleep but couldn't wait any longer. Meet me at the barn ASAP."

I grinned and typed, "Be right there." I stretched and kicked aside the covers. I padded through the house to see if Lark was up. She wasn't in her bed.

"Lark Bird?" She wasn't in the bathroom, but all of her gear was. I rolled my eyes. Despite her scrupulous personal care and appearance, Lark had always kept the messiest room, the floor perpetually strewn with clothes and belongings. I had finally given up on making her straighten it when she was in high school. One fewer battle.

Dean had told me to wear jeans for riding and that there was sure to be a pair of one of his sisters' paddock boots to fit me at the barn. I pulled my hair into a ponytail, slid my feet into flip-flops, snared a granola bar from the kitchen and headed for the barn.

Entering the gloom of the barn from the bright sunlight, I blinked and saw my missing daughter stepping from a stall door, pulling an Amazon length of green hose behind her. I stooped to pet Charlotte, who had appeared behind me and nudged my leg. "There's my missing daughter. I *wondered* where you were."

Lark turned, disheveled and thrilled. Hay clung to her water-splashed T-shirt and jeans. She looked about eighteen. "I've been out here since six. I'm doing all the watering this morning." She looked down at herself and laughed. "If Ben could see me now." She disappeared into Lady's stall, and a calico cat, hair standing up on her back like toothbrush bristles, streaked out. "That's Penelope," Lark called to me. "She sleeps in Lady's stall." Hearing our voices, Dean came around the corner. He and I were alone. He stalked hipshot in my direction and pulled me to him by the hips. His eyes were dark with longing. He gave me a thorough kissing as Penelope twined around our legs.

"Excuse me," a lilting female voice said. Stepping back from Dean, my face pinking, I regarded a young girl with curly black hair who was dressed in khaki britches and paddock boots and hauling a bucket of what looked like brown trail mix.

"Robin Hamilton," Dean said, "this is Andi DeFelice. Andi's a student at UVA." I smiled politely. "She boards her horse at

Villeneuve in exchange for working sixteen hours a week at the barn."

Cavalier poked his head over his stall door, nickering and bobbing his great head. "Chill, Cav, I'm coming!" Andi called and continued her work.

In the tack room Dean found a pair of Mary's boots that were a good fit for me. Dean settled a black helmet onto my head, bending to kiss my throat as he fastened the clasp. "Let's go get Trolley," he said, "before I end up carrying you into an empty stall."

We walked out to the sunlit corral, Trolley on a lead rope. Mary and Leslie were out in the paddocks working with other horses, so Dean and I were alone. It was as if I were scaling the barn itself trying to get my leg over Trolley's back. "You know what Ian Fleming said," I panted. "'A horse is dangerous at both ends and crafty in the middle.'" Dean chuckled at my discomfiture. Trolley was patient with my attempts, and at last I was in the saddle. I felt exhilarated, though, looking down at my lap, I was sure my round thighs looked repulsive. *Oh, what the hell.* I reached down and stroked Trolley's light-chestnut withers. Dean pulled his phone from his back pocket and took our picture. It would always be one of his favorite photos.

Ten minutes later, I was riding around the corral by myself. By that time Lark had joined us, and with her father's direction, she was comfortably astride Lady in no time. She *was* a natural. Dean leaned against the fence and beamed. Lady tossed her head and pranced, more spirited than Trolley, but that suited me just fine.

That afternoon Laurel taught her granddaughter to can vegetables. Entering her kitchen, I found them in faded aprons, Lark stirring a huge pot of tomatoes: a blonde good witch over a bubbling cauldron. My phone chimed with a text from Dean: "I have a surprise for you. Meet me behind the barn?"

Sure he had something seductive in mind, I felt my pulse speed up. "See you later, gators," I said to Lark and Laurel.

I rounded the corner of the barn almost bumping smack into Leslie leading Cavalier to the paddocks. "Oh ... Hi!" I said. I noticed the horse stopped in his tracks as soon as Leslie did. Cav was almost twice as tall as Leslie. I had to marvel at the control Dean's sisters had over the massive creatures.

"Hi, Robin. Listen ..." She stopped, looking miserable. "I wanted to apologize about the other day. I was drunk and stupid at the pool. My big brother gave me hell."

"Don't think another thing about it," I said with a smile. "I'm sure I've been drunker and stupider. Are you getting Cav ready for the event?"

"Yep." She smiled gratefully, pulled a hunk of carrot from her pocket, and offered it to the horse. "Thanks, Robin." Leslie and Cav moved out, and she called over her shoulder, "We really *are* glad you're here."

Beyond the corral the object of my desire leaned against an enormous tarp-covered object. "What are you up to?" I asked, walking right up to him and twining my arms around his neck. Dean cradled the back of my head as we stood kissing under the beat of the afternoon sun, the muffled drone of mowers up by the road the only sound. He smelled brothy with sweat, his shirt back damp under my hands. I realized it was the first time I'd ever smelled Dean's body odor, and the cumin-like earthiness of it turned me on. There was little about Dean Falconer that did not.

Then he broke away. "Guess what I have here."

Looking down at his tented jeans front, I laughed throatily, "You mean aside from the obvious?"

"Woman, you are killing me," he groaned. Dean grabbed the heavy tarp with both hands. At the first glimpse of large tires and green paint I knew.

"Dean! You still have the Jeep!" Awestruck, I watched as he unveiled the vehicle like a waiting bride, the Jeep in which I'd fallen in love with him that first weekend in DC. I looked from the man to the machine and began to cry. I sat in the passenger seat running my hands over the upholstery and the dash, and a deluge of memory swamped me. Dean climbed in and gathered me to him. "I can't believe you kept it," I sniffled.

"Believe it or not, it still runs like a top. I use it around the farm. I couldn't bear to part with it."

I looked up at him then. "I'm glad you kept it."

Dean pointed to the key in the ignition. "I still have my lucky roach clip." He grinned, indicating the key chain. I ran my fingers over it, recalling another long-buried memory. "Do you want to go for a spin?" he asked.

"Yeah." I nodded, drying my eyes with the hem of my shirt. We went for a fine ride around the property. When we had covered the Jeep again as if putting a much-loved child to bed, Dean and I walked hand in hand toward the main house. A great rumbling announced a huge silver pickup truck rolling down the gravel drive.

"That is a *big* truck," I said.

"Around here we call that a big-ass truck," he said with a grin. "Billy's back." Charlotte and Hudson rose from their places under the giant oak in the front yard and moved toward the truck their tails wagging like metronomes. Dean raised a hand and watched the truck's approach from beneath the bill of his cap.

Shorter than Dean, solidly built and strong looking, Billy Babbitt stepped from the cab with an empty water bottle in hand. He hauled a bag from the truck bed. "Hey, boss," he said, smiling shyly.

"Robin Hamilton," said Dean, putting his arm around my waist, "this is Billy Babbitt, one of my oldest friends and our farm manager." Billy removed his sunglasses and stepped forward to shake my hand.

"Billy, I'm happy to meet you," I said warmly.

"Likewise." Billy had trouble looking me in the eyes and bent to pet the dogs. I wondered if it was shyness or if his cool reserve spoke of something unnamed.

"When you get settled in, Bill, come over to Mom's. I want you to meet my … our daughter," Dean said, smiling down at me. The two of us went in to see how the canning was going.

* * * * *

The next day Dean and Lark took the first of the father-daughter hikes they would take that summer, up to Crabtree Falls. They came back after seven hours, stinky—concentric rings of sweat at their armpits—but happy companions. A scholar of the nuances of my daughter's moods, I could tell that Lark had been crying. Faint, dried snails' tracks of tears streaked her cheeks. I guessed that father and daughter had had at last the opportunity for a long-needed conversation.

Later that afternoon, the hikers freshly showered, the three of us drove out to Blue Mountain Brewery for dinner. We sat on the terrace under a red umbrella, drinking fancy craft beer and sharing a huge, gooey Mediterranean pizza—the kind where the cheese stretches long from your mouth. Lark and I gazed at the perfect view of the mountains that appeared azure in the slanting sun and indigo in the blooming shadows made by clouds.

As we drove home, the setting sun turned the sky a vivid cobalt streaked with orange. Moved, I watched as the blue slipped from purple to gray before darkness blurred the seam connecting land and sky. My sit bones were painfully sore from riding, and I felt every bump with the Jeep, but I was happier than I'd ever been before. Lark fell asleep so quickly and profoundly that night on the guesthouse sofa that I knew I'd been right: the day with her father had been cathartic. I hoped it had for Dean as well, but I never asked either of them. It appeared they each had made peace with the past.

CHAPTER

22

Robin

2013

The weeks were passing like scenery from a car window. On the third of July, Dean took Lark and me to see his Charlottesville office. The firm resided in a narrow, character-filled, old house, a rabbit warren of rooms, drafty in the winter and hot in the summer. It smelled of tobacco from James's clandestine cigars and of the peppermints that their administrative assistant Divya kept on her desk. The conference table where they met with clients anchored the dining room of the house. The guys had added gas logs to the fireplace there for warmth and ambience.

Dean had completed a big project just before Lark and I arrived and was keeping only one office day for the summer, one of the perks of having a partner, and the firm was running smoothly in James's capable hands.

The forecast promised that Independence Day would be much cooler than the previous days. The evening was letter perfect, even cooler on Carver Mountain, where the family, Billy, James, and Jill gathered for an open-to-the-public picnic and firework event with summer food from local food trucks and plenty of cold beer. At dusk, sitting back against Dean on a quilt and savoring his solid warmth, I gazed at the panoramic view below—the silhouetted small towns amid ridges of night-navy mountains. The rising apricot moon suddenly seemed full of portent. A shiver crept along my arms, but I let it pass unexamined as the fireworks began—red, white, and blue bursts, glowing spidery tendrils against the indigo sky. As the others exclaimed and clapped, Dean took my chin and turned my face to his. From the next blanket, Mary said, "You two! You need to get a room." Lark was having a blast somewhere up ahead in the group drinking beer with Leslie, Rob, and Billy. I could hear her laughter and smiled as I kissed her father.

Minutes later we were gathering up blankets and coolers, giddy and singing all the patriotic songs we knew, laughing as we stumbled over the words. We picked our way through the trees and the other revelers back to the cars, the moonlight our only guide. Then something I heard Mary say sobered me as if I had plunged headlong into a glacier-fed lake. She and Jill were tripping along arm in arm for support in the gloom behind Dean and me. Jill was saying something about how happy James had told her that Dean was, and Mary said evenly, "Thank goodness Robin came along when she did, or we might have ended up with Heather De Hart."

"Oh, God, *Heather*," Jill said.

Who the hell is Heather De Hart? I thought. I glared at Dean.

"What?" he said, laughing in surprise. "What was *that* look for?"

"Nothing," I said. We reached the Jeep, and Lark and Billy hopped in the back to ride back with us. It gave me a few minutes to collect my tortuous thoughts and will myself not to overreact.

At Villeneuve again, Dean and I walked into the pool area. Dean asked if I wanted to take a late swim. "I'll sit this one out," I said and sat down on a chaise longue.

"*Okaaayy.* Then I'll be right back." His handsome face bewildered, he walked to his house. I sat there stewing, prickly, bitchy. When Dean reappeared, he sat silently down on the edge of the pool in his red trunks. Why did he have to look all sexy at this moment? The full moon—that portentous moon—seemed to hover above his right shoulder. "What's all this, Robin?" he asked, annoyed.

"I don't know, Dean. You tell me. Who is Heather De Hart?" I sat unyielding, my arms crossed over my chest.

He whipped his face around to stare at me, astonished. "Where did you hear about Heather?" he asked. I was perversely glad to have shocked him.

"Something I overheard Mary say to Jill tonight ... Exactly what she said was that she was glad I came along when I did or they may have ended up with Heather De Hart," I said, defiant and childish.

"Sweetheart, will you come sit over here and let me explain?"

After a moment I moved to sit on the side of the pool, leaving enough space between us for a sumo wrestler. "I told you that first night at ... Crispo ... in New York ... that I had dated someone recently—it was last winter actually—and I also remember telling you that I hadn't found anyone I wanted to spend my life with." Dean raised and lowered his feet in the water; I watched the ripples spread in circles on the water, dreading what he would say next. "It was Heather," he said. "She had a catering business here that everybody used. Robin, I broke it off with her as soon as you called me in February."

"In *February!*" I said.

"Yes!" He was defensive and angry now. "As soon as you and I started talking in February, I knew I wanted to make something happen with you. I was never serious about Heather, and at that point, any ... thoughts of *her* ... flew out of my head." He paused. "But she wanted me to marry her. Everybody knew it."

"Heather," I spat, getting up to pace the pool's apron. The name conjured an image of some wispy blonde waif with enormous blue eyes.

"Robin, you're not being reasonable. I feel like I've been sent to the principal's office. How the hell was I supposed to know you were about to come back into my life?" he demanded. And when I didn't answer, he barked gruffly, "Huh?"

I sat as silent as granite, irrational, unwilling to concede. Dean lowered himself into the water and began swimming laps. After five or six, he was back, running his hands over his face and head.

He rested his arms on the side of the pool, studying me again, his breathing heavy.

"It's not just that I'm more ridiculously jealous than I can believe," I said, continuing my rant. "But you should have told me that you were seeing someone, someone who wanted to marry you!" My voice rose and quavered on the "marry you." I would not cry.

"Shhhh, Robin, I'd rather our daughter not hear this." Lark had disappeared into the guesthouse after the picnic.

"I'd rather her not hear it either ... *and* I think *I've* heard enough myself." I stood and stomped back to the guesthouse, as effectively as I could manage in my flip-flops, and shut the door without turning to see his face. I crept to my room and saw that Lark's door was closed. I hoped she hadn't overheard the ugly conversation. I lay awake most of that night replaying the fight. Burning with righteous indignation and throwing the covers aside, I realized it was humiliation I felt—Heather had wanted to marry Dean, and "everybody knew it." Who was this woman? Had I seen her around? Did she still want Dean? I had to know. But the next morning, my pride and I stayed in the guesthouse when Lark left for the barn. I drank coffee, sulking tiredly.

At ten I received a text from Dean: "Baby, I'm sorry. I should have told you. Will you forgive me?" At eleven he sent the same message again.

This time I typed a terse "Not sure yet," milking my resentment. Dean replied that he was leaving the next morning to see a client in North Carolina and returning the day after that. I replied with a brusque "Have a good trip." He was *leaving* at a time like *this*? I got up and stalked to the closet, hauled my big suitcase from the top shelf, and tweaked my lower back. *Shit!* My eyes filled. I would get myself back to New York City tonight, I would. I had lived without Dean Falconer for thirty-five years. I had a career I had worked assiduously to build. Good riddance to bad rubbish.

My silent rant lasted about five minutes. But I stayed inside the entire day and night for good measure. Lark, sensing that something was afoot, treaded softly around me and spoke little, only remarking as she came in from the barn the next morning, "Dean just left for his trip."

Laurel knocked on the door and invited Lark and me to go to a movie. "I saw in the paper the downtown cinema is showing a revival of *Pretty Woman*. Wouldn't it be fun to see that on the big screen again?" Itching to get out of the house, I said I'd like to go. Laurel gave Lark a conspiratorial wink. *What was that about?* I thought as my daughter chimed in, "Let's go to dinner too. Leslie told me about a French place, Petit Pois, that she likes."

Billy saddled Trolley for me, and I rode for a while, feeling bummed that Dean had gone away while we were at odds. I wondered if Lark and I should stay in Virginia. I handed the mare off to an obliging Andi for grooming and went in to shower. The three of us had delicious dinners of mushroom risotto; trout with green beans, almonds, and brown butter; and glasses of creamy Virginia viognier. But Julia Roberts's on-screen fairy tale left me feeling sulky and timorous, as if I were coming down with something: Would the tale of Robin and Dean have a happy

306

ending? We stepped onto the lamp-lit cobblestoned mall again afterward, and Laurel spotted a friend. She waved her over to introduce us. Lark was introduced as "my granddaughter, Lark," while I was "Lark's mother, Robin." I felt the woman's eyes appraise me and shrank from the unspoken question that leaped and lingered there.

Though the forecast called for a summer storm, I walked to the barn the next afternoon to see Trolley. Billy was hauling hay from the back of his truck to the barn. Lately, he had been even quieter than usual, introspective. "How are you, Billy?" I asked.

"I'm good," he answered shortly, but his smile didn't reach his eyes. The storm was beginning to brew, the slate sky roiling. The horses grew restless and nickered as warm gusts blew through the barn and raised the dust.

We heard the familiar sound of the Jeep's engine before we saw it. My heart flipped over, concern for Billy momentarily forgotten. In that moment I knew I could no more live without Dean Falconer again than without physical nourishment. The first drops of rain spattered the dusty ground like bacon grease on a stove. Charlotte, whose broad tail had been thumping against my legs, cantered out to meet the Jeep. Billy and I walked out accompanied by Hudson, who had emerged from his favorite spot under Billy's truck.

Smiling tentatively in my direction, Dean stepped down onto the gravel drive and then turned to fish the back of the Jeep for an umbrella. "Welcome back, boss," Billy said. Then he seemed to sniff out the tension that stretched like a partition between Dean and me and said, "I'll catch you later, man." He called to the dogs, "Come on, pups," and limped back to the barn. The limp had become more pronounced, I noted. Dean raised the umbrella over us, and we stood facing each other alone.

"Hello, Dean." I flinched as a great boom of thunder crashed at the heels of a flash of light from the west.

"Hello, Robin," he said, his mouth twisting. "Let's take cover. Want to ride back to the house with me?"

"Sure," I said, nonchalant. We got into the Jeep, and Dean put the car in reverse and his hand behind my headrest to look back. The familiar smell of his skin in the warm, rain-spattered shirtsleeve caught me by surprise. I closed my eyes. We drove the two hundred yards in silence. Dean parked the Jeep and turned off the engine.

I spoke first, my heart an undigested bolus behind my breastbone. "Dean, first, I'm embarrassed that everyone knew about Heather but me, and second, how do you know she's over you?"

Dean rubbed his eyes tiredly and looked at me. "I won't lie to you. Heather was supremely pissed when I broke it off with her. I'm considered ... a catch ... at least around here." I raised my eyebrows at him. "Well, it's true," he said. "I saw her one more time after that in April."

In April? I opened my mouth to object, but he jumped right back in. "I ran into her at the farmers' market one Saturday morning and bought her a lemonade. We talked for a few minutes, and she told me she was moving north to Middleburg to be close to her folks. Her parents run an old inn and train foxhunting dogs. *That's* how I know she's over me. Heather's long gone."

"Well," I said, slightly mollified, "I just wish you had told me about her, before I heard it from someone else."

"I regret that. I was thoughtless … It was a stupid error in judgment."

"But, Dean … I've had this in the back of my mind: Are you absolutely certain you're not interested in me simply because I'm the mother of your child? Sometimes I worry that I'm just … part of a package deal. If that's the case, *please* tell me the truth right now." My eyes implored him as great drops battered against the roof and made opaque the expanse of windshield.

Dean unhooked his seatbelt and opened the door. "Let me change clothes, and I'll pick you up with the big umbrella when the storm passes. It's time I showed you something."

An hour later the two of us walked to the barn beneath the umbrella. A light rain continued to fall. The farm looked crazily green. Dean led the way to Kirby's stall. The horse was busily chomping forage in the corner. "Stay here; I'll be right back," he said to me and entered the stall. I waited in stillness, inhaling the scent of dampened hay and animal. Dean's voice floated over the stall door. "When I was a kid, I made a secret hiding place here. It was my horse Wahoo's stall then." I heard the screech of wood against wood and the sound of something sliding. Dean sneezed once, twice, and reappeared with a cobwebbed and dusty old shoe box. He wiped his nose with his shirt sleeve. Derelict masking tape strapped the box's lid to its bottom. Across the top in black marker DEAN'S was written in his hand. Dean blew across the box and sat down on a tack box. Mesmerized, I watched as dust motes drifted in the dim light. "Sit here with me?" he asked. "When I knew I couldn't find you and had to ... move on ... I packed you away in this box." My pulse quickened as Dean pulled away at the strips of tape.

He lifted the top, and a spindly daddy longlegs scrabbled from its depths. "Ooooh!" I started as he flicked it away. In the box were envelopes from my old pink-and-green floral-bordered stationary. My throat began to ache with an ineffable sadness. One at a time Dean handed me the funny little cards I'd sent to cheer him and the scrap of notebook paper with my name and phone number in DC. He removed the letters, the deeply emotional ones I had written when only I had known I was pregnant with his child. "I read them a dozen times," he said. I scanned the letters, penned in my careful, youthful handwriting, through the bright sheen of tears. His hands in the box again, Dean untangled a tinkling item and held the St. Thomas medal aloft. A sob escaped me as I took the necklace and wound it around my hand, peering at the inscription. Dean reached inside once more and lifted the photograph of the two of us—the twin to mine—and his Eagles' concert ticket stub from the bottom. Dean's lashes were dark with tears as he said, "These were all I had of you; I couldn't part with them ... but I didn't want anyone else to see them either." I gulped, nodding my head. "Robin, I was in love with you when we were ... kids, before we ever even thought about having a child." He took my face in his hands, the box across his knees. "I'm in love with the woman you are now, with *you and only you*." I smiled at him with trembling lips and closed my eyes. "Look at me, Robin. Don't you know you're the girl for me?"

"Yes. I do know. I love you so, Dean," I answered in a wash of love, forgiveness, and hope. He held me then. Outside the rain had stopped, and light once more filtered through the boards of the barn.

That weekend, the whole family gathered at Nelson Mountain Vineyard for an afternoon of relaxation. The staff was pouring twelve wines for the afternoon's tasting, and by the time we had sampled the sweeter wines, we were all feeling merry. We took bottles of chilled summer rosé out to the terrace where comfortable rump-sprung furniture waited, the hazy blues and greens of the mountains a breathtaking backdrop. "How beautiful is this?" I exclaimed, utterly charmed. I gazed down at a small, picturesque lake, a battered yellow rowboat bobbing at its edge.

Languorous, Mary said, "Robin, you wouldn't believe how gorgeous it will be here in October. The vines will be tinged with fall color—red, purple, gold. You just want to hold the swollen grapes in your hand like …"

"Ba-by!" Rob grinned. "How 'bout coming over here to sit with me?" We all laughed.

I knew I would have to come back to Virginia in the fall when the trees would burnish the mountainsides in jewellike colors and see the vines for myself. And the farm. Villeneuve would be ablaze in the autumn. What would it be like when Lark and I went back to New York? Would the summer haunt my days? I looked about at the family I was coming to know. Mary and Leslie had become dear, spontaneously affectionate with Lark and me. Robert and Warren were what Anita Roth would call *menschen*: honorable, good guys you knew you could rely on. And Laurel. Dean's mother's sweet ways had begun to patch the tear in my heart torn by my own mother's death. It was hard to believe the spirited and sturdy woman I knew had once been institutionalized for depression. Before we left that afternoon, Leslie asked a staff member to take a picture of the whole tipsy group of us, Dean and me front and center.

The next morning, Dean made a run into town. Lark and I did a yoga practice. My daughter was pleased with my progress. My warrior poses and sun salutations were much steadier, my balance improving. Over lunch at Laurel's, Dean asked me to take a trail ride with him that evening. He and Lark had taken a long ride together, and now it was my turn.

When it was cool enough to be comfortable for the horses, we saddled Trolley and Dean's aristocratic Kirby and headed out, a picnic of cheese and sausage, a baguette, fruit, and a bottle of Pinot Noir in a canvas tote secured to Kirby's saddle. Dean urged the horses down the road and through the back woods of the farm. Trolley, shoes clopping over the rocky places, followed Kirby through the narrower trails at a comfortable pace. I felt authentic and pleased with my appearance wearing new britches, riding boots, and a smart helmet that Leslie and Mary had bought for me. Charlotte and Hudson trotted along behind until they grew tired and turned back for home.

When we reached the summit, I was captivated by the view below. I could just make out the doll-sized gray gambrel roof of the barn. Its copper weather vane winked like a flame through the trees at Villeneuve. We dismounted, tied the horses off, and spread out an old wedding ring quilt made by Dean's grandmother Helen. We peeled off our boots and reclined, deeply inhaling the clean air. Dean poured us some wine. It wasn't long before we were making out. At once, Dean sat up, his breath fast in his throat. "Robin, there is nothing in the world I would like more right now than to make love to you, here in this perfect place, but I need to talk with you about something." Grimacing, he tucked his shirttail in. I sat up and crossed my legs in lotus position, curious.

He began, "I've thought of at least a half dozen ways to say this."

My thoughts spiraled crazily. Did he want to take a step back? Had things been happening too fast between us? Could I have misread all the neon signs? I gazed at him mildly though my heart inched toward my throat. Dean's eyes penetrated mine. I could see the tiny flecks of blue around the gray.

"I never wanted to lose you when you left DC … and then all the years I spent alone. It was a miracle when you came into my life again. And you gave me a daughter." He paused, choked with emotion. "I don't want to lose you again. I know it's only been a month. But I love you more than I've ever loved anyone on this earth."

My chest filled with suppressed sobs of hope.

"I want you to be my wife. I want you to live with me here at Villeneuve. Robin, will you marry me?"

Tears flowed as my entire being flooded with happiness. Looking into the eyes of the man that I adored, I breathed, "Yes. Only yes."

Dean dug into the pocket of his jeans and withdrew a tiny black box. Opening its hinged edge, he carefully removed a ring. The oblique rays of early-evening sunlight captured the brilliant flash of gems. "Dean," I breathed, "it's exquisite." He smiled shyly at me and slid the gold ring onto my finger. "I couldn't love you or the ring more," I said, gazing at the two-carat, emerald-cut diamond, surrounded by about a dozen luminous emeralds. Something stirred in my memory.

Dean asked, "Do you recognize the diamond, sweetheart?"

"No," I said slowly. Then, "Yes ... I do, I think." I looked at him questioningly.

What he said next left me speechless: "It's your mother's diamond." He told me then about his covert mission. I sat gaping at him as if he were channeling Scheherazade. He had met my father, quite literally for the first time, in Raleigh and spent an evening with him. A week earlier he had asked an ecstatic Hank for my hand by telephone, and my dad had brought my mother's wedding ring to Raleigh. Unbeknownst to me, my dad had kept my mother's diamond with the hope that Lark or I would one day wear it. In the years after Mom's death, I had never thought to ask him about it. With my father's blessing and the ring in pocket,

Dean had sought a Charlottesville jeweler, who had extricated the diamond from its original setting and created a new piece, adding jewels "the color of my eyes" around it.

"So *that's* where you went," I said softly. "Oh, Dean, I'm sorr—"

He placed a finger over my lips and smiled and then kissed my hands, cheeks, forehead, and lips. We began to laugh, kissing and kissing. Finally he said, "There's more." I searched his face. What more could there be? "Robin, I want to give you the wedding ... *and* the wedding *night* that you should've had, that *we* should have had, all those years ago." He paused. "Let's wait to make love on that night." Dean looked down at his hands. "What can I say? I've become a very traditional man. It just seems the right thing."

Dean and I were living another lifetime. After so many years, it would almost be like making love for the first time. I found that I loved the idea.

"That being said, can we get married tomorrow?" he deadpanned. I hooted, and we were off in a fit of cackling.

When we got ourselves under control, we spread the picnic. As Dean sliced the sausage on the diagonal, he asked, "What sort of wedding would you like, sweetheart?" I pensively chewed a piece of creamy Havarti, and a vision passed before my eyes: a small outdoor wedding at Villeneuve. Perhaps I would walk from Laurel's house down the steps to him in the sheltering of one of the great oaks. We sat facing each other, finishing the meal and the wine, and talked of plans until the sun dipped low, darkening the blues of the mountains.

We mounted the horses again and moved along the narrow wooded corridor that rose steeply above the farm. As Trolley and I bumped down the trail, my eyes slid to the beautiful ring on my finger over and over again. My thoughts leapfrogged over themselves. *When? Can I get ready for a wedding from Villeneuve? Will I stay here until the wedding? And what about my home? My practice? Lark needs to get back to New York for teacher in-service and the start of school.* It was all too much to get my head around.

At the barn we handed the horses off to Billy. He listened to our news as dispassionately as if watching a grocery clerk scan his purchases. We walked hand in hand to Laurel's to share the news with her and Lark. Dean asked, "What the hell's wrong with Billy?"

"I've noticed too! He seems depressed to me. You know him better than anyone. Does he get like that?"

"I've never noticed him acting depressed, and he's been my manager for thirty-five years." We had come to the main house and, without consultation, sat down on the terrace. Dean continued, his brow furrowed, "I wasn't around after Billy had his accident in seventy-six. I was at UVA and then in DC. I don't really know what he was like then. But when I came home again and asked him to manage the farm, he was really happy. He loves this place. When Victoria died … and when Mrs. Babbitt died, Billy was pretty resilient."

"Talk to him, sweetheart," I said. "See if you can find out what's going on."

We stepped through Laurel's mudroom, and I realized how I had come to love the old house, its idiosyncratic creaks and groans, its smells of lemon-oil polish and old wool. Lark and Laurel were sitting in the wing chairs in the kitchen watching the news, sipping from mugs of tea. We shared our news with them and showed them the ring that of course they already knew about. Laurel cried, her eyes shining, "Oh, Robin, it's stunning! And your mother's diamond. Aren't you thrilled, honey?"

"I am!" I said, my heart filling again. "I can't wait for Dad to see the finished piece." I loved that he and Dean had been coconspirators.

Lark grinned, her eyes polished pewter. "Well played, Dad." And to me, she said, "Mom, it's gorgeous and so unique."

I couldn't wait to call my dad and show Leslie and Mary the ring … and Theresa! I had to call Tee! We had talked a couple of times that summer. Now she needed an immediate update.

I woke the next morning with a goofy grin on my face. Dean and I were engaged! I walked outside in my robe and saw Dean and Billy getting into the Jeep. I knew Dean must be taking Billy somewhere to talk and wondered where they were headed. They waved as they pulled out. After a yoga practice I dressed and went to the barn to see Mary and Leslie. They were working with a beautiful yearling they had named Mercury in the corral. "Hot damn!" Leslie said, sliding her sunglasses up into her hair. She removed her leather gloves to examine the ring. "It's fabulous! Dean pulled it off," she said to her sister. "Were you surprised?"

"It's fabulous," said Mary. "We're so happy for you both." And then she cried, "Sister hug!" swooping Leslie and me in her arms.

"Welcome to the family," they said together, and we all laughed.

Lark and I went into town to shop for groceries and dog food. When we returned, the Jeep was still missing from its parking spot. About three o'clock, Dean tapped on my door. "Just hold me," he said, his voice hollow. Over the next hour, Dean told me what he had learned from Billy. The two had driven over to their former high school baseball field and had sat on the bleachers in the sun and watched the kids play. At one point Billy had said to Dean, "You know, before Robin came along, I felt like you and I were in the same boat. Man, I haven't had a girlfriend since ... Becky Park and I broke up ... senior year of high school." Dean had looked at him in surprise. "I mean, sure, I've had *women*," Billy had said with a shrug, "but I've never had anyone ... that *loved* me ... like Robin loves you. Now here you are getting married." Dean's heart had ached at Billy's naked expression of despair. "I'm sorry, man. I just feel left out ... you know? How will I ever have what you have? I'm lonely, Dean."

Dean said he felt terrible. He'd been so wrapped up in me and in Lark that he hadn't really thought about Billy this summer.

"How could you have known?" I asked.

"I should have. He considers me his best friend. I feel like shit."

"Look at me, Dean," I said. "Billy considers you his best friend because you *have* been to him. You turned his life around when you

318

brought him to Villeneuve. He's just going to have to sort this out. Why does he think it's too late for him to find love?"

"I don't know … the short-term memory stuff and the limp, I guess."

"His little memory glitches wouldn't be a deal breaker, and the limp? A woman couldn't love Billy because of a limp?" I said nonplussed. "He's a good-looking man, a talented man, a thoroughly nice man!"

"Maybe you should tell him that," Dean said, kissing me on the nose and smiling for the first time. "I tried to build him up this afternoon, but you sound much more convincing."

"I will. When we get back from the honeymoon, we are going to find somebody to fix him up with."

"Yes, ma'am," Dean said and pulled me into his lap.

We chose a wedding date of August 10, a Saturday morning, four days before Lark began teacher in-service. She would leave for New York the day after the wedding. Dean wanted to go to Paris for the honeymoon; he had never been. I would stay in Virginia until the wedding and after the honeymoon would return to New York long enough to attend to the details of relocating my life. I spent hours on the phone with my excited father, and with John Hicks, discussing what we would do with our practice. John was nearing retirement age, and my leaving would present immediate problems for him, but it couldn't be helped.

One night after Dean and I had been to Jill and James's for dinner, I tossed and turned, uncomfortably warm though I wore only a short cotton gown. I had had too much wine and knew what I needed was a huge glass of water. I padded to the kitchen thinking of the fun we'd had that night. How fun it would be to do couples things with the Culpeppers after Dean and I were married. Drifting back to my room, I stood at the window, looking for the moon, and drank deeply from the glass. A bright gibbous moon hung low in the sky and spotlighted the roof of the main house. I became aware of what looked like an enormous swarm of gnats in the air. Curious, I stepped outside onto the concrete of the pool's apron, cool now with the night, and saw more of the swarm gathering. And I knew with a prickling chill up the base of my neck that it was smoke before I smelled it. *Laurel wouldn't be burning her fireplace in the summertime. Or in the middle of the night.* I shook my head to clear it.

The air was now filling with flickers of ash—the gnats I had seen—and then I could see the red glow of flames at the roofline on the back corner of the main house. *"Dean!"* I screamed, running for his house and banging through the door. "The main house is on fire!"

Lark came out of the guesthouse in short pajamas. "Mom?" she cried, alarmed. Dean stumbled through the door pulling a pair of jeans up his hips. "Lark! Call 911!" he yelled. The two of us ran in bare feet through the grass.

"Mom!" Dean screamed, sprinting ahead of me. He reached the back terrace, overturning two chairs with a series of loud, metallic clangs and burst through the back door. I glanced up and saw Laurel's startled face framed by her upstairs bedroom window. I could hear Dean screaming to his mother as he made his way through the house.

"Oh my God," I said as Lark caught up with me, her phone clutched in her hand. I watched as Laurel, who appeared to be sleepwalking, turned slowly from the window. Lark and I stood clinging to each other and blubbering. "Are they on the way?" I asked her desperately, my heart trip-hammering in my chest.

"They said six to eight minutes," Lark sobbed. I began to pray.

Dean, half-carrying his mother, stumbled from the back door, and the two tumbled onto the terrace in a heap, coughing and gagging, their eyes streaming. "Robin! Get back!" Dean shouted. He got up again and pulled Laurel across the terrace and onto the grass where Lark and I waited in dismay.

The windows at the corner of Dean's boyhood room exploded with a roaring flash. Shattered shards of glass flew several feet and showered the ground below. Lark and I could feel the heat from where we stood. We turned as we heard trudging footfalls from the direction of the barn and something heavy slithering across the grass. A wild-haired Billy Babbitt tugged the big hose behind him, the surge of water making a stream through which his bare feet slogged toward the house. *Billy!* I looked from the man back to the blown-out windows, where shadows of flames now leaped and danced. I imagined Dean's old mattress ablaze. Dean ran to Billy, and together they aimed the hose at the windows.

From the main road then we heard the thin yowling of sirens. Relief suffused me, and I turned to Laurel and Lark. Laurel's hair was an untidy gray nimbus around her pale face, her open mouth a rictus of incredulity. Her body trembled in her long nightgown. *She's in shock.* "Lark, run and get your grandmother a blanket," I yelled. I led Laurel to a safer distance and lay her down in the grass. I sat on the damp ground and cradled her head in my lap. Lark reappeared with two blankets, and we covered Dean's mother.

Big Hudson paced up and down, whining at the commotion and pawing at the ground. We could hear the horses moving in the barn, alarmed and restless, the mares whinnying loudly. Billy and Dean were slipping and sliding in the fallen glass as they grappled with the hose, but they halted and turned as the emergency vehicles screamed down the drive. "Charlotte …" Laurel moaned, trying to sit up. "She nudged me awake. Is she still in the house?" *Little Charlotte!*

Lark and I dragged our eyes to the open back door through which smoke now rushed. The dog appeared like an apparition. She limped down the steps, her eyes bloody and crazed. Foam flecked her muzzle. We watched in impotent horror as the dog staggered across the terrace, a great spate of diarrhea spattering the brick. As Lark ran to her, Dean screamed, "Get back, Lark!" Lark dragged Charlotte by the collar to where we sat, stricken and paralyzed. Lark curled her body around the animal whose sides heaved with laboring breaths, her tears falling on the dog's sooty fur. The firefighters tumbled from the truck and yelled for Dean and Billy to get out of the way. In moments torrential blasts of water were arcing through the air. I ran to meet Dean. His hands and feet were cut and bloody, his eyes dazed. He pulled me into a tight embrace for a moment and then moved to Lark and his mother on the grass.

The fire was out, and the sun began to rise. Early pale-yellow light filtered through the great oaks, the dew on the grass like tears the night wept. The firemen stomped into the house in their dirty boots, one with an axe in his hand. "Oh, Lord, what are they going to do to my house?" Laurel moaned. As we waited for the crew to reappear, we appraised ourselves. Billy had a gash down one cheek that needed tending. Both men were soaked to the bone and bled from their feet. Bright poppies of their blood bloomed across our grass-stained nightgowns. Lark hurried back to Dean's to get a first aid kit, and we bandaged the men in the dawn. The firemen tromped back out onto the terrace, their faces calm. Billy's efforts with the hose had slowed the conflagration until the firefighters had arrived to quench the remaining blaze before it could spread to the rest of the house. But smoke had escaped through the door and vents, and heavy soot limed the upstairs. Capricious old wiring was most likely the cause of the blaze; the upstairs of the house hadn't been remodeled in many years. With the windows blown out and gaping, their frames blackened, the corner of the house looked like the shell of a war-torn building. The flames had licked onto the roof, and a large swath of it had burned away.

As Lark and I walked Laurel to Dean's house, Dean and Billy surveyed the wreckage. The room was a dripping black cube, the stench of melted plastic and fabric unbelievable. In some spots one of the firemen had gashed through the walls to the outside wall with his axe to make sure embers did not smolder there. The next day a professional cleaning crew came, and Dean and Billy went into town to pick up enormous scrubbers—air-cleaning filters—and installed them throughout the house. We heard the low roar of the scrubbers day and night, but they took care of the lingering charred odor in a week's time. Laurel moved in with Dean until the house and roof could be repaired. "I always did want to redo that room," she wryly said. Charlotte lay quietly on Dean's den floor, her head on her paws, her red-streaked eyes drowsy for a couple of days, healing herself the way animals do, and made a full recovery.

One afternoon Dean, Lark and I finally visited Monticello. The docent who led our tour was a fount of information on the life of Thomas Jefferson. Dean's appreciation for Jefferson's architectural genius enhanced the experience for us. Lark and I loved seeing Jefferson's inventions, the fine antiques and portraits in the home. That evening Dean and I prepared a dinner of smoked salmon and Caesar salad for Lark and Laurel. After the meal I told them I had a surprise. "We're due for a good surprise," Laurel said as I dashed back to the guesthouse. In my packing for the summer I had included the first volumes of the photograph albums from Lark's childhood.

Lark said, "Uh oh, here we go," but with good humor. Mother and son sat, their heads together, as Dean opened the leather album.

The first picture was of two-day-old Lark in the sweet little gown with pink embroidered rosebuds. I remembered propping her on my hospital bed pillow as my father took the photo. "That was taken just before we brought her home from the hospital," I said.

Dean looked at me and then at the picture for a moment, and a closed sign settled over his handsome features. He stood and walked from the room.

"He just needs a minute," Laurel said, looking after her son and nodding once. I rose and stepped around the corner into the living area where Dean stood, looking out the broad expanse of window at his farm. I wrapped my arms around him and lay my head between his shoulder blades. He turned to me and put his arms around me, his cheek atop my head.

"I just felt this crushing … regret … remorse … when I saw that picture. That incredible baby girl … that was *mine* … I should have been there. I should have been the one holding the damned camera."

"I know, sweetheart," I said. We stood that way for several moments. Dean seemed to draw strength from our embrace. I heard the vacuum seal of the refrigerator door opening, a cabinet door closing, the sighing of cork pulled from a bottle, the murmur of voices.

"I can't believe how tiny she was, and already so pretty," he said. "I bet I could've held her in one hand." He stretched out a palm and cupped it. I told him about the day in the hospital I had unwrapped Lark from her little gown to examine her and had discovered the feet and toes the image of his own.

"I'd like to think I would've been a good father. You did it all by yourself … I still can't wrap my head around that."

"I had lots of help from my parents," I reminded him. "You'll be there for her the rest of your life, darling." I smiled, kissing his cheek. "And she loves you, you know."

"I do know," he said and smiled a little. "Let's get back. I want to see the rest of the pictures. But I may need some Kleenex."

Laurel handed Dean and me glasses of steel-aged Chardonnay, and we returned to the album. I knew in time Dean would make his peace with the past. "It's such a gift to see these," Laurel said. "And, Lark, I still can't get over how much you look like Leslie, even then. We need to show her these."

"Oh no, the naked ones," Lark said, cringing as they flipped a page. "Mom, that was just *wrong*."

"Everybody takes those pictures of their babies," Laurel said. "I have a couple of your father in fact," she added impishly.

"Uh, let's not go there," Dean said.

I laughed. "I would *love* to see Dean's pictures sometime, Laurel."

"Well, remind me to dig them out for you, honey." I flashed a victorious grin in Dean's direction.

The next day Lark, Leslie, Mary, and I escaped the clamor of the construction crew working to repair the house (Laurel insisted she stay and supervise) and drove to Richmond in search of a wedding dress. At the fancy bridal salon Leslie recommended, a woman discreetly regarded my figure and directed us away from the strapless gowns to a collection of dresses for the mature bride. "The *old* bride," I said, wrinkling my nose. "I may end up looking like the Queen Mum."

Leslie laughed and linked my arm with hers. "You are going to look *fabulous* and *sophisticated*." The salon owner seated the four of us in Louis Quatorze chairs, and an associate brought a tray of champagne in flutes. The first gown they brought out was undeniably dowdy, beige with horizontal pleats. Horizontal pleats! The second was an elegant ivory lace, but the big bow on the behind was out of the question. The third selection knocked us out. Leslie, Mary, and Lark said I had to try it on immediately.

I reappeared grinning and sent the trio into rhapsodies of approval. Tinged with the palest shade of apricot, a color so subtle it sneaked up on you, the gown was made of exquisite, finely wrought Burano lace layered on organza. The softly scooped neckline and modest short sleeves flattered my figure. And the way the A-line skirt flowed so softly and easily about my hips and thighs … It was the one. "It was *made* for you, Robin," Mary said smiling, her champagne flute raised in a toast.

"You have to wear your hair up, so the lace in the back will show," said Leslie.

The price of the dress made me feel as though I'd put a cake in the oven and forgotten to add the sugar, with company coming. But my sweet father had insisted on paying for the dress and the flowers. "Indulge the old man," he had said. "I've been waiting for this for decades."

Late that afternoon, Dean and I sat by the pool talking about the wedding. We both wanted it to be intimate—just family and our closest friends—and we wanted to honor the people who meant most to us. I had already asked Tee to be matron of honor. Dean said he had thought he would ask James to be best man but asked me what I thought about him choosing Billy instead. I reflected on Billy's recent feelings. "I think it's perfect ... In fact, it's *completely* brill!" He grinned and grabbed his phone to text Billy and ask him to come to the pool. Billy and Hudson strode across the grass from the barn. Billy looked sheepish as he came through the gate in his work clothes.

"Our hero!" I called to him, pretending to swoon. Laurel and I had been teasing him with the title since the night of the fire.

Billy smiled diffidently. "What's up, boss?" he asked Dean.

"Mr. Babbitt," said Dean expansively, "have a seat. We're about to have this wedding, and I need a best man. If you're free, I'd like *you* to do it."

Billy sat back against the chair and grinned his old easy grin. "Honored to, man."

I jumped up and hugged him. "I'm taking you handsome guys into town tomorrow for new suits!"

The next day we met at a men's store where we found a pair of elegantly cut gray suits and ties. "How come you get to see me in my suit and I don't get to see you in your dress?" Dean asked.

"It's traditional. Remember tradition?" I asked saucy and grinning.

That night Dean and I invited Lark and Billy to go to Blue Mountain Brewery with us for dinner. Billy was sun burnished and attractive in a plaid madras shirt and khakis. Dean and I observed Billy's interactions with women. Shy, away from his milieu of the farm, he was definitely rusty. But in the following days we noticed that Billy seemed happier, his limp less obvious again. We vowed to include him in our plans more often.

I turned my attention to a dress for Theresa. A cool aqua would be a lovely summer color and flattering for her high color. I called her with the assignment of finding a dress in Paris. *What a hardship.*

Lark had had a perpetual smile on her lips since Ben had booked his travel itinerary for the wedding. He was due to arrive two days before. Lark couldn't wait for Ben and Dean to meet.

The mother of the groom was in a fevered ecstasy of plans for flowers, a minister, a caterer, musicians, and a photographer. I was happy for her to take the lead on those details, for she knew the area resources. Laurel, Dean, and I put together the small guest list one night after dinner, and the sisters helped me send out simple invitations.

Dean and I went into town for blood tests, simple gold wedding bands, and a late lunch date. We were usually up late at night, looking at online information on Paris hotels, transportation, and excursions. After Victoria had died, Dean had made trips to

Germany and Czechoslovakia and later to Italy and Greece, but he had always believed Paris to be a gap in his architectural education. Of course I was thrilled. This time I would be visiting the City of Light for a purely happy reason. Theresa was ecstatic. "I hoped you'd come here, *cherie*!" she exclaimed. "I'm going to find the perfect little *intime* hotel—a little jewel box—for you and Dean!" I laughed with pleasure at her perpetual enthusiasm. Theresa and Laurent would fly over for the wedding, and afterward the four of us would fly to Paris together. The hotel Theresa found seemed perfect and was near their apartment building on the boulevard Saint-Germain. Dean and I booked it immediately. We were ready for a wedding.

CHAPTER

23

Robin

2013

The beautiful people arrived. After a week's visit with Colleen in Chicago, Theresa and Laurent made it to Villeneuve the day before the wedding. Tee stepped from the rental car looking impossibly young and svelte in tight jeans, a black T-shirt, and big glam sunglasses. I ran to swoop her up in a hug. Laurent, immaculate as always, launched his frame from the rental smiling broadly.

The Pelletiers and Dean and I sat around Laurel's kitchen island drinking iced tea. Theresa, hands darting like barn swallows, described the hotel she had found for Dean and me. I felt butterflies the size of kites in my stomach at the thought of leaving for Paris after the wedding. Dean asked Laurent about what architectural attractions he should see in Paris in addition to the obvious. From his artist's perspective, Laurent described *les incontournables*—the must-sees. Laurent in turn asked Dean about running a horse farm. I saw they would become friends as they walked out for a tour, Dean smiling proudly. No one could believe the lovely main house had been devastated by fire just weeks before.

Lark had been sitting on the stoop with her laptop since Ben had called from Richmond. Tee and I walked out to join her. As Ben's rental car rolled up the drive, Lark was on her feet. Before Ben could turn off the engine, she was in his lap. "They haven't seen each other in a month," I said to Tee with a grin.

"Jeunes amoureux," she sighed as we slipped back into the house. "Ben's as beautiful as Lark!" she whispered.

Lark brought Ben in to meet her grandmother just as Dean and Laurent returned to the house. "Hey, Robin!" Ben said, pulling me into a hug. I regarded the pair with pleasure as Lark made the introductions. With Lark's light features, the two made a striking couple, a chiaroscuro. I mentally crossed my fingers hoping the wedding would put Ben and Lark in the marrying mood. They would make such beautiful babies. Lark's eyes seemed lit from within as she introduced Ben to her father. My chest felt as effervescent as if I'd inhaled champagne bubbles.

The rest of that day Lark and Ben disappeared a few times. Tee and I speculated they were finding places to make love. "Don't make me think about that," Dean said with a moue of distaste. "She's my baby girl!"

When my father and Anita Roth arrived late in the afternoon, I was awash with familial completion, perfection. My jean pockets were full of mascara-smeared tissues. That evening, we had a lovely rehearsal dinner at nearby Keswick Hall with family and friends. Seeing Laurent for the first time, Mary, Leslie, and Jill were agog. I thought Theresa looked a bit smug as she held his arm. Billy, as best man, made a simple but eloquent and poignant toast to the bride and groom. It meant so much to Dean and me after our friend's confession a few weeks back.

Back at Villeneuve by nine thirty, we were all too keyed up to go to bed. Laurel, Billy, Dean, Laurent, and Dad sat drinking wine in Dean's living room. Laurent was staying the night at Dean's house along with my father. Ben would sleep at Billy's apartment over the barn. Lark and Ben said they were going for a walk, to more than one set of raised brows and amused twitching of mouths. Theresa and I went to relax in the guesthouse. It had been a long time since one of our sleepovers and a chance to really talk.

When I walked over to kiss Dean good night, he and Ben were sitting by the pool drinking beer, talking about baseball teams and the pennant races. The two had hit it off right away. Lark sat on the end of Ben's chaise longue watching them, her face incandescent.

Theresa and I got ready for bed. Lark's room was still dark. She and Ben had disappeared again. Tee and I finally reclined on my bed in our pajamas, glasses of scotch in hand as we'd done so many times before. Tee said, "Rob, Dean has aged *well*. He's *très sexy!*"

I grinned like the Cheshire cat. "We're waiting for our wedding night to make love. It was Dean's idea."

Tee's eyes widened over the rim of her glass. "You're kidding me," she finally said.

"Nope, and I'm convinced it's going to be ... well worth the wait. He was so sweet about wanting to give me the wedding we should have had and a proper wedding night."

"Rob ... you're killing me," she said, dipping to wipe her eyes on the hem of my pillowcase. She smiled then and pulled me into a hug. "Let's see that fabulous ring again." Tee rocked my hand like a cradle so that the stones captured the lamplight. "*Olivia's* diamond," she said, shaking her head with wonder.

"But, Tee," I fretted after a moment, "Dean hasn't seen me naked. Things are a lot ... you know looser and *bobblier* than they used to be."

Theresa snorted with laughter. "Rob, the man practically worships you. Do you really think he's going to be thinking about that in the heat of the moment?"

"I don't know!" Theresa was still as slender as a girl, her champagne-glass B cups fairly perky. My DD cups were definitely on a downward trend.

"Well, he won't. He'll have his hands full, and I do mean full!" she teased.

I hooted with chagrin, choking a little on my Scotch. "What if I'm too set in my ways from living alone my entire adult life?" I whined.

"Robin, stop it! This is your miracle. I'm not going to feed your paranoia. It's going to be fine. This is your fairy tale ending, *cherie*. You're going to be married. To *Dean Falconer.*"

We heard the front door open and close softly. We looked at each other and giggled. The conversation turned to other things: Tee's mother, my dad, my thoughts for wrapping up my New York life, Lark and Ben, and Theresa's career—she was spending more and more time at the gallery and was thinking about leaving the magazine for good. Then drowsy, our glasses empty, we hugged good night and crawled beneath the covers. Theresa wriggled into her customary stomach-sleeping position, and I onto my side. After a moment I said into the darkness, "I love you, Tee."

And she murmured through layers of linen and down, "Love you too, baby. Forever and always."

It rained the next morning, which everyone insisted was good luck for brides. About nine thirty, the dogs barked the arrival of John Hicks, who had traveled from New York on the red-eye. And less than an hour before the ceremony, the sun made its appearance. Those working outside stopped what they were doing to stand and look upward. The swath of beautiful colors that arched across the sky was a brilliant reminder of God's grace in Dean's and my lives. As the trees dripped away the remnant of the rain, the catering team had the chairs for the ceremony and the lunch-reception tables and chairs set up in the paddock with the symmetry of a chorus line. Laurel had insisted I be secluded in her house with Tee and my father until time for the ceremony. Peering out the front windows, I watched Dean's mother, still in work pants and clogs and clearly in her element, directing the florist to wire the lush white peonies and trailing English ivy to the makeshift altar and along the aisle I would walk. She called to Charlotte and Hudson, who seemed to be supervising it all, and tied great white bows to their collars.

Lark came in to see me and slipped a hand into mine. She murmured, "You look perfect, Mom." She squeezed my hand three times. I squeezed her back four and smiled into her eyes. Laurel came back inside to get dressed and shooed us from the windows.

With just a few minutes to go, Dad took me aside. "I am so glad you have your mother's ring," he said, looking down at the engagement ring. "And soon you'll have a wedding band to wear forever."

Tears stung my nose. "Thank you, Dad. I love you." I kissed his cheek, fragrant with vetiver, and then, as if orchestrated, Theresa appeared to hand me my bouquet. The peony-and-rose combination smelled like heaven must.

"Are you ready, Rob?" she asked.

We heard our cue—the violin and guitar strains of Pachelbel's Canon in D. Laurel, clutching a hankie, blew us a kiss and stepped out to proceed to the front row and sit with the rest of the family. Dad gulped and offered me his arm. I took it, full of love for him. I knew he was thinking of my mother. Stepping into the sunshine, we moved down the steps to the sibilant sound of appreciative whispers. Theresa followed, graceful in exquisite aqua lace.

My eyes sought Dean's face at the altar next to the minister and Billy. I gazed at him all the way down the aisle, and he at me. Our traditional ceremony began. When the minister asked, "Who gives this woman to be married to this man?" my father solemnly said, "Her mother and I do." We both sniffled as he kissed my cheek before taking his seat beside Laurel. I handed my bouquet to Lark in the front row next to Ben. The guests spoke a collective *"Aww"* as Dean leaned to kiss his daughter.

I turned to him then, gorgeous and distinguished in the gray suit that matched his eyes. We fought to keep our composure as we exchanged vows and rings. When the minister pronounced us husband and wife, Dean kissed me lingeringly, amid applause and laughter. As he pulled back, I tossed my head, and for the first time he noticed the little silver bird earrings, darkened with age. He murmured in my ear, "The robins. You kept them." He kissed me again, and we turned to the congregation as Mr. and Mrs. Dean Thompson Falconer.

We moved en masse into the paddock, where tables waited under shady oaks for a lunch reception. From beneath one of the great trees, a string quartet spilled the music of Mozart. Later, sated with delicious food and wine, I leaned against the back of my chair and gazed languidly around at family and our closest friends. Dean, holding my hand, was chatting with Billy on his right side. Lark was feeding Ben bites of wedding cake. I watched as she wiped crumbs from his chin and leaned to kiss his laughing mouth. How I wanted them to be as happy as Dean and I were. Those two would get it right the first time.

To Ben's right my dad sat talking with elegant, silver-tressed Anita Roth. What memories the two shared from their years as neighbors in New York. And how they had loved my mother. Dad leaned back in his chair, relaxed and happy in a dark-navy suit, a white rose in his lapel. He had gained weight in the last year, but it suited him.

Beside Anita, James was whispering something in Jill's ear. She giggled and sipped from her glass of champagne: a ripe peach in a silk wrap dress and chunky gold necklace. And I was astonished to see that across the table my mother-in-law was flirting with an attentive John Hicks on her left. It seemed that anything was possible on this day. Regal in an aqua silk suit that accentuated her sun-browned décolletage, she fingered the lustrous pearls at her throat and swung one crossed leg up and down. Her shoe actually dangled from her toe! John appeared to be teasing her about something.

On my other side sat my darling Tee. She and her splendid Frenchman were kissing, and as I looked down, I saw that one of his large hands cupped her bottom, not much bigger than a skein of wool. I remembered they had celebrated their thirty-fifth wedding anniversary that spring. *Ahh, love,* I thought contentedly. Dean turned back to me. "Sweetheart, how are you? Happy?"

A sphere is the easiest shape for nature to assume: a bubble, a planet, a drop of water. Our journey of love had come full circle— assuming a sphere of profound wholeness. "Happier than I ever imagined," I answered.

He kissed my neck and murmured, "How would you like to go on a honeymoon with me, pretty girl?"

"I'm all yours," I whispered.

Dean tapped his water goblet with his spoon and stood. "Fill your glasses," he instructed everyone. He thanked our guests for their love and support on our special day as we had rehearsed. And then he surprised me.

"In eighteen seventy-seven my paternal grandparents established a new settlement in Virginia, and they named it Villeneuve." He looked at his mother and smiled. "My mother came to Villeneuve as a bride. She and my father were always happy." He grinned and looked at his sisters. "They raised two daughters and a fine, upstanding son." Everyone tittered, and Leslie hooted.

Dean looked down at me then. "In *nineteen* seventy-seven, one hundred years after Villeneuve was established, I met the love of my life Robin Courtwright Hamilton. Coincidence?" He reached down and took my hand. "I was happy here all my life, but I've never been as happy as I am at this moment. I'm sure my grandparents would be pleased to know that another bride will make her home at Villeneuve." He reached to pick up his glass. "To my beautiful bride, Robin Hamilton Falconer." Everyone stood.

"Hear, hear," the men chanted. And at once we were surrounded with hugs and kisses. Dean and I went back to our separate quarters to dress for the trip to Paris. We had a five o'clock plane to catch from Richmond. Theresa giggled at my excitement. I was practically vibrating with it as we skinned out of our wedding finery and dressed in comfortable travel wear, me back into my dark New York clothes for Paris. We assembled at the Pelletiers' rental car with the family.

Dean and I turned to Lark. I realized that all summer she'd seemed very young, almost girlish in the uncharted territory of her father's presence, but since Ben had arrived, our daughter had again become the sophisticated and sexy woman I knew. The three of us, now a family in the truest sense of the word, had a private moment together.

Two hours later Dean and I were seat belted in aboard the jet for Paris. Across the aisle from Theresa and Laurent we toasted our happiness with good champagne (Laurent was an endless reservoir of resources). The flight attendants to whom Theresa told our story were charmed and then especially attentive. Dean and I snuggled under a blanket together for the nine-hour flight. While walking the aisles to stretch our legs once, he murmured, "Hey, green-eyed lady, want to join the mile-high club?"

I laughed and elbowed him. "We've waited this long; I'm not about to do it for the first time in a gross public toilet!"

Laurent drove us to our hotel as the sun rose over Paris, the early sky a rosy pink. Tee was curled like a tawny kitten in the passenger seat, her pink mouth slack. We would meet up with them later for a late lunch. Dean had made reservations for us at the Ritz Hotel.

Dean and I entered the lobby of the small Hotel Juliette St. Germain replete with nineteenth-century furnishings and art. Laurent, acquainted with the owner, had known we would be pampered there. Although it was very early, Monsieur le Patron himself emerged to greet us. Dean registered us as Mr. and Mrs. Dean Thompson Falconer while I suppressed the goofy grin that tugged at the corners of my mouth and managed a decorous expression.

The luxuries waiting in our suite were assaults on already overstimulated senses. First we were met with the heady scent of a great bouquet of fresh flowers—peonies, roses, and stock. The attached card read "Theresa and Laurent Pelletier." "Oh, from Tee; how lovely!" I said. "Oh my gosh," we then said at the same time as we found *two* bathrooms—his and hers— a Jacuzzi large enough for water polo in between. In the bedroom, the king-sized bed was turned down. Luxe white toweling robes lay across it, their arms crossed as if daring us to hurry up and get it on. Slippers peeked from beneath the dust ruffle. "Whatever happened to your water bed?" I asked, thinking of where we had first made love.

"The water bed!" Dean laughed. "It sprang a leak … *before* I could get rid of it. The landlord was *pissed*."

On one of the pillows was a white box wrapped with pale blue ribbon. My curiosity piqued, I wondered, *What* more *could there be?* Atop layers of blue tissue nestled another little card, this one handwritten by Theresa: "He'll howl like a wolf. Love, Tee."

"Tee!" I hooted, tucking the note in my pocket. "I better open this by myself," I said to Dean. He went into his bathroom chuckling softly. I unfolded a length of silky fabric from its tissue nest: an exquisite emerald green lace peignoir—the most beautiful piece of lingerie I'd ever seen. Dean and I had spoken of jumping into the shower together as soon as we arrived, but as I held the peignoir against me, I found that I wanted to come to him fresh and glowing from the shower in the delicate robe. I pushed it back into the box as Dean reemerged.

As I showered, I was flooded with gratitude and at last desire. Hastily drying my hair, I slipped the peignoir over my skin. My heart suddenly feeling as if it had left the building, I opened the door.

Dean lay on one elbow in the great bed under sumptuous Egyptian cotton, his face flushed with longing. I approached the bed and stood before him. He gulped and uttered, "Robin," as he scanned my body in the filmy robe. Mesmerized, he peeled the covers back. I saw that he was gloriously naked and quite ready for me. I let the peignoir drop to the floor with a whisper and shook my hair to sweep my shoulders. I moved into his embrace.

"Madame Falconer," he said huskily. "That body ... your body has *always* looked like it was carved ... to adorn the pillar of a palace."

Tears prickled at my lashes. "Oh, Dean ... I love you so."

As we kissed deeply, our hands explored each other again as if blind and reading texts of braille. We made our first married love. I heard sounds like mourning doves on the zinc roof above and realized they were coming from me. And then the urgency came crashing in; thirty-five years of waiting to join together again rose on a tide that took us far, far down. Our cries rose as if in homage to the one who had created love just for us. Finally sweetly sated with each other, our lassitude from the wedding and jet lag complete, we slept entwined until twelve thirty. Dean made love to me again, tantalizingly slowly this time.

We found it was time to get ready for our lunch with Tee and Laurent and reluctantly rose to dress. Blinking like night creatures as we stepped into the early-afternoon sunlight, we were like any married couple on holiday. Almost. I wondered how many other pairs could possibly share a history like ours. My heart seemed weightless as we strolled hand in hand in one of the world's most beautiful cities. Theresa and Laurent met us in front of their building, Tee beaming at us. "Did you rest well?" she teased. Already late, we hopped quickly into Laurent's sedan, and he aimed it for the Ritz.

The hotel was magnificent; even the ladies' room was opulent. "Tee, have you seen that bathroom?" I hissed. Lunch was as beautiful as it was delicious. On my third glass of champagne I quoted Hemmingway: "When I dream of afterlife in heaven, the action always takes place in the Paris Ritz."

"Hear, hear." Dean grinned, raising his glass. We laughed a great deal and shared bites from each other's plates of delicacies: poached sole and artichokes; glazed sea bass and grapefruit peas; lobster salad with lemon balm and baby lettuces; and fragrant French bread and butter. Dean and I spooned poached peaches in pink champagne with raspberry glacé into each other's mouths and sealed the bites with little kisses.

That evening, Dean and I stayed in and ordered a light room service dinner. We soaked in the great tub and made love with exuberance. At fleeting illusory moments I saw glimpses of Dean's young face. I know I slept that night, but my heart stayed awake.

I awoke before Dean did that morning and turned to see his head on the next pillow. *We're married*! I thought with a rush of deliciousness. I could wake up in the mornings with Dean Falconer for the rest of my life. Dean lay on his back breathing softly. The sunlight that filtered through sheers at the windows revealed his stubble of blond and silver whiskers. Abruptly the alarm on his phone sounded from the bedside chest, and he shot out an arm to silence it. He turned to look at me, and unadulterated happiness registered in his eyes. "Good morning, wife," he said, stroking my hair.

An hour later we grabbed croissants and cups of café crème to go and hurried to the Metro. We strolled the streets of bohemian Montmartre. And on a guided tour of Sacré-Coeur, I thought Dean's eyes would tumble out of their sockets. We had a leisurely lunch with glasses of summer rosé at a little bistro and took a boat cruise along the Seine. That night, we walked to the Pelletiers' for a scrumptious dinner deftly prepared by Madame Heloise. "*Allons-y*," Laurent said. He held his fork aloft and grinned at Dean. We tucked into the meal. Dean closed his eyes and moaned with pleasure with his first bite of Heloise's goat cheese, caramelized onion, and tomato tart. This was followed by bacon-wrapped figs, salad greens, and for dessert chocolate tartlets with candied grapefruit peel. It was a blessing to be in Tee and Laurent's home again, this time with a healthy and whole Theresa *and* my very own dream husband.

On a couple of days Dean and I made no plans at all, finding that we only wanted to wander and discover. Once on a bridge arching the river, a jazz band with saxophone and cello materialized. A rotund little man in a red jacket accompanied them with aplomb on a tiny console piano mounted on a child's wagon axle. On other bridges we were intrigued by hundreds of combination locks, like the ones on high school lockers, fastened to the metalwork. A Japanese man being walked by a slobbery mastiff told us that couples sealed their love by placing locks on the bridge.

Later at Laurent's gallery, Dean fell in love with Laurent's work. His architect's eye appreciated the precision with which Laurent depicted homes, buildings, and cathedrals. On two soggy days, Dean and I explored the Louvre and the Musée D'Orsay. One fine day, the sky vivid and blue again, we ambled through the Tuileries Gardens and ate lunch al fresco at a small café under the chestnut trees. On our last day I wanted to take Dean to the Luxembourg Gardens I had loved with Theresa those years ago. We packed a picnic although the sky was leaden. And the park was just as enchanting as I remembered.

Theresa and Laurent drove us to the airport that evening. We had a drink in a bar before boarding, talking of plans for the two to come and spend time with us the next summer, at Villeneuve and the Outer Banks. Finally, Theresa and I faced each other arms outstretched and shared a long, bittersweet embrace.

* * * *

As our Jeep crunched down the oak-lined drive at Villeneuve again, my heart soared. I would no longer sleep in the guesthouse:

that night I would share Dean's bed as his bride. Smiling, I reached for his hand and squeezed it three times. "Are you sharing that with *me* now?" he asked happily and squeezed mine back four.

We passed Billy in the paddock and waved to him. He smiled and raised his hat in salute. We climbed out of the Jeep to pet the ecstatic dogs. Laurel was happy to see us and anxious to hear about the trip. Typically thoughtful, she was busy preparing dinner for us. I saw the colorful postcard I'd sent from Montmartre posted on her refrigerator door. She asked about a huge parcel that had arrived from Paris. "I had the man prop it against your back door under the awning. I've been dying to know what it is." Dean and I looked at each other and shrugged. We had no clue. The little gifts we'd bought for family and friends had been carefully tucked into our carry-on bags in case our luggage was lost. Laurel said she would bring dinner over later, and we invited her to stay and eat with us. Dean brought the box—whose torn return address was unreadable—inside. We would shower and take a nap before dinner and open the parcel with Laurel after dinner.

We ate our fill of delicious pasta primavera and spoke of what we had done and seen in Paris. I gave Laurel the elegant little silver clock we had found in the Marais for her dressing table. We took our coffee into the living room and regarded the curious package. Inside was a wooden crate that Dean had to use tools to pry open. Incredulous, we stared at the painting of the Paris Opera House Dean had most admired at Laurent's gallery. I translated the note scrawled in Laurent's heavy back-slant script: "May you be ever joyful in your marriage. Theresa and Laurent." Overwhelmed, and although it was late in Paris, Dean called Laurent immediately to thank him.

Dean propped the painting against our mantle, and we stood admiring it again, toasting our happiness with glasses of good Virginia Cabernet Franc.

My mind turned to the business I had to take care of in Manhattan. After Dean and I unpacked and rested for a few days, I flew to New York to meet my father. Dad had offered to come and help me supervise the packing and moving of the furniture I wasn't selling. We would hold an estate sale with Anita's help and put the brownstone on the market.

I met with John again about the sale of my share of the firm. He was seriously considering retiring and leaving the city. Extraordinarily, he was interested in courting my mother-in-law! I learned that John had stayed on at Villeneuve an extra couple of days after the wedding getting to know Laurel and a spark had been set alight between them. Why had Laurel not told us? Dean and I had some romantic investigating to do.

Later in the week I met Nick for lunch at PJ Clarke's. Despite our intimate history there had never been any awkwardness between us. I had invited Nick to the wedding, but he and Dakota were expecting their first baby in two weeks. "I'm finally going to be a father," Nick said with a grin, as smug as if he'd invented fatherhood himself. "But I'll be seventy-four and decrepit when she graduates high school."

Burning the candle at both ends, I was able to take care of most of the details of relocating with Dad's and Anita's help. The unresolved loose ends would have to be handled long distance. I was exhausted and ready to get back to Dean.

The day after I returned to the farm the huge orange moving
van trundled down the gravel drive. Charlotte and Hudson ran
in front of it as if it were their job to herald its arrival. After the
movers left, Dean and Billy indulged me by moving some of the
furniture again to suit me. The panoply of pieces and the memories
they evoked provided an eclectic and interesting look and feel to
our home. We loved the monks' table in its new setting, and my
family clock looked perfect atop Dean's rough-hewn mantle. What
wouldn't fit went to the guesthouse to complete its furnishings.
Neither of us could wait for Lark to come and visit.

It was time for Dean to return to work. I unpacked boxes and
settled my belongings. I had the wedding photos and pictures we
had taken over the summer handsomely framed and placed them
about the house. Most days I took time to ride Trolley. Mary
taught me how to rise to a trot and to bathe and groom the horse
myself after a ride. I enjoyed shopping and lunches in town with
my mother and sisters-in-law and learned my way around Dean's
kitchen, mingling my pretty dishes with his plain ones. After doing
all his own cooking for so long, Dean loved having dinner prepared
for him each night. It became our ritual that Indian summer to
have a swim and drink by the pool before dinner. Sometimes we
even skinny-dipped and made love in the night-cool water.

I talked with Dean about practicing law again. As full as my
life had become, I'd begun to miss my work. Dean and I had
thrown around a few ideas. The best was that I would set up
an office in Dean and James's building on High Street. Dean
approached James with the idea of using a canted room, currently
cluttered with ancient files and boxes that neither of them knew
what to do with, things that their assistant Divya was dying to

throw out. James agreed. "Not only," he'd said with a grin, "will we get that room cleaned up, but having Robin here will give the office an immediate upgrade."

One chilly night in early October Dean and I relaxed on a sofa, reading by the first fire of the season. The dogs lay companionably on the hearthrug—Charlotte's tail giving the intermittent thump, her eyes watchful, and Hudson snoring and occasionally farting in his sleep. Logs of white birch cracked and popped, filling the room with the aroma of wintergreen. I inhaled deeply. "Mmmm, the wood is nice!"

Billy and Laurel had come for dinner that evening for a batch of chili and buttermilk cornbread muffins. Billy had been palpably nervous. His first date with his old high school friend Margo, whom he had run into at Trader Joe's, was coming up that weekend. "Man, she's still *hot* for fifty!" he had told Dean confidentially, but of course Dean had told me. Laurel and I were proud of him for asking Margo out and had good-naturedly coached and teased him about it throughout dinner. I presented Billy with a good-looking new denim button-down shirt, just for luck.

My telephone rang, interrupting my reading of the *New York Times*. It was Lark. "Darling!" I said after one ring. My eyes fell on a black-and-white photograph in a pretty silver frame on Dean's end table, a laughing Lark at a vineyard that summer.

Lark and I exchanged chitchat, and then she asked, "Mom, is Dad there with you? Will you put me on speaker?" With a flicker of excitement, I told Dean what I was doing.

He put his book aside. "Larkster!" he called.

"How are you, Dad? I miss you. Mom, Dad, Ben's here with me. We have news."

"Hi, guys," Ben said. I could hear a smile on his handsome face.

"Hi, Ben, darling! How are you?" I called.

"Mr. Holland!" said Dean.

Lark interrupted, "Ben has a new job."

"Well, that's great! What will you be doing?" I asked.

Ben said, "It's a new gig with Coloma actually—director of sustainability."

Lark's voice was buoyant. "He'll be working from New York!"

"That's wonderful news!"

"Congratulations, Ben," Dean said warmly and asked him more about the job.

Ben told us what the position entailed and then stopped. "Listen, folks, Lark is about to burst."

I heard Lark laugh, the fumbling of the phone, the sound of a kiss. "Well," Lark said, "how would you guys like to be part of another wedding soon … like in two weeks?"

Stunned, Dean and I looked at each other and stammered, "*Really?*" I said, "It's about time!" and Dean added, "In *two weeks?*" Lark and Ben laughed at us.

Lark said, "But there's more ... It seems I'm going to have a baby." I let out a whoop of joy, jarring Dean, who blinked and then grinned as if he'd learned he'd inherited the Palace of Versailles. They told us of their plan for a simple wedding. They wanted to be married at Dad's house on the beach on Lark's fall break from school. She would continue to teach until the baby was born in April. We ended the conversation telling them we loved them, foolish grins plastered on our faces.

Dean's face was full of wonder as he said, "Well, I'll be damned." He studied the calendar on his phone. Then he looked up at me. "How can I be a good grandfather when I'm just learning how to be a father?"

"We'll cross that bridge when we come to it." I smiled, rising to let the dogs out the back door. I went to the bookcase where Dean had connected my old turntable. I glanced at the framed photos on the shelves—the beautiful eight-by-ten wedding picture, a five-by-seven photo of me astride Trolley the first time, the grainy little snapshot of Dean and me from 1977, and the picture taken of the whole Falconer clan at the vineyard. I raised the cover on the record player and dropped the needle on the album that had brought us together all those years before. I padded back to my husband and hitched a leg up to straddle his lap. Slowly, I began to unbutton my blouse. Dean waited, brows raised, his eyes darkening to slate.

"What's your pleasure, Grandpa?" I asked.

ABOUT THE AUTHOR

Elizabeth Wafler's passion for a story told with heart led her to write her own fiction. A former elementary school teacher, she lives in the foothills of the Blue Ridge Mountains of Virginia with her husband and Cairn terrier, Mirabelle. The author can often be found at a local farmers' market in search of the perfect heirloom tomato or bouquet of flowers or at one of the area's beautiful vineyards enjoying a glass of Virginia wine. She is currently at work on her second novel, *A Faculty Daughter.*

ACKNOWLEDGEMENTS

Merci bien to Debbie and Greg Ketchum: to Deb for her loving support, even while planning a wedding; and to Greg for his editorial perspicacity and endless reservoir of encouragement.

Thanks are due to the team at AuthorHouse, especially Rob Clarkson and Viola Willis for their availability, enthusiasm and patience.

I owe deep appreciation to my enthusiastic beta readers, Mary Sumner, Anne Chambers, Alice Fitzpatrick and Beth Lofton.

I am grateful to Alice Vargo whose beautiful painting graces the cover of *In Robin's Nest*, and to photographer Kim Veillon for the fetching author photos.

I thank Shelley Payne for educating me on all things horses. She helped me imagine Villeneuve and send it galloping onto the page.

A fond bow is due newlyweds Katie and Ben Fitzpatrick for the sweet engagement ring story.

Special thanks are also due to Theresa Jackson and Mary Tillson, the besties who inspire and keep me laughing, and to lovely Joyce Seibert for her unflinching faith and encouragement.

I am especially grateful for my family. Without my husband Porter's unconditional love and support of *In Robin's Nest* this novel wouldn't have seen the light of day. His keen eye for inaccuracies and help in making Dean's sports analogies work were invaluable. My daughter, Liv, was my cheerleader from afar. It is a truly special moment when your adult child tells you she is proud of you.

This book is a work of fiction. All errors of fact or supposition are mine alone.

December 2015, Keswick, Virginia